Counting Women's Ballots

How did the first female voters cast their ballots? For almost 100 years, answers to this question have eluded scholars. *Counting Women's Ballots* employs new data and novel methods to provide insights into whether, how, and with what consequences women voted in the elections after suffrage. The analysis covers a larger and more diverse set of places, over a longer period of time, than has previously been possible. J. Kevin Corder and Christina Wolbrecht find that the extent to which women voted and which parties they supported varied considerably across time and place, defying attempts to describe female voters in terms of simple generalizations. Many women adapted quickly to their new right; others did not. In some cases, women reinforced existing partisan advantages; in others, they contributed to dramatic political realignment. *Counting Women's Ballots* improves our understanding of the largest expansion of the American electorate during a transformative period of American history.

J. KEVIN CORDER is a professor of political science at Western Michigan University in Kalamazoo. His research has appeared in the *American Political Science Review*, *The Journal of Politics*, and other outlets in political science and public administration. Much of his work focuses on economic policy, and he is the author of two books on the Federal Reserve System. In 2013, Dr. Corder received a Fulbright–Schuman European Affairs program grant to study the regulation of banks in Malta and the United Kingdom. He shared a National Science Foundation grant and the Carrie Chapman Catt prize with Christina Wolbrecht for the research design that inspired *Counting Women's Ballots*.

CHRISTINA WOLBRECHT is an associate professor of political science and director of the Rooney Center for the Study of American Democracy at the University of Notre Dame. She is the author of *The Politics of Women's Rights: Parties, Positions, and Change*, which received the Leon Epstein Outstanding Book Award from the Political Organizations and Parties Section of the American Political Science Association (APSA). She is coeditor of *Political Women and American Democracy* as well as other edited volumes, and the author or coauthor of articles appearing in *Perspectives on Politics*, *American Journal of Political Science*, *The Journal of Politics*, and other leading political science journals.

Counting Women's Ballots

Female Voters from Suffrage through the New Deal

J. KEVIN CORDER
Western Michigan University, Kalamazoo

CHRISTINA WOLBRECHT
University of Notre Dame, Notre Dame, IN

CAMBRIDGE
UNIVERSITY PRESS

CAMBRIDGE
UNIVERSITY PRESS

32 Avenue of the Americas, New York NY 10013-2473, USA

Cambridge University Press is part of the University of Cambridge.

It furthers the University's mission by disseminating knowledge in the pursuit of education, learning, and research at the highest international levels of excellence.

www.cambridge.org
Information on this title: www.cambridge.org/9781316505878

First published 2016

Printed in the United States of America by Sheridan Books, Inc

A catalog record for this publication is available from the British Library.

ISBN 978-1-107-14025-7 Hardback
ISBN 978-1-316-50587-8 Paperback

Contents

Illustrations

Figures

Tables

Acknowledgments

This book would not have been written if it were not for John Sprague.

This is true in a general sense. John Sprague was a teacher, mentor, dissertation chair, and friend to both authors from the time we were graduate students at Washington University in St. Louis in the 1990s. John's wisdom and perspective have shaped both of us deeply as social scientists and inform every aspect of this book, from the concern for the role of context in shaping political behavior to attention to the effective visual display of information.

This is also true in a specific sense. When Gary King made his forthcoming book, *A Solution to the Ecological Inference Problem*, available to the academic community in the mid-1990s, it was John who alerted both of us to the potential of bringing these new methods to bear on important unanswered questions. His initial enthusiasm and insight sparked the two decades of collaboration that produced this book.

We also owe a great deal to Gary King. As we discuss in Chapter 4, the identification of the ecological inference problem by William Robinson more than sixty years ago (along with the emergence of high-quality survey instruments) led to a significant and regrettable turn away from aggregate election data collection and analysis in the second half of the twentieth century. Many interesting questions – regarding not only elections, but also a wealth of puzzles across multiple fields – went unanswered as a result. Gary's book helped reignite work on approaches to ecological inference, including the Bayesian approach proposed by Jon Wakefield that we employ in this research. Gary also has been a long-time supporter of this project in particular, inviting us to a 2002 conference on ecological inference at Harvard and continuing to provide useful advice and feedback as the project progressed.

We are indebted to our friends Andrew Martin and Kevin Quinn as well. The estimates that form the key empirical basis for this research were produced using a modified version of MCMCpack, an R package for Markov Chain Monte Carlo estimation they developed with Jong Hee Park. Even more important has been their ongoing consultation on the considerable data and estimation challenges this research has confronted. For that, and for many fine meals, we are grateful.

Kristi Andersen's book *After Suffrage* provided essential guidance to this period and these issues when our project was in its infancy, and Kristi herself has been a valuable sounding board and supporter over the years. We also benefited from the advice and encouragement of other colleagues around the country, including Karen Beckwith, Lisa Baldez, Lee Ann Banaszak, Dianne Bystrom, Gerald Gamm, Dan Galvin, John Geer, Robert Huckfeldt, Holly McCammon, Ken Kollman, Rick Matland, Bruce Oppenheimer, and Rick Vallely. Some of the conversations were many and wide-ranging, some few and specific, but each person helped us to develop further the ideas and approach we articulate in this book. To those who have provided insight but whom we have inadvertently and regretfully failed to list here, please know you have our gratitude as well. The opportunity to present and receive feedback on our research from seminar participants at the University of Notre Dame, Western Michigan University, Loyola University Chicago, Northwestern University, Ohio State University at Marion, Swarthmore College, Vanderbilt University, Washington University in St. Louis, and the European Conference on Gender and Politics, as well as from discussants and audience members at multiple American Political Science Association (APSA) and Midwest Political Science Association (MPSA) meetings, has been invaluable. As the finish line neared, Dave Campbell read the entire manuscript, cover to cover; his insights and encouragement made the final push possible. All of these fine colleagues are of course blameless for any errors that remain.

A multitude of undergraduate and graduate students performed essential tasks as research assistants, including tracking down and verifying citations and sources; scouring newspaper microfilm; and above all, entering column upon column of electoral and census data, some of it written in pencil and then copied on to microfilm decades ago. We are grateful to Notre Dame graduate students Brian Krueger, Patrick Flavin, Catherine Borck, Jill Budny, Jay Johnson, Ana-Tereza Lemos-Nelson, Noman Sattar, Cheryl Schotten, Claire Smith, Yizhong Sun, Michele Waslin, Annabella

España-Najera, and Justin McDevitt; Notre Dame undergraduates Mary "Chrissy" Prina, Megan DiPerna, and Lauren Willoughby; and Western Michigan University graduate student Uisoon Kwon.

Financial support has been essential to this project. In particular, this research would not have been possible without National Science Foundation grants SES-9905843 and SES-9905307, which supported the original data collection and analysis. A research prize from the Carrie Chapman Catt Center for Women and Politics Research at the Iowa State University provided early support and encouragement. We also benefitted from ongoing funding from our home institutions, particularly the Institute for Scholarship in the Liberal Arts (College of Arts & Letters), Faculty Research Program, and the Rooney Center for the Study of American Democracy at the University of Notre Dame, and the Research Development Award Program at Western Michigan University.

Tracking down historic election records is an adventure. In pursuit of the exceptional Illinois election records (recorded by sex in 1916 and 1920; see Chapter 3) we contacted all 102 Illinois counties (save Cook, where the data were already available in published form) via telephone. Though most election records below the level of the county were lost to history, we are grateful to the county clerks and staff who dug through their archives in search of the data we required. A few were able to copy and send us records; others opened their doors to Christina Wolbrecht and her husband during one memorable spring break so that we could enter the data directly off of the poll books that were too large for a standard copy machine. We also visited and/or called a number of state, university, and presidential archives and libraries across the United States in search of election records and other information and were repeatedly impressed by the professionalism and knowledge of the staff who answered our questions, and in more than a few cases, followed up with large packages of photocopied material that made this project possible.

Lew Bateman, senior editor at Cambridge University Press, has been an unfailing and patient supporter of this project for many years. It was a pleasure to work with him, and with the staff at CUP, to bring this book to press. We are grateful to the three anonymous readers, whose careful and thoughtful feedback sharpened and improved the final manuscript.

Our families and friends have been patient as well. J. Kevin Corder thanks his wife, Susan, for her good humor as she endured hundreds of claims about how close the "Christina book" was to actual completion. For unflagging optimism and encouragement, he also appreciates his Western colleagues, particularly Tom Bailey and Katherine Joslin.

Christina Wolbrecht likewise is grateful to her colleagues at Notre Dame, in particular Alexandra Guisinger and Karen Graubart, for advice and support of all kinds. She thanks her husband, Matt, for all the ways he makes her professional life possible and her personal life meaningful. And for only occasionally saying, Just finish it! Christina Wolbrecht also thanks her daughters, Ella and Jane, both of whom were born after this book project was initiated, for their love and joy. They were outraged to learn that women were once denied the right to vote; we hope this book is just one more piece of evidence for them of the myriad ways in which women should and do count in this world, in politics and beyond.

ILLUSTRATION I.I. Prior to the ratification of the Nineteenth Amendment, some states enfranchised women for a limited set of offices, necessitating separate voting procedures. (Box for women's ballots, unknown state and date, from the suffrage collection of Dr. Kenneth Florey)

1

Counting Women's Ballots

On August 18, 1920, Tennessee became the thirty-sixth state in the union to ratify the Nineteenth Amendment to the United States Constitution. After a more than seventy-year battle, women throughout the United States secured the right to vote. The national enfranchisement of women represented the largest expansion of the electorate in American history, nearly doubling the size of the voting age population.[1] Millions of citizens who had never cast a ballot became eligible to do so.

This dramatic expansion of the electorate generated a great deal of activity and uncertainty. Newspapers offered advice to new female voters. "You Can't Drag Your Husband Into The Booth When You Vote on Tuesday!" explained the *Bridgeport Post* (Bridgeport, CT), helpfully adding that "There Are No Mirrors Inside ... Hubby Cannot Legally Offer You a New Hat to Vote for His Candidate."[2] Political parties and women's organizations designed "play elections" and practice voting booths to teach women how to fulfill their new civic obligations.[3] Cities

[1] We say "nearly" because eleven states allowed women to vote in the 1916 presidential election. On the other hand, restrictive interpretations of registration rules (ratification occurred after registration deadlines in a number of states) denied women access to the ballot in Arkansas, Georgia, Mississippi, and South Carolina in 1920, delaying women's participation in presidential elections in those states until 1924 (Gosnell 1930). Together with black men, many black women continued to experience systematic exclusion from the franchise until the second half of the twentieth century.

[2] "You Can't Drag Your Husband Into The Booth When You Vote Tuesday!" *Bridgeport (CT) Post*, October 31, 1920. See also: "What the Woman Citizen Should Know" (repeated column). *St. Paul Dispatch*, July 24, 1920, p. 2; "To Women: Register!" *Chicago Tribune*, August 21, 1920, p. 1.

[3] "Play Election Devised to Teach Women How to Vote." *Boston Globe*, August 10, 1920, p. 2; "Women Taught How to Run an Election." *Boston Globe*, August 13, 1920,

and states extended registration times; added days for women to register; and shifted women's names from earlier, limited vote lists, all in an effort to accommodate new female voters.[4]

Expectations were high that women would play a key role in the election. "Women Take the Ballot Seriously" declared one headline just days after ratification.[5] "Registration of Women Is Heavy" advised the *St. Paul Dispatch* as the election approached.[6] "Women Filled Lines at Every Voting Booth" proclaimed a *Boston Globe* front-page headline on election day.[7] Suffrage leaders predicted a "marked change because of women's entrance into the electorate."[8]

Both political parties actively sought the support of new female voters (Bagby 1962; Barnard 1928a, b; Jensen 1981; Lemons 1973).[9] Yet, all of these new voters were apparently a source of considerable anxiety for political organizers: "Women's Vote Baffles Politicians' Efforts to Forecast Election" warned one newspaper headline.[10] The *Boston Globe* reported that "anxious politicians of both parties are sitting up nights worrying about [women's votes]" in an above-the-fold, front-page article entitled "How Will the Women Vote?"[11]

Almost 100 years later, that question – How did newly enfranchised women vote? – remains to be answered satisfactorily. The decades-long struggle for women's suffrage involved conflicting claims about whether and how women might cast their ballots if permitted to do so. Although the experience of female voters in early enfranchising states had provided some clues, the national enfranchisement of women brought about by the Nineteenth Amendment provided the opportunity to evaluate the electoral behavior of women conclusively. Yet, our knowledge of how

p. 2; "Women Learn How to Vote at Fair." *St. Paul Dispatch*, September 6, 1920, p. 5; "Registration Week Begins Tomorrow." *The New York Times*, October 3, 1920, p. 4.

4 For example: "Mayor Extends Time for Registration." *Boston Globe*, August 19, 1920; "Wednesday Only Day for Women to Get Votes." *Chicago Tribune*, August 20, 1920, p. 3; "Women Now Registered Stay on Lists." *Bridgeport Post*, September 22, 1920, p. 1.

5 "Women Take the Ballot Seriously." *Boston Globe*, September 8, 1920, p. 1.

6 "Registration of Women Is Heavy." *St. Paul Dispatch*, October 23, 1920, p. 1.

7 "Women Filled Lines at Every Voting Booth." *Boston Globe*, November 2, 1920, p. 1.

8 "Women Transforming Polls, Says Mrs. Catt After Vote for Cox." *Minneapolis Morning Tribune*, November 3, 1920, p. 3.

9 For example, "Democrats Lay Plans to Snare Women's Votes." *Chicago Tribune*, August 10, 1920, p. 7.

10 "Women's Vote Baffles Politicians' Efforts to Forecast Election." *Bridgeport Post*, October 29, 1920, p. 1.

11 "How Will the Women Vote?" *Boston Globe*, September 5, 1920, p. 1.

women first voted and with what consequence remains contradictory and incomplete.

Two somewhat conflicting sets of conclusions characterize current understandings of the behavior and impact of the first female voters. One perspective emphasizes the failure of women to employ their new right distinctively and of women's suffrage to effectuate any meaningful political change. In this assessment, women took up their right to vote in only very limited numbers, and those who did cast ballots voted just as men did. As a result, the impact of female voters on American politics was virtually nonexistent. As early as 1924, writers were asking, "Is Woman-Suffrage a Failure?" (Russell 1924; see also Blair 1925; Rice and Willey 1924; Tarbell 1924), and that characterization was soon accepted as scholarly wisdom (Alpern and Baum 1985).

Other scholars, however, have claimed that in some elections and in some places, women exercised their new right in ways distinctive from those of long-enfranchised men. Women have been implicated as major contributors to the Republican landslide of 1920, and many have concluded that women's suffrage initially benefited Republican candidates (e.g., Brown 1991; Lane 1959; Smith 1980; Willey and Rice 1924). An association of women with the Progressive movement led many to expect women to be particular supporters of Progressive causes and candidates, such as third-party presidential candidate Robert La Follette in 1924 (e.g., Allen 1930; Flexner 1959; Ogburn and Goltra 1919; Russell 1924; Tarbell 1924). Others describe women – mobilized by issues of religion and prohibition – as playing a particularly important role in the presidential election of 1928 (Andersen 1996; Burner 1986; Burnham 1980; Matthews 1992; Sundquist 1983). Still others have proposed and uncovered data consistent with the claim that men and women followed distinct paths to New Deal realignment in the 1930s (Andersen 1979; Gamm 1986).

Yet, the evidentiary basis for *any* conclusions about women's electoral behavior and impact after suffrage turns out to be surprisingly thin. The reason is that we actually possess very limited useful data on how women voted after suffrage. With rare exceptions, official records report only the total number of votes cast overall and for each candidate. Whether women cast ballots, for which candidates, and with what consequences cannot be determined directly from the vote record alone. Reliable public opinion polls – the modern solution to this problem – were virtually nonexistent during this period. Early researchers attempted to draw conclusions from the available aggregate election and census records, but since Robinson (1950) social scientists have understood the dangers of what is known as the ecological fallacy (see Chapter 4) and generally shied away from such analysis. Meticulous empirical work has told us something about how women voted in a few places at a few times (e.g., Andersen 1994; Gamm 1986; Goldstein 1984), but this time- and effort-intensive research is limited both geographically and temporally. As a consequence, more than ninety years after women won the right to vote, and despite a conventional wisdom that can sound quite confident in its conclusions, we actually know far less than we should, or than we believe we do, about the behavior and impact of female voters in the period after suffrage.

This book seeks to fill this lacuna and in doing so, to deepen and improve our understanding of an important period in American electoral history and political development. The enfranchisement of women, the largest expansion of the electorate in American history, transformed the relationship between women and the state (Andersen 1996). The extension of suffrage rights to women is a key example of the sort of "durable shift in governing authority" (Orren and Skowronek 2004, 123) that shapes the path of American political development by disrupting and transforming relationships of influence and power. Yet, our current knowledge of how women employed the vote once won remains quite limited, almost 100 years after the fact.

Combining unique historic election data and recent methodological innovations, we are able to estimate the turnout and vote choice of new female voters in the five presidential elections following suffrage (1920–1936) for a larger and more diverse set of places – a sample of ten American states – than has previously been possible. This is a major accomplishment. Previous studies were limited to a small number of places over one or a small number of elections. Estimating how particular groups behave based on the available aggregate data on population characteristics and overall election returns has long been considered an insurmountable methodological challenge, particularly for a group as evenly distributed across locales as women are. Our ability to generate reliable estimates of women's turnout and vote choice during this era is a central contribution of this research.

These estimates permit us to observe and evaluate the behavior and impact of new female voters. In doing so, we consider the accuracy of the traditional and often conflicting narratives of the behavior and impact of new female voters found in contemporary and scholarly sources. Moreover, we place those long-standing accounts within the context of more general expectations about the turnout and vote choice of women as newly enfranchised citizens derived from elections and voting research. The result is a thorough and extensive theoretical and empirical accounting of the incorporation of women into the American electorate.

While highlighting the contributions we are able to make, we also acknowledge important limitations. Women, like men, are not an undifferentiated bloc in any sense, including politically. A number of characteristics, such as class, ethnicity, immigrant status, and race, surely shaped women's political experiences and incorporation into the electorate. Our methodological approach permits us to offer insights into the electoral behavior of women in general during this period, but it does not allow us to reach any conclusions about the electoral behavior of women in different social groups.

We recognize that different groups of women very likely had different opportunities and propensities to take advantage of their newly granted right to vote. To use one particularly important example, we have every reason to expect that the myriad formal and informal institutions that kept black men from the polls in the 1920s and 1930s certainly barred most black women from participating as well, despite their concerted attempts to do so. Black women faced particularly strong barriers in the South, where the vast majority of African Americans resided in the 1920s and 1930s (Lebsock 1993; Terborg-Penn 1998). Our data cannot tell us the race of those women who did turn out to vote, but everything we do know about the period leads us to expect there were few African American women in their ranks. Thus, while our data and estimates can only speak of the electoral behavior of male and female voters in general, we are cognizant of the fact that any description of women as an undifferentiated whole masks important variation among and between them. We seek to be attentive to these dynamics when discussing turnout and vote choice in our various states.

In this introduction we first review current understandings of the impact of women's suffrage on American politics. We then turn to a discussion of expectations for the mobilization – both overall and by particular political parties – of newly enfranchised women. Next, we argue for a broader and more nuanced standard for evaluating the contribution of women to elections after suffrage. Finally we preview our findings and map out our plan for the rest of the book.

The Supposed Impact of Women's Suffrage

This book inquires into the behavior and impact of female voters after suffrage. For many, these are settled, and easy to answer, questions. Women were initially (and for quite some time) reluctant to turn out to vote. When they did vote, women cast ballots that were largely indistinguishable from those of long-enfranchised men. These claims emerged almost immediately after women won the right to vote (see Alpern and Baum 1985; Andersen 1996; Baker 1984). Contemporary writers debated whether, in what ways, and to what extent women in politics were a "failure" (Blair 1925; Russell 1924; Tarbell 1924), while in a widely cited study, scholars described women's "ineffective use of the vote" (Rice and Willey 1924). By the 1930s, the standard textbook on American politics, Ogg and Ray's *Introduction to American Government*, could report that the experience of female voters had clearly revealed that "women voters are strikingly like men voters" (1932, 112). These early, largely impressionistic accounts became the basis of the conventional wisdom as "[m]any conclusions drawn in the 1920s were incorporated into standard histories of the impact of the adoption of the Nineteenth Amendment" (Alpern and Baum 1985, 45).

Indeed, many contemporaries and later scholars concluded not only that the enfranchisement of women had no discernible impact on elections, but that women's suffrage had no impact on politics at all. That is, the belief that women's suffrage was a "failure" described not only elections, but also effects on public policy, politics more generally, and the cause of greater equality for women (see Andersen 1996; Baker 1984). Despite women's extensive activism in the Progressive movement, women's suffrage failed to generate more reform-oriented and female-friendly public policy. Despite women's supposed natural purity and morality, women's suffrage failed to transform the corrupt world of politics. Despite the great promise of the vote as the sine qua non of democratic politics, women's suffrage failed to dramatically empower women or fundamentally challenge their unequal position in American society.

The "women's suffrage as failure" conventional wisdom has been challenged on a number of fronts. Cott (1990) argues cogently that looking for dramatic political change in the wake of women's enfranchisement ignores the extent and ways in which women were politically active both before and after the "great divide" of 1920. Goss (2013) shows how the conventional narrative of women's organizational collapse after suffrage misses the ways in which women's organizational activism diversified in the 1920s and the degree to which women's advocacy continued apace. As women were already active and influential within movements and as advocates for policy change before enfranchisement (see Clemens 1997; Wilkerson-Freeman 2003), we should not expect to see dramatic change when the – one could argue, relatively less powerful – act of casting ballots was added to women's available repertoire of political action (see Pateman 1980). Cott (1990, 153) also challenges electoral impact as the standard by which women's political influence should be judged: "Concentrating on suffrage and the electoral arena means viewing women's politics through the conventional lens where male behavior sets the norm." Many writers, both at the time and since, have emphasized that most politically active women of the period explicitly rejected any expectation of a female voting bloc, arguing instead that women, as diverse and independent human beings, rather than a gendered class, would be similarly diverse in their political choices (e.g., Alpern and Baum 1985; Cott 1990; McConnaughy 2013; Roosevelt 1940).

Others argue that the failure claim ignores important achievements. At the national level, scholars have credited women's suffrage with providing the impetus for a number of important bills in the early 1920s, most notably the Shepard–Towner and Cable Acts pertaining to maternity and infant care and women's citizenship, respectively (Andersen 1996; Ogg and Ray 1932). These successes and the general dearth of other new policies responsive to women must be viewed, Andersen (1996) argues, within the broader context of the 1920s, a decade of conservative retrenchment and Progressive movement weakness. At the state and local levels, legislators initially responded to women's enfranchisement with various reform policies, many aimed at women and children, and women's suffrage often translated into political influence and activism in complex and important ways (e.g., Schuyler 2006; Scott 1972; Wilkerson-Freeman 2003).

Moreover, whatever the direct impact on elections, policy, and politics, the passage of the Nineteenth Amendment transformed women's contested relationship to the political sphere, as well as the "boundaries between male and female" (Andersen 1996, 15). As we discuss in detail in Chapter 2, by granting women access to the ballot, the Nineteenth Amendment clearly recognized women as political actors in their own, independent right, challenging long-held norms about the appropriate place of women and the nature of politics itself (DuBois 1978). Women's suffrage was thus a key step in a long, not always straightforward process of expanding political equality for women.

We certainly endorse the unambiguous evidence that women acted politically and affected political outcomes long before, and after, the extension of suffrage rights. We also agree that suffrage represented a fundamental transformation of women's relationship to and place within American politics. What remains less well understood is how and with what consequences women exercised their new rights – that is, how women actually voted. Whatever indirect impact enfranchisement might have had, at its core, suffrage transformed women into *voters* – or at least *eligible* voters – and thus our knowledge of the impact of women's suffrage remains far from complete.

Women won the right to vote at a time of great transition in American politics. The 1920 election, the first after the end of World War I, was heralded as a "return to normalcy" and the decade of the 1920s is often viewed as a relatively tranquil and prosperous interlude between two world wars and before the Great Depression. Yet this apparent lull masks a great deal of change and disruption. Electoral participation, historically high and widespread in the late nineteenth century, fell dramatically in the early twentieth century (cf. Burnham 1965; Converse 1972; Rusk 1974). A third-party presidential candidate garnered 17 percent of the vote in 1924, signaling a growing dissatisfaction with the options offered by the two major parties (Rosenstone, Behr, and Lazarus 1996). Throughout the decade, new lines of cleavage and an evolving population were transforming the political parties. By 1928 – just the third presidential election after the ratification of the Nineteenth Amendment – the process of what would become known as New Deal realignment was underway, dramatically disrupting previous electoral patterns and ultimately resulting in a dominant Democratic majority after decades of Republican ascendancy.

What did women's suffrage contribute to these developments? Did women – as new and inexperienced voters – contribute to electoral instability and change? Did particular issues and parties mobilize women and attract their votes? Were women – undermobilized and with presumably weaker partisan ties – at the forefront of New Deal realignment? Or, as many have claimed, did women's votes have little or no impact at all? In other words: Did women's votes count?

Our challenge to the suffrage-as-failure narrative is thus found not (only) in the electoral data we analyze, but also in the questions we ask. A misguided focus on suffrage success or failure can obscure many interesting and relevant questions about the experience of female voters in the first elections after suffrage. The behavior and impact of newly enfranchised women is, we argue, best understood in terms of *mobilization*: the decision to turn out (mobilization into the active electorate) and the decision to cast a ballot for a particular party's candidate (mobilization by and into particular parties). Both choices defined women as political actors – turnout made women voters, and vote choice made women active partisans. Both decisions were shaped by women themselves – their interests, characteristics, and experiences. Both choices also were shaped by the political context in which women entered the eligible electorate – the ways in which communities facilitated and/or discouraged women's political engagement and preferences. Both choices are intertwined: People turn out to vote largely to (or because they have been encouraged to) cast ballots for particular parties and candidates: "Deciding whether to vote is a choice made not in the abstract, but in the context of particular candidate choices, party images, and issue agendas" (Andersen 1996, 74). Jointly, both kinds of mobilization determine impact. The effect of any group of voters is a function of the mobilization of that group, overall and for particular parties, relative to the mobilization of other groups. Thus, our expectations for the electoral behavior and impact of women after suffrage are shaped by the characteristics of newly enfranchised women themselves and the varying political contexts in which women first had the opportunity to exercise their new suffrage rights.

In the next two sections, we discuss expectations for the mobilization of female voters overall (turnout) and for particular parties (vote choice), respectively. We then return to the question of the impact of women's suffrage, arguing that examining turnout and vote choice together allows us to provide more nuanced evaluations of the contributions of women in the first elections in which they were eligible to participate.

The Turnout of New Female Voters

One direct impact of women's suffrage has been universally acknowledged: Overall turnout declined as a result of adding women to the eligible electorate. What remains unsettled is how much of the decline in turnout in the early twentieth century can be attributed to women. According to many observers and scholars, women's failure to embrace their new right played a major role. As a population without electoral experience and burdened by strong norms discouraging participation, it is not surprising that women are implicated in many of the major treatments of declining turnout at the turn of the last century (e.g., Converse 1972; Rusk 1974). According to Converse (1972, 276), "while definitive research on the precise effects of female suffrage remains to be done," women's suffrage unambiguously played a (or even the) major role.

There is in fact no question that women initially turned out at lower rates than did men, which, given the size of the eligible female electorate, certainly dampened turnout rates (Andersen 1996; Burnham 1980; Dugan and Taggart 1995). Yet, others have challenged the assumption that all or most of the 1920s decline in turnout can be attributed to new female voters, noting the many factors that discouraged participation more broadly during the period, including widespread one-partyism and the introduction of increasingly restrictive registration rules (e.g., Cott 1990; Kleppner 1982b). Burnham (1965) points out that much of the early twentieth-century decline in turnout occurred before 1920, suggesting that other factors were driving the long-term trend. Similarly, Kleppner (1982b) argues that turnout patterns are not consistent with a hypothesis that women's suffrage was the dominant cause in the 1920s, but rather point to the impact of factors such as declining party competition. Andersen (1990) notes that the "System of 1896" produced a large number of citizens with weaker-than-usual partisan attachments, also contributing to decreased turnout. Finally, a focus on women's low turnout per se ignores the more complicated effects of women's suffrage in tandem with other long-term shifts in American political culture. The introduction of the Australian (secret) ballot, combined with the shift in polling locations from saloons and barber shops to schools and churches, transformed election day from a raucous, social, and largely masculine spectacle to a placid, bureaucratic proceeding (see Edwards 1997). It is perhaps not surprising that these changes were associated with decreased turnout (see Andersen 1990; Baker 1984).

Although it is clear that women's turnout initially (and indeed for decades) lagged that of men, basic features of women's mobilization – the level of turnout; the difference in turnout between men and women; and in particular, the variation in the turnout level and gender gap over time and across space – remain largely unknown. Lamenting that women's turnout initially and for some time lagged behind men's, as a general rule, has often obscured the considerable variation in women's turnout across time and space after suffrage. Understanding the causes and consequences of this variation can provide important insight into the nature and potential of women's engagement with electoral politics in this era. What might we expect of women's mobilization into the active electorate in the presidential elections following enfranchisement?

Expectations for Women's Turnout

New female voters shared many characteristics with long-enfranchised men: socioeconomic status, race, religion, region, age, and immigrant status, to name a few. They differed from men in two specific ways: They were *new* (to the electorate) and they were *women*. These two characteristics were, of course, closely related. The condition of being female was the defining factor that excluded women from suffrage,[12] and the Nineteenth Amendment expanded access to the franchise on the basis of sex alone. In other words, female voters in the 1920s and 1930s were *new* because they were *women*.

Both their newness and their gender were expected by both contemporaries and later scholars to have important consequences for how and with what impact women employed their new right. It is not surprising that the turnout of women, as new voters, lagged behind that of men. Voting has long been characterized as a learned behavior and an acquired habit; turnout in the past increases the probability of turnout in the future (see Gerber, Green, and Shachar 2003; Plutzer 2002). Those who have been systematically denied the opportunity to participate are likely disadvantaged in the future; experience, it is hypothesized, reinforces attachment to the political system and generates higher turnout across the life cycle (cf., Niemi, Stanley, and Evans 1984). Contemporary activists expressed the concern that women's turnout was hampered by lack of experience (Gerould 1925; Wells 1929). At the same time, the experience of other newly enfranchised groups suggests that acquiring the habit of voting may not be that difficult; other new voters appear to have turned out at nearly equal rates and in much the same manner as those already in the electorate (Kleppner 1982a; Niemi, Stanley, and Evans 1984).

New female voters, however, confronted unique conditions as a result of their sex. As Andersen (1990, 196) writes, "viewing women as simply one instance of the class of 'newly enfranchised voters' is inadequate" because women were not only denied the vote, but had been taught to understand themselves as "*by nature unsuited* to politics" (italics original). Dominant (but evolving) social customs equated femininity with the private sphere of home, as opposed to the public world of politics (Kraditor 1981; Lane 1959; see Chapter 2).

Thus, women entering the electorate in the 1920s had been socialized during a period of widespread female disenfranchisement and

[12] For women of color and immigrant women, race and citizenship also were exclusion factors, both before and after the passage of the Nineteenth Amendment.

norms against women's political engagement. Social scientists have long recognized that the "times" in which one is born and socialized shape attitudes and behavior throughout life. Critical events, such as national enfranchisement, can disrupt beliefs and transform behaviors. Yet, not everyone changes in response to new information, and the likelihood of changed attitudes and behaviors is not uniform; younger people appear more open to change whereas the attitudes of older people are more "crystalized" and thus resistant to alteration (e.g., Beck and Jennings 1991; Mannheim 1952; Stoker and Jennings 2008). For these reasons, we should not be surprised that attitudes about appropriate roles for women continued to discourage some women from voting in the years after 1920 (Andersen 1996; Baker 1984). For example, nearly 8 percent of respondents (one-ninth of all female nonvoters) in Merriam and Gosnell's (1924) classic study of nonvoting in 1920s Chicago gave "disbelief in women's voting" as a reason; another 1 percent cited "objections of husband" (see also Gosnell 1927). In an explicit test of the effect of generations (e.g., Mannheim 1952), Firebaugh and Chen (1995) find that women who were older at the time of enfranchisement were less likely to turnout to vote throughout their lives (i.e., to change their behavior) than women who were younger in 1920, or who were born after the ratification of the Nineteenth Amendment (cf. Beckwith 1986).

Thus women's turnout was believed to be hampered by both their newness and their gender. And indeed, that women's turnout after suffrage lagged that of men is not in dispute. Because female turnout was not observed directly in most states, we have very few available indicators of turnout by sex. Nonetheless, to our knowledge, every known instance of available US data reveals a lower rate of turnout or registration among women as compared to men in the first elections in which women were eligible to vote (Arneson 1925; Berman 1993; Gamm 1986; Goldstein 1984; Lebsock 1993; Pollock 1939; Sumner 1909; see Chapter 3). In other nations, where data on the sex of voters are available, women consistently turn out at lower rates than men immediately after suffrage (Duverger 1955; Tingsten 1937). Postwar survey work indicates that women's participation, although increasing over time, continued to lag that of men from the advent of survey research in the late 1940s and 1950s through the 1970s (Berelson, Lazarsfeld, and McPhee 1954; Campbell et al. 1960; CAWP 2014; Wolfinger and Rosenstone 1980).

The rationale for and evidence of women's lower turnout, relative to that of men, is overwhelming. We are thus confident in treating women's lower rate of turnout as an assumption of this research, rather than a hypothesis to be tested. As we detail in Chapter 4, the noncontroversial assumption that male turnout exceeds female turnout makes it possible for us to estimate women's turnout and vote choice with available aggregate data. However, it is important to emphasize that we assume only that male turnout exceeds female turnout; we do not assume anything about the *size* of the turnout gender gap. The few available studies reveal considerable variation in the level of female turnout and the size of the sex differential both within the United States and within and between other nation states (Burnham 1980; Duverger 1955; Goldstein 1984; Niemi and Weisberg 1984; Tingsten 1937). The circumstances in which women were eligible to vote were clearly consequential. Thus, our analysis focuses on understanding variation in women's turnout at different times and in different places.

Explaining Variation in the Mobilization of Women

Although most accounts share the assumption that women entered the electorate as less politically experienced and engaged than men, the implications of this lack of experience and engagement on variation in turnout are ambiguous. As inexperienced voters, women may have been particularly susceptible to political cues and stimuli. Alternatively, women's isolation from politics may have made them resistant to traditional channels of influence and affect. Or, perhaps women's experience with and exposure to politics prior to suffrage resulted in responsiveness to political context similar to that of long-enfranchised men. We consider the possibilities in turn.

More Responsive to Context. A dominant characterization – both at the time and among many later scholars – is that newly enfranchised women were politically disengaged, uninterested, and inattentive (see Chapter 2). Even if we do not share contemporaries' expectations that women were *inherently* (i.e., by their very nature) less interested in politics, socialization and social norms during the period, as well as the experience of disenfranchisement, likely gave women less opportunity to learn about and develop an interest in politics.

As so understood, women shared fundamental characteristics with other low-propensity, or – to use terms long popular in political science – "peripheral" voters. Peripheral voters are less engaged – both in terms of interest and activity – in political affairs than "core" voters. Core voters' interest in and attention to politics produces reliable electoral participation; the default behavior for core voters is turning out to vote. Although an unusual circumstance may keep core voters from the ballot box from time to time, those cases are the exception rather than the rule. Peripheral voters, on the other hand, pay little attention to and have little interest in, political affairs. As a result, their default behavior is nonvoting; unless given a strong reason to be active, peripheral voters tend to abstain from participating in elections (see Campbell 1960, 1964; Glaser 1962; Kaufmann, Petrocik, and Shaw 2008; Kleppner 1982a).

As this discussion suggests, context – both across place and over time – is especially important for peripheral voters whose baseline propensity to vote is low. Core voters participate regardless of the circumstances. Peripheral voters require strong stimuli to overcome their basic disinclination to political activity. For example, close elections have long been identified as a spur to turnout (cf. Campbell et al. 1960; Holbrook and Van Dunk 1993; Patterson and Caldeira 1983). Close competition is consequential for a number of reasons: It induces parties and candidates to expend greater effort on voter mobilization, encourages heightened press coverage, generates excitement and greater interest in the election, and increases the perceived value of any one vote (see Aldrich 1993; Rosenstone and Hansen 1993). The mobilization efforts associated with close competition have particularly strong effects on low-propensity voters (Arceneaux and Nickerson 2009; Hillygus 2005); while high-propensity core voters are already at, or near, their limits for mobilization, many peripheral voters remain available for mobilization.

Similarly, campaigns that involve highly salient issues with widespread interest and appeal and/or particularly charismatic or compelling candidates bring peripheral voters to the polls (Kaufmann, Petrocik, and Shaw 2008). The expectation that less politically engaged voters, such as women, are particularly affected by the nature of the campaign or candidate, or the closeness of the election, has a long history. For example, Glaser (1962, 38) writes, "when the glamour of campaigns and public concern vary, *women*, the young, and the lower class will fluctuate more in turnout than will men" (emphasis ours).

A similar logic leads us to expect barriers to voting to weigh particularly heavy on those already disinclined to turnout to vote. In particular, stringent legal requirements for voting are known to discourage participation (Patterson and Caldeira 1983; Powell 1986; Rosenstone and Hansen 1993; Wolfinger and Rosenstone 1980). Requirements that citizens register long before campaigns have made elections salient, pass literacy or citizenship tests, or pay a poll tax all add to the real and perceived costs of voting. For voters already disinclined to participate, the effort demanded by bureaucratic hoops may be a price they are unwilling to pay. Many of the major Progressive Era reforms, particularly the Australian ballot, were in widespread use by the time women entered the electorate. Yet, states and localities varied considerably in the types and stringency of the provisions they employed (Keyssar 2000). If women are rightly understood as peripheral voters, we would expect that women's turnout was especially responsive to variation across locales in the legal costs associated with voting. Black women were particularly singled out for oppressive implementation of the poll tax and other registration requirements, surely dampening their turnout (Lebsock 1993). Some observers reported that Southern poll taxes also bore heavily on white women, perhaps to a greater degree than they did on poor white men or even African Americans (Bunche 1973; Wilkerson-Freeman 2002). Further evidence of the perception that the poll tax suppressed women's votes can be found in the considerable activism for poll tax reform by women's organizations in the decades following suffrage (Ogden 1958; Scott 1970; Tyler 1996).

There is some evidence that new female voters indeed behaved as peripheral voters in their turnout behavior. Within other countries, where turnout was generally low, male–female turnout differences after suffrage were relatively large. Where turnout rates increased, the gap between male and female turnout narrowed, sometimes considerably (Tingsten 1937). Thus whatever encouraged male turnout appears to have had an even greater effect on female participation. In the United States, Kleppner (1982b) finds the closeness of the election to have a particularly strong stimulating effect on the turnout of new female voters. Thus, the expected lower levels of political interest and attentiveness among women may have resulted in turnout behavior that is more responsive to contextual shifts than men's: More depressed by barriers to voting and more stimulated by incentives.

Less Responsive to Context. Alternatively, new female voters may have been *less* responsive to context than were men. Some would argue that women were strongly disinclined to any political activity during this period. It was not simply that women were not well socialized into politics, but that they were strongly socialized into a *nonpolitical* role (Stucker 1976). As we discuss in Chapter 2, during the nineteenth and into the twentieth century, dominant conceptions of a woman's role clearly assumed she belonged within the confines of the home, where she was naturally suited to the responsibilities of the household, above all motherhood. Men and women were believed to occupy "separate spheres" with men's domain the public sphere of business and politics, and women's place the private sphere of home and family (DuBois 1998; Kerber 1988).

As a result, women's reluctance to challenge dominant norms may not have been overcome by any contextual stimuli; many women may simply have been unwilling to vote and no external conditions could convince them otherwise. For example, mobilization efforts may have little or no impact on those with the lowest propensity to vote because their disinclination to political activity is so strong that no outreach or stimulation can overcome it; only among intermediate-propensity voters (those with at least some inclination to political engagement) can mobilization efforts spur turnout (Matland and Murray 2012; Niven 2004, 2001).[13] Women's presumed lack of interest also may have led them to pay less attention to or gather less political information, insulating them from contextual effects. All of these factors point to women's turnout being less responsive to the political context than was men's.

Equally Responsive to Context. Finally, perhaps the turnout of newly enfranchised women responded to their political context in much the same manner as men's did and thus, the size of the turnout gender gap was not systematically related to the political context. Political parties had an incentive to mobilize women as well as men, and as we discuss in the empirical chapters, there is good evidence that both sought to reach out to new female voters. Despite being characterized as apolitical, women did not arrive at polling places in 1920 completely devoid of political information or experience (see Cott 1990). Women engaged in various non-electoral forms of participation prior to their enfranchisement (Clemens 1997). Women's activism had both facilitated and benefited from an expanded definition of the political that encompassed issues about which women were expected to have special expertise, such as social reform, perhaps increasing female interest in politics (Baker 1984). Although political intensity and participation were declining by 1920, most voting-age women nonetheless had been socialized in a period characterized by strong partisanship, highly salient and intense political debates, and widespread political participation (Burnham 1965). This socialization may have facilitated the assimilation of women into their new political role. As a result, women may have responded as men did to changes in the political context.

In Chapters 5 through 8, we evaluate each of these competing perspectives on women's turnout with the particular goal of understanding how

[13] As Arceneaux and Nickerson (2009) point out, much of the research finding no mobilization effect among the lowest propensity voters examines low salience local and state legislative races. They find that in more salient elections (such as the presidential elections examined here), mobilization efforts do impact even very-low-propensity voters.

specific institutional and political features of the various states encouraged or discouraged the incorporation of women into the electorate. Did context have a greater impact on the turnout of women, as we would expect of a politically uninterested and inattentive group? Or were women so uninterested in and inattentive to politics that even the most politically stimulating contexts could not overcome their disinclination to turnout? Alternatively, did previous political experience and interest make newly enfranchised women as responsive to their context as long-enfranchised men? The answers to these questions, we find, emphasize the contingent and complex nature of women's incorporation into the electorate – where women were first eligible to cast ballots had important consequences for whether they did so.

The Vote Choice of New Female Voters

Generations of students and scholars have received a conventional and unremarkable account of the extension of suffrage. As early as 1946, historian Mary Beard (61–62) complained that "textbooks on government" (she singled out political science luminary V. O. Key in particular) "pay little or no attention to what women have done with the vote, to their political agitation, to their ideas of government." Modern college-level American politics textbooks usually include the story of the women's suffrage movement and the ultimate success of the Nineteenth Amendment in their coverage of the extension (and retraction) of voting rights over time. In most cases, however, the story ends there; women won the right to vote, and then female voters disappear from discussion until the discovery of the gender gap in the 1980s. As this timeline suggests, the inattention to women's electoral behavior after suffrage can be attributed to the prevailing understanding that women failed to emerge as a distinct and influential voting bloc after suffrage. For example, in their American politics textbook *We the People*, Ginsberg, Lowi, and Weir (2009, 298) conclude that "Although proponents of women's suffrage had expected women to make a distinctive impact on politics as soon as they won the vote, not until the 1980s did voting patterns reveal a clear difference between male and female votes."

The failure of a women's voting bloc to emerge has been traditionally attributed to the widespread belief that women voted as their husbands and thus only replicated the male vote (see Alpern and Baum 1985; Flanagan 1995). The expectation that women would defer to their husbands and simply "double the existing vote" was pervasive even before the Nineteenth Amendment was ratified (McConnaughy 2013, 11). According to a 1916 *New York Times* article,

> The theory of the woman suffragists that, when accorded the right to vote, the women will vote independently of the men and cast their ballots according to their own convictions is not borne out by the returns from Illinois, where the votes of the women are counted separately. The women of that State voted squarely with the men on the main issue. Their voting nearly doubled the cost of the election and greatly increased the labors of the poll clerks, but the only way it affected the result was to make the Republican majority in Illinois larger than it would have been … The lesson of Illinois is, therefore, that woman suffrage tends to increase the number of voters without affecting the result of the voting.[14]

As soon as women began exiting polling places nationwide, observers declared the expectation confirmed: "American women vote as their husbands, brothers, or fathers indicate," claimed journalist Charles Edward Russell (1924, 729). "Most of the women I know … vote as their husbands vote," echoed writer Katharine Fullerton Gerould (1925, 450). In his popular treatise on American life in the 1920s, *Only Yesterday*, journalist Frederick Lew Allen (1931, 95–96) described the "American woman:" "She won the suffrage in 1920. She seemed, it is true, to be very little interested in it once she had it; she voted, but mostly as the unregenerate men about her did." Pioneering pollster George Gallup claimed in 1940: "How will [women] vote on election day? Just as exactly as they were told the night before" (quoted in Berinksy 2006, 506). Histories of the period soon followed suit. For example, citing examples from journalists and political activists, historian William H. Chafe (1972, 31) writes that "observers noted the same tendency of women to defer to men when it came to politics."

The idea that women took political direction from their husbands also characterizes many of the original, influential studies of American voting behavior. The Columbia scholars, describing data showing that, among married respondents, a larger percentage of women than men report that they "would go to a family member to discuss a political question" and "discussed politics with a family member," conclude (Berelson, Lazarsfeld, and McPhee 1954, 102): "The men discuss politics with their wives – that is, they *tell* them – but they do not particularly respect them. On the side of the wives there is trust; on the side of the husbands, there is the need to reply or guide" (emphasis original). It is not clear on what

[14] "The Illinois Women Voters." *The New York Times*, November 8, 1916, p. 12. See also: "The Women Who Voted." *The New York Times*, November 10, 1916, p. 12.

evidentiary basis Berelson and his colleagues infer this set of attitudes or behaviors to explain the observed discussion patterns, other than the received conventional wisdom about the dependence of women on their husbands for political information and preferences.

Emphasizing women's reported lower levels of political efficacy, the authors of *The American Voter* likewise describe most (although not all) women as strongly influenced by their husbands (Campbell et al. 1960, 492): "The wife who votes but otherwise pays little attention to politics tends to leave not only the sifting of information up to her husband but abides by his ultimate decision about the direction of the vote as well." (Ladd [1997, 118] notes that "The stereotyping achieved in this 'classic' account has rarely been equaled and never surpassed.") In his influential paper, "The Nature of Belief Systems in Mass Publics," Converse (1964, 233) concludes that due to women's lesser sophistication, knowledge, and interest, "The wife is very likely to follow her husband's opinions, however imperfectly she may have absorbed their justifications at a more complex level."

Students of American elections rarely asked women or men directly about the reasons for the similarity of the votes of husbands and wives, but available comparative work provides some support for the assumption of dependence on the husband's expertise. Duverger (1955, 49), in his UNESCO report, *The Political Role of Women*, describes the results of a 1953 French survey in which

> Nearly a third of the women questioned state that they voted in the same way as their husbands primarily because they were not interested in politics themselves and preferred to rely on their husbands' judgment. No man gave such a reply. One-fifth of the women questioned said that they wanted 'to avoid arguments', but only *one* man gave this answer. (italics in original)

It is presumably on this basis that Duverger (1955, 129) later concludes

> But, while women have, legally, ceased to be minors, they still have the mentality of minors in many fields and, particularly in politics, they usually accept paternalism on the part of men. The man – husband, fiancé, lover or myth – is the mediator between them and the political world.

Not everyone followed the "vote like husbands" script. Political scientist Charles Merriam wrote in 1929 (154-155):

> … the general testimony has been that votes are not primarily determined by sex lines, but by other social considerations. This cannot be taken to mean that women follow the lead of men, for in many instances the contrary is true, and the woman may persuade or cajole or intimidate the man.

Yet even many of those who allow that women of the era may have exercised independence of thought and judgment still expect that women voted the same as men did. The reason was not women's deference to men but that women, like men, voted in ways consistent with relevant group characteristics such as socioeconomic status, race, or religion (e.g., Chafe 1972; Goldstein 1984). As no less an authority on women and politics than Eleanor Roosevelt wrote in 1940 (45), "I think it is fairly obvious that women have voted on most questions as individuals and not as a group, in much the same way that men do, and that they are influenced by their environment and their experience and background, just as men are." Given the fairly equal distribution of women across demographic groups, the expected outcome is still little or no difference in partisan mobilization, and thus electoral impact, associated with the entrance of women into the electorate.

Although the "voted like their husbands" conventional wisdom is popular, a closer read of previous research reveals a number of expectations for divergent vote choice among men and women. Many assert that Republicans held an advantage among women in the first elections in which women were eligible to vote, for example (see Alpern and Baum 1985; Brown 1991; Goldstein 1984; Willey and Rice 1924). Women were often expected to be stronger supporters of Progressive causes and candidates (e.g., Ogburn and Goltra 1919). The issues of Prohibition and religion were believed to have particularly stimulated female mobilization – both for and against Democrat Al Smith – in 1928 (Andersen 1996; Burner 1986; Burnham 1980; Matthews 1992; Sundquist 1983). Others have suggested women – whose limited experience with the ballot made them uniquely available for both mobilization and conversion – played a distinctive role in New Deal realignment (Andersen 1979; Gamm 1986). From these various accounts it is clear that there are a number of open questions about women's mobilization and incorporation into the partisan electorate. The empirical chapters describe and evaluate these election-specific claims in detail. In the section that follows here, we consider general expectations for female voters' patterns of partisan support overall.

Expectations for the Partisan Mobilization of Women

Accounts of women's suffrage include both claims that women voted exactly like men and claims that women were distinctive in their vote choice. Research on vote choice and elections more generally also supports various expectations for the partisan mobilization of women, depending in large part on our assumptions about both newly enfranchised women and the contexts in which they first cast their ballots. We consider the competing claims below and evaluate them in Chapters 5 through 8.

Women as Swing Voters. There are a number of reasons to expect female voters were particularly susceptible to election-specific partisan swings. As we have noted, women were widely assumed to be politically uninterested, inattentive, and disengaged, the classic description of so-called peripheral voters. In addition to being less likely to turn out to vote, peripheral voters are less loyal partisans and more swayed by election-specific factors than long-term allegiances. The same factors – salience, competition, unusually appealing candidates, compelling issues – that are expected to stimulate turnout among peripheral voters also drive their vote choice when they do participate. Because peripheral voters' partisan attachments are less grounded in experience, information, and reasoning, they are more susceptible to the election-specific messages that favor one candidate over the other (Kaufmann, Petrocik, and Shaw 2008; Miller and Shanks 1996).

Other characteristics of new female voters also point to swing voter behavior. Women's lack of experience meant missed opportunities for reinforcing commitment to the electoral system and to a particular partisan preference. Converse's (1969, 1976) classic statement on partisan stability emphasizes the importance of reinforcement via electoral participation for explaining the increasing stability of partisan identity over time, an expectation confirmed by later research (e.g., Jennings and Markus 1984; Stoker and Jennings 2008; see also McPhee and Ferguson 1962). Converse (1969) predicted that those enfranchised later in life would have particular weak partisan attachments (and turnout), not only because of the lesser time for reinforcement through electoral participation, but also because of the missed opportunity for the establishment of political affiliations during the early life socialization process.

There are gender-specific rationales for the expectation of less loyalty to the two major parties as well. Contemporaries often described women as more committed to ideals than to party (Barnard 1928c; Monoson 1990; Rogers 1930). The Progressive movement denounced political parties as corrupt and inefficient, so to the extent women were Progressive minded, they were expected to shun traditional parties (see Andersen 1990). Finally, women's lack of influence in the parties and the selection of nominees led some to argue that neither parties' candidates represented the interests of women, discouraging loyalty to either party (Fisher 1947; Flanagan 1995; Martin 1925).

Thus, we might expect newly enfranchised women to be, on average, less loyal partisans and more susceptible to election year swings than established voters (Lemons 1973; Rusk 1974). Evidence in support of this hypothesis in the case of new voters, including women, has been mixed (e.g., Cain, Kiewiet, and Uhlaner 1991; Claggett 1980; Niemi, Stanley, and Evans 1984; Niemi et al. 1985; Wong 2000). Claggett (1982) considers the case of female enfranchisement explicitly, noting that Converse's framework would predict weak partisan ties among new women voters, which would in turn lead to greater electoral instability following suffrage extension. He finds no such surge in electoral instability after 1920.

Women Mobilized by Particular Parties. On the other hand, some contemporary observers and later scholars concluded or expected that new female voters gave particular support to one or another of the parties, what we term the "particular partisanship hypothesis." Specifically, a number of accounts suggest women's suffrage benefited the Republican Party, at least initially (e.g., Bagby 1962; Brown 1991; Burner 1986; Gould 2003; Lemons 1973; McCoy 1971; Pateman 1994; Smith 1980; Willey and Rice 1924; see Chapter 5). The most cited evidence in support of this expectation is the fact that in 1916, the Democratic incumbent received 9.1 million votes to his Republican challenger's 8.5 million. In 1920, following the passage of the Nineteenth Amendment, the Democratic candidate again received 9.1 million votes, while the number of votes secured by the Republican almost doubled to 16.1 million votes (Brown 1991).

Why might the first female voters favor the Republican Party? The Republican Party was the major party most associated with Progressivism during the first elections in which women were eligible to vote, and it was a Republican Congress that passed the Nineteenth Amendment. Moreover, there is some evidence that Republicans more directly and overtly appealed to women voters, while Democrats chose not to depend on sex-specific appeals (Barnard 1928a, 1928b; Jensen 1981). Suffrage leaders themselves were overwhelmingly middle-class Protestants, characteristics associated with Republican identification in the mass electorate. Many expected that the first women to take advantage of their new right likely shared those characteristics, and attribute the Republican bias among women voters to which women voted, rather than to women as a whole (Rymph 2006).

As this discussion suggests, an expectation that women favored the goals and ideals of the Progressive movement underpins many expectations for particular partisanship. Women (and women's organizations) had been active and prominent participants in the Progressive movement, and Progressive ideals, particularly moral reform, were consistent with the qualities associated with women during the nineteenth and early twentieth century (Baker 1984; Evans 1989; see Chapter 2). Indeed, concern that women would use the vote to achieve Progressive goals, particularly prohibition, galvanized a number of active opponents to women's suffrage, most notably the liquor industry (Flexner 1959; McDonagh and Price 1985). Many expected women's votes to be particularly influenced by Progressive issues such as prostitution, gambling, poverty relief, child labor, workplace health and safety, good government, and especially prohibition (Allen 1930; Flexner 1959; McCormick 1928; Ogburn and Goltra 1919; O'Neill 1971; Rice and Willey 1924; Russell 1924; Tarbell 1924; Toombs 1929; Wells 1929; Willey and Rice 1924). As we have suggested, in 1920, the party most closely associated with Progressivism was the GOP. In 1924, however, recently enfranchised women had the option of casting a ballot for an actual Progressive Party candidate, Robert M. La Follette. Thus, we might expect women were more likely than men to cast their ballots for Republicans, or when available, for candidates associated with the Progressive cause.

Women Mobilized by Locally Dominant Parties. We also consider a third possibility – that the first female voters may have favored locally dominant parties. Harvey (1998) argues that long-established political parties had an advantage over new interest-based women's organizations in mobilizing female voters into electoral politics. Both parties and interest-based groups had experience with and expertise in mobilizing male voters, and thus both were responsible for bringing men to the polls. Women's groups, however, had little experience in voter mobilization and difficulty transitioning to that new role, and thus new women voters were mobilized almost exclusively by parties. As a result, Harvey (1998, 147) predicts that

> ... male registration and voting behavior during the 1920s should reflect not only the mobilization efforts of the two parties, but also the efforts of independent benefit-seeking organizations attempting to mobilize male votes for their own purposes. Conversely, women's registration and voting behavior would reflect only the efforts of the parties to mobilize their loyalties.

Thus, "holding the partisan strength of any area constant, we should see women registering and voting disproportionately with the local dominant party, relative to registering and voting men" (1998, 148).

Other processes may have contributed to greater mobilization of women by the locally advantaged party. The period preceding 1920 was characterized by strong partisanship and widespread one-partyism (e.g., Burnham 1981a). Even when denied the right to vote, women would have been exposed to communities where in most cases one political party dominated in terms of loyalty among the mass electorate and control of political office. One-partyism likely shaped the consistency and strength of the political messages that women received (what we might describe as partisan socialization), influencing their sense of partisan identification and their vote choice once enfranchised (e.g., Beck and Jennings 1991; Mannheim 1952; Stoker and Jennings 2008).

Both men and women would have been exposed to these strong partisan messages, but women may have experienced more homogeneous and reinforcing partisan cues. During this period, men were more likely than women (particularly middle-class, white women) to work outside of the home or immediate neighborhood, thus exposing them to a greater diversity of partisan cues. Presented with conflicting messages, we might expect men to be less consistent in their vote choice (Berelson et al. 1954; Huckfeldt et al. 1995). To the extent that women were less likely to work outside the home or neighborhood, the partisan cues women received may have been more uniform, resulting in more consistent and stable vote choice. For example, in his classic study of Jews in 1950s Boston, Fuchs (1955) notes that Jewish women's interactions were far more circumscribed than were their husband's (most women rarely left their own ward), resulting in distinct political patterns: Men, exposed to the non-Jewish community, were more likely to defect from traditional Jewish patterns in vote choice than were women. Many women in the suffrage era may have experienced similarly homogeneous political environments in their homes and neighborhoods compared to the greater diversity of cues to which men may have been exposed. Such experience may have inculcated greater loyalty and responsiveness to the locally dominant political party. For these several reasons, then, we might expect the first female voters to be particularly likely to support the locally dominant party, what we term the "local party hypothesis."

Women Mobilized as Men Were. Finally, we might expect, as many have long concluded, that women's vote choice was, on the whole, indistinguishable from that of men. The justifications for such an expectation run in at least two directions. In one framing of this expectation, women are once again understood as politically uninterested and inexperienced. However, Campbell and his collaborators (1960, 492) argue that because women relied on their husbands for political information and other guidance, women's partisanship and vote choice was more stable than we might expect for a similarly inexperienced group: "Since the partisan decision [of women] is anchored not in these fragments [women's lesser political information] but in the fuller political understanding of the husband, it may have greater stability over a period of time than we would otherwise suspect." In other words, unlike most new voters, and unlike the typical uninterested and inattentive citizen, women had easy access to political knowledge and information via the men in their lives (husbands, fathers, sons). As a result, their political preferences were rooted in stronger attachments than is the case of most new or uninformed voters. The authors of *The American Voter* thus do not challenge the characterization of newly enfranchised women as inexperienced and uninterested, but they do provide a rationale for the popular "voted like their husbands" conclusion (e.g., Alpern and Baum 1985; Gerould 1925; Russell 1924) grounded in established theories of partisanship and political knowledge.

A second – alternative or additional – way we might explain women's vote choice as similar to that of men emphasizes that women did not enter the electorate entirely devoid of political experience, interest, or opinion. As discussed in the preceding text and in detail in Chapter 2, although women were denied the right to vote, they were not absent from political activity and activism prior to 1920 (Clemens 1997; Cott 1990), experiences that would have exposed them to the same sorts of political knowledge and cues to which men were exposed. As we have noted, the heightened partisanship of the period likely made political information relatively easy to come by. Suffragists themselves, particularly those who put forward equality rather than difference arguments (see Chapter 2), had argued that women were fully capable of engaging in politics in just the same manner as men did (McConnaughy 2013). While Campbell et al. (1960) expect that in shared households and communities, men influenced the vote choice of women, we note that men and women in shared households also likely shared ethnicity, race, nativity, class, religion, and a host of other politically relevant characteristics. To the extent that we expect such factors to predict male vote choice, we might expect them to have a similar impact on women, with the result of similar partisan mobilization patterns among men and women. As Goldstein (1984, 147) argues: "The mere fact that the men and women in an area voted similarly does not imply the either sex was dominated by the other. Members of both sexes acting independently of the other could easily arrive at the same solution of the voting calculus." Thus we might expect to see the first women who entered polling places mobilized by parties in much the same way men were.

In Chapters 5 through 8 we examine the evidence in support of each of these hypotheses. Were women "peripheral voters" – swinging from party to party in response to election-specific forces? Were female voters "particular partisans" – more likely to support specific parties, such as the Republicans or Progressives? Were female voters more loyal to the locally dominant party than were men? Or were women "normal" partisans, indistinguishable in their vote choice patterns from long-enfranchised men? As we will see, each of the five presidential elections between 1920 and 1936 provides a particular type of leverage for examining these questions.

Evaluating the Contributions of Female Voters

A full understanding of the electoral behavior of new female voters requires attention to both mobilization in general (turnout) and mobilization by and into particular political parties (vote choice). It is the combination of these forms of mobilization, particularly in comparison to the mobilization of long-enfranchised men, by which we can understand and evaluate the impact of women's suffrage on electoral politics immediately following enfranchisement.

What might we expect in terms of the impact of new female voters? As we have suggested, almost immediately after women exited the polling places in November 1920, a conventional wisdom emerged that women's suffrage produced no impact: New female voters took up their right in only very limited numbers, and those who did cast ballots voted so similarly to men that the impact of female voters on American politics was virtually nonexistent. The often-unstated standard was a rather dramatic political change: Women suffrage would be judged to have an impact if and only if women voted in such numbers and so distinctively as to change election outcomes.

In one sense, this is not an unreasonable standard. Elections are contests for the selecting of political representatives, and influence over – or better yet, determination of – that choice is power indeed. Given their share of the population, women certainly had the potential to play such a pivotal role in election outcomes. Such an impact, however, requires women to turn out at levels nearing or even surpassing those of men, and/or to cast their ballots for different candidates and parties to a significant and dramatic degree. Neither of those conditions strike us as likely during the period examined here. As we have detailed, we have every reason to expect women's turnout to lag behind that of men during this era (although we expect the size of the gap to vary considerably across time and place). Similarly, even without an expectation that women voted like their husbands, the fact that women were similarly distributed among socioeconomic, religious, and other politically relevant groups suggests that vote choice differences, while certainly possible and meaningful, are unlikely to be large. Since the dawn of modern survey research, the gap between the presidential vote choice of men and women has never exceeded 15 points[15] – enough to influence election outcomes, but only in the context of considerable female turnout and/or a very close partisan divide between male voters. Although possible, on the whole, we do not expect to find that women changed the outcome of presidential contests at the state or national level in the first elections after suffrage.

Does this reality mean that women's suffrage did not matter? Changing the outcome of an election is not, we argue, the only way in which newly enfranchised women may have had an effect on elections and electoral politics. Indeed, a single-minded focus on that high standard has, we believe, obscured the many possible other ways in which women's presence affected elections. Instead of emphasizing who determines the outcome, we focus on who contributes to the outcome, and how, thus permitting us to observe the ways in which women's presence made elections different than they might otherwise have been. What did women contribute to the Republican landslide in 1920? What role did women play in the impressive showing of the Progressive Party in 1924, or alternatively, the ability of the Republican Party to successfully stave off the Progressive challenge? Perhaps most importantly, what was the contribution of women to the shifting partisan alignments of the 1928, 1932, and 1936 elections? Did women, as many expected, play a significant role in dampening enthusiasm for Democrat (and Catholic) Al Smith in the Republican (and Protestant) Midwest? Did undermobilized immigrant (Catholic) women in the Northeast contribute to dramatic Democratic inroads there? Were undermobilized women responsible for large portions of the new voters who entered the active electorate during the New Deal realignment period? Were women more likely to convert from one party to another? What did women contribute to both stability

[15] Source: American National Election Studies. http://electionstudies.org/nesguide/2ndtable/t9a_1_1.htm (Accessed May 21, 2013).

and change in partisan alignments across this period? How might patterns of mobilization overall and by each party been different if women had remained disenfranchised?

We combine both forms of mobilization – turnout and vote choice – to investigate the contribution of female voters to the global patterns of electoral stability and change in each presidential contest. We give particular attention to the transformative elections of 1928, 1932, and 1936 as the "System of 1896" (Burnham 1970, 1981a) unraveled, giving way to the New Deal realignment. By doing so, we offer a richer and more nuanced account of the impact of women's suffrage on American elections which takes into account the varied ways in which new female voters may have contributed to electoral patterns across this dramatic period in American political history.

A Brief Preview

Our research reveals that the behavior and impact of new female voters was both complex and contingent. Women's use of their new right was dependent – more so than men's – on context: Women's turnout was especially stimulated by a competitive political environment, and particularly dampened by restrictive voting laws throughout the period. As we have outlined, this responsiveness to context is consistent with what political science expects of a group that is characterized by a lower level of political engagement (peripheral voters), but not as completely disengaged from politics as many expected of women of the period. As a result, both the level of women's turnout and the size of the turnout gender gap varies considerably from state to state; as early as 1920, we estimate women's turnout to exceed 55 percent in highly competitive Kentucky, while fewer than 5 percent of Virginian women turned out to vote in that same election. These findings challenge attempts to characterize women's political engagement as solely determined by their gender or inexperience. Where encouraged and motivated to do so, newly enfranchised women were capable of impressive levels of mobilization. *Where* women were enfranchised mattered more for women's turnout than the fact that they were women.

On the whole, we conclude that women did not cast ballots for dramatically different parties and candidates than did men. Yet the partisan mobilization of women did differ from that of men in particular places and at particular times. In the first presidential elections, we find that women are particularly mobilized by the locally dominant Republican Party in the Midwest, but are not more Republican than men nationwide, contrary to conventional accounts. In 1924, we find women were as likely, or in a few places less likely, to cast Progressive votes than were men, again contrary to expectations that women were particularly inclined to support Progressives and/or fickle, inexperienced, and loosely tied to the major parties. This set of findings suggests women were initially mobilized by and loyal to the parties traditionally dominant in their state, consistent with the local party hypothesis, and contrary to the expectations of many that women were less dependable partisans.

We find that women were dramatically mobilized in 1928, both for and against Smith, as many have long expected. Yet, contrary to the conventional wisdom, women were not unique in 1928; men also experienced a massive surge in turnout and shifts in vote choice in 1928, equalling or exceeding that of women. Finally, as the New Deal realignment unfolded over the 1932 and 1936 elections, women and men were mobilized into the electorate in large numbers as Democrats. Although we cannot trace conversion and mobilization definitively, our estimates do provide insight into general patterns. We conclude that women were, as expected, more likely than men to defect to the Democratic Party (we observe this most clearly between 1928 and 1932). However, given the larger number of men already in the active electorate, we also conclude that conversion likely played a larger role for men, and mobilization a larger role for women, in generating new Democratic votes. Despite the fact that the number of men participating in presidential elections was much larger, the combined impact of conversion and mobilization in our sample states nets about 1.5 million new Democratic female voters and 1.5 million new Democratic male voters. A mere sixteen years after the extension of the franchise, women's ballots made up an equal share of the gains that underpinned the new Democratic majority. Thus, our research both confirms some aspects of traditional or conventional accounts and challenges others.

What Follows

In the chapters that follow, we review the theoretical and historical background of American women as political actors prior to suffrage with the goal of informing our understanding of their electoral behavior after suffrage, as well as assess what previous scholarship has already told us about how women first used the vote. We describe the design of the research reported in this work, including the original data and innovative methodological approach used to estimate women's and men's turnout and vote choice in these five elections. We use those estimates to investigate a number of puzzles about the behavior and impact of female voters in the five presidential elections after suffrage, and conclude by summarizing our answers to the major questions raised and considering how the experience of the first female voters relates to the decades of female electoral participation that have followed.

We begin by placing our investigation into the behavior and impact of female voters after suffrage into a broader understanding of women and the vote in American history and American politics. In Chapter 2, we examine how conceptions of voting as an act of citizenship and about women as political actors in a democracy evolved over time in the United States. We briefly review the history of the struggle for voting rights for women, emphasizing how that battle shaped the expectations for women's contribution once the vote was won. We examine the other ways in which women affected politics, both before and after the ratification of the Nineteenth Amendment. Denied access to the dominant mode of mass politics in the nineteenth century – voter mobilization – women helped to invent new forms of political influence through social movements and interest group politics. In doing so, they helped shift the distinctions between public and private, both by helping to bring politics into arenas that had previously been considered beyond the reach of the state (particularly the home), and by bringing what were traditionally considered women's interests – care of children, social purity, food and other consumer goods – into the public realm. This process had important consequences for twentieth-century politics writ large, but also directly shaped the expectations for and experience of new female voters.

Interest in the electoral incorporation of half the population has inspired a number of efforts to gain insight into women's voting behavior after suffrage. In Chapter 3, we review what we know from available data and research. In some cases, scattered pieces of actual hard data on registration, turnout, party identification, and even vote choice are available by sex, either because the information was tabulated in that way or researchers have scoured archives for registration lists or voter rolls. In other cases, scholars have, with varying success, sought to estimate female voting behavior during this era, sometimes despite (or without awareness of) the hazards of relying on aggregate data. By detailing what we do know, with some confidence, about women's electoral behavior immediately following the extension of suffrage, we also identify the very real limits of that knowledge, and the need to expand upon our evidentiary basis to more fully evaluate women's electoral behavior and impact after suffrage.

Some ninety years after the ratification of the Nineteenth Amendment, why don't we know more about the behavior and impact of female voters? As scholars have long lamented, "male and female ballots had been fatally co-mingled" (Alpern and Baum 1985, 44), and reliable voter surveys of the period are more or less nonexistent. Chapter 4 introduces our approach to this challenge. As this chapter focuses on data and methodological details, some readers may prefer to skip to the substantive findings reported in the chapters that follow. We first describe how and why we constructed our ten state sample, discuss the election returns and census data we gathered at various levels of aggregation, and compare our sample to the broader United States. We discuss the politically relevant state-level variation captured by our sample, with particular attention to region, party competition, and the legal obstacles to voting. We review, in broad strokes, the evolution of methods of ecological inference since Robinson (1950) identified the ecological fallacy. We describe the Bayesian approach to ecological inference employed in this research to estimate women's turnout and vote choice at the state level. We consider the problems and possibilities inherent in ecological inference in the case of gender, specifically the low variation in proportion of women – the population of interest – across geographic observations. We verify the accuracy of our estimates by reference to available "true" data from Illinois where male and female ballots were counted and reported separately in 1916 and 1920. An appendix provides detailed information about statistical programming choices and evaluation of convergence and other properties of the estimator.

The heart of our empirical analysis is reported in Chapters 5 through 8, in which we explore the ways in which women did (and did not) turn out to use their new right, for which candidates and parties, and to what effect on American elections. In Chapter 5 we examine the election of 1920, heralded as the "return to normalcy" and at minimum, a return to Republican ascendancy after World War I and the Wilson interlude. The election of 1924, featuring a relatively successful third-party candidate who represented the cause of Progressivism, long associated with the activism and interests of women, is the focus of Chapter 6. In Chapter 7, we take on the high-salience election of 1928, in which both contemporary observers and later scholars expected the historic candidacy of Catholic Al Smith and the central issues – religion and Prohibition – to generate unprecedented interest and mobilization among women on both sides of these issues. Finally, in Chapter 8 we turn to the transformative New Deal elections of 1932 and 1936, when recently enfranchised female voters were particularly available for both conversion (because they lacked repeated electoral experience to reinforce partisan loyalties) and mobilization (because so many women had not yet entered the polling place) into the emerging Democratic majority.

In Chapter 9 we focus on what our findings as a whole tell us about key long-standing questions about the incorporation of women into the American electorate. Using contemporary survey data, we place the first female voters within the broader context of the nearly 100 years of women's electoral participation that has followed. Finally, we return to the central question of this research: Did women's votes count?

The title of this book – *Counting Women's Ballots* – is meant to evoke both the substantive questions and methodological challenges at the heart of this research. The empirical impossibility of counting the ballots of newly enfranchised women separate from those of long-enfranchised men has confounded scholars for almost 100 years. Ballots are not distinguished by the sex of the people who cast them, and the solution employed by later scholars – public opinion polls – are unavailable or unreliable during this era. New advances in ecological inference allow us to "count" women's ballots – that is, to produce unique and reliable estimates of women's turnout and vote choice – for more locales and elections than possible with previous methods and data.

These estimates permit us to gain insight into the central theoretical and empirical puzzles driving this research: Did women's ballots "count" in a substantive sense? Specifically, what did women contribute to electoral stability and change during this transformative era? Using our new evidence to provide greater insight into the electoral behavior and impact of women after suffrage is the goal of this book, and the task to which we now turn.

2

Before Suffrage

Nancy Cott (1990) has rightly critiqued the treatment of 1920 as the "great divide" in the history of women in American politics. The accomplishment of women's suffrage via the Nineteenth Amendment is often viewed as a sharp break separating the experience of women into prepolitical and political periods. Women's political activity after 1920 is treated as wholly distinct from that which came before, and the very fact that women acted politically before 1920, and not just through the suffrage movement, can be overlooked. Certainly the attainment of suffrage represents a signal transformation in the character of female citizenship (see Andersen 1996). Yet, as Cott persuasively argues, women's political engagement before and after 1920 is in many ways characterized by more similarity than difference (see also Goss 2013).

We can understand the political behavior of women after suffrage only within the context of women's political behavior before suffrage and of the rapidly evolving political milieu in which women first entered polling places. Enfranchised women were not summoned out of the ether in 1920. A long tradition of Western political thought placed women in a particular, nonpolitical realm and assigned women particular virtues and interests. Yet, the extended struggle for suffrage rights, activism and organization in movements and clubs, and a culture in which politics were highly salient imbued many women with extensive political experience, knowledge, and skills before the vote was attained. Unable to employ the ballot, the central mechanism for political influence of the period, women helped create other forms of political influence. At the same time, the vote itself – its place in the American democratic system and the practical ways in which ballots were cast – evolved dramatically across this period.

This chapter provides an historical and theoretical background to the empirical findings in the chapters that follow. We first trace the ways in which conceptions of politics, especially voting rights, and of female nature, particularly with regard to politics, developed across US history. We then turn to a brief overview of the American suffrage movement, with an emphasis on the ways in which that movement shaped the expectations for and experience of women at the polls in the 1920s and 1930s. We next describe how, despite being denied access to the ballot, women helped to pioneer an expanded repertoire of political activity across the nineteenth and into the twentieth century. We discuss how those new forms of political activism, combined with other developments, contributed to a shifting political context by the first decades of the twentieth century. In the conclusion, we summarize how this background helps us understand the behavior of the first female voters, the central task of this book.

Women and Politics in Theory and Practice

That the franchise was made available to voting-age women only ninety-some years ago strikes most twenty-first century Americans as strange and anachronistic, a sign of the absurdity of bygone norms and traditions. Yet most citizens in the nineteenth century and before found women's suffrage so outlandish that even the first women's rights advocates were reluctant to endorse the idea. The women's suffrage movement encountered persistent, widespread opposition. Victory required lifetimes of effort. Disapproval of women's voting did not disappear with the passage of the Nineteenth Amendment (Merriam and Gosnell 1924). To comprehend the expectations both of contemporaries and later scholars, and the actual voting behavior of women during the 1920s and 1930s, requires an understanding of why women were denied access to the ballot for so long.

The exclusion of women from political life, including electoral politics, has a long history and deep roots in liberal and republican political theory (Pateman 1994). As those ideas intersected with the trajectory of American political development in the nineteenth and early twentieth centuries, ideas about the place of women in the American political order were both invigorated and challenged. American history has been characterized by repeated extensions and retractions of suffrage rights as the definition and qualities of political citizenship were continually renegotiated in light of economic, social, and political change (Keyssar 2000).

Women's struggle for and eventual enfranchisement should be understood both as one of many controversies over voting rights, and as uniquely shaped by interrelated conceptions of gender and power. Many of the reasons for the exclusion of women from the franchise are consistent with those used to justify the exclusion of other groups – concerns about independence, competence, and power-sharing – but as Carole Pateman (1980, 567) argues, conceptions of womanhood as distinct from politics were so pervasive that "the opposition to women's enfranchisement was much stronger, longer lived, and ran much deeper than the opposition to manhood suffrage, even black-manhood suffrage." Distinctive beliefs about the essential qualities of women and the relationship between femininity and political power motivated the ways and extent to which women were expressly denied access to the ballot (DuBois 1978). It was within this context that women advocated for enfranchisement and then entered polling places.

Women's Suffrage and the American Constitutional Order

The Framers spent little time debating the right to vote during the Constitutional Convention of 1787. The US Constitution itself contains only a few, mostly indirect, references to suffrage rights. Article I, Section 2 states that in elections to the House of Representatives "the Electors in each State shall have the Qualifications requisite for the Electors of the most numerous Branch of the State Legislature." Article II, Section 1 grants states power over presidential voting, allowing that presidential electors will be chosen "in such Manner as the Legislature thereof may direct." Indeed, Article II does not even necessitate popular election of the electors who select the president and vice president, and in some early elections, presidential electors were chosen directly by state legislatures (Esptein and Walker 1995). A basic commitment to democratic government is expressed in Article IV, Section 4: "The United States shall guarantee to every State in this Union a Republican Form of Government" (see Keyssar 2000; Smith 1997).

The impact of the Constitution's silence on suffrage was to leave intact the disenfranchisement of women under most state constitutions (Smith 1997). In 1874, in direct response to the claims of women's suffrage advocates, the US Supreme Court unanimously confirmed that, even with the addition of the Reconstruction amendments, "the Constitution of the United States does not confer the right of suffrage upon anyone" (*Minor v. Happersett*; see DuBois 1998). Attainment of women's suffrage thus required either state action or a constitutional amendment.

Although the original Constitution did not specify *manhood* suffrage, it is clear that the Framers did not expect women to vote (Lewis 1995). Specific language disenfranchising women was unnecessary, as it was widely understood that voting would be the province of (white, propertied) men. At least one delegate to the Constitutional Convention was made aware of the possibility of greater participation for women, however. In a now famous exchange of letters, Abigail Adams implored her husband John to "Remember the Ladies," suggesting only partially in jest that "If particular care and attention is not paid to the Ladies, we are determined to foment a Rebellion, and will not hold ourselves bound by any laws in which we have no voice, or representation." John Adams' response – "I cannot but laugh" – suggests the views of the Framers and their contemporaries regarding women's participation in politics (Rossi 1973).

Early Rationales for Suffrage Exclusion

The Framers failed to offer a rationale, but female disenfranchisement was a consistent assumption of the liberal and republican political theories that undergird the US Constitution. The contrast between women's (perceived) nature and the requirements of suffrage formed the crux of the reasoning. Both liberal and republican thinkers of the eighteenth century considered independence a crucial prerequisite for citizenship, particularly the exercise of the franchise. Debates over property restrictions, for example, were often grounded in the claim that the dependence of the poor renders them unable to express a will of their own (Keyssar 2000). Yet, even propertyless men could be construed as independent heads of their households, and thus as voters (Pateman 1980). Women, on the other hand, were "dependent on men almost by definition" (DuBois 1998, 84), and thus necessarily excluded from the franchise.

Other aspects of female nature, such as natural delicacy and physical weakness, further justified women's disenfranchisement. As defense of the republic was a critical aspect of citizenship, the perception that women were unable or unwilling (owing to their moral aversion to the use of force) to take up arms disqualified them from the central right of citizenship. Independence was again an important concept; a man's ability to engage in physical combat was evidence of, and served to protect, his independence (see Kerber 1988; Pateman 1980). Perhaps most fundamental was a simple understanding that politics was outside of women's sphere of interest and ability, in part because of women's particular qualities, but more generally because dissociation from politics was itself a quality of femaleness, while "citizens should be as masculine as possible" (Smith 1997, 131).

Republican Motherhood: A Place in Politics

If women could not participate at the polls, what then was their place in this new political order premised on a contract between citizen and state? Eighteenth-century political thought offered little guidance on the place of women in the polity other than the widely accepted proposition that women lacked the qualities necessary for republican citizenship. Historian Linda Kerber (1985, 1980, 1976) has shown how the "revolutionary generation" overcame this lacuna by developing an ideology of Republican Motherhood to bridge the gap between the republican ideals of equality and the perceived inability of women to perform the same responsibilities of citizenship as men. The concept of Republican Motherhood introduced a political component to women's role in the private sphere, and allowed women to contribute indirectly to the republic without leaving the domestic realm. Imbued by nature with piety and morality, a woman's contribution to the polity was to educate and encourage civic virtue in her sons and husband. In doing so, women served to temper the passions of men that might harm the republic, and made it possible for them to perform the duties of citizenship.

By inoculating women from ambition and corruption, female exclusion from the political sphere was not only natural but also necessary to the accomplishment of their role. Because women were inherently selfless and disinterested, they lacked personal ambition for political power, status, or influence. Prohibitions against direct female political participation provided added guarantees against the development of such selfish goals. As a result of women's disinterestedness, their counsel on civic matters was believed to be motivated solely by moral virtue. Restriction to the private realm also protected women from the corruption inherent to political life, again ensuring the purity of female guidance (Andersen 1996; Marilley 1996). The concept of Republican Motherhood thus both justified the continued exclusion of women from the political arena while also proscribing a means by which women might fulfill unique obligations of citizenship.

The Evolving Vote

Thus, at the time of the founding, citizens understood the political role of women to be limited to a very specific set of duties and obligations. Despite the prevalence of these views, some women did vote in the early days of the republic and before. A few propertied women, especially single women and widows without husbands to represent the interests of their households, exercised the suffrage in New Jersey, New York, Connecticut, and several towns in Massachusetts in the late eighteenth century. For example, after independence, the New Jersey state constitution provided suffrage rights to "all inhabitants" of particular means, and a 1790 legislative act confirmed that female inhabitants were included in the provision. As property-holding became a less important qualification, however, sex became more important. When the New Jersey constitution was rewritten after the elections of 1807, women were specifically disenfranchised (Keyssar 2000; Klinghoffer and Elkis 1992; Young 1975).

As these examples suggest, American's ideas about the place of the ballot, as well as the laws governing its use, evolved considerably over time. The Framers' relative silence regarding suffrage generally highlights the degree to which they viewed the vote as a relatively minor aspect of the political order they had established. In the first decades of the nineteenth century, however, property restrictions were eliminated or considerably scaled back, creating a system characterized by universal white manhood suffrage and mass participation in politics. Voting began to emerge as a central symbol of American democracy. The term democracy itself was transformed into a widely acclaimed characteristic of the American system (Smith 1997). The Jacksonian revolution, with its attack on elitist mechanisms for political choice ("King Caucus") and exaltation of democratic populism, further glorified electoral mechanisms and popular participation. As the primary way in which most Americans interacted with their government, elections became rituals of democracy and voting the foremost act of citizenship.

Separate Spheres and Continued Suffrage Exclusion

Across the nineteenth century, veneration of the rights and equality of the common man also contributed to heightened advocacy for political and social reform. Many women participated in reform efforts, particularly the abolition and temperance movements, experiences that provided both the ideas and tools for a movement for women's rights (DuBois 1998). The movement for women's suffrage, described in greater detail in the text that follows, emerged as a relatively small, fringe effort before the Civil War, but developed into a mass movement during and after Reconstruction. In the some seventy years between the first demand for women's suffrage at Seneca Falls (1848) and the ratification of the Nineteenth Amendment in 1920, advocates and opponents of votes for women constructed and refined both new and old rationales to understand women's relationship to the state in terms of voting rights. Indeed, the emergence of an active women's movement, combined with other political developments (most notably the enfranchisement of African American men), forced those who favored the status quo to articulate the rationale for disenfranchisement as never before (Kraditor 1968).

Women's nature remained the central rationale for the exclusion of women from the electorate. During the nineteenth century, the emphasis on a woman's unique character, particularly her virtuous place in the home, was strengthened and elaborated into what has alternatively been termed the Cult of True Womanhood (Welter 1966) or Cult of Domesticity (Kraditor 1968). Women – meaning middle-class white women – were believed to be naturally characterized by piety, purity, submissiveness, and domesticity. Inherently devout, women served as the carriers of religious values and practices to their husbands and children. Purity, especially sexual purity, was similarly essential to female virtue. In particular, women's purity provided a check against the natural sexual aggressiveness of men. As with female piety, the purpose of women's purity was to encourage men to lead more virtuous and moral lives. While women provided religious and moral guidance, their proper position still required submission to their husbands or fathers. Women's role clearly required her to stay within the confines of the home, where she was naturally suited to the responsibilities of the household, above all motherhood. True Womanhood thus provides a complement to and furtherance of the ideology of Republican Motherhood as both emphasize that motherhood was not only women's natural occupation, but also, by raising sons to be good citizens, her contribution to society at large (Cott 1975; Kerber 1988; Welter 1966).

Men and women thus occupied "separate spheres," with men's domain the public sphere of business and politics and women's place the private sphere of home and family.[1] Although belief in natural gender difference and distinct roles precedes the nineteenth century, the concept of separate spheres was strongly articulated and elaborated during this period (DuBois 1998; Kerber 1988). Ironically, an emphasis on women's difference flourished just as democratic ideals of equality were trumpeted. At the same time, economic and social forces contributed to increasing

[1] There is considerable debate among scholars concerning the uses and misuses of the separate spheres concept. See, for example, Kerber et al. 1989; Kerber 1988.

disparities as industrialization led to a disconnect between men's and women's work and lives. In an agricultural society, men and women worked, often side by side, on the shared project of maintaining a farm and home. With industrialization and urbanization, the work of both men and lower-class women increasingly shifted to the factory and office, leaving the home the sole province of middle- and upper-class white women (Pateman 1980). Glorifying the home and domestic responsibilities as the natural and divine order for women demarcated not only men from women, but lower-class women from their middle- and upper-class sisters as well. In the words of historian Gerda Lerner (1969, 12), "It is no accident that the slogan 'woman's place is in the home' took on a certain aggressiveness and shrillness precisely at the time when increasing numbers of poorer women *left* their homes to become factory workers" (author's emphasis). That the domestic ideal of the protected and proper homebound wife and mother failed to describe the lives of many women did not prevent women's suffrage opponents, and later proponents, from emphasizing this supposed defining aspect of women's nature in their arguments.

Rationale for the opposition to women's suffrage took many forms. In the eyes of many female suffrage opponents, separate spheres were viewed as a source of power and influence. Indeed, one of the reasons some women opposed women's suffrage is that it was viewed as a threat to the independent power and influence women supposedly wielded in their separate sphere (Baker 1984). Women did not expect to be able to compete with men on equal footing if they were forced to enter the public sphere, and at the same time, felt that they would be losing the authority, influence, and independence they enjoyed in the private sphere. Opponents also appealed to religion, which was really "no argument at all, but the mere announcement that God has ordained man and woman to perform different functions in the state as well as in the home" (Kraditor 1981, 16). Access to the ballot would lead to strife within the home, undermining marriages and resulting in the neglect and abandonment of children. Finally, opposition arguments emphasized the biological differences between the sexes. Innate physical weakness made women unfit for the rigors of the polls and unable to defend the republic against threats, foreign or internal, particularly from immigrants and African Americans. Women were naturally emotional (and thus unstable and impulsive), while logic was the province of men. The intellectual and physical demands of voting were too taxing for women's weaker constitutions (Kraditor 1981).

Evolving Arguments for Women's Suffrage

Before and immediately after the Civil War, women's rights advocates critiqued the Cult of True Womanhood and emphasized the essential equality of men and women. With their roots in the abolition movement and radical Republicanism, it is perhaps not surprising that early feminists focused on the unjustness of the unequal treatment of women in light of essential similarity to men. Early suffragists declared women human beings and citizens first and foremost, emphasized women's common humanity and fundamental equality with men, and adapted the ideals on which the American republic was founded – natural rights, popular sovereignty – to argue for the extension of the suffrage to women (Kraditor 1981).

Yet, when women's suffrage failed to materialize after the Civil War, and in the face of increasingly entrenched opposition, many late nineteenth century suffragists adopted arguments that did not challenge, but instead appropriated, the Cult of True Womanhood. Rather than asserting that women should have the vote because they were no different from men, women increasingly argued that women should be given the right to vote *because* of their difference (DuBois 1998; Kraditor 1981).

This shift in argument and strategy has been rightly criticized as conservative and exclusionary, and often racist and nativist. Instead of challenging the fundamental assumptions from which many had argued women's oppression sprung, many suffragists accepted – and used as a justification for suffrage rights – an understanding of female difference and women's nature as more moral, self-sacrificing, and domestic than that of men. These values, suffragists argued, were desperately needed in politics. This change in strategy coincided with other conservative shifts, particularly the emergence of nativist and racist themes. If "lower" elements were allowed to vote, why should pious and respectable (i.e., native white) women not be allowed to do the same? In the context of widespread concern about corruption and scandal, suffragists argued that women's votes could inject morality as well as effectively counter the dangerous and destabilizing influence of immigrants and racial minorities (see Kraditor 1981).

These arguments, although deeply problematic, highlight the way in which the Cult of True Womanhood contained, in Welter's words, "the seeds of its own destruction" (1966, 174) or at least the potential for radical opportunity. First, the denial of voting rights to women was based in part on the idea that within a household, men's and women's political interests were inseparable. A woman did not need a vote because her husband cast his ballot on behalf of the household as a whole (Siegel 2002). By emphasizing women's difference, particularly that their concerns and preferences were unique to their sex, at some level the Cult of True Womanhood held out the possibility that husbands may not adequately represent the interests of wives. Indeed, given men's predilection for political corruption and in the context of debates over good government, social purity, and temperance, women might be expected to hold distinct preferences and interests that were quite relevant to political choice (see DuBois 1998). In the words of Carrie Chapman Catt in 1897, paraphrasing Wendell Phillips, "If women are like men, then they certainly possess the same brain and that should entitle them to the ballot; if they are not like men, then they certainly need the ballot, for no man can understand what they want" (Keyssar 2000, 196).

Second, as the scope of government action expanded and evolved, the Cult of True Womanhood provided a justification for women's inclusion, rather than exclusion, from the political sphere. As the nineteenth century came to a close and the twentieth dawned, government at all levels became increasingly involved in social welfare and economic regulation (Skocpol 1992), topics on which women arguably held particular expertise. Much of this change was driven by female reformers who, denied access to the ballot, had employed and pioneered alternative forms of political influence via early interest group politics (see fuller discussion in the text that follows). Women defended their efforts to shape public policy as entirely consistent with True Womanhood: Women were simply bringing their natural concern for the protection of others, for social purity, and for morality to the political sphere, where scandal and corruption showed that such virtues were sorely needed (Skocpol 1994). This extension of women's private sphere to encompass part of the public sphere was justified as a form of "municipal housekeeping." Women were performing the same tasks, but in a wider context. At the same time, as government became increasingly involved in areas that might be considered women's natural province (e.g., the regulation of food, consumer products, and moral purity), it appeared increasingly nonsensical for women to be denied political voice (Baker 1984; Pateman 1980).

The Changing Nature of Electoral Politics

As Progressive reform efforts highlighted, one reason that many Americans opposed women's enfranchisement is that the conduct of politics was considered a dirty, corrupt, and above all, masculine endeavor. The dominant images of politics included the smoky backroom deal-making of party machines, military-style campaign marches, and back-slapping, boisterous political debate. Voting was not immune: The generally brief, bureaucratic, and sterile voting procedures of the modern age occur in public places, such as schools, churches, and municipal buildings. In the nineteenth century, in contrast, ballots were often cast in saloons, barber shops, and other "male" spaces as part of an all-day affair involving parades, rallies, and other festivities (see Bensel 2004). In the words of one 1920s party leader, "Many women have felt in the past that there was something not in keeping with their sheltered life in going out to vote. The polls were not considered wholesome places" (Crawford 1924, 8).

Dominant conceptions of womanhood not only made it difficult for citizens to imagine women engaged in political activity, so defined and understood, but as Baker (1984) has argued, these rituals and activities also drew some of their power from the exclusion of women. Politics provided affirmation of men's common bonds and political power (Andersen 1996; Baker 1984). These arguments increasingly lost force as Progressive reforms bureaucratized the process of voting and the state rapidly took over the conduct of elections at the turn of the century. The possibility that women might participate in elections seemed less outlandish as the process became less overtly masculine. At the same time, dominant images fade slowly; to most voters in the 1920s and 1930s, elections continued to be viewed as forays into a less than civilized milieu where proper women's presence was not entirely appropriate.

Thus, evolving understandings of the inherent qualities of women shaped contemporary observers' understanding of the (political) nature of women and their presumed interests. Women were understood to be inherently apolitical, yet their supposedly innate differences provided a rationale for an independent political voice for women. The political arena was no place for women, yet politics increasingly intruded on women's sphere, as political processes themselves became less overtly masculine. In the next section, we track the development of the campaign for suffrage itself, and how claims of its supposed failure tell us more about the standards to which women were held than about women's actual employment of the vote.

The Struggle for Women's Suffrage

The struggle to attain suffrage rights for women consumed more than seventy years and lifetimes of effort on the part of activists. In this section, we briefly review the history of the suffrage movement and how contemporaries and later scholars understood the consequences of the movement's eventual success for women and American politics.

The Suffrage Movement

The conventional dating of the women's suffrage movement to the Seneca Falls Women's Rights Convention of 1848 is, as Banaszak (1996, 5) argues, "at once too late and too early." Too late because the focus on 1848 can obscure the extent to which women were already engaged in activities outside of the private sphere since before the American Revolution (Kerber 1988). The 1848 origination of women's suffrage also can miss the stirrings of debate over women's condition in the preceding decades. Women's central complaints revolved around the legal concept of coverture, inherited from English Common Law. Married women were legally "covered" by their husbands and ceased to possess a separate legal identity. Under coverture, women could not inherit property, testify in court, or sign enforceable contracts. By 1848, state legislatures already were beginning to legislate property and other rights for women (although more as a reaction to changing economic conditions than to achieve women's equality) through various Married Women's Acts (Smith 1997).

Yet regarding women's suffrage specifically, 1848 is also too early. Attendees at the 1848 Seneca Falls Women's Rights Convention did not consider female disenfranchisement a primary concern or suffrage a central goal; there was in fact considerable debate over whether to include such a demand at all. Conference organizers, most notably Elizabeth Cady Stanton, drafted a Declaration of Sentiments, modeled after the Declaration of Independence. The catalog of women's grievances and demands ranged from religious and social to political and economic inequality. The only resolution to which delegates did not unanimously agree was that calling for women's suffrage; many attendees believed the demand so outrageous that it would taint the rest of the document. Stanton and renowned abolitionist Frederick Douglass were able to convince a narrow majority of the centrality of political rights. Yet, despite the prominence of Seneca Falls, women's rights were a very limited movement in the antebellum period. A series of women's rights conventions brought together similarly minded reformers and a loose network of women lobbied state legislatures for various reforms, including women's suffrage. However, no women's rights or women's suffrage organizations were created and other than the Married Women's Acts, few proposals received legislative consideration before the Civil War (Banaszak 1996).

The Civil War and the reforms that followed greatly raised the hopes of women's rights activists. The abolition movement in which so many activist women had labored for so long had accomplished its grand goal, albeit at an exorbitant cost. If such an inconceivable outcome could be achieved, the equally outrageous demand for women's political equality seemed attainable. Women's hopes were quickly dashed as it became clear that Republicans, the party that had provided the most encouragement to female reformers and women's rights proponents, intended to limit the extension of the suffrage to black men. Not only did the Reconstruction amendments to the US Constitution fail to enfranchise women, but Section 2 of the Fourteenth Amendment also connected, if indirectly, the word male to voting rights in the Constitution for the first time (Edwards 1997; Evans 1989).

For the fledgling women's rights movement, the fallout from the Reconstruction Amendments was extensive. First, the emphasis on voting as a central aspect of African American citizenship focused women's rights advocates' attention on the suffrage goal. Activists and observers increasingly referred to the woman suffrage, rather than the women's rights, movement (Evans 1989). The second effect was to divide suffragists strategically and organizationally. Many activists, including Lucy Stone, Henry Blackwell, and Frederick Douglass, held that "this hour belongs to the negro" and supported the Republican Party's decision to pursue black manhood, rather than universal, suffrage. Despite their similarly long-standing activism within the abolition movement, Stanton, Susan B. Anthony, Sojourner Truth, and others refused to support amendments that failed to encompass women's suffrage. In 1869, the two camps established separate women's suffrage organizations. The American Woman Suffrage Association (AWSA), headed by Stone and Blackwell, favored a state-level fight for women's suffrage, rather than national enfranchisement via constitutional amendment. The AWSA generally supported and worked within existing institutions, including the nationally dominant Republican Party. The National Woman Suffrage Association (NWSA), founded several months earlier by Stanton and Anthony, tended to take a more radical approach in both demands and tactics and offer a more wide-ranging critique of social and political institutions (Banaszak 1996; Evans 1989). Both were overwhelmingly white organizations. A few black women were active in both the AWSA and NWSA, but black women faced widespread exclusion in state and local organizations. Those black women who campaigned for suffrage tended to do so through separate African American suffrage organizations (Terborg-Penn 1998, 1978).

Despite splits and controversies, the cause of women's suffrage gained momentum and achieved a few early successes. For a variety of complex and often idiosyncratic reasons (see Keyssar 2000), frontier states led the way: Kentucky had allowed school suffrage (voting only for school boards) to white widows with children as early as 1838 (Young 1975), a full ten years before Seneca Falls. In 1869, the newly organized territory of Wyoming granted full suffrage to women, a provision that it retained on achieving statehood in 1890. The official record claims that one delegate to the state constitutional convention put an end to debate by declaring, "if consideration is given to disfranchise half of our people, it should not be the better half" (Erwin 1946, 528). Colorado extended the franchise to women in 1893, followed by Utah[2] and Idaho in 1896. The enfranchisement of women received extensive consideration in states outside of the South; between 1870 and 1890, an average of more than four states per year took up the issue of women's suffrage (Banaszak 1996). The success of state-level suffrage campaigns appears to have hinged on the ability of pro-suffrage organizations to forge mutually beneficial coalitions with third parties and other reform movements (McConnaughy 2013).

Over time, the goals and tactics of the NWSA and AWSA grew increasingly similar. In 1890, the two organizations merged into one organization, the National American Woman Suffrage Association (NAWSA). Yet unification accompanied a period activists referred to as "the doldrums." No new states adopted women's suffrage between 1896 and 1910. Suffragists were similarly stalled at the national level, where suffrage bills failed to be reported out of committee. Despite the lack of advance, the suffrage movement expanded dramatically during this period, drawing in an increasingly wide and diverse range of women. Also during this period, the first generation of suffragists were gradually replaced by a second generation of leadership, which adopted new strategies and arguments for women's enfranchisement (Banaszak 1996; Kraditor 1968).

The doldrums came to an end in 1910 when Washington State enfranchised women. Over the next ten years, more than twenty states enacted some form of women's suffrage reform, via referendum or legislation. The ability to establish and maintain coalitions with other groups remained an important factor for suffrage success (McConnaughy 2013). Where referendum were held, success was correlated with population characteristics

[2] Women were enfranchised in the territory of Utah in 1870, but the women's suffrage was later revoked as part of the political struggle between the Church of Latter Day Saints (Mormons) and the federal government over polygamy. Women's suffrage was reinstated in 1896 when Utah achieved statehood (Keyssar 2000).

such as ethnicity, religion, and education, as well as contextual factors such as population density and industrialization (McDonagh and Price 1985).

Success of the state efforts, as well as of other Progressive reforms that many woman activists also advocated, further energized the movement. At the same time, differences over tactics and priorities once again divided the suffrage movement, foreshadowing the conflicts that would characterize the post-suffrage period. Alice Paul took over leadership of the NAWSA's Congressional Committee in 1913, eventually founding a separate suffrage organization, the Congressional Union. Paul and others were influenced by the growing international movement for women's suffrage, including the militant strategies – mass demonstrations, hunger strikes, and jail protests – practiced by English suffragists. In particular, Paul sought to adopt the British strategy of holding the party in power responsible for failing to achieve women's suffrage. Because Democrats controlled Congress, Paul mobilized her supporters to campaign against Democrats around the country. Although both the Democratic and Republican parties endorsed women's suffrage in their 1916 platforms, the national effort remained stalled. Paul's Congressional Union staged an ongoing picket of the White House, chaining themselves to public property and risking jail. At the same time, the second generation of leadership at the NAWSA, most notably Carrie Chapman Catt, developed the "Winning Plan," designed to capitalize on the threat of women's votes in states where women had the ballot to push for both national and state-level enfranchisement.

The renewed and expanded agitation for women's suffrage, both radical and traditional, combined with a growing sense of inevitability, the impact of World War I (particularly the attendant shift in attitudes toward women workers), and the election of a Republican Congress in 1918 set the stage for the accomplishment of the suffrage movement's ultimate goal.[3] In 1918, the House of Representatives passed the Nineteenth Amendment, but it was voted down in the Senate. Suffragists continued their campaign, and both chambers passed the Nineteenth Amendment in

[3] This brief discussion does not do justice to the myriad factors that contributed to women's eventual enfranchisement, both in the United States and elsewhere. For example, Pateman (1980) notes the increasing dependence on universal suffrage as a means to insure against the sort of class revolution underway in Russia. Rather than a grant of power to the previously disenfranchised, extension of suffrage rights was elites' way of ensuring widespread commitment to the liberal democratic state. See McConnaughy (2013) for a further discussion of the factors that contributed to suffrage victory in 1920.

1919 (Wheeler 1995). The campaign shifted to the battle to achieve ratification in the states before the next election. By August of 1920, suffragists were just one state short, with Tennessee viewed as the last chance for victory. As the final vote approached, suffragists expected to lose narrowly, but at the last minute, Representative Harry Burn (at twenty-four, the youngest member of the Tennessee House) switched his vote from nay to yea in response to an appeal from his suffragist mother. The proclamation certifying the ratification of the Nineteenth Amendment was signed on August 26, 1920 (Evans 1989; Flexner 1959).

The (Perceived) Failure of Success

The extensive mobilization of female activism through the women's suffrage movement raised expectations that enfranchisement would translate into significant political power, or at least political influence and policy change. Conventional wisdom has long maintained that neither followed from the incorporation of women into the electorate. Not only were women widely believed to have failed to turn out or vote as a bloc, but also the high levels of female organizational activism sustained before enfranchisement appeared to drop off significantly in the 1920s (Chafe 1972; Lemons 1973; O'Neill 1971). The preeminent suffrage organization, NAWSA, transformed itself into the League of Women Voters (LWV), which focused on political education and a program of progressive political reform (Young 1989). Traditional accounts emphasize that the LWV lacked the political influence and vitality, not to mention membership, that the NAWSA boasted at its height, and that most other women's organizations lost membership, became less influential and active, or ceased to exist after 1920 (see, e.g., O'Neill 1971). Scholars have since disputed this characterization, noting that while some pre-1920 organizations waned or disbanded, others, many with large and active memberships, continued or were established in the decades following enfranchisement (Cott 1990; Goss 2013; Nichols 1983). Few, however, dispute that after a brief period in which a few policy gains were made, most notably the 1921 Sheppard–Towner Maternity and Infancy Protection Act, policymaking responsive to women's specific concerns had generally ceased by the late 1920s; it is often noted, for example, that Congress failed to reauthorize Sheppard–Towner in 1929 (Harvey 1998).

Why did women fail to wrest policy concessions from policymakers once enfranchised? Many have claimed that the central problem for female organizing after suffrage was a failure to achieve consensus on the next course of action. Activists before 1920, this account suggests, had agreed on only one thing – the desirability of the vote. Once that goal was achieved, female activists were unable to coalesce around a shared agenda, but were instead split sharply on a number of issues, particularly whether legal equality, as embodied in the newly proposed Equal Rights Amendment, or protective legislation were in the best interest of women (Becker 1981; Breckinridge 1933; Chafe 1972; Lemons 1973; O'Neill 1971). Others emphasize that female organizing must be put in the context of other Progressive Era organizations, most of which declined in size and efficacy during the conservative 1920s. Progressive policymaking in general, and not just related to women, slowed dramatically after World War I (Freedman 1979; Sarvasy 1992).

Perhaps the dominant explanation is politicians' widespread perception that a unified women's vote had failed to materialize and thus women posed no threat and wielded no influence (Chafe 1972; Lemons 1973). Harvey (1998) has offered a more nuanced account, arguing that women's suffrage organizations were unable transform themselves into effective voter mobilization organizations before the political parties, which had significant information and resource advantages and were already organized for just such tasks, could step in to mobilize women voters. As a result, female voters were mobilized through office-seeking political parties rather than benefit-seeking interest organizations. Political parties had little incentive to advocate policies of interest to women, and thus as it became clear that women's organizations would not emerge as an effective force for counter-mobilization, policy concessions dried up. Finally, as we explore in greater detail in the text that follows, women's inability to translate ballot access to political influence points to the indeterminate nature of the vote as a mechanism for policy change, particularly compared to other forms of political activity (Pateman 1980).

Thus the seventy-some year struggle for suffrage rights ended with what many viewed as a hollow victory, as politicians and journalists trumpeted the failures of women's suffrage as a mechanism for political power and of women as an organizational force (see Blair 1925; Gerould 1925; Kenton 1924; Russell 1924). This narrative of failure and disappointment has been strongly challenged by later scholars on many fronts (e.g., Andersen 1996; Baker 1984; Cott 1990; Goss 2014; Nichols 1983), but the story may be most significant for what it reveals about the standards to which new female voters were held. Anything short of widespread turnout, clearly distinct patterns of vote choice, and resultant significant policy change suggested women's suffrage had failed and female voters did not merit political – or scholarly – attention. These standards are simply unrealistic for a group characterized by strong social norms against political participation and systematically denied access to the voting booth for virtually all of American history, while simultaneously socialized in communities and homes characterized by strong and salient political interests and identities premised on shared characteristics other than gender. In other words, women's lack of direct electoral experience and experience of gender bias likely continued to discourage many women from exercising their right to vote once it was secured. At the same time, women's previous political experience, activity, and exposure, the context in which they first entered the polling places, and their various political identities likely influenced – as much or more as their gender per se – the ways in which women who did exercise their new right cast their ballots. In the next section, we document the myriad ways in which women experienced politics prior to the Nineteenth Amendment.

Politics by Other Means

A focus on suffrage can obscure the ways in which continuity characterizes the pre- and post-1920 political behavior and interests of women, particularly the extent to which women engaged in political activity prior to their enfranchisement (see Cott 1990). Throughout the nineteenth century women's repertoire of political action expanded and evolved, transforming both women's relationship with the state and American politics itself. The causes with which women were associated – abolition, temperance, social purity, political reform – were employed by both supporters and opponents to predict what effect women's suffrage would have on electoral and policy outcomes. In seeking to influence politics without access to the vote, women pioneered new means of political influence – interest group politics – which would become the dominant form of politics in the twentieth century (Baker 1984; Clemens 1993; Cott 1990, 1987). At the same time, women participated, often indirectly, in traditional forms of electoral politics. Women thus had many opportunities to develop political knowledge, experience, and perspectives prior to suffrage. Understanding women's political activities when direct participation in electoral politics was not an option thus gives us insight both into the ways in which women were expected to and did in fact wield the vote after enfranchisement.

If one understands mass politics as (among other things) activities pertaining to the selection of rulers and public policies, and to the creation and reproduction of political attitudes and identities, American women have been political since the Founding (see Young 1975). As we have discussed, in the period immediately following the American Revolution, the concept of Republican Motherhood prescribed a particularly indirect form of political influence via women's effect on husbands and sons (Kerber 1988). But from the Founding of the Republic, women's actual behavior did not always fit this circumscribed role, both because of their own choices and as a result of the changing political, economic, and social environment in which women lived their lives.

The "Age of Association"

Historian Sara Evans (1989) describes the mid-nineteenth century as the "age of association" for women. Women, particularly middle-class white women, were identified with and central to many of the social and political movements of the nineteenth century. In the first half of the century, women took part in the debate over slavery, the central political, social, and economic issue of the era. Women were active participants in the abolition movement, gathering petition signatures, organizing meetings (including a separate Female Anti-Slavery Society), attending conventions and demonstrations, authoring antislavery tracts, and otherwise seeking to influence political outcomes. The Antebellum period also saw women's activism through other social reform and moral purity campaigns that were often closely linked to abolitionism (Evans 1989).

The impact of this participation cannot be overstated. To the extent that the debate over abolition was cast in moral and religious terms, women's particular qualities provided a rationale, even requirement, for female participation; as a result, women were able to use "religious and moral commitment to create new public spaces and female solidarity in the name of Christian duty" (Evans 1989, 74). Through their involvement, women gained the skills and resources that would help drive female activism in the nineteenth century. Abolition was particularly important to the development of the women's movement. Abolitionism contributed theoretical and moral underpinnings to feminism, but far more important was the abolition movement's role in giving women the tools with which to counter that oppression. Women already were pressing for reform of the practices of coverture when the abolition movement was in its infancy. What women gained from the abolition movement were the skills for organizing as an effective political movement (DuBois 1998; Evans 1989).

Women continued to be active in public debates after the Civil War, when the moral reform issue of temperance coalesced into a large and influential movement characterized not only by female participation but by female leadership. Indeed, the central organizational actor in the struggle, the Woman's Christian Temperance Union (WCTU), explicitly denied membership to men (Evans 1989). As with the abolition movement, temperance activism gave women an opportunity to acquire and develop political resources and skills. Although temperance activism often started in narrow arenas defined by gender roles, it frequently facilitated a natural transition to the wider political realm. As Evans (1989, 128) argues, in pursuit of prohibition, women took part in a broad critique of societal structure, an experience that naturally lent itself to extension and evolution: "Anger at alcoholic men who failed to fulfill their familial responsibilities and provide for their wives and children thus grew into a broader challenge to the male mismanagement of the entire political/public arena, a criticism easy to sustain in the last quarter of the nineteenth century."

The involvement of women in the temperance movement also contributed to expectations for women's use of the vote. Many women participated in both the suffrage and temperance campaigns. The Women's Christian Temperance Union (WCTU) endorsed women's suffrage in 1883 and was an important part of the pro-suffrage coalition in the United States (Banaszak 1996). Rhetorically, suffragists often claimed that the achievement of prohibition would be a direct benefit of women's enfranchisement (Kraditor 1981). Although the extent and effectiveness of liquor interest opposition to women's suffrage is difficult to gauge (in part because such interests carefully hid their involvement), brewing and liquor businesses clearly provided significant funding to efforts to oppose referenda and legislative votes on suffrage in a number of states (Flexner 1959) and the presence of liquor interests was associated with legislative opposition to women's suffrage (McConnaughy 2013). The association of the two causes also contributed to the hostility of many immigrant groups to the cause of women's suffrage (McDonagh and Price 1985). Prohibition, as well as good government campaigns directed against urban political machines, were correctly recognized by many immigrants as, at least in part, culturally motivated attacks by middle- and upper-class native whites. Combined with the nativist rhetoric of pro-suffrage arguments around the turn of the century, the temperance–reform–suffrage link likely alienated many immigrant groups, particularly Germans and Irish, from women's suffrage (Banaszak 1996).

Women's suffrage was associated with other reform efforts of the nineteenth and early twentieth century, ranging from Jane Addams's settlement movement to labor activism to consumer protection to good government campaigns. Women established and led important organizations that advocated for social, economic, and political change during this period, including the Women's Trade Union League (WTUL), the International Ladies Garment Workers Union (ILGWU), and the National Consumers League (NCL). Women also were linked to important third-party political movements (e.g., Wilkerson-Freeman 2003). Although characterized by some dissent over the issue, Populists and later, Progressives, supported women's suffrage as part of a broad reform agenda and as a means to the achievement of other goals. In somewhat different ways, both Populists and Progressives emphasized a program of protection – of workers, farmers, and other oppressed and downtrodden groups, but also of the home and of women (from prostitution, dangerous work conditions, and violence). Protection was considered an outgrowth of women's natural inclination toward care and nurture; Populists and Progressives favored women's suffrage in part because they expected female voters to support their proposals and goals (Banaszak 1996; Edwards 1997) and to benefit from the organizational skills and resources of the women's suffrage movement (McConnaughy 2013). Together with temperance activism, the impact of women's activism for various political and social reforms was to help associate women with specific political preferences and ideals in the minds of contemporaries and later observers.

Women's association with reform movements also raised the suspicions of Democratic and Republican Party leaders. A major component of Progressive Era reform was a "good government" indictment of political parties, which in the late nineteenth and early twentieth centuries meant the political machines that dominated many rapidly expanding American cities. Good government reformers sought to introduce scientific management principles and order to the conduct of city governments, replacing the corrupt, chaotic, and inefficient regimes of the party machines. It is not a coincidence that reformers tended to be native, white, and middle- or upper-class, while party machines were characteristically dominated by recent immigrants and the working classes (see Judd and Swanstrom 1994). Given women's participation in municipal reform efforts and their supposed inclination toward idealistic virtue, rather than base partisanship, observers generally expected partisanship to matter less for female voting behavior (cf. Barnard 1928c; Monoson 1990; Rogers 1930). Party leaders, preferring predictability and loyalty, were considered unenthusiastic about the prospect of adding female voters to their electoral calculations.

At the same time, women became increasingly involved in the civic affairs of their local communities. The nineteenth century was a period of immense flourishing of civic membership groups in the United States (see Skocpol 2003). Women were active in mixed-gender organizations, such as the Grange and the American Red Cross, but also had opportunities for participation and leadership within organizations limited to women. Clubs in which (especially educated, middle-class) women met together for mutual support began to appear in the Antebellum period. After the Civil War, their numbers exploded, resulting in thousands of women's clubs around the United States. Even the most progressive white women's clubs tended to systematically exclude women of color, so African American women created a separate black women's club movement in the late nineteenth century (Terborg-Penn 1998).

In more than a few cases, these organizations graduated from social and literary functions to civic concerns, seeking to improve their communities through the establishment of parks, libraries, and other public facilities. Some took on larger projects, pursuing public improvements such as electrification, water and sewer construction, programs to benefit the welfare of children and women, and so on. Organized nationally through the General Federation of Women's Clubs and other organizations, most clubwomen saw themselves as simply using their womanly skills to improve their communities rather than engaging in politics per se. Yet in seeking to achieve even the smallest of goals, clubwomen gained civic skills (speaking in public, organizing a meeting), interacted with public officials, and influenced the direction of public policies in their cities and states (see O'Neill 1971; Skocpol 2003). These experiences challenge the expectation that all newly enfranchised women lacked political experience, interest, or knowledge.

A Diverse Political Repertoire

Participation in movements and clubs, as well as the emerging focus of political debate on topics considered women's sphere (see "The 'Domestication of Politics'"), increasingly directed women's attention toward the political arena. Yet, women were denied direct access to the dominant tools of political power during the era – electoral and party politics. For most of the nineteenth century, the effective organization of voting blocs via parties represented the principal means of exerting political control and influence. Although women participated in party politics, they were tangential to such efforts, and their association with political reform contributed to significant distrust of parties among many female activists (Clemens 1997). As a result, women developed many alternative means for political activism. Since the earliest days of female activism for Married Women's Acts and abolition, women pioneered such now-commonplace interest group tactics as petitioning, influencing public opinion, delivering speeches and addresses, writing editorials, producing publications, testifying before legislative committees, conducting empirical analyses, endorsing candidates, sponsoring initiative and referendum drives, and meeting with political decision makers. Women were by no means alone in their use of these tools, but their formal exclusion from electoral politics made them far more likely to employ these tactics as a central political strategy (Cott 1990, 1987; McGerr 1990).

This is not to say that women were entirely absent from party and electoral politics; indeed, given the pervasiveness of party politics, it would have been difficult for women to avoid the realm of parties and elections entirely. With the expansion of universal manhood suffrage in the first decades of the nineteenth century, voting and electoral politics emerged as the central means of political influence. Through extensive organization and the effective use of group referents and patronage to mobilize blocs of voters, political parties of this era were the primary instrument for the attainment and exercise of political power. In many cities, enterprising politicians used machine style politics to further consolidate the power of the political party (Judd and Swanstrom 1994). Prior to 1896, the two major parties were both fairly competitive outside of the South (Burnham 1965) and elections offered an important form of public entertainment. Party identification was closely tied to salient ethnic, racial, class, and immigrant group referents that knit political identification to other forms of social loyalty. The salience of electoral politics contributed to turnout among the enfranchised at rates exceeding 80 and even 90 percent, and heightened interest in elections among voters and nonvoters alike (Burnham 1965). Nineteenth century women were thus immersed in a context in which party politics were highly salient and elections were public rituals confirming fundamental racial, ethnic, and religious identities – identities that women shared, even if they were denied expression of those loyalties at the ballot box. These identities surely influenced women's employment of the ballot once suffrage was won.

Given the heightened salience of electoral politics during this era, it is thus not surprising that women still participated in electoral politics, of which actually casting a ballot was only a minor aspect of a larger pageant of expressive group politics. On an individual basis and through organizations, women attended rallies and meetings; staffed party barbecues, picnics, and suppers; organized ladies' auxiliaries; canvassed wards; endorsed candidates; and even publicly sought to "buy" the votes of enfranchised men (Edwards 1997; Freeman 2000; Monoson 1990). Beginning in the late 1880s, both parties sponsored ad hoc women's leagues through which women could campaign on behalf of presidential candidates. More permanent local women's partisan organizations also were established and organized into national associations (Sainsbury 1999). While often rejecting the label "political," many women identified as partisans, just as they recognized other social identities. And although women themselves were excluded from direct electoral participation, gender itself was central to party rhetoric of the period as parties campaigned on "home protection" and the defense of female virtue. More generally, displays and defenses of masculinity (and accusations of femininity against opponents) were principal components of political campaigns after the Civil War, as politics became a defining aspect of what it meant to be male (see Edwards 1997).

Even before the ratification of the Nineteenth Amendment, women also participated in politics as candidates, office-holders, and party convention delegates (Freeman 2000); indeed, by one estimate, more than 3,000 women pursued political office prior to 1920.[4] As women gained the vote in specific states, increasing numbers of women had access to the electoral franchise. By the time the Nineteenth Amendment was ratified, 339 of 531 votes in the Electoral College were accountable to both sexes, although many of those states had enfranchised women just a year or two before 1920 (Wheeler 1995). Women's participation in the early suffrage states was watched closely for indications of the possible effects of suffrage expansion (e.g., Sumner 1909). Where women had yet to win the vote, some women attempted traditional electoral participation anyway. The best known case involved Susan B. Anthony and a group of fellow suffragists who were arrested for attempting to register and vote in Rochester, New York in 1872. Anthony alone was tried and fined (she refused to pay and the state did not attempt to collect). Her trial and bold defense received widespread publicity (Young 1989).

In the eighteenth and nineteenth centuries, dominant conceptions of women emphasized their inherently apolitical nature. Yet, a closer look at women's activities and the political, social, and economic context in the decades prior to suffrage suggest that women had ample opportunities

[4] See: Her Hat Was In the Ring!, a database of women campaigning for elective office prior to the ratification of the Nineteenth Amendment: www.herhatwasinthering.org/

to be exposed to political information and to develop political identities and attitudes. Moreover, multifaceted political activism before 1920 offered women opportunities to develop political skills and the capacity to engage effectively in the political arena, including, presumably, the ability to cast ballots once granted the right to do so.

The Shifting Political Context

While women's political role was evolving, so was the American political context. In particular, the expansion of the state into new areas of regulation and influence helped both facilitate the achievement of suffrage rights for women and shape expectations for women's use of the ballot once secured. At the same time, the increasing dominance of group-based, rather than party-based, politics – partially pioneered by women (Clemens 1993) – ironically contributed to a devaluing of the vote itself at just the moment that women won the right (McGerr 1990). In this section we examine the shifting political context into which women were enfranchised, as well as the limits of the ballot for gaining political power at the time that suffrage was granted.

The "Domestication of Politics"

In their varied forms of activism, nineteenth century female activists expanded the sphere of acceptable activity for women (Baker 1984). The line between the public (men's sphere) and the private (women's) became increasingly blurred, as women rationalized activity outside of the home on the basis of the very qualities – moral purity, selflessness, dedication to home and family – that were used to justify women's restriction to the private sphere. Women and others framed women's participation as "municipal housekeeping," the idea that women had a responsibility to apply the skills at which they excelled in the home to particular problems of the public sphere, such as good government, temperance, education, social welfare, and so on (Spain 2001).

While many reform organizations originally favored private solutions, reformers increasingly turned to government to take up these responsibilities, and in fits and starts, the state and federal government adopted an increasingly broad set of responsibilities for the care and welfare of it citizens. Although the greatest expansion of government responsibility would come with the New Deal, the roots of this transformation in government's role can be traced to the preceding period, and in many cases, to the activism of women (Skocpol 1992). Thus, women's political activism in the late nineteenth and early twentieth century both contributed and reacted to an expanding definition of the responsibility of the state for the social welfare of its citizens. Government at various levels began, for example, to regulate the production of food and medicines, protect children from dangerous working conditions, and enforce moral standards regarding alcohol and sexuality. Many of these tasks involved objects and arenas understood to be the primary jurisdiction of women – the food women purchased for their families, the children women were responsible for raising, and the moral norms women were expected to guard and transmit.

In the long term, the effect was what historian Paula Baker (1984) has called the "domestication of politics." Instead of challenging ideas about the nature of women, female activists changed the nature of politics by expanding the definition to include the economic, and more importantly, social conditions of citizens, areas in which women were believed to have particular expertise. Politics thus increasingly infringed on women's sphere, and women were increasingly entering the male sphere of politics. As a result, women's activism had an impact on society's willingness to accept political activity by women, including voting, as well as an impact on the nature of political activity itself.

The Declining Value of the Vote

As we have seen, in an age in which mass political participation was central to political influence, women found ways to participate in politics even without the ballot. It may not be coincidental, however, that the final barriers to full electoral participation came under real threat only once elections themselves became less important to the achievement and exercise of political power. Perhaps the most prominent sign of the waning importance of elections at the end of the nineteenth century was the declining interest of citizens in participating in them. Mass participation in politics, specifically turnout, began its long, infamous decline after the election of 1896. The causes are many. In a seminal paper, Burnham (1965, 1002) attributes voter demobilization to "the establishment of industrial-capitalist political hegemony;" that is, economic elites wresting political power from the masses, who responded with weakening partisanship and reduced electoral participation. Capitalist consolidation helped bring about the shift from the fairly evenly matched party competition outside of the South after the Civil War to a period of widespread Republican ascendancy after 1896 (Bensel 2000). One-party dominance (the Democratic Solid South and Republican control in the North) provided little incentive for parties to actively mobilize voters, dampened interest in elections, and lessened the perceived value of any one vote, all contributing to alienation and declining turnout among voters.

Others give greater causal weight to widespread institutional change in the late nineteenth and early twentieth century (Converse 1972, 1974; Rusk 1970, 1974), most notably, ballot reform (specifically state-printed Australian ballots with office bloc, rather than party line, format), personal registration systems, the direct primary, civil service reform, nonpartisan elections, and female suffrage. These developments weakened parties; hampered straight-ticket voting; lessened voter fraud (especially repeat voting); decreased the ease of voting; heightened information costs (by removing or weakening party cues); and, in the case of female suffrage, added a large group to the electorate who lacked experience with and socialization in the practice of voting.

With the declining role of elections and parties came the ascendancy of legislatures and lobbying as the central sites of political power. As we discussed in the preceding text, by pioneering forms of interest group politics and participating in the pursuit of political reform, women facilitated this transformation:

> At an institutional level, women's groups were central to a broader reworking of the organizational framework of American politics: the decline of competitive political parties and electoral mass mobilization followed by the emergence of a governing system centered on administration, regulation, lobbying, and legislative politics. (Clemens 1993, 760)

The result, ironically, was that women helped undermine the political power of the tool they so valiantly pursued for more than seventy years: "To the extent that women deprecated partisanship and pioneered interest group lobbying, they helped create the political system that devalued the vote" (McGerr 1990, 883).

As a result, enfranchisement meant a change in women's status as citizens, but it did not necessarily mean a change in actual power or influence. For much of American history, voting has been trumpeted as the ultimate act of democratic citizenship, which is, of course, one of the reasons that suffragists believed their denial of suffrage rights was so egregious. Voting is how citizens – those to whom a democratic state is expected to be responsive – formally register their preferences. Yet, as Pateman (1980, 575) writes,

> 'Democratic participation' may be key to women's emancipation, but periodic exercise of the franchise to choose national and local representatives at a time, on

issues, and for candidates about which the elector has no choice is an exceedingly weak and minimal form of democratic participation compared with that in, say, the suffrage movement itself.

This is the great irony. As feminist Suzanne La Follette wrote in 1926, "It is a misfortune for the women's movement that it has succeeded in securing political rights for women at the very period when political rights are worth less than they have been at any time since the eighteenth century" (quoted in Cott 1990, 160). Progressive reforms were weakening the power and influence of political parties, while those seeking to influence politics – including, as we have seen, women – were increasingly adopting what we now recognize as interest group politics, rather than working through the party and electoral system. This reality ought to shape our expectations for the way in which women would take up the ballot, for whom, and with what possible impact once suffrage was granted.

Conclusion

The passage of the Nineteenth Amendment is rightly recognized as a signal transformation of women's place in the American political order. Suffrage is a central right of democratic citizenship, and in gaining that right, women's relationship with the state was made more direct, equal, and influential. Beyond the ability to cast a ballot, enfranchisement reconfigured power relations between men and women "because it exposed and challenged the assumption of male authority over women" (DuBois 1978, 46). Before women ever entered the polling place and regardless of how they voted or with what consequence, the enfranchisement of women represented a centrally important redefinition of the boundaries between public and private and between male and female (see Andersen 1996).

Political participation, particularly voting, was long considered foreign to the very nature of womanhood. A women's natural piety, domesticity, and purity made her unfit for politics, except indirectly, by imbuing her sons and husband with civic virtue. That *any* women advocated for or took advantage of the right of suffrage once granted must be considered an impressive accomplishment in light of these pervasive social norms. Yet despite the theoretical constructs of Republican Motherhood and the Cult of True Womanhood, the reality is that many women entered the electorate with myriad experiences of political activism, interest, and exposure. Participation in social movements, organizations, and clubs, particularly those associated with abolition, suffrage, and temperance, helped women develop political resources and tools. The pervasive nature of party politics and its links to other social identities gave women knowledge and loyalties with which to adapt to their expanded political role. The changing nature of the political agenda, particularly the encroachment of government into the realm of social welfare and protection, contributed to a further blurring of the separate spheres. Politics increasingly infringed on the traditionally private, and those supposedly limited to the private sphere increasingly entered into political debate.

The political history and context outlined in this chapter informs our understanding of women's turnout and vote choice in the 1920s and 1930s in at least four important ways. First, a long and well-established tradition in Western political thought portrayed women as inherently and appropriately apolitical. The presumption that women are characterized by lesser political interest, knowledge, and experience has fueled expectations for and interpretations of women's electoral behavior throughout the almost 100 years since women were enfranchised. Thus, for example, a number of scholars have assumed that women's suffrage meant the entrance of a large group of voters ignorant of and disinterested in politics who would contribute to lower turnout and electoral instability (Converse 1969, 1972, 1974; 1976; Rusk 1974). Separating reality from assumption is key to how we approach and interpret the electoral behavior we can observe.

Second, women's political activism and the evolving political climate helps explain a number of expectations for women's use of the ballot. For example, newspaper reports are replete with predictions (from both supporters and opponents of women's suffrage), later endorsed by scholars, that women would not be swayed by the traditional and corrupt political parties (Barnard 1928c; Monoson 1990; Rogers 1930) and that female voters would aid both temperance and Progressive reform (Allen 1930; Flexner 1959; McCormick 1928; McDonagh and Price 1985; Ogburn and Goltra 1919; O'Neill 1971; Rice and Willey 1924; Russell 1924; Tarbell 1924; Toombs 1929, Wells 1929; Willey and Rice 1924). These predictions were grounded in the reality that women were indeed active in the Progressive movement. Yet expectations about how those experiences would translate into electoral behavior have been subject to only very limited empirical evaluation (e.g., Goldstein 1984), and the findings have been mixed (e.g., Claggett 1982; Kleppner 1982b).

Third, a broader view highlights the general salience of partisan politics during this period, and recognizes that women were exposed to and participated in politics, including elections, before suffrage. As a result, many newly enfranchised women were likely already engaged in and knowledgeable of electoral politics; given the heightened salience of elections during this era, it is hard to imagine how they would not be. Moreover, the strong links between group and party identity made traditional political loyalties and socialization less foreign to women than many expected, likely reducing the disruptive initial effect of women's enfranchisement. These identities, it is important to emphasize, were predicated on shared ethnicity, religion, nativity status, class, and other characteristics other than gender. Thus, even in the context of formal disenfranchisement, we have reason to expect women had opportunities to develop political knowledge, preferences, and skills that would shape their incorporation into the electorate once suffrage was granted.

This perspective can inform both our expectations about whether and for whom women would cast ballots, as well as our interpretations of the patterns of electoral behavior we observe. A general similarity in the voting behavior of men and women may indeed be indicative of women blindly following their husbands. Such patterns might also, given what we know about women's political engagement and opportunities before and after suffrage, be consistent with a conception of many women as engaged and attached to politics in much the same way as similarly situated men.

Finally, women's political participation prior to national enfranchisement also helps us understand the context in which women's initial voting behavior should be understood. Women's entrance into the polls was largely judged in relation to the standards of widespread and highly organized participation that had characterized American politics in the second half of the nineteenth century. By 1920, however, rates of turnout among enfranchised men had been declining sharply for more than twenty years. A politics dominated by parties and elections was being replaced by a political system in which interest-based legislative politics was ascendant (Clemens 1993). Women's inability to exhibit high levels of turnout and cohesive bloc voting was derided as evidence of the failure of women's suffrage (Blair 1925; Gerould 1925; Kenton 1924; Russell 1924). Yet, the extent to which women exercised the right to vote should be understood within the context of the declining relevance of mass democratic politics regardless of sex. When asked in 1924, "Is woman suffrage failing?," the reformer Jane Addams responded that the more appropriate question was "Is suffrage failing?" (Cott 1990, 160).

The political thought and history described here helps us to understand both why women were denied the vote for so long, and more importantly for our purposes, many of the expectations and assumptions about how women would exercise the right once granted. Evaluating those expectations has been hampered by a dearth of reliable information about women's turnout and vote choice during this era. In Chapter 3, we review the efforts of previous scholars to address this lacuna, before introducing our own unique data and methods for answering these questions.

ILLUSTRATION 3.1. In line to vote at Clarendon, Virginia. November 4, 1924. Source: National Photo Company Collection (Library of Congress).

3

What We Already Know

What do we already know about how women voted after suffrage? As we argued in Chapter 1, the conventional wisdom rests on a sparse empirical base. As a general rule – but with at least one important exception – ballots in the United States are not distinguished by the sex of the person who drops them into the ballot box. As a result, very little hard data on the turnout and vote choice of male and female voters are available from official election returns. The modern solution to this problem – the mass survey – is generally unavailable or unreliable during this era, with a few notable exceptions.

In this chapter, we review what is actually known – not what we think we know – about how women voted after suffrage from previous research and available data. Our current understanding of the first female voters rests on several different sorts of data, each of varying reliability. In some cases, scattered bits of actual hard data on registration, turnout, party identification, and even vote choice, by sex, are available, either because the information was tabulated in that way or researchers have dug into registration lists and poll books. In other cases, scholars have, with varying success, sought to estimate female voting behavior during this era, without awareness of or (later) working around the ecological inference problem. We first examine reports based on the available hard data, and then turn to published estimates. Our goal is to gain a clear understanding of what the available, reliable research tells us about female voters after suffrage, and – as importantly – what the real limits of that knowledge are.

What we find is that available data and previous research provide valuable pieces of insight into women's voting behavior after suffrage in a small number of places over a small number of elections. The best data come from one state (Illinois) over two presidential elections (1916 and 1920) and one city (Boston) over a set of elections (1920–1940). A few other scattered bits of data exist. These data allow some conclusions (e.g., women's turnout lagged men's in every known case) but largely testify to the considerable variation in women's electoral behavior across place and time. Although quite useful, and certainly an improvement over no data at all, it is difficult to generalize from the available hard data about female voters after suffrage. Early estimates are generally plagued by serious problems of logic and methodology. Later scholarly work offers appropriately cautious conclusions, mostly about turnout; previous scholars generally have been unable to offer much in the way of useful estimates of women's vote choice. Thus opportunities to improve the evidentiary base of our knowledge of how and with what consequences women voted after suffrage are considerable.

Available Hard Data

As a general rule, ballots tend not to identify the sex of the person casting them; election returns are reported by geopolitical unit (e.g., county or state), not by demographic characteristic. During the period examined here, important exceptions to this rule fall into two general classes. The first type of exception, truly a class of its own, is represented solely by the State of Illinois, where the general rule was violated: From 1916 (1913 in the City of Chicago) through 1920, male and female ballots were counted and reported separately. In Illinois, then, it is possible to directly observe the actual turnout and vote choice of women and men in two presidential elections and a number of other contests for a brief period of time.

Women in Illinois were granted the right to vote in school elections in 1891, which in most counties simply meant that women could vote for the trustees of the University of Illinois. The Illinois Constitution of 1870 limited suffrage to men, but an 1891 Illinois state supreme court decision held that the constitutional prohibition applied only to offices established by the state constitution, that is, state-level offices, such as governor, secretary of state, and so on. Thus when the Illinois state legislature enfranchised women in 1913, it could do so only for nonstate elections. Because women could vote only on a subset of offices (including US president), and in an effort to discourage fraud (women casting votes for prohibited offices), the State of Illinois printed separate male and female ballots.[1] Although this had been the practice since school suffrage was established in 1891, it was not until 1916 that counties began to report the separate male and female vote totals for the offices in which both could participate. The City of Chicago, however, began reporting separate election returns in 1913, and reported separate male and female registration figures at the ward level through 1932. While the Nineteenth Amendment negated the need for separate ballots in the 1920 election, the state legislature did not amend the law to allow for uniform ballots until 1921 (Goldstein 1984).

Although there are other states where registration and even turnout figures are sporadically reported by sex, Illinois is the only state – to our knowledge – in which the *vote choice* of men and women can be *directly* observed, not just during the initial incorporation of women into the electorate, but at any time in American history. The most extensive analyses of these data are reported in Joel H. Goldstein's University of Chicago dissertation, *The Effects of the Adoption of Woman Suffrage: Sex Differences in Voting Behavior – Illinois, 1914–21* (1984). As we would expect of such unique and valuable data, a number of other scholars have relied on some or all of the Illinois data as well (e.g., Abbott 1915; Gosnell and Gill 1935; Kleppner 1982b; Merriam and Gosnell 1924; Rice and Willey 1924; Willey and Rice 1924). As we explain in Chapter 4, the valuable Illinois data also play a key role in our research.

The second class of exception to the rule that official election records do not contain information related to the sex of the voter is the information contained in registration lists and, more rarely, poll books. In some cases, registrars recorded the sex of the person registering or entering the polling place, and statistics are thus available on the numbers of men and women registering and/or actually voting. In rarer cases (e.g., Boston), the party with which the voter identified at the time of registration is also recorded, affording insight into party, if not actual vote, choice. In still other cases, ambitious researchers have combed preserved registration lists and poll books in an effort to identify (with some error) the sex of the voter based on the name recorded.

Given the considerable time and effort uncovering such data requires, we have only a few examples covering a few places at (usually) a small

[1] Printing separate male and female ballots was only one possible approach to the problems caused by states granting women suffrage for specific offices. For example, in Connecticut, where women had school suffrage before 1920, women used special women-only voting machines ("Fair Voters Will Line-Up with Men," *Bridgeport (CT) Post*, August 25, 1920, p. 5).

number of elections. For example, in their efforts to demonstrate the advisability of women's suffrage, the Collegiate Equal Suffrage League of New York employed Helen Sumner (1909) to undertake an investigation into the electoral behavior of women in Colorado who were enfranchised in 1893. Included in her wide-ranging evaluation is a detailed study of 1906 registration records. Sumner determined voter sex from the names on registration and poll books for a sample of nine counties she describes as representative of the state as a whole. Although not without flaws, Sumner's data afford rare insight into the early voting behavior of women in one of the first states to pass women's suffrage.

In another example, the Boston Board of Election Commissioners reported registration and party identification by sex at the level of the precinct (subdivision of wards) during the two decades following women's enfranchisement. These data thus do not offer direct measures of turnout and vote choice, but provide useful indirect measures (registration and party registration). Given the rarity of measures of political preference, the party registration data is particularly welcome. Using detailed precinct-level census data, Gamm (1986) analyzes a subset of precincts chosen for racial and ethnic homogeneity. By focusing on homogeneous Jewish, Italian, Irish, native white (which Gamm terms "Yankee"), and black precincts, Gamm can make reasonable inferences about the electoral behavior of specific racial, ethnic, religious, and in a few cases, class and immigrant groups without committing the ecological fallacy. While we emphasize that Gamm's central goal is to trace New Deal realignment, the data he reports provide a rare and valuable opportunity to observe how men and women of different racial and ethnic groups were mobilized into the active electorate (registered voters) over a considerable period of time – 1920 through New Deal realignment.

There are a few additional studies that report more limited actual data on registration or vote behavior by sex. For example, Pollock (1939) uses registration and poll lists in Ann Arbor, Michigan, reported by sex, to examine twenty-four different local, state, and national elections and primaries over an eight-year period (1924 to 1932). Andersen (1994) examines county-level registration data in Oregon, where separate male and female registration lists were kept from 1912, when women were enfranchised, through 1924. Berman (1993) employs 1916 registration lists from Arizona (where women gained the right to vote in 1912), which report separate totals for men and women in each precinct.[2] Lebsock (1993) reports registration figures for black and white women for a number of counties in Virginia in 1920 based on a survey conducted by a state-wide good government organization.

What We Know from Available Data

The limited available hard data provide a glimpse into the electoral behavior of women after suffrage in a few particular places at a few specific times. What can we learn about women's turnout and vote choice from these data?

Turnout

The available data are unanimous on one conclusion: Women initially took up their new right at rates that lagged behind those of long-enfranchised men (e.g., Anderson 1994; Gamm 1986;[3] Goldstein 1984; Sumner 1909).

[2] In another example of creative efforts to employ available registration data, Smith (1980) examines a sample of women who registered to vote in San Diego (CA) in 1920, comparing their reported characteristics (address, occupation, political party, and marital status) to the general population of women in San Diego. The nature of her data (she only collects information on women) makes it difficult, however, to draw any conclusions about women's turnout or vote choice, overall or in comparison to men, from her report.

[3] We note that the data Gamm (1986) presents, although entirely appropriate to his purposes, are less well suited to estimating the *level* of turnout among women or men in the general election, particularly in 1920. Gamm's chief interest is in the partisan composition of the electorate, and his data source reports registration *by party* only for the state primary. Using registration figures from the primary likely underestimates both registration and turnout in the general election for both men and women in all elections, but particularly for women in 1920. The Nineteenth Amendment was ratified on August 26, and the Massachusetts state primary took place just twelve days later, on September 7. The city of Boston made special arrangements to accommodate new female voters, including extending registration times before the primary (two evenings) and again before the general election (three evenings) and adding additional registrars to the staff (see *Annual Report of the Board of Election Commissioners*, 1921). Moreover, women in Boston did have an opportunity to register before August 26: As ratification became more likely, officials urged women to register for school elections (women in Massachusetts had school suffrage), because school election registration lists would be converted automatically to general election registration lists after ratification. However, the *Boston Globe* reported that few women took advantage of this means to early registration, and instead "flocked" to register after ratification ("How Will the Women Vote?" *Boston Globe*, September 5, 1920, p. 1). It seems reasonable to expect that women's ability to register before the primary was constrained by the short timeline. More generally, Massachusetts allowed registration between the state primary and the general election; registration in Boston closed thirty days before the election (Blakey 1928). Thus, registration figures from the state primary almost certainly underestimate the potential turnout in every election (keeping in mind that all registered voters do not turn out on election day), and most likely strongly underestimate women's potential for turnout in 1920.

In many cases, the available data require researchers to rely on registration data, rather than turnout itself, but registration was a widespread voting requirement during this period, and thus although not every registered citizen turned out to vote, every person who voted had to have registered at some point.

Although consistently less likely to turnout than were men, women's rates of turnout and the gap between men and women varied considerably across time and place. In Sumner's (1909) 1906 Colorado data, for example, the male–female turnout differential ranges from 36 points in Delta County (which Sumner describes as agricultural) to a mere 6 points in Teller County (characterized by mining). In Boston, women's registration rates vary (across precincts and elections) from as little as just 3 percent to as high as 66 percent. The registration gender gap also varies across precincts and elections – from more than 50 points to fewer than 10 (and just 3.5 points in black precincts in 1940!). About 35 percent of women in Arizona (1916) registered to vote compared to 49 percent of men, a 14-point gap (Berman 1993). In Ann Arbor, even women who had taken the step of registering turned out at a somewhat lower average rate (about 9 percentage points) than registered men. The largest gender differences in turnout were for low salience elections (off-cycle municipal elections). In one instance, the presidential election of 1928, the percentage of registered women voting exceeded the turnout of registered men, although the percentage of registered men continued to far exceed the percentage of registered women (Pollock 1939).

Time. In general, women's turnout and registration rates tended to increase with successive elections, although this did not always mean a

A comparison of rates of registration for men and women at the time of the state primary (September 7, 1920) and at the general election (November 2, 1920) confirms this expectation. In Boston as a whole, men's registration increased 8 percent between the primary and general elections (51 to 55.1 percent). Women's registration increased 123 percent over the same period (12.9 to 28.7 percent). As a result, the difference in rates of registration suggested by the primary data is in most cases considerably larger than that suggested by the general election data. Certainly, women's registration lags significantly behind men's in 1920, but not quite as dramatically as the primary data would lead us to believe. Only in 1920 is the error introduced by using primary registration data likely sex specific. Note, however, that while primary registration figures likely slightly underestimate general election rates in 1920, when women had only twelve days to register between ratification and the primary, it is unlikely (although we unfortunately lack the data to confirm this) that women's registration behavior changes as dramatically between the primary and general in subsequent elections. For that reason, although the primary registration data for 1924–1936 may underestimate the *level* of registration among both men and women, it is likely a reasonable approximation of the difference between male and female registration rates.

smaller male–female turnout/registration gap over time. Female registration grew modestly between 1917 and 1924 in Oregon, but male registration rates increased to an even greater extent, so the registration gender gap actually grew (Andersen 1994). In Illinois, on the other hand, women's rates of registration did not increase significantly between 1916 and 1920 (Goldstein 1984; see Chapter 5). In Boston, both men's and women's registration rates tended to increase steadily across elections, but women's turnout grew at a faster pace in most precincts (Gamm 1986).

The extent to which the registration gender gap narrows varies considerably across groups in Boston (Gamm 1986). For most racial, religious, and class groups – native whites, Jews, Irish, African Americans – women made dramatic gains in registration, particularly in the 1930s, which resulted in large declines in the size of the registration gender gap. In middle-class Irish precincts, to give just one example, the turnout gender gap declined from almost 48 points to just about 8 points between 1920 and 1940. This enormous gain was achieved despite the fact that women in middle-class Irish precincts were some of the most highly mobilized in 1920: almost a quarter of women in those precincts registered to vote in 1920 compared to just 10 to 15 percent in other precincts.

Rural versus Urban. Rural and urban women may have adapted to their new right differently. In Oregon, purely rural counties tended to boast higher rates of female registration than counties with larger (2,500 plus) towns; registration rates were lowest by far in Multnomah County (Portland) (Andersen 1994). On the other hand, in Sumner's 1906 Colorado data, women's electoral behavior in comparably urban Denver County is not particularly distinguished from that in the other more rural counties. Cities themselves appear to vary considerably. The registration gender gap in 1906 Denver wards rarely exceeds 15 points (Sumner 1909). In Boston, on the other hand, the registration gender gap routinely exceeds 20 to more than 30 points in some precincts, especially in the first elections after suffrage (Gamm 1986).

The impact of an urban versus rural context may have intersected with other factors. For example, Lebsock (1993) finds that women, both white and black, were less likely to register to vote in rural Virginia counties compared to urban. She attributes this difference to the considerable difficulty in fulfilling Virginia's stringent electoral requirements in rural counties (Lebsock 1993, 86):

> Virginia lawmakers had intentionally made the registration process complicated. One had to locate the county or city treasurer, pay one's poll tax, and then proceed with receipt in hand to find the registrar. In the largest cities, this was not

usually difficult; the registrar was required to sit for thirty days in a centrally located public building. In the country, registration was handled by local precincts by registrars who were required to sit for only one day out of the thirty-day registration period. They were not required to announce when that day might be or where they might be located.

According to one activist, "Our rural women had a lot of trouble running all over the country trying to catch registrars, who were out plowing or fishing or doing various things" (Lebsock 1993, 86). Rural registrars in particular had a great deal of latitude in judging an applicant's fitness to vote, and it was widely understood that this latitude was used particularly to suppress the vote of newly enfranchised black women.

Social Class. As was the case for men, higher social class appears associated with higher turnout among women. Gosnell and Gill (1935), for example, claim that the 1932 Chicago registration data show that women of higher social class registered at higher rates than women of lower social class. Using crowding as a gauge of class, Andersen (1994) also finds evidence that wealthier women were more likely to register to vote in Oregon than were poorer women. Gamm (1986) is able to provide a breakdown by class for the many Irish and Jewish precincts in Boston. Registration rates for women are generally higher in the higher class precincts, especially in the first years of enfranchisement. While men in higher class precincts also were generally more likely to register than men in lower class precincts, women in higher class precincts in Boston were much more likely to register than their sisters in lower class precincts.

Ethnicity and Immigration. The impact of ethnicity and immigration on the political incorporation of female voters can be seen most clearly in Gamm's (1986) Boston data. For example, the Irish in Boston were famously well-organized in politics during this period. Not surprisingly, then, Irish precincts, particularly those of relatively higher class, boast some of the highest rates of registration of the groups represented in Gamm's Boston data, including among newly enfranchised Irish women. Indeed, ethnicity may have trumped gender, although Boston's powerful political machines may have been an exceptional case. By 1936, all but the poorest Irish women are more likely to register to vote than Yankee, black, Italian, and almost all Jewish *men*. In general, variation in the rates of female registration lines are consistent with the patterns seen among men; where male turnout was higher, so was female. There are important exceptions, however, in which class and ethnicity intersects with sex in interesting ways. For example, Irish (especially higher class) and higher class Jewish men are the most highly mobilized. Irish women are similarly highly mobilized, but upper middle-class Jewish women, although highly mobilized compared to other women, lag behind their male counterparts to a much larger degree than do Irish women of similar class status.

Women were enfranchised during a period of massive immigration. Available evidence suggests women in immigrant communities were particularly reluctant to embrace their new right. In Illinois, men in immigrant wards were more likely to register than those in wards with more native-born citizens, but women did not follow a similar pattern, suggesting that a unique gender dynamic suppressed immigrant women's electoral participation (Goldstein 1984). In Boston, turnout was lower for both men and women in Italian wards with newer immigrants compared to wards with more second-generation (native born) Italians before 1936. Women in the more native-born wards are at least twice as likely to register in every election before 1936 than are women in the more recently immigrated wards. The effect is smaller, but in the same direction, for men during these elections, suggesting that recent immigrant status may have dampened female participation more than it did male.

Race. We have very little data on the voting behavior of women of color. In one rare exception, Lebsock (1993) reports on a survey of registration figures in the State of Virginia conducted by a state good government group and published in the *Richmond Times Dispatch*. Nearly 30 percent of the population of Virginia is African American, so the survey provides a unique opportunity to learn about the impact of race on participation (US Census 1922). Black women were consistently less likely to register than were white women. However, the gender gap may have been considerably smaller among blacks than among whites. Lebsock estimates that in the state capital of Richmond in 1920, about 12.5 percent of voting-age black women registered compared to 14.8 percent of black men, an almost imperceptible gap. Among whites, however, 27 percent of women registered compared to more than 79 percent of men, an enormous difference. Black women were least likely to register in counties where the African American population was largest, including a number of black majority counties where registration rates among black women ranged from a high of 2.5 percent to a low of zero. Registration of black women was higher where the black population was relatively smaller and "competition between Democrats and Republicans was keen enough to encourage the Republican leaders to cultivate their black constituencies" (Lebsock 1993, 86). Unfortunately, Lebsock does not report comparable figures for black and white men, outside of Richmond, so we cannot determine if the differences among black and white women were comparable or different than the differences among black and white men; that is, the extent to which gender or race explains these patterns. On the whole, Lebsock (1993, 87) notes that in 1920, the white majority was "slightly larger than it had been," but whether as a result of lower relative registration among black women compared to white, or more white men registering in response to the threat of black women's access to the polls (or other causes), is not clear. Despite concerted campaigns to aid their registration, black women faced similar resistance and resultant low rates of registration in other Southern states as well (Gilmore 1996).

Gamm's (1986) Boston data are another important source, although unlike in Virginia, blacks were just 1.2 percent of the population of Massachusetts in 1920. In 1920, women in black precincts register at rates (around 11 percent) that exceed those of women in some precincts (such as Italian and working class Jewish precincts), are on par with women in others (such as poor Irish and other Jewish precincts), and lag behind (by as much as 10 to 15 points) women in still other precincts (such as other Irish and native white precincts). Clearly, race, class, and immigration interacted in important ways. Importantly, as in Virginia, gender gaps are consistently quite small among African Americans in Boston: From 1920 to 1940, African American precincts account for some of the smallest male–female differences Gamm reports; by 1928, women in black precincts come within fewer than 10 points of their male counterparts, and they are almost indistinguishable by 1940 – just a 3.5-point difference. The only precincts that come close to as small of a registration gender gap in 1940 are the native white (8.8-point gender gap) and most prosperous Irish precincts (7.8 points). The small gender gap among black populations (compared to whites) in both Richmond, Virginia and Boston, Massachusetts suggests race may have been more determinative of black women's electoral participation than was their gender.

Vote Choice

Although scholars have been able to use registration lists to track male and female registration and turnout, data on how women actually cast their ballots are even more difficult to come by. The only known instance of actual vote choice reported by sex for presidential elections is limited to Illinois in 1916 and 1920 (Goldstein 1984). Gamm (1986) uses party registration (at the time of the state primary), recorded by sex, as a measure of party attachment. These data can give us some indication of which parties mobilized women into the active electorate.[4]

Loyalty. As we discussed in Chapter 1, many observers and later scholars expected women to be less loyal partisans than men. The Illinois data offer limited support for this hypothesis. For example, Goldstein (1984) finds some evidence of greater ballot rolloff and split-ticket voting among women compared to men. Willingness to defect from the two major parties is also an indicator of weaker partisan attachment. Goldstein (1984) concludes that newly enfranchised women in Chicago were indeed slightly more likely to favor Progressive Party candidates for University of Illinois trustee.

Progressive Values. On specific bond issues, Goldstein indicates that women were more favorable than men on moral issues of social reform, namely Prohibition and Sunday blue laws (see also Gosnell and Gill 1935). On political reform proposals advocated by the Progressives (introduction of initiative, referendum reform), however, women were less favorable. On other bonds involving such matters as street repair and hospital construction, no sex differences emerged.

Partisanship. Did women's enfranchisement benefit the Republican Party in particular? The evidence is mixed. Data from Oregon (Andersen 1994) and Illinois (Goldstein 1984) suggests women were more likely to vote for Republican Harding in 1920 than were men. On the other hand, Gamm's (1986) data on the party identification of women in Boston do not suggest that women, as a group, favored one party over another immediately following enfranchisement or in the years to come. Reflecting the traditional party strength in those communities, Jewish, black, and Yankee women were initially more mobilized by Republicans than Democrats, while the reverse was true among Italian and Irish women. This mobilization by the locally dominant party, rather than a general bias toward Republicans or Progressives, is consistent with the state-level findings for 1920 and 1924 we report in Chapters 5 and 6.

Realignment. As we explore in Chapters 7 and 8, under- and recently mobilized women were particularly available for New Deal conversion and mobilization (Andersen 1979). In Boston, as throughout most of the United States, the twenty years following enfranchisement were

[4] Unfortunately, Gamm (1989) was unable to locate party registration data for most precincts for 1932.

characterized by a general shift to Democratic support. Not surprisingly, then, both men and women of all groups increased their Democratic mobilization over time. In most cases, however, women increased their Democratic mobilization to an even greater degree than did men across this era, narrowing the gap between the Democratic mobilization rates of men and women (Gamm 1986). To preview our own findings, we also uncover evidence of greater relative female mobilization into the Democratic Party during realignment (see Chapter 8).

Among most ethnic groups, women's realignment came somewhat later than did men's. Among East Boston Italians, for example, men experienced their greatest surges into the Democratic fold before 1936, while women's greatest gains came in 1936 and after. While Italian men and women display the greatest differences in their realignment timing, the basic pattern of earlier male realignment followed by female realignment appears to characterize most groups (Gamm 1986). This finding for Boston diverges from traditional accounts of the role of women in New Deal realignment. Scholars have long assumed that Democratic growth in 1928 came in large part from urban and immigrant women who had been less likely to turnout than their rural and native sisters in the first elections after suffrage, but were moved to turnout both for and against Al Smith (e.g., Andersen 1979; Brown 1991; Burner 1986; Huthmacher 1959). The explanation made logical sense as the low levels of mobilization among women in the early 1920s made women one of the only groups among whom large increases in turnout were possible. Nonetheless, the data from Boston do not support that interpretation. As we explore in detail in Chapter 7, our analysis provides further evidence (beyond the City of Boston) that women were not uniquely mobilized in 1928 – overall or by either party.

Limitations of Available Hard Data

Previous scholars have made impressive and quite successful attempts to uncover what sex-specific electoral data can be discerned from the sparse historical record. These data give us a unique and rare insight into how women used the ballot after suffrage. In particular, the distinct male and female returns for the State of Illinois have been closely studied, and for good reason. As the only source of "true" data on the turnout and vote choice of male and female voters immediately after the Nineteenth Amendment, the Illinois data provide a rare opportunity to observe with some certainty, and test a number of hypotheses regarding, the electoral behavior of women voters. As have other authors (e.g., Alpern and Baum 1985), we take advantage of the Illinois data in this project to verify assumptions and evaluate estimates (see Chapter 4).

Yet, there are real limits to the general conclusions about female voting behavior that can be inferred from the experience of just one state. For example, Alpern and Baum's (1985) analysis suggests that the gap between male and female turnout in Illinois was substantially larger than in other states. As a result, the Illinois data may have contributed to the overly pessimistic conventional wisdom about the extent to which recently enfranchised women failed to exercise the right. Moreover, Illinois, although a diverse state in many ways, is not fully representative of the diversity of contexts in the United States. Illinois represents just one region of the country, and only limited variation on such factors such as electoral competition and party strength.

Other data sources have similar limits. Boston (Gamm 1986) is a large, highly urban center. Even compared to other major cities, Boston's unique characteristics (e.g., Irish political machine, colonial history) make it distinctive. Even if we treat Boston's population as representative of city dwellers, the majority of the American electorate did not live in or even around cities exceeding a population of 100,000 in the 1920s and 1930s.[5] Finally, Gamm's data, as truly impressive as they are, are not even necessarily representative of Boston itself. The homogeneous precincts, although extremely useful for making inferences about specific social groups, comprise only a subset of the population of Boston and cannot tell us about the behavior of citizens in more heterogeneous contexts.

The comparability of these data also is a challenge. Although many measure the same activity (registration), they do so at fairly variable times, both historically and within the election cycle (primary vs. general election). The Boston (Gamm 1986), Oregon (Andersen 1994), and Illinois data (Goldstein 1984) provide information on registration immediately following enfranchisement but others provide a snapshot of an election or two past the first one in which women had the ballot: the Colorado data (Sumner 1909) are from 1906 (suffrage granted in 1893), while the Ann Arbor data (Pollock 1939) cover 1924 to 1932 (1920 suffrage). The available data cover three entire states (Arizona, Illinois, and Oregon) at limited times (and except for Illinois, for registration only

[5] A total of 34 percent of the US population were categorized as "metropolitan," residents of central cities and their suburbs, in the 1920 census. The comparable figure in the 2010 census was greater than 83 percent. In 1910 and 1920, central cities were defined as cities of 100,000 or more (US Census 1912, 1922, 2012).

and one election), one partial state (Colorado) in one early election, and two quite different cities (Boston and Ann Arbor, as well as Chicago, Portland, and Denver in other data). Few data sources cover more than one election, making it difficult to track how women's electoral participation changed over time and from election to election. Most data sources include information about presidential elections, but a number of the sources cover multiple types of elections (sometimes not reporting them separately so distinctions can be made). Comparisons are thus difficult, limiting our ability to draw general conclusions.

Comparative Data

Before we turn to efforts to estimate women's turnout and vote choice in the United States, we note the availability of data on the experience of women after suffrage in other Western nation states.[6] In contrast to the United States, a number of other countries tallied male and female votes separately for at least a short period of time after enfranchisement. Differences in year of suffrage extension, variation in conditions of enfranchisement (some countries initially assigned a higher age of enfranchisement to women, required property ownership, and so on), and diversity in terms of the date and nature of specific elections, make comparison of the electoral incorporation of women across nations extremely difficult. Yet the experience of women elsewhere also can inform our expectations and understanding of the behavior and impact of women in the United States.

Female turnout consistently lags male turnout, although the size of the differential varies considerably both across and within nations (Duverger 1955; Tingsten 1937). In Yugoslavia, for example, where turnout of both sexes exceeded 88 percent, women trailed men by fewer than 2 points in the first national elections after suffrage extension. In France, on the other hand, polls (not actual turnout data) suggest sex differences around 10 points. There are a few instances, largely in cities and towns rather than the country, in which female turnout even exceeds male turnout slightly. Turnout was consistently higher in cities and towns compared to rural places, and male–female differences were larger in rural areas than they were in urban locales. More generally, differences between men and women tended to be smallest where overall turnout was highest

[6] Specifically, the authors cited here report on data available from Sweden, Norway, Denmark, Iceland, Finland, Estonia, Germany (certain districts only), Austria, Australia, and New Zealand (Tingsten 1937), and from Norway, Germany, France, and Yugoslavia (Duverger 1955).

(Duverger 1955; Tingsten 1937). There is substantial variation across countries, but in general, female turnout tends to increase, and the size of the male–female differential tends to decrease, over time. Given only Chicago for comparison, Tingsten (1937, 32) concludes that "the difference in participation between men and women is considerably larger in the United States than in most other countries."

Less information is available regarding vote choice, but the general conclusion is that women were generally more likely to support conservative and Christian parties and less likely to support socialist and communist parties (Duverger 1955). Tingsten (1937) concludes that religion appears to have played a more determinative role in women's vote choice, while class seemed to be less important to women compared to men.

Previous Efforts at Estimation

Given the paucity of good data on women's electoral behavior and the significant costs in gathering what little data might exist, a number of scholars have sought to estimate female voting behavior immediately after enfranchisement from mostly aggregate-level available data sources. In this section we examine prominent early (pre-Robinson [1950]) attempts to estimate women's turnout and vote choice, as well as examples of later, more cautious efforts.

Early Scholarship

Women's suffrage was becoming reality at the same moment as the advent of the modern social sciences; the American Political Science Association, for example, was founded in 1903. By the early twentieth century, a few of these recently professionalized political scientists turned their attention to the highly contested issue of female voting behavior. Lacking survey data (with one exception, noted later), scholars relied on available aggregate data sources. As a result, they not surprisingly often encountered, and in some cases clearly committed, the ecological fallacy.

William Ogburn and Inez Goltra's 1919 *Political Science Quarterly* article, "How Women Vote," is distinguished by a number of firsts: The first to use a multivariate statistical technique in a political science journal. The first (apparently) attempt by political scientists to use "indirect" methods to estimate the percentage of women voting for particular outcomes in an election. And in offering a few caveats, the first to suggest the theoretical possibility of what later became known as the ecological fallacy (see King 1997, 1–2).

Ogburn and Goltra use a 1914 Portland, Oregon election to investigate a number of hypotheses related to women's use of the vote. (Women were granted the vote in Oregon in 1912). Although sophisticated for its time, Ogburn and Goltra's method of estimation is straightforward: They report the partial correlation between the proportion of registered voters who are women and the proportion of the voters in the precinct supporting various ballot measures, holding constant the "conservatism" of the precinct. They estimate precinct conservatism with support for six ballot measures in 1912, prior to the extension of suffrage. From these correlation coefficients, they infer "the sex more in favor of the measure." For example, they conclude that women were more likely to favor restricting the franchise to citizens (anti-immigrant), less likely to support an eight-hour work day (contrary to expectations about women's support of Progressivism), and far more supportive of Prohibition.

In their first footnote, Ogburn and Goltra (1919, 415, fn. 1) acknowledge that, technically speaking, all a negative coefficient shows is that "precincts where larger percentages of women vote are the ones that vote more heavily against the measure." Although they interpret such a coefficient to mean that women were, on average, more opposed to the measure than were men, they acknowledge, but do not think likely, that "it is also theoretically possible to gerrymander the precincts in such a way that there may be a negative correlation even though men and women each distribute their votes 50 to 50 on the given measure." We now know that the authors were correct to acknowledge this theoretical possibility, and that the potential for incorrect inference – the ecological fallacy – was likely greater than Ogburn and Goltra recognized (see Chapter 4). Thus their estimates of the early voting behavior of women are considerably suspect and of limited utility.[7]

Ogburn and Goltra were not the only scholars of their generation to employ statistical techniques to discern the voting behavior of newly enfranchised women. In their influential piece "American Women's Ineffective Use of the Vote," sociologists Stuart A. Rice and Malcolm M. Willey (1924) primarily estimate female turnout in 1920 by assuming that male turnout had declined between 1900 and 1920 at the same rate as it declined between 1880 and 1900 (the authors use decennial census years to avoid estimating the size of the population). Using

[7] King (1997) notes that the Ogburn and Goltra data appear lost to history. Our own work in the Oregon State Archives uncovered what appear to be the original signature sheets submitted to place the initiative measures on the ballot, but not the actual precinct-level votes on the measures themselves.

that assumption, Rice and Willey conclude that female turnout in 21 Northern states where women did not have the ballot before 1920 averaged 34.7 percent. They acknowledge that the figure constitutes a lower bound, because (as others have since pointed out; see Goldstein 1984) the decline in the turnout rate of men was likely significantly steeper from 1900 to 1920 than from 1880 to 1900. They place the upper bound at 46.5 percent, based on the known turnout of women in Illinois. They expect that figure is also higher than average "because the tendency to vote in Illinois is more marked than elsewhere …, the women of that State had enjoyed limited suffrage at a relatively early date, and had been influenced by extensive educational campaigns designed to bring out their votes" (Rice and Willey 1924, 643). Rice and Willey's research was widely cited on the question of women's electoral participation after suffrage, reinforcing "for years the popularly held notion that women were primarily responsible for the sharp drop in voter turnout in 1920" (Alpern and Baum 1985, 46).

The general approach employed by Rice and Willey of estimating women's initial turnout or vote choice by comparing the size of the active electorate or vote for a particular party before women's enfranchisement (when male turnout and vote choice is known) to the size of the electorate/vote after women's enfranchisement, often given some consideration to the likelihood of a decline or increase in the male turnout/vote around the same time, has been popular (e.g., Converse 1972; Titus 1976). All conclude, not surprisingly, that women were less likely to turn out to vote than were men in those initial elections, although the degree of difference, inferred or stated, varies with the author.

Notably, we have almost no examples of estimation of female turnout or vote choice via the type of scientific surveys or polls that now dominate the study of electoral behavior. A rare exception is Arneson's (1925) survey of the "typical Ohio community" of Delaware. Arneson and his students polled some 4,390 citizens (nearly half the town!) and found a turnout rate of 72.9 percent of male citizens compared to 57.1 percent of women, a gap of 15.8 points. Arneson and a colleague (Arneson and Eells 1950) repeated the survey some twenty-four years later; by 1948, the gap between men and women had narrowed to just 1.6 points, with male turnout at 63.1 percent and female at 61.5 percent.

Press Accounts

The conventional wisdom also was shaped by early press reports concerning women's turnout and vote choice. While recognizing the impressionistic and anecdotal nature of most such reports, the lack of alternative reliable data has provided a void into which journalistic coverage is often treated as the best alternative to no information at all. Reporters sometimes had access to registration figures broken down by sex from which they could predict the relative size of the male and female vote. For the most part, however, journalists reported the predictions and impressions of party leaders, local experts, and polls workers. Interest in the electoral behavior of women in the years immediately following their enfranchisement was high. States where women were enfranchised early received particular attention as bellwethers for the rest of the country.[8]

Although some reports predicted massive turnout of women in 1920, exceeding that of men,[9] most were far more judicious and accurate, describing women's turnout as lagging behind that of men. Most news items indicated an expectation that women's vote had favored the GOP, especially in rural areas. In some cases, this expectation was backed up by reasonable inferences from hard data (e.g., an increase in the total vote, but with most of that increase benefiting one party[10]), but in most cases the basis was unreliable sources such as straw votes or estimates of party leaders.[11]

In each successive election after 1920, party leaders and observers predicted an unprecedented increase in women's presence at the polls.[12] This was especially true in 1928, when the contest between Democrat Al Smith and Republican Herbert Hoover – immigrant Catholic versus native Protestant backgrounds, and wet (i.e., anti-Prohibition) versus dry – was expected to particularly excite and interest women voters.[13]

[8] For example: "Women Voters Fail to Follow Leaders." *The New York Times*, November 10, 1916, p. 5.

[9] See, e.g., "Women Outvoting Men 3 to 1 in New York." *Bridgeport (CT) Post*, November 2, 1920.

[10] For example, "Women Help Win State by Record Vote." *Minneapolis Morning Tribune*, September 14, 1920, p. 1.

[11] For example, "Recapitulation of Straw Ballot." *Boston Globe*, October 16, 1920, p. 1; "500,000 Illinois Women to Vote on Wednesday." *Chicago Tribune*, September 12, 1920, p. 2.

[12] For example, "Record Vote Is Expected by Women's League." *The Duluth (MN) News Tribune*, October 24, 1924; "Women Will Cause Big Vote." *Houston Post-Dispatch*, October 27, 1924, p. 1.

[13] See "Women Play an Important Part in Presidential Campaign." *Santa Fe New Mexican*, October 20, 1928; "What'll Women Do? Is Chicago Election Enigma." *Chicago Daily Tribune*, October 4, 1928; "Women Will Decide How Missouri Goes." *The New York Times*, October 27, 1928; "Forecasts Big Vote by Women of State." *The New York Times*, October 7, 1928; "This Year's Woman Vote to Set a High Record." *The New York Times*, October 21, 1928, p. 8; Sullivan, Mark. 1928. "Election Will Bring Biggest Vote on Record." *The Duluth (MN) News Tribune*, October 28, p. 1.

Again, in many cases, these predictions were pure speculation, but many were grounded in registration figures that either showed general increases (often attributed mostly to women by reports from registrars and party leaders) or specifically indicated increased registration of women.

For the most part, however, the coverage of women's turnout and vote choice in the elections immediately following the ratification of the Nineteenth Amendment is characterized by a signal reluctance to offer any solid information on women's actual voting behavior for the simple reason that so little hard evidence existed. Party leaders on both sides predicted that women's turnout would be large and would benefit their party, but journalists were unable to validate those claims after the fact, even if they had been inclined to do so. Registration data might have provided some insight into women's turnout and even vote choice, and in some cases it did, but for the most part, the major newspapers of the day diligently reported the latest party leader's or political expert's claim about the impact of women's votes, and left it at that. Well-read citizens would be left with the impression that women's turnout was constantly increasing, always potentially consequential, and in most cases, Republican.

Later Scholarship

In contrast to early research, more recent scholars acknowledge the pitfalls of ecological inference, but seek to use available data and defensible logical assumptions to do what they can to evaluate women's turnout and vote choice after suffrage. For example, Kleppner (1982b, see also 1982a), in keeping with the earlier approaches, estimates female turnout by using previous male-only elections to predict male-only turnout for the year in which women were enfranchised, and uses the difference between the predicted and actual turnout as the estimate for female turnout in that year. He emphasizes that the 1920 overall turnout decline clearly was not caused by female enfranchisement alone, but also by other factors that suppressed male turnout. In general, Kleppner finds that the male–female differential varied considerably with the legal and political environment, particularly the degree of partisan competition, with highly competitive states having smaller differentials.

Alpern and Baum (1985) are specifically interested in the impact of female voters on the 1920 election. Employing a sample of 612 counties grouped into three regions (Midwest, New England, and Mid-Atlantic), they regress the 1916 Republican presidential vote (all males) on the

1920 votes for the Democratic, Republican, and all other party presidential nominees at the county level. The coefficients from the regression can be used to recover the proportion of men who voted Republican in 1916 and Democratic in 1920. Across a series of regressions and with some adjustments for logical inconsistencies, the complete accounting of the behavior of male voters can be recovered for the entire region. The difference between the predicted male votes in 1920 and the total votes is the estimated female vote in 1920. Comparison against the Illinois true values suggest that this approach underestimates the difference between male and female voters: the actual turnout Illinois differential in 1920 is 27 points compared to the estimated 18-point gap. Alpern and Baum conclude that the influx of female votes inflated Republican Harding's large majorities in the Mid-Atlantic states and Illinois, but helped Democrat Cox in New England and the Midwest (other than Illinois), although not enough to change the outcome. Like other ecological regression approaches, the method requires the assumption that what are known as transition probabilities – the percentage of men who vote Democratic in 1916 and also vote Democratic in 1920, for instance – are constant across counties in the sample. While this might be somewhat reasonable for the 102 counties in Illinois, we are less confident that this would hold for the 344 counties spread across the Mid-Atlantic region. The estimates are clearly inconsistent with data uncovered by Gamm: His 1986 work indicates that female turnout was substantially lower than male turnout in the New England, at least in Boston. Nevertheless, Alpern and Baum offer the most rigorous attempt to test the conventional wisdom with aggregate data.

With these few exceptions, most recent scholars, cognizant of the pitfalls of inferring individual-level behaviors from available aggregate-level data, have shied away from attempts to estimate women's turnout or vote choice in the period following suffrage. The precipitous decline in turnout in 1920 is sufficient evidence for many to conclude that women were initially extremely reluctant to take up their new right (e.g., Converse 1972; Rusk 1974). The surge in Republican mobilization in 1920 similarly leads some to describe early female voters as favoring the GOP (e.g., Brown 1991). Most authors interested, directly or indirectly, in female electoral behavior after suffrage fall back on the available hard data or accept the established conclusions concerning the impact of suffrage: Few women turned out to vote, and those who did voted either like men, or were slightly more mobilized by Republicans.

Conclusion

Meticulous efforts by several scholars have provided tantalizing insights into women's voting behavior after suffrage. For the most part, this research concludes that women's entrance into the electorate was slow but steady. Women's turnout lagged men's consistently, but did tend to increase over time. There was considerable variation in women's turnout – both overall and relative to men's – across time, place, and groups. Even less information on vote choice is available, but what we can learn from Illinois and Boston indicates that women's party preference was shaped by ethnicity, race, class, and immigration, just as was the case for men. Women in Boston appear particularly mobilized by the locally dominant party in the first elections after suffrage. These conclusions are drawn from a limited sample, however, covering a handful of states and communities.

At the same time, the general conventional wisdom that emerged from the 1920s is that women's turnout failed to match the promise of female activism on display in the suffrage movement: Despite preelection hype, turnout is universally described as low, which is attributed to women's general disengagement with political life. Historians and social scientists generally accept the characterization of women's votes as either mirroring men's or perhaps initially favoring the Republican Party, despite the limited amount of hard evidence on which to base that contention. Much of the conventional wisdom is based on speculation, questionable analysis, and gender stereotypes.

Thus, there is considerable room for improving the empirical bases on which our understanding of women's incorporation into the American electorate rests. It may indeed be the case that the conventional wisdom is correct, but that is, as they say, an empirical question. Our quest in the chapters that follow is to develop an approach to estimating women's turnout and vote choice that will improve the empirical basis on which we understand and evaluate women's use of the ballot in the elections following their enfranchisement.

4

Estimating Women's Turnout and Vote Choice

Since women first entered polling places, scholars and political observers have lamented the difficulty of observing the distinct electoral behavior of women and men. The methodological challenge is described simply by Ogburn and Goltra (1919, 413): "women's ballots are not distinguished from those of men but are deposited in the same ballot box." As a result, in virtually all cases, official records report only the total number of votes cast and the number of votes cast for each candidate. Whether women cast ballots, for which candidates, and with what consequence cannot be directly determined from the actual vote record. Or, as *The New York Times* concluded in 1932, "No one will ever know exactly what part the women played in the final result since voting machines tell no tales on them."[1]

This chapter explains how we overcome these challenges and generate estimates of how women and men voted in the first elections following suffrage. As this chapter focuses on technical issues related to data and methods, some readers may prefer to skip to the substantive findings reported in the chapters that follow. However, because of the unique data and statistical techniques we employ, as well as the considerable challenges that have hindered previous work on this question, substantial attention to data and methodology is warranted.

Some early scholars combined aggregate election returns and census data to draw conclusions about social and economic determinants of electoral behavior, including sex (e.g., Ogburn and Goltra 1919; Rice and Willey 1924). Since Robinson (1950) identified the inherent dangers

[1] "The Women's Vote." *The New York Times*, October 25, 1932, p. 18.

of this approach, now known as the ecological fallacy, social scientists have tended to shy away from using aggregate data to analyze voting and elections (for exceptions, see Brown 1991; Kleppner 1982a; Nardulli 2005). In place of aggregate data, most contemporary work on electoral behavior relies on mass surveys. The introduction of reliable public opinion polls, beginning in the 1930s and accelerating with the establishment of the American National Election Studies (ANES) in the 1950s, has greatly advanced our understanding of electoral behavior (Berinsky 2006; Berinsky et al. 2011; Rubenstein 1994). Yet, mass surveys have obvious limitations for historical research: If the period of interest precedes the development of surveys, available aggregate data are often the only available alternative (cf. Andersen 1979).[2]

As we saw in Chapter 3, some hard data as well as useful estimates of women's turnout and vote choice in the 1920s and early 1930s do exist, but are limited in spatial and temporal coverage. With so little data available, some concluded that conjecture and speculation are the only available options. Writer Edna Kenton threw up her hands in despair in 1924: "Absolutely no statistics are available [on how women vote], and one guess is as good as another" (1924, 44). We do not accept this pessimistic conclusion. Although we cannot know the truth with certainty, some "guesses" – we prefer the term, estimates – are in fact better than others. As this chapter explains, our approach to this challenge is to combine available aggregate election returns and census data, recent innovations in methods of ecological inference, and information from the historical record to estimate women's use of the ballot in ten states during the five presidential elections following national enfranchisement. With this approach we are able to confront the lament of *The New York Times*: Voting machines may not record women's and men's ballots separately, but with a few reasonable assumptions and a lot of computing power, voting records can indeed "tell tales" about how women voted.

We first describe the available data that underpin the analysis. We construct a sample of ten states and collect census data and election

[2] Some embryonic polling did exist in the 1920s, including the famous *Literary Digest* straw polls that accurately predicted presidential elections from 1916 to 1932 and then failed spectacularly in 1936. While acknowledging the shortcomings, Erikson and Tedin (1981) use the *Literary Digest* data to analyze New Deal realignment, but others have argued that the data are not a representative sample throughout the period (Brown 1988; Shively 1971–1972). Berinsky and his colleagues (2011) have compiled historic public opinion polls into a usable form for scholars, but their data begin in 1936, the final year of our analysis.

returns at various levels of aggregation. We describe how our sample provides variation on important aspects of political context, and the specific measures of state-level political context we employ. We then evaluate the degree to which our sample does, and does not, represent the entire United States.

We next outline, in general terms, the evolution of methods of ecological inference since Robinson (1950) identified the full extent of the challenge. Work is ongoing, but current tools and approaches offer unprecedented opportunities to extract reliable estimates of individual-level behavior from aggregate data. We then turn to the approach to ecological inference adopted in this work. Capitalizing on recent work in Bayesian data analysis, we rely on a Bayesian hierarchical model to estimate women's turnout and vote choice at the state level. (Technical details – statistical programming choices and post-estimation diagnostics – are described in an appendix to this chapter.)

Next, we explain the problems and possibilities inherent to ecological inference in the case of gender. In particular, low variation in the characteristic of interest – sex – across geographic observations makes inferring the distinct electoral behavior of men and women a serious challenge. The Bayesian approach we employ has the advantage of letting us introduce substantively meaningful assumptions in direct and clear ways that permit us to overcome these challenges, a major achievement that permits us to quite dramatically expand on what we know about how the first female voters used the ballot.

Finally, we evaluate the performance of the data collection and estimation strategy, in particular in terms of our ability to accurately recover the observed or reported vote choice of women and men in the Illinois presidential elections of 1916 and 1920. The performance of the estimator is impressive by this standard. The estimates, spanning five elections and a diverse set of ten states, comprise the empirical basis for our investigation into women's turnout and vote choice after suffrage in Chapters 5 through 8.

Identifying and Gathering Appropriate Data

Our estimation strategy, described in the text that follows, produces state-level estimates of the turnout and presidential vote choice of women and men. Generating those state-level estimates requires data on the population (specifically, number of voting-age men and women) and electoral behavior of citizens in multiple geographic units within each state. In this section, we describe the challenges to gathering such data, our ten-state sample, and the measures of political context employed in this research.

Aggregate Election and Census Data

We constructed a sample of states with two objectives: (1) to obtain as many observations as possible in each state (preferably in excess of 100), and (2) to produce cross-state variation in politically relevant variables such as region, party control, competition, and legal context. Our estimation strategy requires election returns and census (population) data for multiple observations in each state and election. More observations per state is useful because more units increases the variation – the range – of observed behavior, both turnout and vote choice. This variation improves the efficiency of the estimator, meaning less uncertainty about our findings.[3]

Counties are the standard geopolitical subdivisions of states and have a long tradition of use in historic election analysis (e.g., Key 1949). However, the number of counties per state varies systematically by region (see discussion of regional definitions below). Of the seventeen states with more than seventy-five counties in 1920, all of them are located in the Midwestern and, to a lesser extent, the Southern and Border regions of the United States. Several large states have more than ninety-nine counties; of the nine such states, six are included in our sample (four Midwestern, one Southern, one Border). We add two additional states (one upper Midwest, one Border) with more than seventy-five counties. Doing so is especially useful since this choice adds Minnesota to our sample, a state where Progressives were quite successful in 1924, and thus a good case for examining the expectation of particularly strong support for Progressives among women (see Chapter 6). Relying on county-level data, we are thus able to construct a sample that includes strong representation of the Midwest (Minnesota, Iowa, Illinois, Kansas, and Missouri), and reasonable representation of the Border (Oklahoma, Kentucky) and Southern (Virginia) regions of the United States.

In the other regions of the United States – most notably the Northeast and the West – states either have very few counties and/or we confront

[3] Methods of ecological inference hinge on this variation, rather than on the number of available observations. Unlike regression or other techniques familiar to political scientists, methods of ecological inference are not characterized by statistical consistency: Every additional observation adds a few pieces of information but many new parameters, so larger numbers of observations do not necessarily yield more precise estimates than smaller numbers of observations.

data challenges that frustrate efforts to merge election and census information. In the Northeast, states tend to have relatively few counties. In this region, we are able to address this problem by shifting to the subcounty level of geopolitical aggregation, what the US Census calls the Minor Civil Division (MCD). Although there is some variation from state to state, in most cases, MCDs are towns, townships, and villages. These units completely overlay the entire US land mass. While historic MCD-level election records have not been systematically reported or preserved by states nationwide, a number of Northeastern states do report election returns at the level of the MCD in their official election reports available from state libraries or archives (Swisher 1933; see Burnham 1981b on the value and difficulty of obtaining MCD-level election records). Moreover, contrary to what we observe in states in other regions, MCD boundaries in the Northeast tended to be stable across the sixteen-year period we examine. This stability makes the merging of election records and census data possible. Using these smaller levels of aggregation not only increases variation in observed behavior, but it also simply makes estimation technically possible; in our two Northeastern states, Connecticut (eight counties) and Massachusetts (fourteen counties), estimation with county-level data alone would not have been possible.

Unfortunately, data challenges proved insurmountable in the West. In several states, populations were so small (e.g., the voting-age population of Wyoming in 1920 is fewer than 120,000 people) that even had a sufficient number of observations been available, the resulting very small populations per observation would have made estimation impossible. In Western states with larger populations, we faced other challenges. In some cases, there were too few counties and no MCD or other smaller aggregation (e.g., ward) election data available. In other cases, MCD election return data were available, but the MCD and even county boundaries were not stable in these "new" states. We estimate election year population by drawing from the decennial census enumerations before and after the election (e.g., we estimate the population in 1924 from the 1920 and 1930 censuses). The practical impossibility of matching census and election returns where boundaries are still shifting necessarily eliminated these states from analysis. For these reasons, our set of sample states does not include any states for the Western region of the United States. As we demonstrate in the text that follows, even with the omission of these mostly sparsely populated states, the sample is representative of the United States on a number of key dimensions (see "Comparing the Sample to the Broader United States").

TABLE 4.1. *Available Data Aggregation for Each Sample State, 1920*

State	Geographic Units	Average Size[a]	Largest Observation
Connecticut	167 MCDs, 10 wards	4,767	98,163 (City of New Haven)
Illinois	96 counties, 103 MCDs, 35 wards	16,855	92,577 (Chicago Ward 25)
Iowa	99 counties	14,431	98,241 (Polk County)
Kansas	105 counties	9,754	74,346 (Wyandotte County)
Kentucky	120 counties	10,746	187,090 (Jefferson County)
Massachusetts	346 MCDs, 26 wards	6,482	112,158 (City of Worcester)
Minnesota	86 counties, 25 wards, 10 cities	11,412	61,063 (City of Duluth)
Missouri	114 counties	17,884	574,687 (St. Louis County)
Oklahoma	77 counties	13,267	71,751 (Oklahoma County)
Virginia	118 counties	10,229	107,327 (City of Richmond)

[a] Total number of men and women 21 and older.

Our resulting sample of ten states is presented in Table 4.1.[4] Our data include six states for which county-level data is sufficient for estimation. Extremely large observations can minimize observed variation in electoral behavior and complicate estimation, so we attempt to disaggregate large MCDs or counties where possible. In Illinois, we address the presence of one extremely large observation – Cook County (Chicago), with a population of more than 3 million in 1920 – by adding available data on the thirty-five still-large wards, as well as MCD-level data where available. Similarly, in Minnesota, we are able to disaggregate several large counties into ten cities and twenty-five wards.[5] In the two Northeastern

[4] The available data for 1920 are described in Table 4.1, but the number of observations – counties, wards, or MCDs – varies across the elections. For instance, we located MCD-level data for five additional counties in 1932 Illinois, so the total number of observations increased to 315. To match census population data with election returns, we relied on thirty-five ward groupings in the City of Chicago, rather than fifty wards (see Anderson 1979 for details).

[5] Unfortunately, we were unable to locate usable data to disaggregate the large observation in the State of Missouri, where St. Louis County is represented as a single observation with more than 500,000 age-eligible residents. Despite the inclusion of this unusual

states, we also disaggregate major cities into their constituent wards to further increase variation and minimize observation size.

Despite the use of different geographic units – counties, MCDs, wards – in various combinations in various states, the number of geographic units and population of these units implies a roughly similar source of data for each sample state. The typical state has about 100 observations averaging about 10,000 eligible voters with a single observation containing as many as 100,000 voters. The state with finest level of disaggregation, Connecticut, has an average of fewer than 2,500 men and 2,500 women in each of the 177 observed MCDs or wards. Illinois has the highest average number of voters per observed unit, principally due the size of wards in the City of Chicago (each averaging nearly 50,000 voters in 1920).

Creation of the dataset required us to merge election returns with population information derived from the US Census for each unit. For the states for which appropriate county-level data are available, we are able to rely on available digitized election returns and census data (ICPSR 1992, 1999; see also Heard and Strong 1950; Scammon 1965). In states where we rely on subcounty-level data, MCD and ward election returns were merged with MCD- and ward-level census information available in print form. Specific data sources are described in detail in the online appendix available at the publisher's website.

Merged census and election returns permit us to estimate overall turnout in each geographic unit. Our measure of turnout is the number of votes cast for all presidential candidates (any party) divided by the sum of the total male and female population age twenty-one or older in that year.[6] The US Census adopts a standard similar to report turnout in the P-20 series on voter participation (US Census 1998). This is a conservative estimate of turnout. The presidential vote excludes ballots that are spoiled or include no presidential vote, so the number of total ballots cast often exceeds the presidential vote by a small margin. More importantly, a variety of state laws excluded particular potential voters, including long residency requirements, literacy tests, and restrictions applied to felons. Many of these laws were applied in racially biased ways, particularly in the South. In addition, some states had large numbers of resident aliens

(in terms of population size) observation, we were able to obtain estimates from the Missouri data.

6 The total number of age-eligible (twenty-one and older) men and women was reported by the census only at lower levels of aggregation (wards and MCDs) beginning in 1930, so even the most basic quantity needed to report turnout in 1920 is a complex estimate.

who were in varying stages of the process of securing US citizenship. As a result, the voting-*eligible* population is likely smaller than our denominator (an estimate of the voting-*age* population), meaning that the turnout of eligible voters is likely somewhat higher than our estimates. In the Northeastern states (Connecticut and Massachusetts) in particular, unnaturalized foreign-born residents make up more than 20 percent of the voting-age population in 1920, and in two Midwestern states, Minnesota and Illinois, about 10 percent of the voting-age population. Like Gamm (1986), we view these voters as important elements of the potential electorate, residents who, when naturalized, were important targets of partisan mobilization. The naturalization of huge numbers of immigrants during the 1920s and 1930s made for a large number of potential new voters. By focusing on the age-eligible proportion of the electorate that turned out to vote we are able to see clearly, for example, the massive new mobilization in the Northeast in 1928, the result of two complementary developments, the growing numbers of immigrants who were eligible to vote and the nomination of a candidate, Al Smith, of particular appeal to immigrant voters. Even with this conservative, downwardly biased estimate of turnout, overall combined male and female turnout levels reach remarkable levels by the 1930s, exceeding 70 percent of the age-eligible population in four sample states.

The Political Context

We sought to generate a sample of states with variation across politically relevant features, such as region, partisanship, competitiveness, and the legal context for voting, all of which we are attentive to in the analysis that follows. Table 4.2 reports the restrictiveness of voting laws, competitiveness of elections, and leading party in each sample state, along with the date presidential suffrage was extended to women, the region in which each state resides, and Electoral College vote share. Our ten sample states include a few large states, particularly Illinois, so the total share of the Electoral College vote (and population) represented by the sample is more than 25 percent. Two states, Illinois and Kansas, extended presidential suffrage to women before the 1916 presidential election.

One central hypothesis we examine concerns whether and to what extent men and women's electoral behavior was shaped by the political context in which they were first eligible to vote (see Chapter 1). Women were enfranchised at the tail end of the "System of 1896," a period characterized by highly regional partisanship and one-partyism at the state-level, with Democratic supermajorities in the states of the former

TABLE 4.2. *Political Context of Sample States*

State	Date of Presidential Women's Suffrage[a]	Region	Electoral College Vote Share (1920)	Party Competition[b]	Restrictions on Voting[c]
Connecticut	1920	Northeast	1.3	One-party Republican	High
Illinois	1913	Midwest	5.5	One-party Republican	Minimal
Iowa	1919	Midwest	2.5	One-party Republican	Minimal
Kansas	1912	Midwest	1.9	One-party Republican	Minimal
Kentucky	1920	Border	2.5	Competitive Democratic	Minimal
Massachusetts	1920	Northeast	3.4	One-party Republican	High
Minnesota	1919	Midwest	2.3	One-party Republican	Minimal
Missouri	1919	Midwest	3.4	Competitive Republican	Minimal
Oklahoma	1918	Border	1.9	One-party Democratic	Minimal
Virginia	1920	South	2.3	One-party Democratic	High

[a] *Source:* Keyssar (2000).

[b] *Source:* Burnham (1981a) for 1914–1930. See text for category definitions.

[c] *Source:* Blakey (1928), Key (1949), and Keyssar (2000). See text for category definitions.

Confederacy, and Republican dominance in the North and West (see Burnham 1981a). Variation on these variables across states in our sample allows us to provide answers to the question: How did political context shape women's electoral behavior?

Region. Politics were highly regional in the 1920s and 1930s (Burnham 1981a), with different trajectories of development, population demographics, and cultures shaping political competition in each area of the country. The Northeast, for example, featured a distinctively large immigrant population: On average, 67 percent of the voting-age population of our two Northeastern states was first- or second-generation immigrant white in 1920, compared to 48 percent, on average, in our Midwestern states, and about 8 percent in our Southern and Border states (US Census 1922). Our Northeastern states also are more dense and urban than the other regions; 88 percent of the population in those two states lived in places characterized as urban in 1920. In comparison, only about half of residents in our Midwestern states, on average, lived in urban areas, and just 27 percent, on average, in our Southern and Border states. Divisions over immigration, ethnicity, and urban versus rural life were central to politics in the 1920s and 1930s (Burner 1986). Thus, for example, while both the Midwest and Northeast were reliably Republican in these periods, we have good reason to expect that these demographic differences made for distinct patterns of politics in these two regions.

We are particularly cognizant of the distinctiveness of the South. The South is idiosyncratic in many ways. The states of the former Confederacy are uniquely racially diverse: In 1920, the voting-age population of Virginia, our one Southern state, is nearly 30 percent African American, while our two Border states (Kentucky and Oklahoma) are both about 10 percent African American (Kentucky is 11 percent, Oklahoma almost 8 percent). No other state in our sample has an African American population exceeding 4 percent in 1920. The South also is distinguished by the long history of American slavery, a labor-intensive agricultural economy, and complex and consequential racial and class social norms and structures, including but not limited to Jim Crow. In particular, by the early twentieth century, Southern white elites had erected a set of formal and informal institutions that suppressed voter turnout among not only African Americans, but poor whites and any opponents of the ruling Democratic Party (Kousser 1974). Legal barriers to voting (including literacy tests, residence requirements, and poll taxes), accompanied by widespread, systematic intimidation and violence, made the cost of voting prohibitive for large swaths of the Southern population. The white-only primary and complete dominance of the Democratic Party further reduced incentives for general election participation (Alt 1994; Lawson 1999; Lewinson 1932; Valelly 2004). Suffrage exclusion was part of a broader antidemocratic political system in Southern states – which Mickey (2015) appropriately terms "authoritarian enclaves" – characterized by a "highly constricted civil society" (Mickey 2015, 56) and a hierarchical and deferential social structure, all of which further depressed political participation, and led to distinctively low turnout rates in general elections.

Region likely shaped women's entrance into the electorate. States with significant immigrant political cultures, such as those in the Northeast, might have discouraged women's turnout; many observers and later scholars have hypothesized that the more traditional gender roles emphasized in many immigrant communities may have held down women's entrance into the electorate (Andersen 1990; Butler 1924; Gerould 1925; Merriam and Gosnell 1924; Rymph 2006). Greater density and more urban context also has been associated with lower female turnout (e.g., Andersen 1994).

Southern culture was widely assumed to be particularly antithetical to female political participation. The suffrage movement had struggled to gain traction in Southern states, and Southern suffragists had developed unique activist repertoires and rhetoric, including appeals to white supremacy (Green 1996; Wheeler 1993), not unlike the claims of Northern suffragists that native female voters would help outnumber ethnic, immigrant voters. African American women faced widespread discrimination and exclusion from the suffrage movement (Terborg-Penn 1993, 1978). The ideal of the "Southern lady" – charming, gentle, obedient, and utterly feminine – sharply constrained women's options for appropriate civic engagement (Scott 1964, 1970). Scholars have shown Southern women to be far more politically engaged (often by subverting traditional civic organizations toward more political ends) in the early twentieth century than the stereotypes accepted by earlier writers presumed (Scott 1964; Tyler 1996; Wilkerson-Freeman 2002, 2003). Yet, none dispute the assumption that women in the South lagged behind their sisters in the rest of the country in taking up their new suffrage right.

We expect that African American women were particularly discouraged from exercising their suffrage rights in the South. The same formal and informal institutions that were intended to disenfranchise black men, among others, also worked against black women. For example, in

1920, Richmond, Virginia appointed additional white women as deputies to handle the rush of white women registering to vote. Appeals for additional black deputies were disregarded, leading to longer lines, more challenges, and more blacks left waiting when the registration office closed at the end of the day. Newspapers and the local Democratic Party warned readers that black women were seeking to register in large numbers, encouraging white women (and men) to exercise their suffrage rights to counter this threat. Not surprisingly, whereas more than a quarter of women in Richmond registered to vote in 1920, only 12.5 percent of voting-age black women did (Lebsock 1989). Although our estimates do not permit us to observe the voting behavior of African American – or any other subgroup of – women, these realities shape our expectations for and understanding of women's turnout in these regions.

In our analysis, we use the same regional classifications the US Census employs with one exception: We divide the Southern region into two categories. South designates the eleven Southern states that formed the Confederacy. Border designates the remaining Southern states. Our ten-state sample includes representation of the Northeastern, Southern/Border, and Midwestern regions of the United States, but as we have explained above, does not include states from the West. In the figures in which we report our estimates in the chapters that follow, we organize our states by region, as well as party context, to highlight important regional patterns in women's electoral behavior and impact.

Partisan Context. Party competition has been identified a key factor in explaining turnout in the early twentieth century (Burnham 1965, 1974; cf. Converse 1972; Rusk 1974), and the general partisan context an important aspect of women's partisan mobilization (Harvey 1998). As we have just discussed, in the South the absence of meaningful two-party competition was part of a broader antidemocratic system that is expected to have had especially strong depressive impacts on turnout during this era. To gauge the partisan context, we rely on Burnham (1981a), who classifies the partisan context of the American states in different eras according to the proportion of the total vote acquired by the major parties in the lower house of each state legislature. A substantial majority of states were noncompetitive in the period, with Republicans or Democrats consistently enjoying seat margins of 40 points or higher. We employ Burnham's measure – derived from the state legislative partisan lead between 1914 and 1930 – as an indicator of the partisan context that shaped early women's votes, both the general level of competition and the specific party advantaged in the state.[7] Specifically, any state in which one party's advantage in state house seat share exceeds 40 points is categorized as one-party Democratic or Republican. States in which the dominant party's advantage is just 0 to 39 points are competitive Democratic or Republican. During this era, thirty-three states are categorized as dominated by one party. Of our ten sample states, six are one-party Republican, two are one-party Democratic, and one each falls into the competitive Republican and competitive Democratic categories. (See Table 4.4 to compare the ten sample states to the broader United States).

The Burnham measure – capturing party vote across elections and time – indicates the grassroots level of party strength in the state, rather than the party advantaged in any particular presidential election contest. This is an advantage of the measure; by focusing on control of the state legislature over multiple elections, this measure ostensibly captures local partisan power, rather than the vagaries of any particular presidential election and the related unique national tides in party support. Because we expect that the impact of partisan control derives from the related levels of local party organization, mobilization efforts, and dominance of social networks, this measure is most appropriate. That being said, the measure also captures the closeness of the outcome of the election in the first elections after suffrage. In the six one-party Republican states, the Republican margin of victory in the 1920 presidential election was at or above 30 percentage points. In the other four states, the margin of the Republican victory was much lower. Only in Virginia (one of our two one-party Democratic states) do we observe a lopsided victory for the Democrats in 1920. As we will see in Chapter 7, the relationship between the Burnham measure and the presidential vote breaks down as realignment gets under way in 1928.

Legal Context. The legal context – the ways and extent to which access to the ballot is regulated or obstructed by such practices as poll taxes or lengthy residency requirements – has long been recognized as an important determinant of the propensity to vote. To gauge the legal context during the five presidential elections examined here, we rely on information

[7] Burnham (1981a) cannot categorize Minnesota in the 1914–1930 period because it shifts to a nonpartisan legislature in 1914. We thus use the 1896–1910 categorization (one-party Republican) for Minnesota. Consistent with that categorization, Harding received more than 70 percent of the vote in Minnesota in 1920, the highest Republican majority in the sample.

provided by the League of Women Voters (Blakey 1928), supplemented by Keyssar (2000) and Key (1949). We distinguish between states that have only a minimal set of restrictions on voters (age, citizenship, and residency requirements of one year or less) and states that impose more stringent restrictions. States with more restrictions impose one or more of several possible provisions: poll taxes, requirements to keep property or other taxes current, English language requirements, demonstration of good character, or residency requirements that extend up to five years. Sample states with these types of restrictions include Massachusetts (ability to read English), Connecticut (five-year resident with good character and ability to read English), and Virginia (two-year resident and current poll tax).[8]

Despite the limited number of sample states, our measures of political context are fairly distinct measures of state characteristics. For example, the sample includes both minimally and highly restrictive states in both one-party Republican and Democratic states. The exception is in the competitive states – both of the competitive states in the sample have minimal restrictions. Regionally, this means we also find highly restrictive laws not only in the South (Virginia), but in both of our Northeastern states as well. In the South, such restrictions were part of a well-known campaign to systematically disenfranchise blacks and empower the Democratic Party (Kousser 1974; Mickey 2015; Valelly 2004). The enactment of such restrictions, particularly in the Northeast, to keep immigrants, particularly the Irish, from the polls is perhaps less well known (Keyssar 2000). Variation in the presence of these provisions across region and party context allows us to gain greater insight into their independent effect on women.

Comparing the Sample to the Broader United States

Previous research on female voters after suffrage was limited to a few states or cities. Our ten state sample permits us to evaluate the behavior and impact of female voters in areas that vary in a number of politically relevant ways – by region, partisanship, competitiveness, and electoral rules. However, we cannot claim that the sample is fully representative

[8] Our two Border states, Kentucky and Oklahoma, required payment of regular or poll taxes in order to vote, but only for the purpose of voting in municipal elections (see Key 1949; Keyssar 2000). Because these requirements did not extend to federal elections, we treat both states as minimally restrictive, which we designate in the empirical chapters which follow as "residency requirement only."

TABLE 4.3. *National and Sample Presidential Election Outcomes, 1916–1936 (Percentage of Total Vote)*

Year	United States (%)		Sample (%)	
	Republican	Democratic	Republican	Democratic
1916	46.1	49.3	48.6	47.1
1920	60.6	34.3	62.3	33.4
1924	54.2	28.9	54.9	28.8
1928	58.3	40.9	57.5	41.9
1932	39.8	57.6	40.3	57.7
1936	36.8	60.6	39.1	57.9

of the broader US electorate. Unfortunately, as we have seen, the type of data required for our estimation strategy precludes construction of a sample that includes each region of the country.

That being said, the ten sample states do share a number of important features with the broader American electorate and population. As Table 4.3 indicates, the sample generally reflects the relevant political experience of the nation as a whole: an overwhelming Republican majority in the 1920 presidential election, a substantial third party surge in 1924, a large Republican majority in 1928, and large Democratic majorities in 1932 and 1936.

The sample states also share a number of important demographic features with the broader United States. Table 4.4 compares the US and the sample states on a number of population characteristics. In terms of the percentage of the population that is white, foreign-born, and resides in urban areas, the ten-state sample is representative of the nation as a whole. On the other hand, the lack of available data in the West and limited data availability in the South does imply some distortions in the regional distribution of states. The Northeast and the Midwest are overrepresented in our sample, while Southern and Western states are under- or unrepresented.

This regional imbalance has consequences for other features of the political context. For instance, because we have only one Southern state, the ten-state sample has a much smaller proportion of the population (27 percent) subject to multiple suffrage restrictions than the nation as a whole (more than 50 percent). For the same reason, the sample underrepresents one-party Democratic states and overrepresents one-party Republican states.

TABLE 4.4. *Characteristics of the United States and Sample States, 1920*

	United States (%)	Sample (%)
Percent foreign born	21	21
Percent white	91	94
Percent urban (2,500 or more)	53	54
Competitive Democratic	3	8
Competitive Republican	23	12
One-party Democratic	23	13
One-party Republican	51	67
Residency requirements only	48	73
Additional suffrage restrictions	52	27
Border	7	14
Midwest	33	59
Northeast	30	20
South	21	7
West	9	0

Note: Percentages are weighted by 1920 state voting-age population.
Sources: Blakey (1928); Burnham (1981a); ICPSR (1992).

Using Aggregate Data to Study Individual Behavior

Ecological inference is a way to learn about the behavior of individuals from aggregate data.[9] The technical objective is to infer unknown individual-level relationships from observed data reported at the aggregate level – states, counties, or other geographic units. The substantive goal of ecological inference is to combine information often collected in entirely separate efforts – population characteristics, election returns – to draw conclusions about individual-level relationships such as the link between voting behavior and sex. Without survey data, we cannot directly assess the voting behavior of individual men and women, but we can use ecological inference to generate estimates of the behavior of those two groups.

Ecological Fallacy

Ecological inference was the basis for much of the early quantitative work in both political science and sociology. The typical approach to compare men and women was to examine the relationship between the percentage of females in particular geographic units and turnout or some

[9] Much of the general discussion of the problem of ecological inference is drawn from Corder (2005).

measure of vote share in the same units. The direction of the relationship was interpreted to indicate whether women were more or less likely to support a candidate or turnout to vote. For example, a positive relationship, indicating that support for Party X increased where the percent female increased, was interpreted to mean that women were more likely to support Party X than were men. (For an example, see Figure 4.2.)

In 1950, Robinson identified what has become known as the ecological fallacy. Robinson demonstrated that observed relationships (such as simple measures of association) between aggregate quantities can be different at varying levels of aggregation, what is known as aggregation bias. The choice of geographic unit – for example, township, county, or state – could influence the observed relationship and substantive findings. For example, the link between gender (percent female) and turnout (percent voting) could be positive, negative, or zero depending on whether the correlation was calculated using data collected at the level of precincts, MCDs, counties, or states.

Robinson thus showed that correlations or other measures of association can produce wildly different results depending on the level of aggregation. It is possible (and in many cases, likely) that the percentage of women could be positively associated with support for Party X in particular geographic unit even if women were *less*, not more, likely to support that party at the individual level. A classic substantive example is Key's (1949, 513–517) finding that voter turnout in Southern counties tended to be positively associated with the size of the African American population. Using a simple correlation to make an ecological inference, a researcher would conclude that African Americans turn out at higher rates than whites. This is, of course, not the case at all. During the period that Key examines, African American turnout is negligible throughout the South. Key argues instead that whites in counties with larger African American populations turn out at higher than normal rates to defend and maintain Jim Crow and the system of white supremacy. If anything, African American turnout was likely lower in these counties than elsewhere. This link between the percentage of African American residents and the behavior of white voters is an example of aggregation bias.

Robinson's observation called into question a variety of results reported by social scientists using aggregate data. Proposals to address the ecological fallacy began to appear soon after the publication of Robinson's study, most notably the work of sociologists Leo Goodman, and Otis Duncan and Beverly Davis, both in 1953. But the search for a satisfactory solution has proven to be both controversial and technically complex.

TABLE 4.5. 2 × 2 *Table with Four Unknown Parameters*

Chicago Ward 27	Vote 45,266	Abstain 44,980
Women 45,680	p_{0i}	p_{2i}
Men 44,566	p_{1i}	p_{3i}

Early Solutions to the Ecological Inference Problem

The problem of ecological inference is typically represented as a problem of missing information. From available aggregate data, observers know the marginal values of a table that describes the relationship between, for instance, the number of women in a geographic unit and turnout in presidential elections. Census data reveal the number of voting-age residents who are women. Election returns reveal the number of people who voted in a recent presidential election. The key information is missing; neither source of data reveals the number of women who vote. Table 4.5 displays the observed and missing information for Chicago Ward 27 in 1920. Ecological inference centers on estimation of the unknown quantity, p_{0i}, the proportion of women who vote.

Early work on the problem of ecological inference relied on two distinct strategies to exploit the information in aggregate data. Goodman (1953) pioneered the use of conventional statistical models for ecological inference. He prescribed what became known as ecological regression. Goodman demonstrated that a simple regression pooling data from a number of geographic units (e.g., the 234 observations in Illinois) could be used to estimate the unknown parameters. The approach requires a restrictive and often implausible assumption that p_{0i} and p_{1i} are constant across all geographic units. Substantively, this would suggest that turnout of women and men is the same in all geographic units. This assumption is rarely satisfied in practice.

At about the same time that Goodman proposed his solution to the problem of ecological inference, Duncan and Davis (1953) introduced a different strategy that is known as the method of bounds. Researchers use information from each geographic unit to identify the logical boundaries on the quantities of interest implied by the table marginals. For example, if a particular group (Group 1) comprises 90 percent of the population in a particular geographic unit, and turnout in the unit overall is 70 percent, the logically possible range of the rate of turnout for that group is fairly narrow. If all of the voters came from Group 1, then the turnout of that group would be 70/90, or 78 percent. If all members outside of Group 1 voted, then turnout for Group 1 could only be 60/90, or 66 percent. Given the large size of Group 1 and high turnout in that area, we can limit the logically possible values of turnout for Group 1 to between 66 percent and 78 percent, a fairly narrow bound.

Information in Table 4.5 reveals the particular challenge that ecological inference presents for estimating behavior of men and women. Because the proportion of the population that is female varies little across units and tends to have a value of about 50 percent, the logical bounds on women's turnout are quite wide (see further discussion of the challenges of ecological inference in the case of gender in the section "Ecological Inference and Gender"). The table marginals reveal that turnout of women could be as high as 99 percent (if each of the 45,266 votes cast were cast by women) or as low as 0 percent (if all 44,566 men voted); both outcomes are possible given the distribution of votes and population. Calculation of these bounds for each of the 234 units in Illinois can reveal information about the likely proportion of women who vote if there are number of counties where turnout is very high (placing a logical floor on the number of women who voted) or very low (placing a logical ceiling on the number of women who voted). As we explain later, introducing more information to the problem – the distribution of votes across parties, combined with the uncontroversial assumption that women turned out less than men – dramatically narrows the logical bounds implied by the simple marginals in Table 4.5.

King's Proposed Solution

Since the problem of ecological inference is so pervasive, and of interest to practitioners in disciplines ranging from geography to epidemiology, a wide range of solutions to the problem have been suggested, typically advancing the early work of either Goodman or Duncan and Davis. In 1997, political scientist Gary King developed a novel approach to the problem of ecological inference that integrated Goodman's statistical approach with the information in the logical bounds identified by Duncan and Davis. At the aggregate level, King proposed an approach – a set of distributional assumptions and computational strategies – that is more flexible than the simple ordinary least squares (OLS) or ecological regression approaches that dominated earlier work on the problem of ecological inference. King relies on a particular assumption about the state-level distribution of the two unobserved parameters of interest (in

TABLE 4.6. 2 × 4 *Table with Eight Unknown Parameters*

Chicago Ward 27	Democrat 7,360	Republican 34,283	Third Party 3,623	Abstain 44,980
Women 45,680	p_{0i}	p_{2i}	p_{4i}	p_{6i}
Men 44,566	p_{1i}	p_{3i}	p_{5i}	p_{7i}

our application, the proportion of men who vote and the proportion of women who vote). King demonstrates how estimation of the properties of this distribution from the observed aggregate data (the entire set of 234 observations from the Illinois data, for instance) can help us further narrow the logical bounds for each geographic unit. By making a simple assumption about the joint distribution of the unknown parameters, King developed an estimation procedure that both satisfied the constraints implied by the logical bounds and relaxed Goodman's assumption. The result was a technical advance that permits application of ecological inference to a wide class of problems.

Our Approach to Ecological Inference

King's work stimulated renewed interest in the challenge of ecological inference in other fields and helped generate a range of new approaches to the problem (see, e.g., King, Rosen, and Tanner 2004). We rely on a Bayesian strategy proposed in Wakefield (2004), but we extend Wakefield's approach in two ways. First, we apply Wakefield's technique – developed for 2 × 2 tables – to the more complex 2 × 4 problem, estimating Democratic vote, Republican vote, other party vote, and abstention (four possible outcomes) for men and women (two population groups). Table 4.6 displays the observed and missing information for Chicago Ward 27 in 1920. Second, we introduce the uncontroversial assumption that male turnout will exceed female turnout in each geographic unit (see Chapter 1 for details).

We estimate the parameters – turnout and vote choice for men and women – for each state in each election separately. The result is a total of fifty-two sets of estimates: Five elections in the eight sample states that introduce women's suffrage in 1920 and six elections (1916–1936) for two states – Kansas and Illinois – that introduce women's suffrage before 1920. The appendix to this chapter describes the estimator in detail.

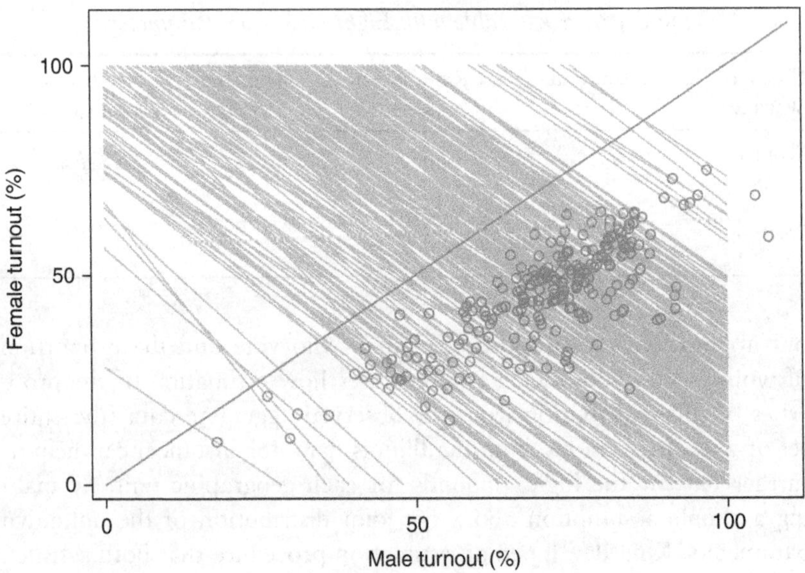

FIGURE 4.1. Logical bounds and observed values, Illinois, 1920.

Ecological Inference and Gender

Using ecological inference to estimate the behavior of women and men is extremely challenging. Even with data that describe small geographic units, we do not observe extremely high concentrations of women or men. This distinguishes gender from other politically-relevant divisions, such as race, class, or immigration, where residential segregation results in high concentrations of various groups in particular geographic areas (often, of course, not by choice). As noted previously, such residential patterns permit the direct (or near direct) observation of behavior for such groups in some especially informative observations. If 90 percent of the population in a geographic unit is white, the logically possible turnout and vote choice rates of white citizens in that unit must be very similar to overall turnout and vote choice in that unit. But, given the typical percent female in any geographic unit is around 50 percent, and a relatively limited variation in percent female across units, the logically possible combinations of male and female turnout range across a very wide interval.

The case of Illinois, where male and female turnout are observed in 1916 and 1920 (see Chapter 3), allows us to highlight the seriousness of the inference problem in the case of gender. Figure 4.1 summarizes two pieces of information. First, the circles are the observed combinations of male and female turnout in the more than 200 observations for which he have information reported by the State of Illinois in 1920.[10] Second, the diagonal lines starting in the upper left of the figure represent the logical bounds, the range of possible values of female and male turnout in each observation implied by the available census and election data. Some of the logical bounds span the [0,100] interval (that is, the logically possible values of women's turnout in those units range from no turnout at all to universal participation), or something very close to that range. However, more than a handful of observations – in the upper right and lower left corners of the figure – feature a more narrow set of possible values for women's rate of turnout.

How can we generate useful estimates, given the wide logical bounds for possible female electoral behavior in most of our units of observation? Note that all of the *observed* combinations of male and female turnout (indicated by the circles) are below the main diagonal, indicating that we do not observe any geographic unit where female turnout exceeds male turnout in that election. By adding the uncontroversial assumption that male turnout was higher than female turnout in 1920, the search for plausible combinations of male and female turnout is restricted to the area below the diagonal line. The combination of the logical bounds and the simple assumption proves, in many cases, to generate relatively narrow range of candidate values for the parameters of interest.

In addition to wide logical bounds, ecological inference in the case of gender faces another serious complication: aggregation bias. As discussed previously, aggregation bias occurs when the aggregate-level relationships revealed by measures of association, such as correlation, are not consistent with the underlying individual-level relationships. We know this is a problem for women and electoral behavior because the Illinois data (where male and female turnout are known) reveal severe aggregation bias in 1920. There are no observed MCDs, wards, or counties where female turnout exceeded male turnout in Illinois. In other words, we know women were less likely to turn out to vote than were men. The ecological relationship – the pattern in the aggregate data – suggests the opposite relationship, as revealed in Figure 4.2, which describes the relationship between total turnout and proportion female in 1920 Illinois. As the proportion of women increases, aggregate turnout increases. The (mistaken) ecological inference is that women turn out at higher levels than men. As we demonstrate in the next section, the approach to ecological inference that we adopt permits us to generate reliable estimates despite this severe aggregation bias.

[10] As the two points outside of the main body of the figure suggest, observed turnout exceeded the estimated voting-age population in two Illinois townships.

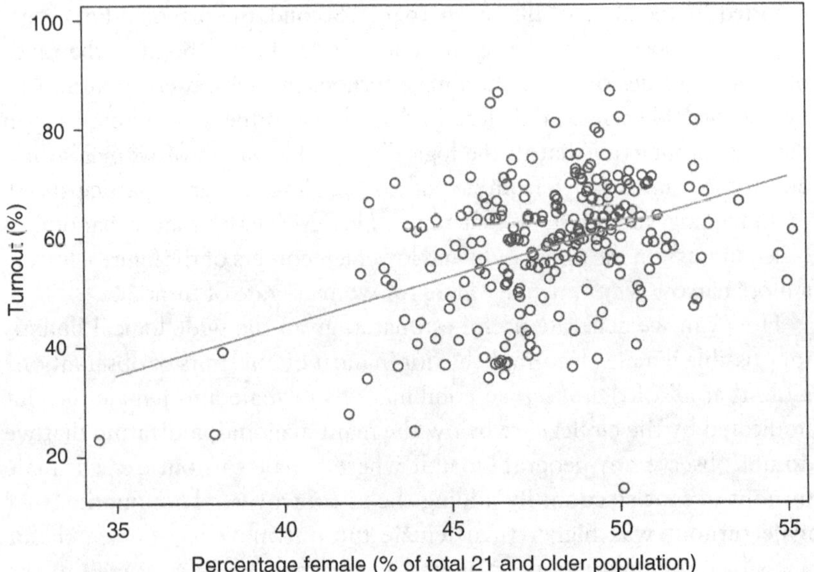

FIGURE 4.2. Ecological fallacy in Illinois, 1920.

Evaluating Our Estimates: The Special Case of Illinois

We estimate female and male turnout and vote choice for each of our sample states in the five presidential elections between 1920 and 1936. Details about model diagnostics and performance are reported in the appendix to this chapter. However, the best indicator of the accuracy of the estimator, in our view, is how well our estimates compare with the known (true) Illinois outcomes in 1916 and 1920 (see discussion of Illinois data in Chapter 3). Table 4.7 reports the actual and estimated quantities for Illinois in 1916 and 1920. The table reveals both the promise of the approach and a few hazards. Despite the substantial challenges to ecological inference in the case of gender – wide logical bounds and the presence of severe aggregation bias in both elections – estimates of turnout and partisan vote share are remarkably close to the observed returns. Indeed, the error or uncertainty associated with the estimate is comparable to the margin of error in the sort of large public opinion survey that forms the basis for most contemporary election research (±3 percent for 1920 Republican vote share, for instance). With the exception of turnout, each of the observed quantities is in the Bayesian credible interval – the range of uncertainty associated with the estimated parameters (see the next section for further explanation of this

TABLE 4.7. *Observed and Estimated Quantities of Interest in Illinois, 1916 and 1920*

	Observed	Estimated	90% Bayesian Credible Interval
Women, 1920			
Republican	70.7	72.0	68.9–75.0
Democratic	24.4	22.7	19.8–25.5
Third party	4.8	5.3	4.2–6.4
Turnout	41.5	37.8	35.9–39.5
Men, 1920			
Republican	65.8	65.4	63.7–67.0
Democratic	26.5	27.3	25.8–28.9
Third party	7.7	7.3	6.7–7.9
Turnout	63.9	67.5	65.8–69.2
Women, 1916			
Republican	52.4	54.4	50.8–58.4
Democratic	43.7	41.9	38.0–45.6
Third party	3.9	3.6	2.9–4.3
Turnout	47.5	43.9	42.2–45.6
Men, 1916			
Republican	52.7	51.4	49.1–53.5
Democratic	43.0	44.1	42.0–46.4
Third party	4.3	4.4	3.9–4.8
Turnout	67.4	71.0	69.1–72.6
Men, change from 1916 to 1920			
Republican	+13.1	+13.9	+11.0 to +16.7
Democratic	−16.6	−16.8	−14.1 to −19.5
Third party	+3.5	+2.9	+2.1 to +3.6
Turnout	−3.6	−3.5	−5.8 to −1.1
Women, change from 1916 to 1920			
Republican	+18.4	+17.5	+12.5 to +22.5
Democratic	−19.3	−19.3	−24.0 to −14.4
Third party	+0.9	+1.8	+0.4 to +3.0
Turnout	−6.1	−6.2	−8.6 to −3.7

Note: 1916 totals include official *estimates* for White, Peoria, St. Clair, and Vermilion counties. No separate ballot totals were reported for men and women in these four counties, so state officials estimated the ballot counts.

interval). In both elections, estimates of overall turnout are very close to the observed, but biased slightly downward for female turnout and slightly upward for male turnout. This small bias, although problematic, does not prevent us from reaching highly accurate conclusions about changes in turnout and vote choice across the two Illinois elections (see the latter part of Table 4.7 for a summary of observed and estimated changes from 1916 to 1920).

The substantive conclusions we draw from the estimates are consistent with what we can conclude from the observed returns. For example, one key question examined in the empirical chapters which follow is whether male and female Republican vote shares differ. In 1920, the 90 percent Bayesian credible intervals for male and female Republican vote share do not overlap; that is, the estimates suggest we should conclude that women supported the Republican Party at higher level than men. This is in fact the case in 1920 Illinois. Women's support for the Republican candidate was more than 5 percentage points higher than men's. In 1916, the estimates suggest we cannot reach this conclusion – the credible intervals do overlap so we must conclude that male and female Republican vote shares are essentially the same. Again, the observed data are consistent with this inference: The observed level of Republican vote share for men and women in 1916 differed by only 0.3 percentage point.

We focus exclusively on state-level estimates in the analysis reported in the empirical chapters. However, the performance of the estimator in Illinois also can be evaluated at the level of individual geographic units. The actual and estimated value of Republican vote share for women and men in 1920 Illinois is summarized in Figure 4.3. A number of points in the top panel are above the main diagonal, indicating that our estimates of female support are below the observed values. On the whole, however, we emphasize that our estimates tend to cluster near the 45-degree line (perfect replication of the observed value by our estimated value), suggesting that despite the considerable challenges of ecological inference in general and for gender specifically, we can be confident in the ability of our methodological strategy to provide reasonable estimates of the electoral behavior of men and women in the years following suffrage. (See the appendix to this chapter for an analysis comparing our estimates to three sets of ward-level data: registration data from the City of Chicago, 1920–1932, registration data from the City of Boston, 1920–1932, and party primary registration data from the City of Boston, 1924–1932.)

Reporting Point Estimates and Measures of Uncertainty

Throughout the text we report two different types of information for each parameter estimated in each state-election case: a point estimate and a measure of uncertainty. We also combine the point estimates with

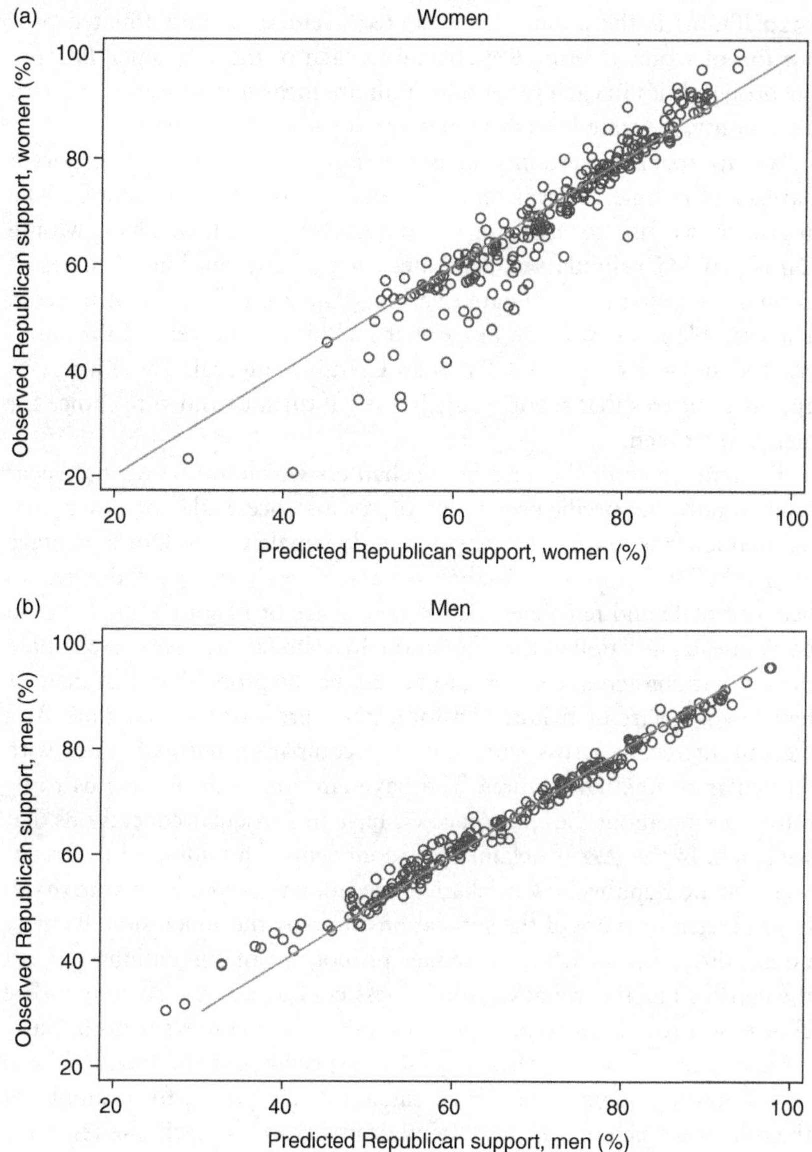

FIGURE 4.3. Observed and predicted Republican support, Illinois, 1920.

underlying census and election returns to produce an estimated count of male and female ballots. The estimates reported in the text are state-level weighted averages of parameters associated with the geographic units in the state. For example, the proportion of women voting Republican in

1920 Illinois is the population-weighted average of the estimated proportion of women voting Republican in each of the 234 units. Because the probabilities in each geographic unit are measured or estimated with uncertainty, the state-level estimates are likewise uncertain.

We approach uncertainty in two distinct ways. First, we report a Bayesian Credible Interval for each posterior quantity of interest. The approach we use to estimate the parameters, Markov Chain Monte Carlo (MCMC) simulation, generates a set of information – a series of estimates or chain of simulated values – for each quantity of interest. The credible interval is the range that includes 90 percent of the simulated values – a 90 percent Bayesian Credible Interval. These intervals appear in figures that report probabilities of turnout and vote choice for men and women.

For many empirical claims in the chapters which follow we also separately report the specific probability of, for instance, male voters supporting Republicans to a greater extent than do female voters. One advantage of the MCMC approach is that we can directly compare differences between male and female estimated vote share or ballot counts for each party at each iteration of the simulation. In a similar way, we can compare the simulations across elections, to determine the probability that male or female vote share or ballots cast for a party grew or fell over time. And we can aggregate across simulations to compare groups of states with particular contextual features. The Bayesian approach permits us to be fairly specific about the confidence we have in particular conclusions that we reach. In the text we claim to be confident of a finding of difference (e.g., female Republican vote share exceeded male Republican vote share) if 90 percent or more of the simulations support the conclusion. We may note a difference in which a smaller proportion of simulations support the conclusions but we acknowledge less confidence in such results. The choice of a threshold of this type in the Bayesian context is notoriously difficult (see Raftery 1995), so we disclose specific probabilities associated with important claims (see our discussion in Chapter 5, for example, of the role of women in the 1920 Republican victory in specific states in the Midwest).

Conclusion

Using a combination of new data and new methods, we estimate the proportion of women who entered the electorate in support of Republican, Democratic, and third-party presidential candidates in ten states over the five presidential elections following the extension of suffrage. The ability to overcome the considerable methodological challenges to ecological inference in general and in the case of women in particular is a major accomplishment. Capitalizing on recent advances in approaches to ecological inference and Bayesian treatments of the ecological inference problem, the estimates recover the true/observed behavior of women and men in 1916 and 1920 Illinois (and other places as well) and permit us to characterize the turnout and vote choice of women and men in other US states.

As a result, we are able to provide insight into the electoral behavior of women (and men) after suffrage across a longer span of time and for a more diverse set of places than possible with previous research. Although not fully representative of the United States as a whole, our ten state sample covers a wide range of political contexts – states in several regions, states that are traditionally dominated by Republicans or Democrats, states that are politically competitive, and states that have a variety of rules pertaining to access to the polls. The sample reflects important aspects of the broader national context, including a number of large cities with a high proportion of recent immigrants as well as geographically large rural areas with a high proportion of native-born whites. We now turn to the central task of this research, employing those estimates to investigate the electoral behavior and impact of women in the five presidential elections after suffrage.

Appendix

Estimation Details, MCMC Diagnostics, and Evaluation with Ward Data

The basic estimation problem treats the observed census and electoral data in each geographic unit as a 2 × 4 table with unknown interior quantities and known table marginals. From census and election data we observe the marginals from each unit in the sample state and we make an inference about the unobserved proportions describing the probabilities of turnout and vote choice for women and men in each election (see Table 4.6). We employ Markov Chain Monte Carlo (MCMC) simulation to approximate the distributions of the parameters of interest. The proportions are estimated by first decomposing the complex 2 × 4 table into 6 simple 2 × 2 tables, then using the Bayesian strategy outlined in Wakefield (2004) to simultaneously estimate the unknowns in all of the 2 × 2 tables. The estimator we use is distinguished from earlier work based on King's 1997 approach because we employ a Bayesian framework and we do not rely on sequential estimates from 2 × 2 tables.

The R × C Problem

Many research problems that could exploit aggregate data cannot be collapsed into a simple 2 × 2 table. Work on more complex tables (more than two rows [R] or two columns [C]) has appeared in the statistical and political science literature (Ferree 2004; Lau, Moore, and Kellerman 2007; Rosen et al. 2001), but application of the R × C strategies is less common and direct comparisons of alternative R × C estimation strategies are rare. We adopt an approach similar to the estimator proposed in Greiner and Quinn (2009). They use a Gibbs sampling approach that simultaneously estimates each of the unknowns, exploiting the fact that any R × C table can be treated as a collection of underlying 2 × 2 sub-tables, each defined by the unique intersection of any two rows and two columns of the joint table. One advantage of this estimator is that uncertainty about estimates in one sub-table (the distribution of male and female votes across Republican and Democratic candidates, for instance), also reflects uncertainty about estimates in other sub-tables (the distribution of votes across third-party candidates or abstentions). The approach developed by Greiner and Quinn ensures that each of the parameter estimates incorporates uncertainty related to all other parameters. Although our approach differs in important ways (we rely, for instance, on cell proportions rather than counts), we exploit this basic insight and apply Wakefield's (2004) approach to the estimation of 2 × 2 tables at each iteration of the simulation. The estimator is implemented with a modified version of hierarchical ecological inference model in the R package MCMCpack (Martin, Quinn, and Park 2011).

The Bayesian Approach

The development of the estimator proceeded over the course of several years and exploited work done in the area of ecological inference by a diverse group of researchers. King (1997) described and implemented a two-step approach to ecological inference that relied on a constrained maximum likelihood approach to estimate the parameters of a state-level bivariate normal distribution of the parameters of interest. Individual unit parameters were then simulated given these estimates. Some particular features of King's approach attracted criticism, particularly in applications where ecological inference involved multiple stages of analysis (Cho and Gaines 2004). The Bayesian approach adopted here – the simultaneous simulation of state-level and individual unit parameters – avoids those particular estimation pitfalls. King, Rosen, and Tanner (1999) introduce a Bayesian modeling approach that, like King's 1997 strategy, relies on a hierarchical structure to introduce information from the aggregate (the state level in our application) to the estimates of quantities at lower levels of aggregation (the county-, MCD-, or ward-level). Generally, Bayesian approaches treat parameters (in this case, the interior cells of Table 4.6) as random variables and use the tools of probability – a likelihood function and Bayes law – to quantify beliefs about what those cells are after having observed the data. The likelihood function simply expresses the probability that we observe particular outcomes or data, given some assumptions about how data are generated. For each simulation, we specify a prior distribution, the value of the parameters that we would accept in the absence of any information in the data. The prior in each case was simply the observed combined or total turnout and vote choice – the same proportions Republican, Democratic, third party, and abstaining for men and women. Any information in the data would move our estimates away from these priors. Any difference we observe between men and women must be a function of the data introduced to the simulation, the likelihood function we choose, and the assumption we introduce about turnout.

The Estimator

The 2 × 4 problem we confront (men and women distributed across Republican, Democratic, other party, and abstention) can be decomposed into six 2 × 2 sub-tables. Table 4.8 shows each of the six tables. At each iteration of the simulation, we randomly select one of the 2 × 2 tables and estimate each probability in the sub-table conditional on the current estimates of each of the other probabilities. The sub-table highlighted in Table 4.8 summarizes male and female support for Republican and Democratic candidates. If we treat the number of male and female abstain and third-party votes as fixed, what is the most likely distribution of male and female votes across the Democratic and Republican candidates – the best estimate of p_{10}, p_{11}, p_{12}, and p_{13}? As the simulation proceeds and other sub-tables are evaluated, the number of male and female abstain and third-party votes is updated, so the row marginals for the highlighted 2 × 2 sub-table vary over the course of the simulation.

At each iteration of the simulation, the random selection of one sub-table fixes half of the parameters based on the previous draw and proposes new values for two parameters: p_{10i} and p_{11i} in the notation

TABLE 4.8. *The 2 × 4 Problem Decomposed into Six 2 × 2 Tables*

	Republican	Democrat	Republican	Third Party
Women	p_{10i}	p_{12i}	p_{20i}	p_{22i}
Men	p_{11i}	p_{13i}	p_{21i}	p_{23i}
	Democrat	**Third party**	**Abstain**	**Republican**
Women				
Men				
	Abstain	**Democrat**	**Abstain**	**Third party**
Women				
Men				

of Table 4.8. The candidate values are on the scale of the logistic (designated μ_{10i} and μ_{11i}) to generate candidate values for the parameters, Martin, Quinn, and Park (2011) rely on the slice sampling procedure described in Neal (2003). Because we had several instances where cell probabilities were zero – no votes for a particular party – we chose to bound or constrain candidate values of the logistic from −5 to 5 (implying probabilities below 0.005 are treated as 0 and probabilities above .995 were treated as 1). The proposed new candidate values are evaluated by assessing the likelihood that each parameter (μ_{10i} or μ_{11i}) would be drawn from the distribution that describes aggregate state-level vote share, in this case, the logit of the Republican candidate share of the major party vote (designated μ_{10} or μ_{11}). If the proposed draw is an improvement – based on the likelihood – over the previous draw and if the candidate draw does not violate the assumption that male turnout exceeds female turnout, then the new candidate value is accepted. We also ensure that each draw is logically consistent – no implied probabilities less than 0 or greater than 1. This evaluation proceeds across each of the geographic units and, when the iteration across units is complete, the state-level parameters (μ_{jj}) are updated to reflect new population-weighted information about the average and standard deviation of the current values of the parameters in the underlying units. The parameters at the MCD level are then converted from the logistic scale and retained as probabilities to set up row marginals for the next iteration of the simulation.

The output from an MCMC simulation is a series of values – a chain – drawn from what is known, in the Bayesian framework, as the posterior distribution. MCMC applications require a "burn-in" period and then a sample of values are drawn from the Markov chain. Each simulation was 11,000,000 or more iterations with the first 10,000,000 iterations discarded as the burn-in. One in 200 – or 0.5 percent of at least 400,000 iterations after the burn – were monitored to recover the parameter estimates, both the point estimates (the average value of the chain) and the endpoints of the 90 percent Bayesian Credible Interval. The MCMC simulation is repeated for each state-election year dataset, so fifty-two simulations were required to generate the estimates.

Replication details and other information about the estimator are available at http://womensballots.nd.edu. The replication archive includes the full set of census and vote data, modified MCMCpack C++ and R language to build the estimator, the state-level estimates, the parameters extracted to evaluate convergence, and details about the distributional assumptions introduced for the quantities of interest and hyperparameters in the hierarchical model.

Markov Chain Monte Carlo Diagnostics

MCMC modeling strategies are introduced and described in the context of Bayesian data analysis in Gill (2002). The technical challenge of Bayesian statistical approaches is the evaluation of high dimension integrals to characterize the posterior distribution for the parameters of interest. Monte Carlo integration is a general approach that permits solutions to these problems and MCMC approaches are a particular strategy for this type of integration. MCMC approaches to Bayesian problems are becoming more common in the political science literature, but there are few conventions for assessing the performance of the estimator and reporting point estimates and confidence intervals. For a general introduction to Monte Carlo statistical methods and sampling approaches we use, see Robert and Cassella (2004).

The key question to be assessed is whether the Markov chain has converged in each case; that is, whether the estimator is sampling across the entire range of the posterior distribution in the observed simulations. Assessing convergence of the Markov chain is not straightforward and remains the subject of considerable work among practitioners of MCMC methods. This is particularly challenging in cases where the Markov chain is slow mixing, meaning that estimates from the current simulation are highly correlated with estimates from the immediately preceding simulation. This is clearly the case with the $R \times C$ estimator, since we hold four of the eight estimated probabilities constant as we update four unknown probabilities associated with a 2×2 sub-table. The problem of slow convergence is widely discussed in the literature on MCMC estimation (see Gill 2002). The basic prescription that emerges from various treatments of the problem is to increase the length of the simulation by permitting very long chain lengths with a long burn-in period.

To assess convergence, we rely on two commonly used diagnostics: Geweke's diagnostic and the Heidelberger–Welch diagnostic. Geweke's diagnostic compares the mean of the estimated parameter in some early proportion of the chain to the mean in some later proportion of the chain. This diagnostic is sensitive to choice of the proportions to evaluate, so we compared the first 10 percent of the chain with the final 50 percent (the default in most applications of this test), as well as the first 20 percent of the chain to the final 40 percent. If any comparison revealed a statistically significant difference in means, we extended the length of the burn-in period. The Heidelberger and Welch diagnostic is similar, but includes a two-step evaluation, first determining if some subset of the early part of the chain should be discarded (based on differences between mean evaluated for an early part of the chain (first 10 percent) and the mean evaluated for the total length of chain). The second stage of the test evaluates the precision of the estimates, comparing the sample mean for the entire chain with the long run variance of the chain (the time series standard error or asymptotic standard error multiplied by 1.96). If this long run variance is more than 10 times larger than the sample mean, then the parameter fails the test. Because we used the scale of the logistic, it was possible for the sample means of the parameter values to be quite close to 0 (equivalent to 50 percent probability). As the parameter estimates approach 0, we did observe several instances where the parameter failed this second-stage test. Ultimately, in fifty-one of the fifty-two simulations we were able to extend the length of the chain to a point at which convergence was unambiguous: each of the twelve state-level logits passed each of the three tests for stationarity and nearly all the parameters passed the second-stage diagnostic which assesses precision. In one case, 1932 Kentucky, a burn-in of 64 million of observations was required. In most cases, a burn-in period of 10 million observations was sufficient. As an example, Table 4.9 reports diagnostic details for a subset of state-level parameters estimated for the 1920 election in Illinois – the state-level logits associated with the four parameters in the Republican–Democrat and Republican–third-party sub-tables from Table 4.8. In this case, a burn-in of 10,250,000 observations was required. Each diagnostic is unambiguously consistent with convergence. Figure 4.4 plots the values of the same parameters at each iteration after the burn-in period. The figures are also consistent with convergence. It is possible for this suite of diagnostics to lead to the conclusion that a chain will fail

TABLE 4.9. *MCMC Diagnostics for Four State-level Parameters, Illinois, 1920*

μ_{10}	logit of the Republican share of major party vote, women
μ_{11}	logit of the Republican share of major party vote, men
μ_{20}	logit of the Republican share of Republican plus third-party vote, women
μ_{21}	logit of the Republican share of Republican plus third-party vote, men

Geweke's diagnostic
Fraction in first window = 0.1
Fraction in second window = 0.5

z-score (less than 2.0 indicates convergence):

μ_{10}	μ_{11}	μ_{20}	μ_{21}
1.30202	−1.63715	−0.28689	−0.10226

Fraction in first window = 0.2
Fraction in second window = 0.4

z-score (less than 2.0 indicates convergence):

μ_{10}	μ_{11}	μ_{20}	μ_{21}
1.3006	−0.4262	−0.24320	0.2168

Heidelberger–Welch diagnostic
Stationarity test

Parameter	Result	Start iteration	p-value
μ_{10}	Passed	1	0.324
μ_{11}	Passed	1	0.499
μ_{20}	Passed	1	0.563
μ_{21}	Passed	1	0.552

Halfwidth test

Parameter	Result	Mean	Halfwidth
μ_{10}	Passed	1.632	0.01567
μ_{11}	Passed	0.946	0.00552
μ_{20}	Passed	2.889	0.00987
μ_{21}	Passed	2.571	0.00607

Note: This output was produced with the R statistical package coda (Plummer et al. 2006).

to converge. In one case, 1936 Massachusetts, the simulation never converged, even with an extraordinarily long burn-in period – 100 million iterations. We include a summary of the 1936 Massachusetts estimates in Chapter 8, but we note that the estimates are suspect.

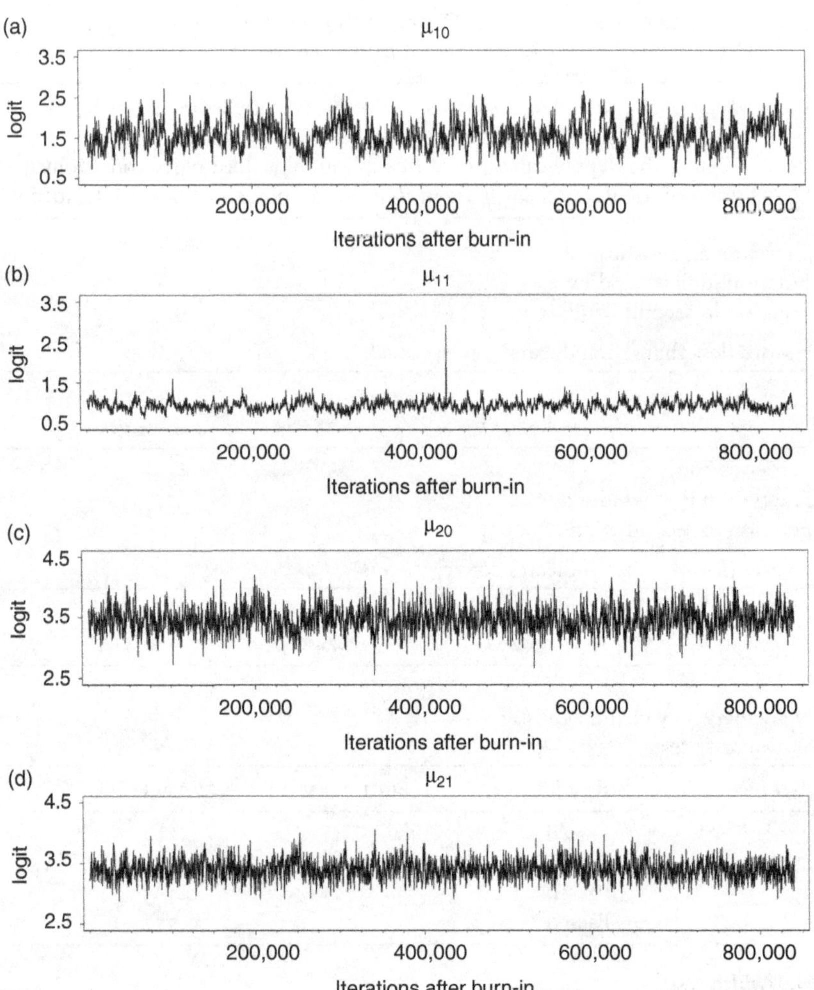

FIGURE 4.4. Trace plots for four state-level parameters, Illinois, 1920. μ_{10}, Republican share of major party vote, women. μ_{11}, Republican share of major party vote, men. μ_{20}, Republican share of Republican plus third-party vote, women. μ_{21}, Republican share of Republican plus third-party vote, men. The *y*-axis is on the logit scale.

Comparing Our Estimates to Known (True) Values

In the chapter text, we compare our estimates to the available data on turnout and vote choice for men and women in the State of Illinois in 1916 and 1920. In addition to these data, there are three other sources of ward-level data with true values: registration information from the City of Chicago, and registration information and primary party preference data from the City of Boston.

The City of Chicago maintained separate registration lists for men and women from 1920–1932. Our estimates are consistent with this registration data in three specific ways. First, despite what we know to be a small upward bias in our estimate of men's turnout, men's estimated turnout does not exceed the proportion of registered male voters in the 1920–1932 elections. Second, estimates for specific elections are consistent with the Chicago reported registration data. For instance, in 1924 men's ward-level registration outpaces women's by 23 percentage points, while we estimate a turnout gap of 25 percentage points. Finally, the increase in size of the electorate indicated by the registration data for the entire 1920–1932 period is consistent with our estimates. The percentage of age-eligible men registered to vote in the City of Chicago increased by 12 percentage points from 1920 to 1932; our estimates indicate that presidential vote increased by 13 percentage points. The percentage of age-eligible women registered to vote increased by 18 percentage points; our estimates indicate the presidential vote increased by 20 percentage points. The change in registration is smaller than the percentage increase in presidential vote for both groups due to a slightly higher proportion of registered voters casting ballots in 1932 compared to 1920.

The City of Boston also maintained separate registration lists for men and women. The Boston ward data reveal a higher upward bias in male turnout compared to the Chicago data, with estimated male turnout exceeding the number of registered males in some wards in some years. But, despite this bias, the increase in the number of registered men (29 percent from 1920 to 1932) is consistent with the estimated increase in men casting presidential ballots (35 percent from 1920 to 1932). The percentage of age-eligible women registered to vote increased by 95 percentage points; our estimates indicate the presidential vote increased by 128 percentage points. As in Chicago, the change in registration is smaller than the percentage increase in presidential vote owing to a higher proportion of registered voters casting ballots in 1932 compared to 1920.

The City of Boston also reported the number of primary ballots cast for each party by sex, so there are some data available about the partisan preferences of men and women in each Boston ward.[11] The data from the primary are not strictly comparable to the estimates for the

[11] We do not report or use the party preference data from the 1920 state primary which took place just twelve days after the ratification of the Nineteenth Amendment.

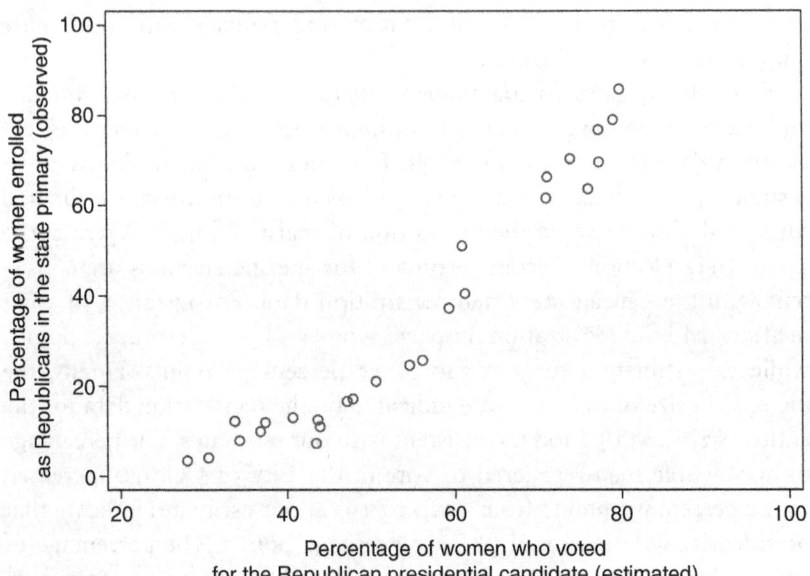

FIGURE 4.5. Observed and predicted Republican support, Boston wards, women, 1924.

general election. Presidential nominating contests were not closely linked to primary elections at the time and the number of primary ballots is much smaller than the number of general election ballots. Nevertheless the party primary data give us some direct information about party differences between women and men, and data about where each party is active. Republican wards should have extensive Republican participation in the primary and large numbers of votes for the Republican presidential candidate in the general election. Figure 4.5 reports ward-level estimates of the female Republican major vote share in the 1924 election and the proportion of women casting a Republican ballot in the 1924 primary election. It is clear that the estimates are consistent with the observed party preference in the primary. The 1928 and 1932 ward data support the same conclusion.

The party primary ballots also indicate that women were slightly more likely to have a Republican preference than were men. Citywide, the percentage of primary voters enrolled as Republicans was about 36 percent in 1924; 39 percent of women and 33 percent of men. In the general election, Coolidge received 54 percent of the presidential vote; the estimates indicate 57 percent of women voted for the Republican and 51 percent of men. In both the observed primary data and our general election estimates, women were more likely to be mobilized as Republicans than were men. The same result holds in Boston in 1928 and 1932.

Finally, the percentage change in observed party preference from 1924 to 1932 is also consistent with our estimates. The number of Democratic primary ballots cast by men increased by about 40 percent from 1924 to 1932; for women the increase was about 80 percent. The number of estimated Democratic presidential ballots cast by men increased by 120 percent – more than double – from 1924 to 1932. The comparable increase among women was 190 percent. The observed primary ballots and our estimates for general election vote choice both indicate that the percentage increase in Democratic support among women was roughly double than among men.

ILLUSTRATION 5.1. Suffrage leaders cast their votes for president in New York City. Left, Mrs. Carrie Chapman Catt. Right, Miss Mary Garrett Hay. November 2, 1920. 111 St. and Broadway. © Bettmann/Corbis

5

Female Voters and the Republican Landslide of 1920

In 1920, Republican presidential nominee Warren G. Harding famously advocated a return to "normalcy" after the destruction of the First World War and the heated political passions of the Progressive Era (Bagby 1962, 158). Many historians and social scientists have accepted the general characterization of the decade of the 1920s as a "return to normalcy." Yet the 1920s in general, and the presidential election of 1920 specifically, were characterized by far more political change than is often recognized. Indeed, it seems odd to describe an election in which the size of the electorate nearly doubled[1] as in any way "normal" (Brown 1991).

The Republican landslide in 1920 – more than 60 percent of voters cast their ballot for Harding – has been portrayed as a "turning point" in which the American public resoundingly rejected internationalism in foreign policy and progressivism in domestic policy making (McCoy 1971, 2349). And indeed, the 1920 election ushered in more than a decade of Republican Party dominance and conservative American public policymaking. What role did new female voters play in that outcome? Although scholars have long maintained that the initial female vote favored the Republican Party, empirical investigation of the question has been limited.

[1] We say "nearly" because eleven states allowed women to vote in the 1916 presidential election. On the other hand, restrictive interpretations of registration rules (ratification occurred after registration deadlines in a number of states) systematically denied women access to the ballot in Arkansas, Georgia, Mississippi, and South Carolina in 1920, delaying their participation in presidential elections until 1924 (Gosnell 1930). Together with black men, many black women continued to experience systematic exclusion from the franchise until the second half of the twentieth century.

In this chapter, we take a close look at the participation of female voters in the presidential election of 1920, the first following national enfranchisement. We first describe the political context in which most women first exercised their right to vote. We then examine expectations for the role of new female voters in 1920, with special attention to predicted partisanship. Finally, we employ our unique estimates of female and male turnout and vote choice to offer new insight into the casting of women's ballots in 1920.

We find that although women were less likely to turn out to vote than were men (an assumption of this research), the turnout gender gap varied considerably across states. New female voters were indeed *more* responsive to their political context than were men, as the peripheral voters hypothesis would predict. To a greater extent than was men's, female turnout was dampened in states with restrictive electoral rules and stimulated in states with a competitive partisan context. At the same time, the considerable turnout of women in a few more competitive states also indicates that under the right circumstances, newly enfranchised women could be effectively mobilized as voters from the start.

Overall, we estimate that 63 percent of female voters in our sample states cast ballots for Harding in 1920. On the whole, then, more women entered the electorate as Republicans than as Democrats. Yet, female voters were not any more Republican in their preferences than were long-enfranchised male voters, 60 percent of whom also supported the Republican nominee. That sample-wide finding masks interesting state-level patterns, however. Female voters were more likely than men to vote Republican in Republican-dominated states, and were at least as supportive of Democrats where Democrats dominated. As we discuss, the implications for our expectations about women's partisan mobilization (see Chapter 1) are complicated by the specifics of the 1920 election. Republican support exceeding that of men is predicted by both the expectations of the peripheral voter hypothesis (in which inexperienced and inattentive citizens swing to the party favored in the election) and the expectation that women were more Republican overall (particular partisanship hypothesis). However, given that we find a Republican advantage *only* in one-party Republican states, we are inclined to view the outcome as consistent with the local party hypothesis that female voters would be more likely than men to favor the locally dominant party. We look to our analysis of later elections to confirm that conclusion.

The presence of women mattered: Across our sample, new women voters contributed to wider partisan variation across states and tended to reinforce the prevailing political power in their own states. But, contrary to some expectations, the Republican landslide cannot be attributed to the mobilization of new female voters; perhaps spurred by the attention to new women voters, men experienced heightened levels of mobilization overall and particularly for the Republican Party in 1920. As a result, Harding netted more *new* Republican votes from long-enfranchised men than he did from newly enfranchised women.

The Election of 1920

The decade between the end of the First World War and the onset of the Great Depression is a study in contrasts. On the one hand, the period stands as something of a reaction against the reformist passions of the Progressive Era. The 1920s were in many ways a conservative period, characterized by ardent patriotism, nativism (particularly in the form of a resurgent Ku Klux Klan), and anticommunism (Burnham 1986; Hofstadter 1955). After a short economic depression in the early 1920s, the economy was generally strong, prosperity was widespread, and economic interests were ascendant, particularly in politics (Fuchs 1971). At the same time, social norms – or at least, women's skirt lengths – were famously liberalized during the "Roaring Twenties" (Evans 1989) and the Progressive impulse, although largely marginalized in both of the major parties, remained an important social and political force, most notably in the relatively successful third-party campaign of Robert La Follette in 1924 (Sundquist 1983).

Important demographic, economic, and political changes were underway during the decade. The United States was experiencing a long-term shift from a mostly rural to a mostly urban population, and from an agricultural to an industrial economy (Gould 2003; Hicks 1960). Where ethnocultural identities had been central to party competition in the nineteenth century, the "System of 1896" is often characterized as one in which capitalist consolidation, declining competition, and electoral reform were loosening partisan ties and dampening rates of mass participation in politics (e.g., Burnham 1965; Converse 1972, 1974; Schattschneider 1960). Within and across the parties, the central political cleavages of the 1920s were both old and new: urban versus rural, agriculture versus industry, immigrant versus native, Catholic versus Protestant, and dry versus wet. Political debate focused on America's place in the world and on Progressive reform, particularly with regard to temperance and economic regulation. Yet, in the first presidential elections of the 1920s, there was little substantive difference between the fairly conservative platforms and candidates of the two major parties, particularly in contrast to the calls for more radical reform emanating from the Progressive, labor, and socialist movements.

The presidential election of 1920 is a case in point. With incumbent president Woodrow Wilson politically hampered by the battle over the League of Nations and physically weakened by a serious illness, Democrats turned to Ohio governor James M. Cox as their presidential nominee, and New York state legislator and assistant secretary of the Navy Franklin D. Roosevelt as his running mate. Cox's nomination was viewed as a something of a repudiation of Wilson and the Democrats produced "only a slightly less conservative platform than the Republicans" (McCoy 1971, 2363). Republicans nominated Ohio newspaper publisher and US Senator Warren G. Harding as their standard bearer over a number of other contenders. The choice of Harding represented a clear victory for the more conservative, business-oriented wing over the reformist and Progressive inclinations of the Republican Party. Harding made efforts to appease the Progressive faction of the Republican Party, but his candidacy and specific policy positions were largely conservative. The 1920 Republican platform eliminated or weakened the Progressive commitments that had characterized GOP platforms in the preceding two decades (Hicks 1960; McCoy 1971).

The two candidates offered some variation on the dominant political issues of the day. Harding was a critic of the League of Nations while Cox defended the position of the incumbent Democratic administration, although both parties were internally divided on the issue. While pledging to enforce all laws (and denying that Prohibition was at issue in the campaign), Cox was largely understood to be a "wet" in contrast to comparatively "dry" Harding. Cox sought to establish himself as the more pro-reform candidate and to cast Harding as a reactionary. Yet Cox was far more pro-business and less radical than true Progressives preferred (Bagby 1962).

Republicans were organizationally stronger than Democrats throughout the country and Harding was the front runner throughout the campaign. But the magnitude of the Republican victory – more than 60 percent of the vote – far exceeded expectations (Degler 1964; Bagby 1962). Hofstadter (1955, 295) goes so far as to claim that "the collapse of the Democratic Party after the war was so severe that it brought about an effectual breakdown of the two-party system and of useful opposition." Cox's only support came from the solid South and Border states, and even there Harding was able to make some inroads. Harding's victory returned the presidency to the Republican Party, thus reestablishing the decades-long pattern of national Republican dominance after the brief Wilson interlude. The election was widely interpreted, both at the time and by later historians, as a repudiation of the League of Nations and of Progressivism as a force in American politics (Bagby 1962; Burner 1986; McCoy 1971).

The 1920 election reflected a sharp break in national patterns of turnout and partisan support. Support for the Republican presidential candidate increased from 46 percent of the total vote in 1916 to 60 percent in 1920, while turnout fell from 60 percent to 45 percent of the eligible population older than the age of twenty-one. The national outcomes obscure the rich variation across states. Changes between 1916 and 1920 were not homogeneous and, in fact, varied dramatically. In Kentucky, for instance, turnout declined only 9 points from 1916 to 1920 – despite the addition of women to the eligible electorate! Republican support in Kentucky increased from 47 percent to 49 percent, a very modest change considering the number of ballots cast for president nearly doubled. In Minnesota, on the other hand, there is also little change in total turnout from 1916 to 1920, but a considerable increase in GOP support (from 46 percent to 71 percent). Still other states (such as Oklahoma and Massachusetts) are characterized by large moves toward the Republicans and sharp drops in turnout. As a result, there is higher variation in turnout and in partisan support across the states in 1920 than in 1916. Clearly the "return to normalcy" involved considerable electoral change and the shape and content of that change varied across states.

Expectations for Female Voters in 1920

The Nineteenth Amendment to the US Constitution was ratified on August 26, 1920, a mere ten weeks – give or take – before election day on November 2nd. Anticipating that ratification would be achieved, a number of states began preparing for female voters before late August. Legislatures were called into special sessions to revise state laws, authorize additional registration opportunities, and otherwise create the legal framework for women's incorporation. In a number of places, registration deadlines were extended, procedures were altered, or women's more limited previous registration (such as for school suffrage in states like Connecticut and Massachusetts) was allowed to suffice for general election registration.[2] Officials installed new voting machines to accommodate the expected increase in turnout[3] and encouraged women to register and vote during the day while men were at work to avoid long lines.[4] For example, the Annual Report of the Election Department of the City of Boston (1921), noting the "additional burden" placed on the department by the Nineteenth Amendment, describes the special measures taken:

> The time of outside registration in wards was extended by direction of the Mayor, 2 evenings before the state primary, and 3 evenings before the presidential election, and 2 additional registrars were added in each ward registration place. Ten addition registrars were employed in the central office and the offices on the first floor of the City Hall Annex ... were used by this department, many days and evening for this registration.

Not all state and local governments were interested in accommodating new female voters, however. In the most egregious cases, four Southern states (Arkansas, Georgia, Mississippi, and South Carolina) chose not to adjust registration laws to allow women to qualify in time for the presidential election; women in those states were unable to vote in a presidential election until 1924 (Gosnell 1930). In the South, in particular, African American women faced the same formal and informal barriers to the exercise of their voting rights as African American men did (Lebsock 1993; Terborg-Penn 1998).

Others interested in encouraging women to exercise their new rights – for either ideological or political reasons – took steps to facilitate the socialization of women to their electoral duty. The National American Woman Suffrage Organization reorganized itself as the League of Women Voters (LWV) six months before ratification and immediately went to

[2] For example, Illinois provided one extra registration day, August 25, for women (and men) before the state primary on September 15 ("Wednesday Only Day for Women to Get Votes." *Chicago Tribune*, August 20, 1920, p. 3). The Boston Election Board permitted women to register in early August in anticipation of ratification ("Women May Register as Voters from August 12 to 18." *Boston Globe*, July 16, 1920, p. 1). See also "Mayor Extends Time for Registration." *Boston Globe*, 19 August 1920, p. 4; "Women Now Registered Stay on Lists." *Bridgeport (CT) Post*, September 22, 1920, p. 1.

[3] See, e.g., "City Ready to Register 'Suff' Vote." *Bridgeport (CT) Post*, July 20, 1920, p. 1.

[4] "Register Early, Women Advised." *St. Paul Dispatch*, October 18, 1920, p. 1; "Women Urged to Do Their Voting Early." *Bridgeport (CT) Post* 28 October 1920. Apparently, however, officials were less accommodating about what the press portrayed as a central female concern, the requirement that registrants give their age. See "Must Women Give Their Age? Special Session to Decide." *Bridgeport (CT) Post*, September 1, 1920, p. 4; "Maine Women, To Vote, Must Give Exact Dates of Their Births." *Boston Globe*, October 13, 1920, p. 1; "Age Revelation a Menace, She Claims." *Boston Globe*, September 2, 1920, p. 1.

work educating women as to both the issues and procedures of elections (see Gordon 1986).[5] The major political parties also acted prior to the ratification of the Nineteenth Amendment to create women's committees charged most centrally with mobilizing new women voters as partisans (Harvey 1998).[6] These party organizations, it should be emphasized, focused on mobilizing white women; efforts to mobilize women of color were limited to churches and other nonparty organizations (Greenlee 2014). In addition to educating women to the issues at play in the election, both organizations and political parties offered practical demonstrations to teach inexperienced women the concrete skills – lever-pulling, ballot-filling – necessary to exercise the right to vote (Scott 1972).[7]

Although some news stories predicted massive turnout of women in 1920, even exceeding that of men,[8] most were far more judicious and accurate, describing women's turnout as lagging behind that of men. Indeed, all available evidence indicates that although millions of women exercised their new right in 1920, far fewer did so than did men (Gamm 1986; Goldstein 1984; Kleppner 1982b; see Chapter 3). Many long-time suffrage activists were gravely disappointed that their grand victory had not translated into more widespread turnout among women and a greater perceived impact on the election (Breckinridge 1933; Young 1989). While pundits continued to herald the emerging political relevance of female voters in subsequent elections, a conventional wisdom that women's votes had little impact began to emerge as early as 1920.

Did women enter the electorate as Republicans? As we note in Chapter 1, a number of scholars have attributed the 1920 Republican landslide in part to the mobilization of new female voters. The belief that most women were first mobilized into the active electorate as Republicans dates to the election of 1920 itself. While both parties' campaigns made efforts to appeal to female voters (Harvey 1998), many news stories reported that the women's vote had favored the GOP, especially in rural areas. In most cases the basis was unreliable sources such as straw votes

[5] See, e.g., "Women Learn How to Vote at Fair." *St. Paul Dispatch*, 6 September 1920, p. 5; "Registration Week Begins Tomorrow." *The New York Times*, October 3, 1920, p. 4.

[6] As Harvey (1998) has argued, the political parties, with considerable expertise and experience with the task of voter mobilization, had a considerable advantage over the nonpartisan and less-experienced LWV.

[7] See, e.g., "Play Election Devised to Teach Women How to Vote." *Boston Globe*, August 10, 1920, p. 2; "Registration Week Begins Tomorrow." *The New York Times*, October 3, 1920, p. 4.

[8] See, e.g., "Women Outvoting Men 3 to 1 in New York." *Bridgeport (CT) Post*, November 2, 1920.

or estimates of party leaders,[9] but in some cases, this expectation was backed up by reasonable inferences from hard data (e.g., an increase in the total vote, but with most of that increase benefiting one party[10]). As we show below, even those reasonable inferences prove faulty in some cases.

Later accounts of the period overwhelmingly conclude that the majority of women voted for the Republican presidential candidate in 1920 (e.g., Bagby 1962; Brown 1991; Burner 1986; Gould 2003; Lemons 1973; McCoy 1971; Pateman 1994; Smith 1980; Willey and Rice 1924). The evidence in support of the general claim is fairly straightforward: In 1916, Democratic incumbent Woodrow Wilson received 9.1 million votes to his Republican challenger's 8.5 million. In 1920, following the passage of the Nineteenth Amendment, the Democratic candidate again received 9.1 million votes, while the number of votes secured by the Republican almost doubled to 16.1 million votes (Brown 1991).

Most attempts to explain this extraordinary mobilization focus on the appeal of the Republican Party to women. Suffrage had been passed by a Republican Congress, and those active in the suffrage movement were expected to be most likely to exercise their new right. Most suffragists were native born white women, who were – in keeping with the electoral behavior of native born white men – expected to be both more likely to turn out to vote and to cast their votes for the Republican Party (Rymph 2006). Prior to the New Deal, the Republican Party was the major party most closely linked to the Progressive movement and its ideals. Women had been active participants and leaders in Progressive organizations, and Progressive ideals, particularly moral reform, were consistent with the qualities associated with the Victorian ideal of womanhood (Baker 1984; Evans 1989; see Chapters 2 and 6). Suggesting "Perhaps Warren G. Harding attracted the vote by his handsome appearance," historian J. Stanley Lemons (1973, 87) notes the Republican candidate "left nothing to chance" in reaching out to female voters. While the Republican platform contained only a few, uncontroversial planks advocated by the new LWV, Harding himself responded to requests from female activists with a long litany of campaign pledges meant to appeal to women, including equal pay for equal work, employment reform (e.g., the eight-hour day,

[9] For example: "Recapitulation of Straw Ballot." *Boston Globe*, 16 October 1920, p. 1; "500,000 Illinois Women to Vote on Wednesday." *Chicago Tribune*, September 12, 1920, p. 2; Crawford, William H. 1920. "Analyzes Power of Woman's Vote." *The New York Times*, October 10, 1920, p. II, 10.

[10] For example, "Women Help Win State by Record Vote." *Minneapolis Morning Tribune*, September 14, 1920, p. 1.

minimum wage, and a ban on child labor), strong Prohibition enforcement, maternity and infant protection, and other social welfare programs (Lemons 1973). Themes related to the home, family, health, and education characterized Republican outreach to women (Greenlee 2014).

Democrats reached out to female voters as well. They highlighted the fact that the Nineteenth Amendment had passed under a Democratic president and that President Wilson had appointed a number of women to major positions in his administration. Candidate Cox emphasized his advocacy for the League of Nations to appeal to women's presumed greater aversion to violence and war, and concern for the safety of their sons (Greenlee 2014). The Democratic platform contained more planks advocated by the LWV than did the Republican platform, but on the whole, Republicans were believed to have the stronger pro-suffrage claim (Lemons 1973). The more radical branch of the suffrage movement, particularly Alice Paul's Congressional Union, adopted the British model of blaming the party in power for the failure to achieve suffrage and campaigned widely against Democratic candidates prior to 1920. After the passage of the Nineteenth Amendment, some suffragists continued to view the Democratic Party as the opposition (Cott 1987; Evans 1989). Nationally, both parties sought to appeal to female voters by highlighting women at their conventions, establishing greater representation of women on party committees, and expanding their separate women's organizations (Andersen 1996; Sainsbury 1999). Newspaper accounts suggested that Republicans had a stronger and more effective organizational outreach to women than did Democrats (Bagby 1962).

In addition to the enormous pro-Republican mobilization nationally in the year in which women were enfranchised, some reports from specific locales, particularly from urban areas in the North, support the contention that Republican efforts to mobilize women were successful. For example, Huthmacher (1959) reports that in Boston voter turnout between 1916 and 1920 increased considerably in old-stock Republican wards, but increased by much smaller margins in Democratic wards (see also Gamm 1986). Andersen (1994) also finds some evidence of greater Republican mobilization among women in Oregon. Goldstein (1984) concludes that female voters in Illinois were more supportive of Harding than were their male counterparts. On the other hand, Gamm's (1986) data on the party identification of women in Boston do not suggest that women, as a group, favored one party over another immediately following enfranchisement or in the years to come. Reflecting the traditional party strength in those communities,

Jewish, black, and Yankee women were initially more mobilized by Republicans than Democrats, while the reverse was true among Italian and Irish women.

These accounts suggest that women's turnout and vote choice can be expected to vary considerably across place. Variation in party competition and strength, mobilization efforts, immigration and nativity, class, and ethnicity all appear to contribute to varying turnout and party support among women in 1920 and other early elections (Andersen 1996; Brown 1991; Goldstein 1984; Harvey 1998). This geographical variation has been one of many factors hampering earlier attempts to understand the partisan impact of female enfranchisement.

Thus, previous scholars have suggested that the Republican landslide may be at least in part attributed to the mobilization of new female voters into the Republican Party. Yet the limited empirical record allows for other possibilities. Perhaps men experienced high levels of Republican conversion and/or mobilization, so that both men and women contributed to the lopsided 1920 Republican victory. Or perhaps the aggregate data mask a Democratic advantage among women so that the Republican landslide was possible only via extraordinary Republican mobilization among men. Distinguishing among the various possible causes of the 1920 outcome has been a challenge for previous empirical work on this period.

The Mobilization of Female Voters in 1920

What can our estimates tell us about the overall electoral mobilization (turnout) of women in 1920? Estimated turnout for men and women in each of our sample states is reported in Figure 5.1.[11] Consistent with our expectations about the effect of context on electoral behavior across our five elections, we organize our states by region and party context in the figures reported in this and later chapters: We start with our one-party Democratic Southern state (Virginia) on the far left, then report on our two Border states, with the one-party Democratic state (Oklahoma) followed by the competitive (Democratic-leaning) state (Kentucky). We then move on to our Midwestern states, starting with the one competitive (Republican-leaning) state (Missouri) and then the four one-party

[11] The error bars in Figure 5.1, as well as in all following figures, designate the 90 percent Bayesian Credible Interval. For details, see "Reporting Point Estimates and Measures of Uncertainty," in Chapter 4.

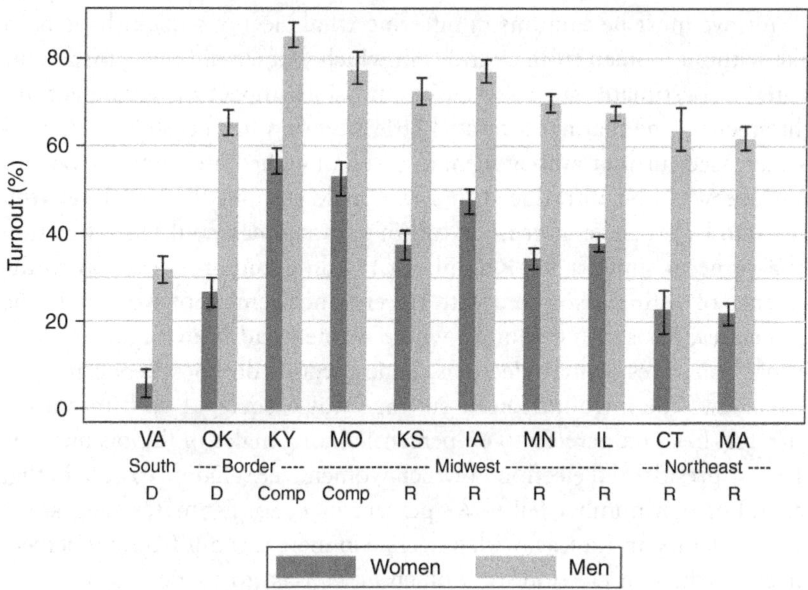

FIGURE 5.1. Turnout of women and men, 1920.

Republican states (Kansas, Iowa, Minnesota, and Illinois). Finally, to the far right we report the findings for our two one-party Republican states in the Northeast (Connecticut and Massachusetts). Both region and our party context measure are indicated, along with state label, on the *x*-axis.

We begin by highlighting that overall, men's and women's patterns of turnout (and vote choice; see Figure 5.4) are very similar in 1920. Where men turn out to vote in higher numbers, so do women. Where men are strong supporters of the Republican candidate, so are women. Despite the burden of historic enfranchisement, women took up their new right in ways that were largely similar to long-enfranchised men.

As many assumed, the introduction of new female voters is almost exclusively responsible for the large decrease in turnout observed between 1916 and 1920. Across our sample, 68 percent of men turn out to vote, compared to just 36 percent of women. Nearly half as many women exercised the franchise as did men. Overall turnout in our sample was 52 percent, suggesting turnout was almost 16 points lower than it would have been had women not been included in the eligible population. The state-level estimates tell a similar story. With the exception of Kentucky and Missouri, fewer than half of women exercised their new right. With the exception of Virginia, men's turnout exceeded 60 percent.

Yet, we must be cautious in inferring what elections might have been like without women from elections in which women did participate. Our state-level estimates suggest that one possible impact of female enfranchisement – one that has attracted little attention from earlier accounts – is increased turnout among men. In seven of eight states where women's suffrage was first introduced in 1920, male turnout increased between 1916 and 1920. The increase in turnout among men could be a function of a surge in support for Republican Harding and/or a reaction to the salience of voting associated with the enfranchisement of women. In the two states, Kansas and Illinois, where women had been eligible to vote in previous presidential elections, male turnout declines between 1916 and 1920. The introduction of suffrage was associated with increasing turnout (from 62 percent to 67 percent) among males in Illinois in 1916, the *first* presidential election in which women were eligible to vote in that state, but that number fell to 64 percent in 1920. Estimates suggest the same outcome in Kansas, with a decline in male turnout from 77 percent in 1916 (the first election for women in Kansas) to 72 percent in 1920. Thus, although the effect appears to be limited to the first election in which women enter the electorate, the increased turnout of men in the states in which women were first able to vote in 1920 may be in part a function of the very presence of those new female voters, suggesting we cannot assume male turnout would have been as high without them. Women may have lowered turnout rates overall, but – at least in 1920 – the overall impact of women on turnout may have been partially offset by the way their presence stimulated the turnout of men.

The willingness of women to take up their new right was highly contingent on context. Overall, estimated female turnout rates vary from 6 percent in Virginia to 57 percent in Kentucky, a difference of more than 51 points! The size of the gender gap in turnout varies from around 24 to 28 points (in Missouri and Kentucky) to more than 40 points in Connecticut.[12]

[12] The size of the difference between male and female turnout, although likely biased upward, is consistent with several of the estimates and pieces of data described in Chapter 3. Gamm (1989) reported precinct-level registration gaps of 5 to 50 percentage points, Chicago ward registration data indicates gaps between 15 and 32 percentage points, and Sumner (1909) found county-level gaps ranging from 6 and 36 percentage points in 1906 Colorado. The notable exception is Alpern and Baum (1985). Estimating turnout prior the publication of Gamm's data, they conclude that male and female turnout (as a percentage of the eligible electorate) was roughly equal in New England and conclude, further, that the Illinois differential was an anomaly. Our estimates and the 1920 data from Boston and Chicago suggest much lower levels of women's turnout, and much larger gaps between male and female turnout.

This enormous variation in female turnout – in general, and compared to male turnout – highlights the challenges of making conclusions about female electoral behavior after suffrage across a set of states and political contexts. The political context in which women entered the electorate as new voters was as important to their electoral behavior as the fact that they entered the electorate as women.

The general pattern that emerges from Figure 5.1 is of a declining turnout gender gap as overall turnout increases. For example, the election in Kentucky was extremely close – the Democrats won the state by 0.4 points. This competition generated extremely high turnout among both men (85 percent) and women (57 percent), the highest state-level turnout estimates for either group, and a relatively small gender gap in turnout of "just" 28 points. Female turnout, like male turnout, tends to be quite low in the other Southern (Virginia) and Border (Oklahoma) states. As we described in Chapter 4, a complex antidemocratic political structure in the South, including, but not limited to, legal barriers to voting, severely restricted turnout in Southern states in general and among people of color in particular. Many also expected that the South's traditional gender norms would make Southern women especially reluctant to take up their new right (Barnard 1928c; Key 1949; Rice and Willey 1924; Schuyler 2006; Scott 1964; see Wilkerson-Freeman 2002). Yet the experience in Kentucky indicates that however strong the traditionalistic Southern culture may have been, a highly competitive political context may have been sufficient for at least some women to overcome it and turn out to vote, and for both parties to make efforts to mobilize their female and male constituencies (see, e.g., Lebsock 1993). Where competition was (relatively) close and both parties had developed the presence and capacity to mobilize voters, women turned out to vote.

Yet election-specific competition alone was not always sufficient to mobilize female voters. Although categorized as a one-party Democratic state during this period (see Chapter 4), Oklahoma had the second closest presidential election in our sample in 1920; the Republican candidate won the state by just 5 points. Oklahoma also was similarly racially diverse; 7.4 percent of the population of Oklahoma was African American in 1920 compared to almost 10 percent in Kentucky. Despite these similarities in competition and racial composition, Oklahoma experienced the fourth lowest female turnout (27 percent) and one of the largest male–female turnout gaps in our 1920 sample (39 points). The differences between Kentucky and Oklahoma may point to the effects of *long-term* political context. While the 1920 presidential election was close in both Kentucky and Oklahoma, Kentucky was a more consistently competitive state during the period overall. Close elections may indeed spur turnout, but the means by which they do so depend in part on party organizations with the capacity to mobilize and propagandize on behalf of candidates. One-partyism in Oklahoma may have undermined the development of Republican (and Democratic) party organization in such a way that effective mobilization was limited, while consistently competitive Kentucky had a more effective two-party system.

Figure 5.1 suggests clear regional differences. Outside of Virginia, women's turnout is lowest in our two Northeastern states, and the gap between male and female turnout is the largest – about 40 points – as well. These states share two features which we expect to limit mobilization of women (restrictive electoral laws and one-party dominance), but the Northeastern states also are characterized by heavily immigrant populations (see Chapter 4). While roughly equal proportions of men and women twenty-one and older were resident aliens in these states in 1920, the presence of significant immigrant communities and their particular political cultures might have discouraged women's turnout; many observers and later scholars have hypothesized that the more traditional gender roles emphasized in many immigrant communities may have held down women's entrance into the electorate (Andersen 1990; Butler 1924; Gerould 1925; Merriam and Gosnell 1924; Rymph 2006). Greater density and more urban context, more common in our Northeastern states, also has been associated with lower female turnout (e.g., Andersen 1994), consistent with what we find here.

Our five Midwestern states, on the other hand, boast the highest levels of women's turnout and the smallest gap between male and female turnout (excepting Kentucky). The Midwest's distinctively large native-born white population (relative to the more immigrant population in our Northeastern states, and the more racially diverse South and Border states) may have contributed to this outcome. Scholars and observers have long expected turnout to be particularly high among native-born white women (e.g., Butler 1924; Gosnell and Gill 1935; Merriam and Gosnell 1924), an expectation confirmed by data from both Illinois (Goldstein 1984) and Boston (Gamm 1986). The rationale for this expectation included the fact that the suffrage movement, particularly its leadership, had been dominated by native-born white women, and native-born whites boasted an, on average, higher social class. Our estimates do not permit us to determine if native-born white women were more likely to turnout; they can only indicate that in the region with the largest native-born populations, female turnout was at its highest levels. The same potential for ecological fallacy that characterizes the relationship between the size of the female population and turnout also pertains to the relationship between the size of the native-born population and turnout (see Chapter 4). For example, it could be the case that the absence of large ethnic minority – a lack of diversity, rather than the particularly dominant group – helps explain this result. Campbell (2008) finds that homogeneous communities foster strong civic norms that are then translated into higher levels of political participation.

The Impact of Political Context

The mobilization of new female voters clearly varied considerably across states. To more fully explore the effects of context, we examine two state-level measures of political context: partisan context and registration restrictions (for details on measurement, see Chapter 4).

Partisan Context. Women were enfranchised at the tail end of the "System of 1896," a period characterized by widespread one-partyism at the state level, with Democratic supermajorities in the states of the former Confederacy, and Republican hegemony in the North and West (see Burnham 1981a). The degree to which new women voters were exposed to diverse or consistent partisan messages, received conflicting or reinforcing political information, and were encouraged or discouraged from exercising their new right were all likely shaped by the partisan context.

As we discussed in Chapter 1, the partisan context is expected to have a particularly large impact on turnout among low-interest "peripheral" voters. A number of scholars expected that competitive contexts would contribute to higher turnout among women during this period (Brown 1991; Burnham 1965; Jensen 1981; Kleppner 1982b). Where competition is heightened, the attendant greater interest and attention, stakes, and mobilizing efforts may alleviate the presumed higher costs of voting borne by women because of social norms and lack of experience. At the same time, given the barriers to women's turnout, a political context dominated by one party may discourage turnout in a way that is especially dampening for women. Contra these expectations, women's presumed lack of interest, lower levels of political attention, and norms against political activity may have isolated them from the effects of context so that women's turnout was even less responsive to the partisan context than is men's. Or, women's previous political experience and exposure may have made them as responsive to context as were long-enfranchised men.

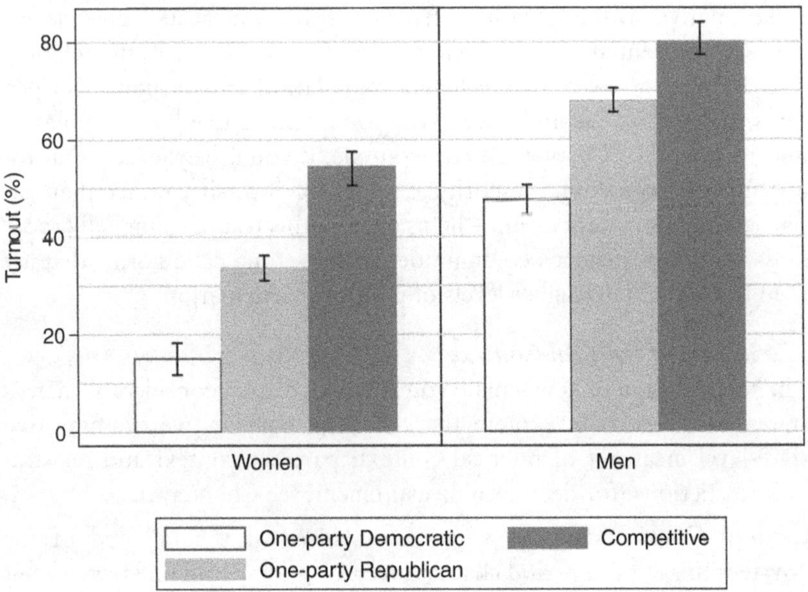

FIGURE 5.2. Partisan context and the turnout of women and men, 1920.

To test these competing hypotheses, we examine turnout, by gender, in the three categories of states: competitive, one-party Republican, and one-party Democratic (see Chapter 4). Figure 5.2 provides clear evidence that partisan context shaped both men's and women's electoral behavior in 1920. As expected, women's turnout is highest in the competitive states, as is men's (100 percent of the pooled simulations are consistent with higher women's turnout in competitive states compared to one-party Republican states, and in one-party Republican states compared to one–party Democratic states). More importantly, competitive partisan contexts stimulate women's turnout more than they do men's: Women's turnout in competitive states is 39 percentage points higher than in one-party Democratic states, compared to a 32 point gain for men, and 20 percentage points higher than in one-party Republican states, compared to a 12-point gain for men (95 percent of pooled simulations are consistent with larger effects of competitiveness for women than men). As a result, the turnout gender gap is smallest in the competitive states (about 26 points) compared to either kind of one-party state (about 33 to 34 points). For turnout, partisan context appears to matter *more* for women than for men in 1920, consistent with the peripheral voter hypothesis.

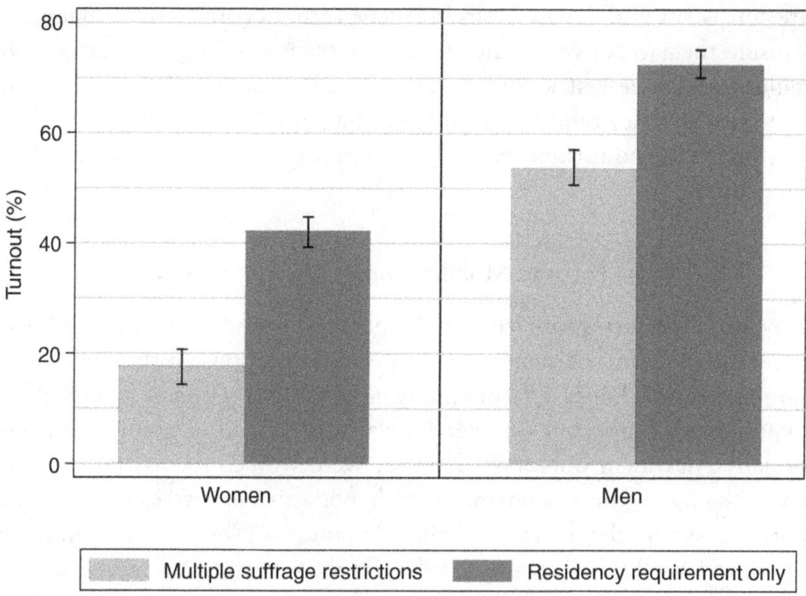

FIGURE 5.3. Legal context and the turnout of women and men, 1920.

Legal Context. The legal requirements for voting have long been understood to discourage participation (Patterson and Caldeira 1983; Powell 1986; Rosenstone and Hansen 1993; Wolfinger and Rosenstone 1980). Here, again, it seems possible that women's turnout was especially responsive to variation in context (see Chapter 1). According to the peripheral voters hypothesis, restrictive electoral laws may have particularly discouraged already disinclined female voters from exercising their rights. Alternatively, women's disinclination to vote might have been sufficiently strong that electoral laws did not dampen their turnout further. Or, finally, women may have responded to changes in the legal context in the same way as did men.

Our measure of the legal context of voting, introduced in Chapter 4, distinguishes between states with residency requirements only and those with multiple suffrage restrictions, including poll taxes, literacy or citizenship tests, and so on. As Figure 5.3 indicates, both male and female turnout is suppressed, as expected, in the more restrictive states, but the impact on female turnout is greater than on male. Female turnout declines by 24 points (a 56 percent drop, in percentage terms) between less restrictive and restrictive states, compared to a 17-point decline (a 23 percent fall-off) for male turnout (99 percent of the pooled simulations are consistent with larger drops in female turnout compared to male). As a result, the gap between male and female turnout is larger in states with multiple suffrage restrictions (a 37-point gap) compared to states with only the residency requirement (a 30-point gap). Again, we find evidence that female turnout is more, not less, responsive to changes in the political context.[13]

The Partisan Mobilization of Women in 1920

How were women mobilized by the parties in the first election following national enfranchisement? The specific conditions of the 1920 election make it challenging to disentangle the various partisan mobilization hypotheses discussed in Chapter 1 because they tend to predict observationally equivalent outcomes in 1920. Were women moved by the partisan swing, as the peripheral voter hypothesis suggests? In 1920, the partisan swing clearly favored the Republicans. Were women initially mobilized by Republicans as a rule? Or were women mobilized by the locally dominant party – which in six of our ten states would have been the Republican Party?

In our sample overall, 63 percent of women voted for the Republican presidential candidate in 1920. In that sense, previous scholars are correct that most women entered the electorate as Republicans. Yet the percentage of men in our sample casting Republican votes was 60 percent, a fairly small difference from women. The state-level estimates (see Figure 5.4) reveal that in all but two states in our sample, women were more likely to cast Republican ballots than men. However, only in our one-party Republican states in the Midwest can we be confident, or nearly so, that these differences are meaningful: More than 90 percent of simulations for Iowa, Minnesota, and Illinois, and more than 80 percent (moderate confidence) in Kansas, indicate women's support for the Republican candidate exceeded men's support. Women voted differently – distinctively more Republican – in those states than did men.

Should we attribute this finding to local dominance by the Republican Party (local party hypothesis), to a general preference for the Republican Party among women (particular partisanship hypothesis), or to the national Republican swing (peripheral voter hypotheses)? The local party hypothesis – women mobilized by and into the locally

[13] This finding is consistent with results we obtained in earlier work, using a different set of sample states and a different modeling approach (Corder and Wolbrecht 2006).

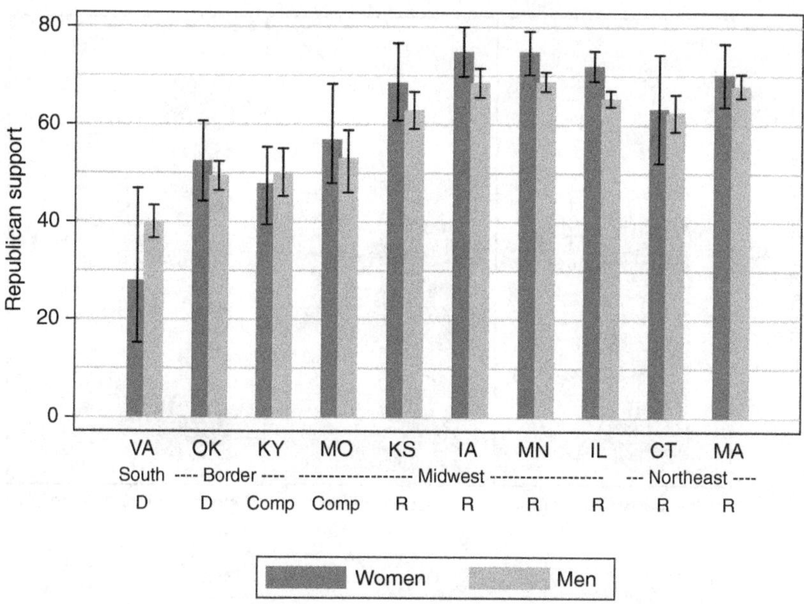

FIGURE 5.4. Republican vote share of women and men, 1920.

dominant party – strikes us as most consistent with the evidence. In the states in which Democrats were dominant (Virginia and Oklahoma) or that were competitive (Kentucky and Missouri), men and women's support for the Republican candidate is indistinguishable; that is, we do not see a general greater female preference for Republicans or surge to the party advantaged in the election (Republicans) in states in which Republicans are *not* the locally dominant party. Indeed in competitively Democratic Kentucky and especially in strongly Democratic Virginia, women may have been more likely to cast Democratic votes than were men; more than 85 percent of the simulations in Virginia indicate female support for the Republican candidate was *lower* than men's support. These results further support the expectation that women were mobilized by the locally dominant party.

The relationship between party context (the Burnham measure introduced in Chapter 4) and women's vote choice, reported in Figure 5.5, provides further support for this conclusion. Men and women in both competitive and one-party Democratic state contexts report similar Republican vote shares, both to the other sex and to voters in the other context. In one-party Republican states, however, not only is the percent Republican much higher for both men and women, as we would expect,

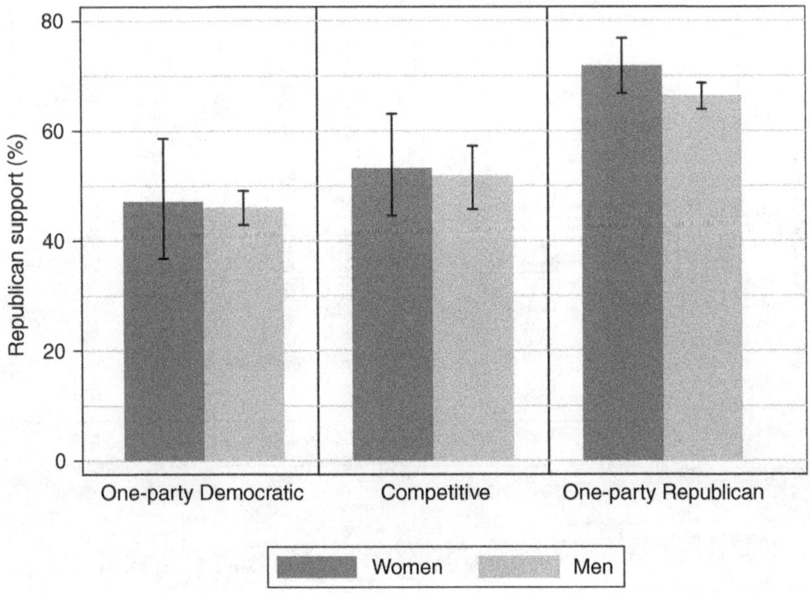

FIGURE 5.5. Partisan context and the Republican vote share of women and men, 1920.

but female voters are even more likely to vote Republican than are male voters in those states (confirmed by over 99 percent of the pooled simulations). In other contexts – competitive or one-party Democratic – only 55 percent of simulations show greater Republicanism among women, which implies no meaningful difference between men and women. Women, these estimates suggest, were not more Republican overall, and were not swept up in a Republican tide. Rather, women were, to a greater extent than men, mobilized by the locally dominant party in their state, which for women in most of our sample states was the Republican Party.

Finally, we note that overall, the range of Republican support is wider for women than it is for men (see Figure 5.4). While male support for Harding ranges from a low of 40 percent in Virginia to a high of 69 percent in Iowa, the range of female support varies from a low of 28 percent in Virginia to a high of 76 percent in Minnesota. The introduction of female voters thus increased electoral variation across states, largely by shoring up the locally dominant party. For example, the addition of women voters increased Democrat's advantage in Virginia, but in Minnesota, the addition of women voters transformed a sizeable Republican majority into an overwhelming one.

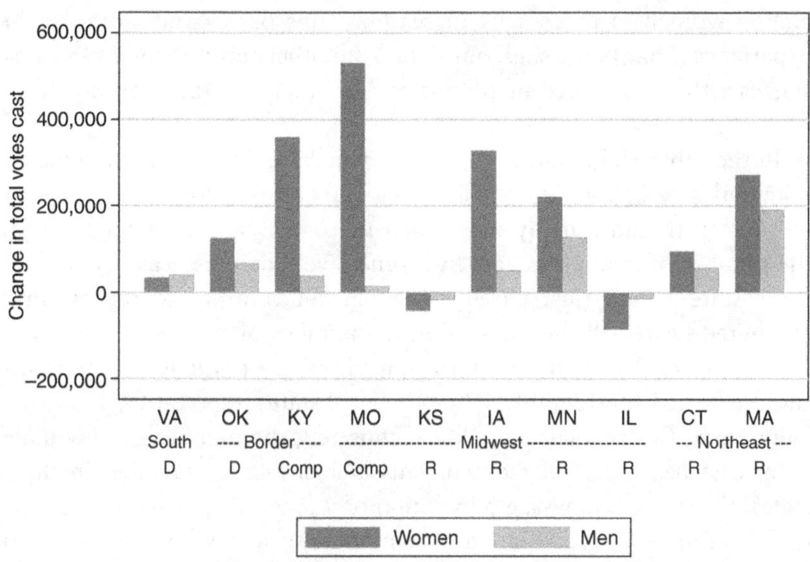

FIGURE 5.6. Change in number of votes cast by women and men, 1916 to 1920.

The Contributions of Women to the Election of 1920

Given what we have determined about women's turnout and vote choice in 1920, what can we conclude about the contributions of women to patterns of electoral stability and change in 1920? With the distribution of votes across the parties in 1916 and estimated support for each party by gender in 1920, it is relatively straightforward to calculate the gains (actual number of ballots) overall and for each party that can be attributed to men and women. The change in number of votes cast by men and women between 1916 and 1920 is reported in Figure 5.6.

The turnout gain estimates reveal several interesting patterns. First, in the two states – Illinois and Kansas – where women were enfranchised prior to 1916, the number of votes cast by both men and women in 1920 actually declines, and *more so for women* than for men (a result found in more than 90 percent of the simulations in Illinois and over 85 percent in Kansas).[14] Since fewer women than men voted in those states in 1916, the rate of decline in turnout was steeper for women than men. These results are not encouraging for those expecting turnout

[14] These estimates are remarkably consistent with the observed or "true" decline in Illinois: The Illinois published returns indicate a decline of over 80,000 women voters from 1916 to 1920 and our estimates suggest a decline of 95,000.

among women to necessarily increase as time passes and women gain experience. That being said, our data from other states in later elections suggests the experience of Illinois and Kansas in 1920 may not have been typical.

In the other eight states, no women voted in 1916, so the number of potential new ballots in 1920 is considerably larger for women than it is for men (because many men voted in 1916). Not surprisingly, then, the number of *new votes* cast by women exceeds those cast by men in every state except (just barely) Virginia. Yet contrary to reports that attributed nearly all the increase in the number of ballots cast in 1920 to women (e.g., Brown 1991), the contribution of women to increased turnout varied considerably. In a number of states (especially Oklahoma, Minnesota, Connecticut, and Massachusetts), the number of new male votes cast nears that of women. This is a dramatic outcome: In these states, the entire voting-age population of women was available for new mobilization in 1920, while only the number of men who had not voted in 1916 could contribute to new votes cast, and still the number of new votes generated by men nears that of women. Notably, these are all states where in 1916, male turnout was on the low end (48 percent to 57 percent) so that there were a sizable number of men available for mobilization. In these states, the mobilization of new (in the sense of not voting in 1916) male voters in 1920 was impressive: The number of men in the electorate expanded by 25 to 35 percent in only four years. In other states (especially Kentucky, Missouri, and Iowa), however, nearly all of the new votes appear to come from women. In these three states (two of which – Kentucky and Missouri – are our only states categorized as competitive), men's turnout was already near 80 percent in 1916, and thus there were simply fewer men available for new mobilization.

What was the contribution of women to partisan mobilization in 1920? Figures 5.7 and 5.8 report the change in number of votes cast for the major party candidates, by men and women, in 1920. Figure 5.9 reports the net Republican gain (increase in Republican vote minus increase in Democratic vote) in 1920. (For women outside of Kansas and Illinois, the number in Figure 5.9 is simply the margin of Republican victory among women in the 1920 election). It is clear from Figure 5.9 that, in our sample states, Republicans picked up far more new female voters than did Democrats. In only two states, Virginia and Kentucky, does the number of new female Democrats exceed the number of new female Republicans. As we have noted, Virginia and Kentucky are states where the Democratic Party was either very strong (Virginia) or competitive (Kentucky). We are

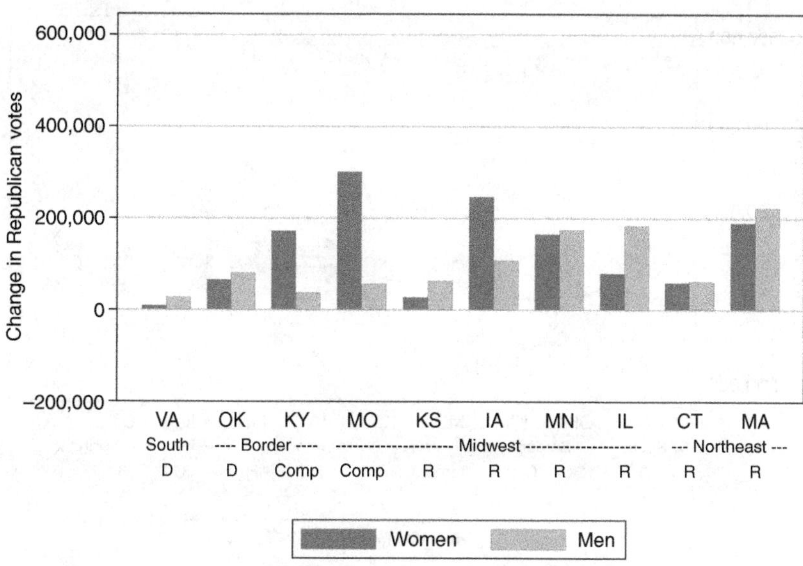

FIGURE 5.7. Change in number of Republican votes cast by women and men, 1916 to 1920.

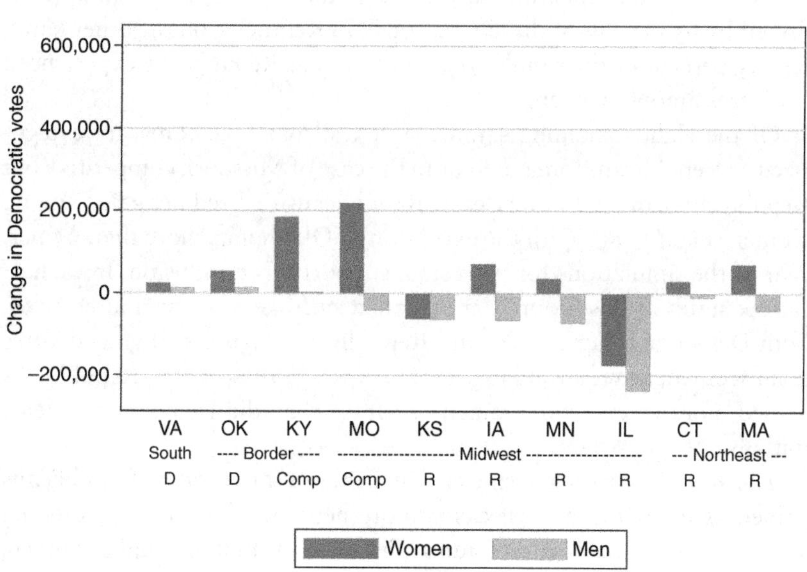

FIGURE 5.8. Change in number of Democratic votes cast by women and men, 1916 to 1920.

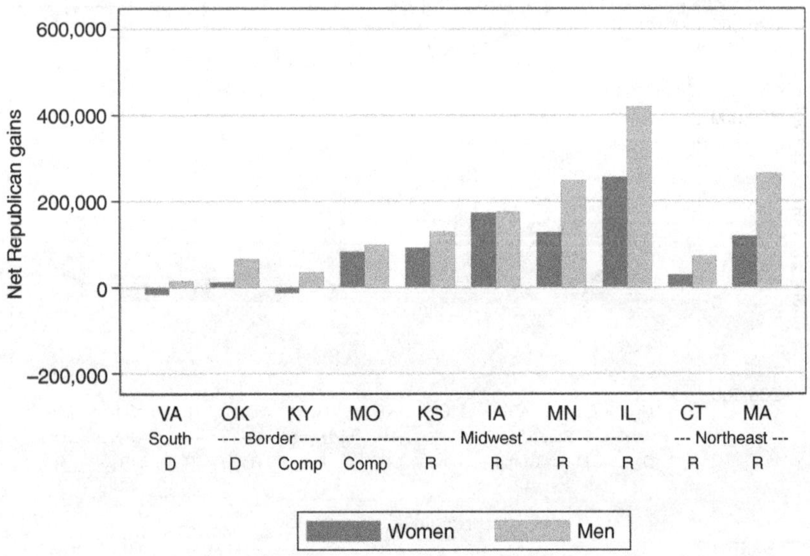

FIGURE 5.9. Change in Republican margin of victory for women and men, 1916 to 1920.

confident of the Democratic advantage among women in Virginia (confirmed by 95 percent of the simulations). In Kentucky, on the other hand, just 65 percent of the simulations indicate that Republicans experienced net losses among women.

Of the eight remaining sample states, all but Oklahoma are categorized as Republican-dominated or in the case of Missouri, competitive but Republican-leaning. In every case, Republicans realized net gains among women (Figure 5.9). With the exception of Oklahoma, more than 95 percent of the simulations for each state support this conclusion. In each of the six states in this group that extended suffrage to women after 1916, both Democrats (Figure 5.8) and Republicans (Figure 5.7) gained votes from women, as we would expect. However, in these states, Republicans gained more voters from women's suffrage than did Democrats, at least initially.

The more surprising result is that in these same states, Republicans gained as many or, in most cases, more net votes from men; exceeding 100,000 votes in six of ten states (Figure 5.9). Indeed, unlike women, Republican gains among men exceed Democratic gains among men in virtually *every single state* (Iowa is a draw). A combination of an increase in the number of Republican male votes (Figure 5.7) and in all but three cases (where the number of Democratic ballots is basically unchanged), a decrease in the number of male Democratic votes (Figure 5.8) results in a huge swing between 1916 and 1920 among men in favor of the Republican party. The net Republican gains were higher for men than for women in *every sample state* save Iowa. Again, this is despite the fact that so many more women are available for new partisan mobilization in 1920 than are men.

We have reason to be quite confident of these conclusions. In Illinois, where we observe male and female ballots directly, the results from the official election records are consistent with our estimates. Both the election records and our estimates show net Republican gains totaled to about 400,000 additional Republican votes from men in 1920, but fewer than 300,000 new Republican votes from women. Specifically, our estimates suggest net Republican gains of 419,000 among men (±80,000) and 255,000 (±80,000) among women. The published returns indicate net Republican gains of 387,000 among men and 297,000 among women. Despite the many challenges of ecological inference, particularly in the case of gender, our methodological approach produces estimates that nicely recover the actual election results and elicit the same substantive conclusions about the electoral behavior of women and men.

The implication of these results is that the increase in Republican support in 1920 is – contrary to the assumptions of previous scholars (e.g., Brown 1991) – more attributable to changing sentiments and mobilization among male voters than it is to the entrance of female voters. Republicans would have had a boon year in 1920 even without female voters; as we have seen, the presence of female voters mostly served to intensify Republican wins in Republican states.

Were Republican gains among men a function of large groups of newly mobilized men, who happened to enter the electorate at the same time that women achieved suffrage? Or did men defect from Democrats between 1916 and 1920, but turnout in roughly the same numbers? Our data do not allow us to reach definitive conclusions about the contributions of new voters (mobilization) versus vote switching by established voters (conversion) to electoral change across elections (see the extended discussion of this challenge in Chapter 6). However, the patterns revealed in our data are suggestive with regards to the extent to which mobilization and conversion characterize the electoral change processes.

In states with relatively high male turnout in 1916 – particularly Iowa, Missouri, and Kentucky – the number of men who could be potentially mobilized between 1916 and 1920 was small, so the introduction of women voters – in large numbers – was not countered by any comparable mobilization of males (see Figure 5.6). In those cases, some conversion of men from Democratic to Republican mobilization is likely to have occurred. In Iowa and Missouri, for example, GOP gains among men exceed turnout gains among men, while Democrats lost male votes in both states (Figure 5.8).

In states with relatively low male turnout in 1916 – such as Connecticut (52 percent), Massachusetts (48 percent), and Virginia (27 percent) – the number of new female voters was matched, partially or completely, by the number of new male voters. In those cases Republican gains appear to be generated from newly mobilized men rather than from defections among Democratic voters; in Virginia and Oklahoma, Democrats also gained a few new male votes and in Connecticut, Democratic losses were far smaller than GOP gains. In most cases, the newly mobilized males and the newly incorporated females did not in some way offset each other – both new male and new female voters were disproportionately Republicans. In the two states with the largest numbers of new male voters (Massachusetts and Minnesota), women and men both support the Republicans, casting more than two-thirds of their ballots for Harding.

Because women in most of our sample states were not enfranchised in 1916, mobilization is the only available mechanism for electoral change among women. The two exceptions are Illinois and Kansas. In both those states, women (similar to men in those states) experienced a loss of Democratic votes cast between 1916 and 1920 (Figure 5.8), and a gain in Republican votes cast (Figure 5.7), for an overall net gain in Republican votes cast (Figure 5.9). Because the number of ballots cast by women and men fell in these states (Figure 5.6), but the number of Republican votes jumped significantly, a substantial number of men and women likely defected from the 1916 Democratic candidate to the 1920 Republican candidate. The decline in Democratic vote share was similar for men and women in Illinois (about 18 percentage points), but slightly larger for women than men in Kansas (22 points compared to 15 points).

Interestingly, despite four additional years of experience with the presidential ballot, the contribution of women in Illinois and Kansas was little different – in terms of turnout or vote choice – than that of women in other one-party Republican states in the Midwest. Distinctly different mechanisms are at work – with conversion likely dominating the new Republican gains for both men and women in Illinois and Kansas, but mobilization largely at work on women in Iowa, Kansas, and Minnesota. But in each of these states Republicans realized large net gains – increasing the margin of victory over the Democrats by hundreds of thousands of votes. And in each state, the contribution of men – in terms of the number of votes – was larger than the contribution of women.

Conclusion: New Female Voters and the Return to Normalcy

Based on the nationwide surge in Republican support between 1916 and 1920, many observers concluded that women voted overwhelmingly Republican when they entered the electorate in 1920. Overall, our results support this conclusion. In the eight states in our sample that extended suffrage for the first time in 1920, 60 percent of women voters supported the Republican Party. But the pro-Republican trend is not a unique characteristic of new female voters; in those same states, 59 percent of men supported the Republican Party. The Harding campaign and the "return to normalcy" appealed to the emerging female electorate as well as the existing and expanding male electorate. The Republican Party netted more votes from new female voters than did Democrats, but, in all our sample states, the number of men mobilized as new Republican voters in 1920 greatly exceeded the number of women so mobilized. Previous explanations that attributed the significant new mobilization of Republican voters in 1920 to women have missed the even greater Republican mobilization of men in 1920.

This is not to say that women failed to contribute to electoral outcomes in 1920. The combined effect of women's patterns of turnout and vote choice meant that the entrance of female voters produced greater divergence in turnout and vote choice across the states. Low turnout states became even more distinct from other states in terms of levels of electoral participation, solidly Republican states became overwhelmingly Republican, and the Republican surge had only a modest impact in Democratic states.

Did newly enfranchised women behave like peripheral voters? In terms of turnout, yes. A party context characterized by close competition spurred women's turnout to a greater degree, and restrictive electoral laws dampened women's turnout to a greater extent, than they did men's. On the one hand, women's turnout behavior is thus consistent with what political science would expect of a group that is generally less interested, attentive, or engaged in politics – a group that has a low propensity for turnout unless an unusually stimulating context helps to overcome that disinclination to vote. We should probably not be surprised to find such an effect among women; denied the ability to develop the habit of voting over time, as well as burdened with socialization and social norms that discouraged political engagement among women, women's propensity to turn out to vote was surely lower than that of men. As a result, the effects of close competition and mobilization efforts not surprisingly had a particularly strong impact on women.

On the other hand, the fact that in some contexts – where competition was close and legal barriers to turnout were low – women's turnout was spurred to an even greater extent than was men's is inconsistent with a characterization of all or even most newly enfranchised women as so fundamentally apolitical that no stimulation could overcome their disinclination to electoral politics. Under the right circumstances, more than half of newly eligible women turned out to vote (Missouri, Kansas, and very nearly Iowa), a level of mobilization that characterizes the eligible public as a whole in some recent presidential elections; turnout in 1988 and 1996, for instance, was about 55 percent overall (US Census 1998). Newly enfranchised women were capable of significant electoral mobilization. *Where* women were first eligible to cast ballots explains more about their level of turnout than the fact that they were women.

In terms of vote choice, the conclusions we can draw from the presidential election of 1920 are less clear. We find that female voters were more likely than men to cast Republican ballots in Illinois, Minnesota, Iowa, and perhaps Kansas. Should we attribute this outcome to a general Republican preference among early female voters (particular partisanship hypothesis), as some scholars have suggested? Or, should this finding be attributed to women being swept up by the Republican swing in 1920, as the peripheral voter hypothesis predicts? Perhaps this finding supports the expectation that women would be mobilized by the locally dominant party to a greater extent than men (local party hypothesis). The particular realities of the 1920 presidential election – Republican swing, many Republican-dominated states – make it difficult to disentangle the competing expectations, and indeed, we cannot conclusively chose among them based on the evidence from 1920 alone.

On the whole, however, we believe the evidence is most supportive of the local party hypothesis that women tended to be mobilized by and into the locally dominated party. We find a significantly greater tendency to support the Republican Party only in states where the Republican Party was dominant. In none of our Democratic-dominated or Democratic-leaning states are women more Republican in their vote choice than are men, and indeed, in Virginia, we have reason to believe women may have been more supportive of the locally dominant Democratic Party than were men. These patterns suggest that the Republican bias was not universal – as both the peripheral voter hypothesis and the particular partisanship hypotheses would suggest – but limited to states where the Republican Party was very strong and well-established. That being said, that is only our inclination at this point; further investigation of other elections should give us additional evidence with which to evaluate these alternatives.

To the many impacts of the enfranchisement of women, our analysis indicates we might add the improved turnout of men. In every state, save one, in which women's right to vote was first exercised in 1920 men's turnout rose over its previous level in 1916. This was particularly the case in states where turnout had been low in 1916, and thus where considerable numbers of men were available for mobilization in 1920. In contrast, in our two states (Kansas and Illinois) in which women had already been permitted to vote, men's turnout fell in 1920 compared to where it had been in 1916. Similarly, while our data begin in 1920, available male and female turnout rates from 1916 in Illinois suggest that men's turnout in 1916 (the first presidential election in which women were allowed to vote in the state) was higher than in 1912. Thus, at least in the short run, nine of the ten states in our sample suggest that the initial enfranchisement of women helped to spur greater turnout of men, in contrast to the general trends toward falling electoral participation during this period.

We can imagine a number of possible mechanisms that might lead men to turnout at a higher rate in the first election in which women were enfranchised. The attention to the electoral franchise generated by the women's entrance into the electorate might have encouraged more men to take advantage of their long-held right. It is also possible that the "threat" of the presence of female voters (believed by many to disagree, in the main, with men on issues such as Prohibition) might have persuaded some men to defend their interests at the ballot box. Alternatively (or concomitantly), we know that when one person in a household votes, others in the same household are more likely to do so (Nickerson 2008). Perhaps enthusiastic new female voters helped bring their husbands, fathers, brothers, and sons to the polling places with them.

The 1920 election has been heralded as a "return to normalcy." Yet, the presence of women at the voting booth was hardly normal politics. In some ways, women did make politics more "normal" – they contributed to strengthening and solidifying the dominant political power in Republican states and to perhaps dampening the Republican surge in

Democratic states like Virginia. If Republicans were the party of normalcy, then women were again "normal" voters, in that most women did enter the electorate as Republicans. Yet, as our analysis shows, men favored the Republican Party at similar levels, and in states where turnout had been low in previous elections, the numbers of new male voters were considerable. As a consequence, on the whole, Republicans netted many more new male voters than they did female voters in 1920.

In 1920, women had just a few short months following the ratification of the Nineteenth Amendment to prepare to exercise their new right. By 1924, however, national enfranchisement had been established for more than four years, and hopes were high that female suffrage had become sufficiently "normal" that women would take to the polling places in large numbers and have a major impact on the presidential election, an election that featured a compelling Progressive candidate. In the next chapter, we turn to the behavior and impact of female voters in the election of 1924.

ILLUSTRATION 6.1. Senator Robert La Follette Sr. speaks to a group of women during his 1924 campaign for President as the Progressive Party candidate. ©Bettman/Corbis

6

Female Voters, Republican Majorities, and the Progressive Surge in 1924

The 1924 election does not rank as one of the more remembered or acclaimed presidential elections in American history. Sandwiched between the "return to normalcy" of 1920 and the dramatic events of 1928, the reelection of Republican Calvin Coolidge in 1924 is in many ways a classic "maintaining" election (Campbell 1966), affirming Republican dominance and leaving basic alignments unchanged. The presidential election of 1924 is perhaps best remembered for the 100-plus ballots required to nominate Democratic "dark horse" candidate John W. Davis and for the relative success of Progressive party candidate Robert M. La Follette.

For our purposes, however, the election of 1924 provides a valuable opportunity to inquire into the behavior of female voters before New Deal realignment got underway in 1928. By 1924, women in every state of the nation had (at least in theory) access to the voting booth,[1] and in the intervening four years since the ratification of the Nineteenth Amendment, presumably sufficient time to adjust to their new civic responsibility. Most importantly, the presence of a viable third-party Progressive candidate provides the best opportunity available to evaluate the widespread expectations that women were particularly sympathetic to the ideals of the Progressive movement and characterized by weaker partisan ties that would encourage more frequent major party defection.

In this chapter, we once again review the electoral context and expectations for female voters before employing our novel estimates to evaluate the behavior and impact of female voters in 1924. We find that in

[1] Formal and informal rules and practices continued to effectively bar many African American and immigrant women from polling places throughout the 1920s and 1930s.

some but by no means all places an increasing number of women were willing to enter polling places compared to 1920. The size of the turnout gender gap narrowed as overall turnout increased. We again find women's turnout more responsive to context than men's, consistent with the peripheral voter hypothesis.

Contrary to expectations, however, new female voters were not uniquely likely to defect from major party loyalties to support the third party Progressive candidate. If anything, male voters were more likely to cast third-party ballots; in a small number of Republican-dominated Midwestern states female voters were more Republican than male voters, and men were more Progressive than women, in their voting choices. Moreover, our estimates suggest that men were more likely than women to defect from major party loyalties to support La Follette in 1924. Thus the results from 1924 reinforce our tentative conclusions from 1920: Women were not more Republican on the whole, or more likely to swing to the party favored by the current election, but tended to be mobilized by and were more loyal to the locally dominant political party than were men, even when offered a credible Progressive Party option. As a result, we ultimately conclude that the presence of large numbers of female voters actually stabilized the electorate, reinforcing the Republican advantage in most states and dampening the Progressive surge in the Midwest, in particular.

The Election of 1924

Calvin Coolidge assumed the office of the presidency following Warren Harding's death from a heart attack in 1923. A former governor of Massachusetts, Coolidge was even more favorably inclined toward business interests than his predecessor (Hicks 1960); in addition to his famous quietude, Coolidge is perhaps best known for his claim that "the chief business of the American people is business" (Gould 2003, 242). Coolidge's ascension to the presidency denied the Democrats their most promising issue in the 1924 campaign, the Harding scandals, particularly Teapot Dome. However, while Republicans remained dominant, the economic recessions of 1920–1921 and 1923–1924 had weakened Republican support substantially: Seventy-eight congressional districts had switched from Republican to Democratic (and none from Democratic to Republican) in the 1922 midterm elections. Coolidge headed off a primary challenge to secure the GOP's nomination, and the brief Republican platform was uncontroversial and conservative (Burner 1971).

On the Democratic side, long-simmering divisions were brought to a head in the battle over the presidential nomination. On one side was William G. McAdoo, representing rural Protestants with nativist leanings who had long been associated with the agrarian William Jennings Bryan wing of the Democratic Party. On the other side was Al Smith, the personification of the emergent urban, immigrant, wet (i.e., anti-Prohibition), and Catholic faction of the Democratic Party. So divided was the party that the convention required more than 100 votes before it could settle on John W. Davis, a fairly unknown compromise candidate, who was not opposed by either faction, but did not excite his party either (Burnham 1986; Hofstadter 1955). Still, Davis had reasonably strong ties to the urban wing of the party, and was viewed as relatively wet, indicative of the continuing shift of the Democratic Party away from its agrarian roots and toward a more urban and immigrant coalition (Burner 1971).

With both parties offering fairly conservative candidates in 1924, various reform groups united behind the candidacy of Wisconsin Senator Robert M. La Follette, the leader of Progressive forces in Congress and a failed candidate for the Republican nomination. La Follette, widely known as a reformer, legislator, and orator, was the obvious choice for Progressive standard bearer. La Follette's coalition sought to unite groups that had never formally cooperated before, including organized labor, farm organizations, and socialists (Burner 1971, 1986; Hicks 1960). Maintaining such a diverse coalition proved difficult for the campaign, but the radical and idealistic La Follette remained popular within the Progressive movement and his candidacy provided the sole alternative to the more conservative platforms offered by the two major parties (Thelan 1976; Unger 2000).

In November, La Follette and the Progressive Party won almost 5 million votes – about 17 percent of the total – and carried his home state of Wisconsin (Burner 1986). In eleven other states, La Follette out-polled the Democratic nominee (MacKay 1947). Nationwide, Coolidge received 54 percent of the vote (down from the 60.3 percent Republicans polled in 1920), and Davis just 29 percent. The electoral disruptions generated by the third-party candidacy of La Follette were largely confined to a handful of states in the Plains and Upper Midwest, namely Wisconsin, North Dakota, Minnesota, Nebraska and, to a lesser extent, Iowa and Illinois. A decline in agriculture prices and resultant farmer grievances had been a major motivation behind the Progressive effort in 1924 (Rosenstone, Behr, and Lazarus 1996) and so Progressive support from states with agricultural economies is not surprising. La Follette drew nearly 1.7 million votes across those six states (more than one-third of the third-party vote in the entire nation). Despite La Follette's strong showing, the Progressive party organization was quickly disbanded after 1924; La Follette himself died in 1925 (Hicks 1960).

Expectations for Female Voters in 1924

Although attention to female voters was not as great as it had been on the heels of ratification of the Nineteenth Amendment in 1920, the press and the public continued to be interested in the potential political behavior and influence of female voters. Many expected, or hoped, that with four years to acclimate to their new political role, women's turnout and impact would be improved over 1920; indeed, some believed women might be decisive in 1924 (Greenlee 2014; Harvey 1998).[2]

The state and national League of Women Voters (LWV), as well as other organizations (such as the Women's Christian Temperance Union), continued their efforts to mobilize female voters with both education and practical political training in 1924 (Breckinridge 1933).[3] These campaigns featured traditional get-out-the-vote tactics, such as social pressure, as well as gender-specific appeals based on popular understandings of the interests of women. The Minnesota LWV, for example, offered a booth at the state fair featuring "a doll representing a woman casting her vote," a "thermometer of civic spirit, indicating the percentage of persons voting in each county of the state in the presidential vote of 1920," and a "series of simple posters tracing the women's vote from the polls to her own home" via the following verse:

> You are the woman who casts the vote that elects the man:
> Who runs the school where Jim and Jane and Johnny go.
> Who gives to youth clean places for his pleasuring.
> Who backs the bill to guard the child in industry.
> Who votes the tax that each year you and I pay
> Who hires the man who tests the milk that baby drinks.
> Who stands for law and for the law's enforcement

[2] For example, Crawford, William H. "A Big Woman Vote Seen by Mrs. Sabin." *The New York Times*, October 27, 1924, p. 8.

[3] See, e.g., "Thirty Million Women to Vote in November Elections: Leaders at Work: Move to Get Rural Vote Out." *Houston Press*, September 3, 1924; "W.C.T.U. Plans Campaign to Get Voters to Polls." *The Duluth (MN) News Tribune*, September 11, 1924; "Sixth Annual Convention of Voters Called; Get-Out-Vote Campaign Stressed by Women." *Duluth (MN) New Tribune*, September 21, 1924.

Who gladly grants good money for good mothering.
Who in the senate has the say on world co-operation.[4]

Political parties also persisted in their efforts to appeal to and train female voters (Freeman 2000).[5] Party appeals also tended to be gender specific; the parties believed they would be most successful at mobilizing women *as women*, emphasizing how the party's candidates and positions were of particular appeal to female voters. Both Democrats and Republicans, for example, organized women's clubs in anticipation of the 1924 presidential election with the goal of increasing female turnout for each party over 1920 (Harvey 1998). At the local level, candidate and party clubs held teas, presented speakers, and made the case for the appeal of the candidate on the issues that presumably mattered most to female voters.[6] Women's traditional, domestic roles were front and center in both parties' appeals to women; for example, the 146-page Women's Democratic Campaign Manual highlighted the party's positions on issues relating to children and family (Greenlee 2014).

The case of La Follette's Progressive party presidential candidacy is a particularly fruitful opportunity to evaluate the different expectations for women's vote choice and partisanship (see Chapter 1). That women would support Progressivism and Progressive candidates was a long-standing expectation of both contemporary observers and later scholars. Women and women's organizations were active and visible participants in the Progressive movement, including Theodore Roosevelt's 1912 Progressive "Bull Moose" campaign (Freeman 2000). Progressive ideals, such as moral reform, were consistent with the qualities associated

4 "Women Voters Will Have a Novel Booth at State Fair." *The Duluth (MN) News Tribune*, September 2, 1924.

5 "To Train Women Speakers." *The New York Times*, September 8, 1924; "Maine Democrats Organize Women," *The New York Times*, September 5, 1924; "Both Old Parties Woo Women Voters." *The New York Times*, October 10, 1924, p. 5; "Appeals to Women to Vote for Davis." *The New York Times*, November 2, 1924, p. 6; "Three Women Debate Campaign Issues." *The New York Times*, November 2, 1924, p. 7; "Women's Vote Will Win 1924 Campaign, G.O.P. Office Says." *Duluth (MN) News Tribune*, September 14, 1924; "Club Prepares Rooms as Headquarters." *Duluth (MN) News Tribune*, September 17, 1924; "G.O.P. Women of State Are Now Organized." *The Duluth (MN) News Tribune*, October 6, 1924; "Davis and Smith at Women's Rally." *Hartford (CT) Daily Courant*, October 26, 1924.

6 For example, "Service to Party Keynote of Talk by Mrs. Fosseen." *Duluth (MN) News Tribune*, September 18, 1924; "Coolidge Club Plans to Hold Precinct Teas; Women Voters to Hear Speakers at a Series of Meetings." *Duluth (MN) News Tribune*, September 25, 1924; "Meriden Women Hear Mrs. Merritt; Hartford Speaker Praises National and State Tickets." *Hartford (CT) Daily Courant*, September 24, 1924.

with women in the nineteenth and early twentieth century (Baker 1984; Evans 1989; see Chapter 2). Progressives were early and ardent advocates for women's suffrage. At the same time, opposition to women's suffrage had been motivated in no small part by concern that women would use the vote to achieve Progressive goals, particularly temperance (Flexner 1959; McDonagh and Price 1985). Progressive issues such as prostitution, child labor, workplace health and safety, good government, and especially prohibition were believed to weigh heavily in women's voting decisions (Allen 1930; Flexner 1959; McCormick 1928; Ogburn and Goltra 1919; Rice and Willey 1924; Russell 1924; Tarbell 1924; Toombs 1929; Wells 1929; Willey and Rice 1924). Consistent with those expectations, Goldstein (1984) finds that women were more likely than men to cast votes for the Progressive candidates in University of Illinois Board of Trustee elections (see also Andersen 1979). Others, however, warned against generalizing about women as a group (Blair 1931; Lippman 1928; Roosevelt 1940), and many party leaders expected female voters would fall into the same ethnic, class, and other patterns as men did (McConnaughy 2013).

The association of Progressivism and the campaign for women's suffrage also contributed to the expectation that women would be more committed to ideals than to any particular party (Barnard 1928c; Monoson 1990; Rogers 1930). Although the strength of party allegiance was weakening from its late nineteenth century zenith, parties still constituted a strong bond between citizens and the political system in the 1920s. The Progressive movement denounced political parties as corrupt and inefficient, so to the extent women were associated with the Progressive movement, they were expected to be wary of the major parties (Andersen 1990; Lemons 1973; Russell 1924). More generally, the legacy of disenfranchisement meant that women had had fewer opportunities to reinforce their partisanship through voting, and might be expected to have weaker partisan attachments and greater likelihood of defection for that reason as well (Converse 1969, 1976). For all these reasons, we might expect women to be especially likely to defect from major party loyalties and to support La Follette and the Progressives in 1924.

The election of 1924 also provides a particularly useful opportunity to evaluate the utility of the peripheral voter concept to describe newly enfranchised women. Peripheral voters are expected to turn out to vote when elections are highly salient, or when there is surge in interest, excitement, and enthusiasm for a candidate or issue. In those cases, peripheral voters are supposedly swayed by whichever candidate or party is most favored by the election-specific conditions that brought them to the polls. Thus, the peripheral voter concept implies the hypothesis that new female voters – unconstrained by the strong party loyalties that characterize "core voters" – were more likely to swing to the Progressive Party where the immediate political circumstances were particularly favorable to Progressive candidates. As we have noted, Progressive strength was concentrated in particular states, allowing us to consider this hypothesis directly.

The election of 1924 thus provides the best opportunity of the elections examined here to observe gender differences in major party loyalty and support for Progressive ideals. The relatively successful third-party campaign of Robert La Follette was a chance for women to defect from the major parties and demonstrate their commitment to Progressive values. La Follette himself had a long history as a strong advocate of women's suffrage and women's rights (such as the appointment of women to political office), and his wife, Belle, had been a popular suffragist speaker (MacKay 1947; Thelan 1976). The Women's Division of the La Follette campaign featured speeches by well-known female activists, such as Hull House founder Jane Addams and Harriet Stanton Blatch, Elizabeth Cady Stanton's daughter and a well-known suffragist in her own right. Yet, compared to the attention given to new female voters in 1920 and the potential role of women in the tumultuous realigning elections of 1928, 1932, and 1936, few scholars have even speculated as to the level of support for the Progressive Party among female voters in 1924 (e.g., Unger 2000). The analysis that follows thus offers unique answers to these questions.

The Mobilization of Women in 1924

How well were women adjusting to their new right four years after the ratification of the Nineteenth Amendment? In our sample as a whole women's turnout was 38 percent, a small increase over 1920, when we estimated women's turnout at 36 percent. Male turnout is basically unchanged from 1920 to 1924: estimated male turnout in our sample is 68 percent in 1920 and 67 percent in 1924. In 1924, then, while women's turnout increased slightly, women continued to dampen turnout overall, and significantly so.

As always, the state-level data (see Figure 6.1) tell a more complicated story. As in 1920, fewer than half of women exercised their right to vote in almost every state; in 1924, the only exception is Iowa. As in

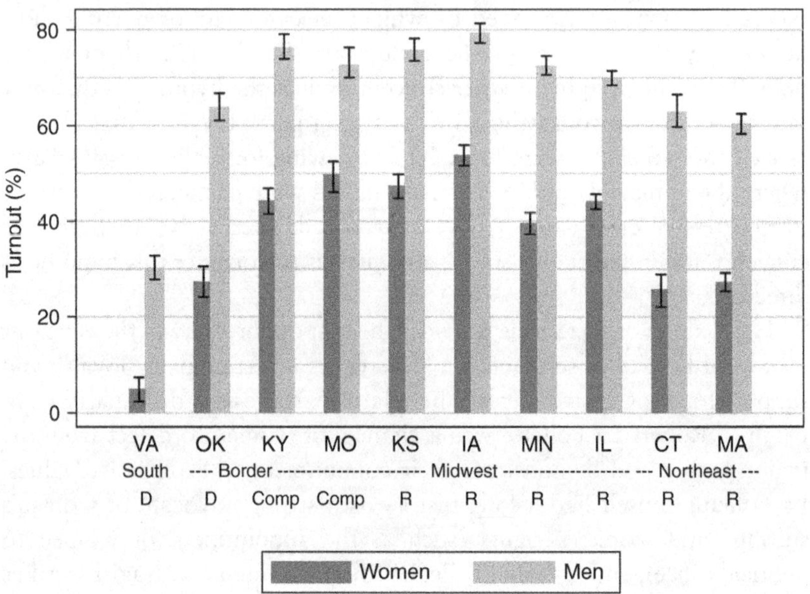

FIGURE 6.1. Turnout of women and men, 1924.

1920, the turnout gender gap narrows as overall turnout increases, suggesting that the factors that encouraged (or discouraged) men's turnout did so to an even greater extent for women. Excluding extremely low turnout Virginia, estimated female turnout ranges 28 points across our sample states (from 26 percent in Connecticut to 54 percent in Iowa) compared to just 19 points for men (from 60 percent in Massachusetts to 79 percent in Iowa). Thus as in 1920, the presence of female voters increased turnout variability overall. Again excluding extremely low turnout Virginia (which puts a ceiling on the size of the gender gap), the largest turnout gender gap is in Connecticut (37 points), where overall turnout was 45 percent (second lowest in our sample), while the smallest gender gap can be found in Missouri (22 points), where overall turnout was 61 percent (the third highest in our sample).

Some evidence of slowly growing acceptance of women's suffrage can be found in small gains in women's turnout at the state level (see Figure 6.2). The increase in female turnout overall is fairly small – less than 10 points in all states – and is largely limited to our one-party Republican states in the Midwest and Northeast. Turnout, for women and men, is virtually unchanged in one-party Democratic Virginia and Oklahoma, and declines in competitive Kentucky and Missouri. In the

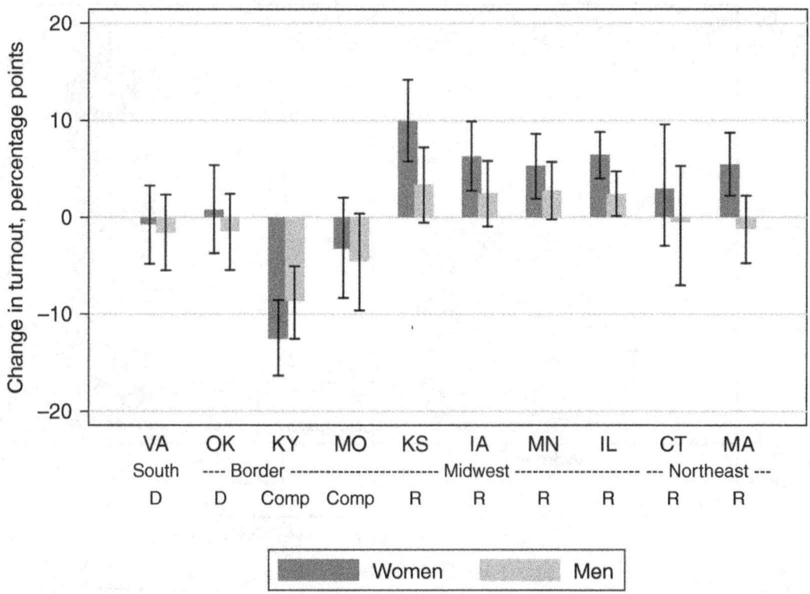

FIGURE 6.2. Change in turnout of women and men, 1920 to 1924.

six states where women's turnout increased over 1920, the estimated growth in women's turnout exceeds the increase for men in every case. We can be particularly confident (more than 90 percent of simulations) that women's turnout increased more than men's between 1920 and 1924 in three states: Kansas, Illinois, and Massachusetts. The result is smaller male–female turnout gaps in 1924 compared to 1920 in nine of the ten states (the exception is Kentucky). With the addition of nearly half a million new women voters in our ten sample states, the gap between male and female participation across the sample states narrowed from 32 to 29 percentage points.

The Impact of Political Context

In 1920, women's propensity to turnout to vote was more sensitive to changes in the political context than was men's, consistent with our expectations for low-motivation peripheral voters. Did this pattern continue in 1924, when women had had four more years to acclimate to their new political role?

Partisan Context. In 1924, as in 1920, and as expected, both male and female turnout are highest in competitive states (Figure 6.3). And as in 1920, women's turnout is more responsive to changes in context

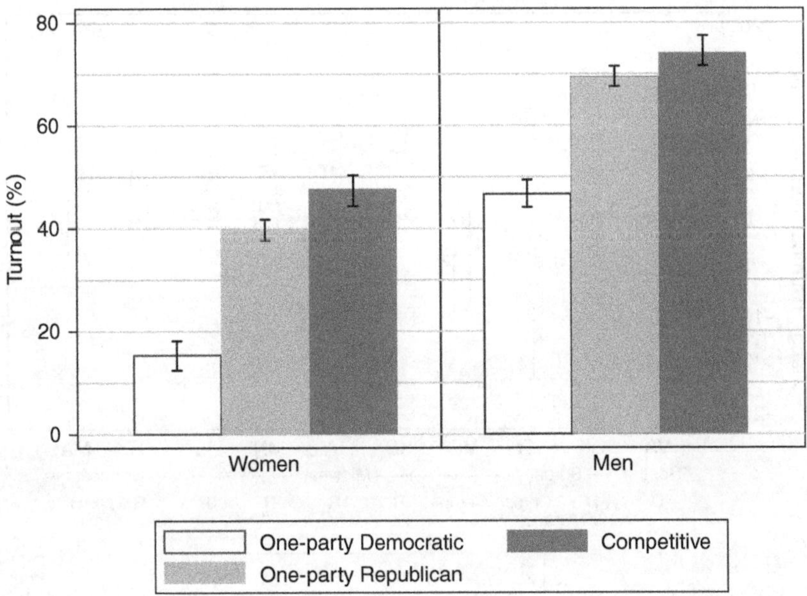

FIGURE 6.3. Partisan context and the turnout of women and men, 1924.

than is men's – higher in traditionally competitive states and dampened by one-party states – as expected of less experienced and less engaged peripheral voters. Specifically, women's turnout is 8 points higher in competitive states compared to one-party Republican states (a 20 percent increase) compared to just 5 points for men (a 7 percent increase). The difference between the turnout of women in competitive states and women in one-party Democratic states is 33 points (a more than 300 percent increase due to the extremely low turnout of women in one-party Democratic states), versus 27 points for men (a 59 percent increase). When simulations are pooled, about 90 percent are consistent with larger effects of competitiveness on women voters than on men.

Legal Context. Similarly, restrictive electoral laws continue to dampen both male and female turnout, with a greater impact on women than men (see Figure 6.4). Female turnout falls 23 points between less restrictive and more restrictive states (a decrease in turnout of more than 50 percent), while male turnout declines just 19 points (a decline of 27 percent). The gap between male and female turnout is 28 points in less restrictive states, but 31 points in the more restrictive states. Again, then, women's electoral behavior shows greater responsiveness to context than does

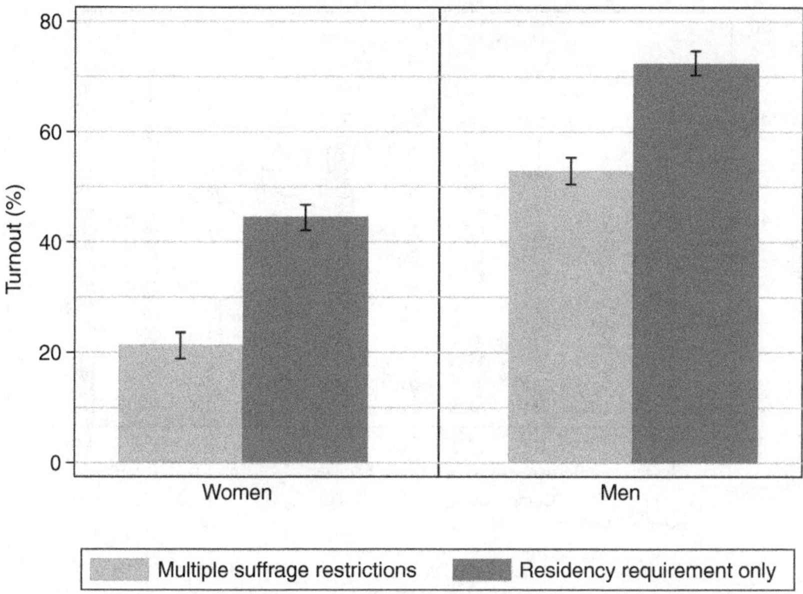

FIGURE 6.4. Legal context and the turnout of women and men, 1924.

men's (confirmed in 96 percent of simulations), as the peripheral voters hypothesis suggests.

The Partisan Mobilization of Women

How were women mobilized by parties – Democrats, Republicans, and uniquely, Progressives – in 1924? In our sample as a whole, the share of women's votes going to the Republican Party declined from 63 percent in 1920 to 57 percent in 1924. Men's Republican vote share also declined, and by about the same amount, from 61 percent in 1920 to 53 percent in 1924. Thus women in our sample were again slightly more likely to vote Republican than were men. Can we attribute this outcome to a general Republican bias among female voters, a swing to the victorious party, or the influence of locally dominant political parties?

Our state-level data (Figure 6.5), arranged by party context and region, can once again help us parse these questions. In one-party Democratic Virginia and Oklahoma, men's and women's vote choice is similar; our point estimates actually suggest that women in Virginia were mobilized by locally dominant Democrats to a greater extent than were men. The

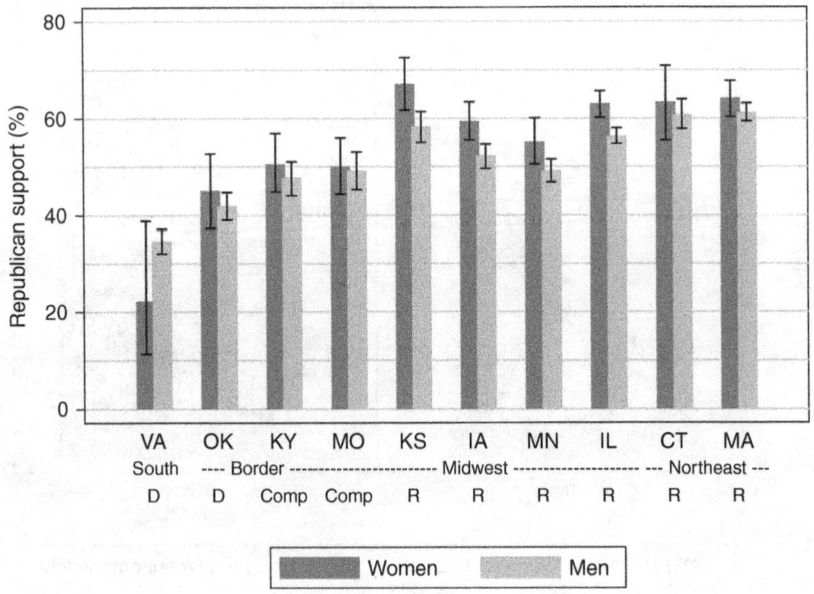

FIGURE 6.5. Republican vote share of women and men, 1924.

extremely low turnout of Virginia women generates wide credible intervals, but even in this case 79 percent of the simulations are consistent with the conclusion that female voters were less Republican than were male. In competitive Kentucky and Missouri, male and female voters are equally likely to cast Republican ballots.

Yet in all four of our one-party Republican states in the Midwest, women are more likely to be mobilized by the locally dominant party than are men. The simulations suggest we can be very confident of this conclusion: In Minnesota, Iowa, Illinois, and Kansas, women's Republican support exceeds men's in 90 percent or more of the simulations; in Illinois, that figure is 99 percent. Region continues to matter: In the traditionally Republican Northeast (Massachusetts and Connecticut), on the other hand, the gender difference in Republican support is negligible. In Connecticut, for instance, women's Republican support exceeded men's support in only 66 percent of the simulations. We have evidence, then, of a persistent distinctly pro-Republican (relative to men) mobilization of female voters, but only in the one-party Republican Midwest, in both 1920 and 1924.

Overall, the incorporation of new female voters, as in 1920, reinforced the advantages for locally dominant parties. In fact, the presence

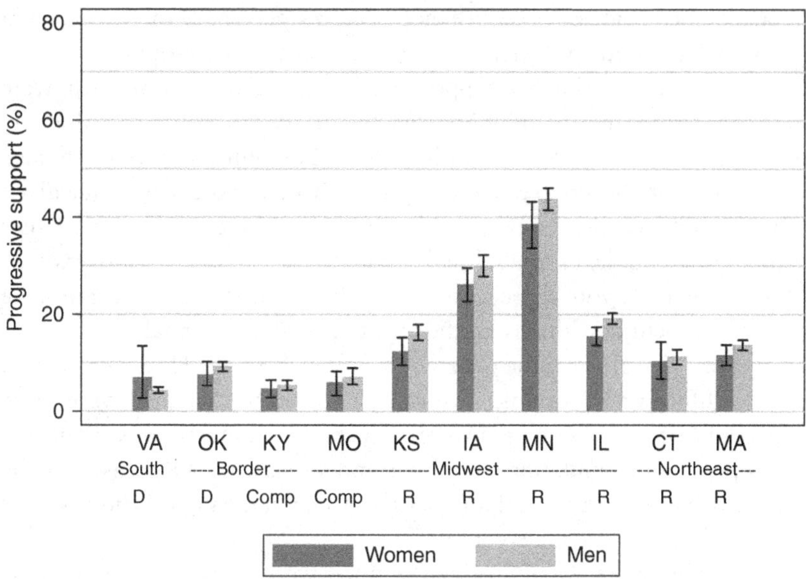

FIGURE 6.6. Progressive vote share of women and men, 1924.

of women in the electorate magnified or amplified differences between one-party Republican and one-party Democratic states even more in 1924 than 1920. The percent of female voters supporting the Republican Party varies by 45 points (22 percent in Virginia to 67 percent in Kansas), about the same as the 44 points that separated the highest and lowest observed Republican vote share among women in 1920. The 1924 male Republican vote, on the other hand, varies just 26 points (35 percent in Virginia to 61 percent in Connecticut), a more *narrow* range than the 33 points in 1920.

Mobilization by Progressives

What about the long-held expectations that women would be weaker partisans and particularly likely to support candidates associated with the cause of Progressivism? As Figure 6.6 shows, Progressive Party support[7] in 1924 was extremely regional. Progressive Party vote share is concentrated in the upper Midwest – in our sample, Iowa and Minnesota

[7] The estimates are support for all third parties (Prohibition, Socialist, and Miscellaneous Independent), but we refer to this as Progressive support because more than 96 percent of the third-party ballots are for La Follette. Owing to difficulties with ballot access, La Follette was listed as the candidate for four different parties, depending on the state (Rosenstone, Behr, and Lazarus 1996; Sundquist 1983).

in particular. Progressives secure more than 25 percent of the votes cast in Iowa and, astoundingly, more than 40 percent in Minnesota.

None of our estimates support the expectation that women were uniquely supportive of or mobilized by the Progressive Party. In only one state in our sample – Virginia – does the point estimate for female vote share for the Progressive Party exceed male vote share, but given low turnout, we cannot be confident of this difference. In every other state in our sample, estimated male Progressive Party vote share exceeds estimated female vote share, contrary to expectations. In most states, we can only conclude with any confidence that male and female Progressive Party vote share were not different from each other. However, in two states – Illinois and Kansas – we can be confident that men were more supportive of La Follette than were women: This conclusion is supported by 99 percent of simulations in Illinois and 91 percent in Kansas. Like the surge for Harding in 1920, La Follette support in the upper Midwest was principally driven by male voters.

What about the possibility that women were more likely to support third parties where third-party support was strongest, as the peripheral voters hypothesis suggests? Figure 6.6 provides no support for this hypothesis. In areas where La Follette and the Progressives were the most popular, the difference between men and women is about the same (3.7 percentage points in Iowa, 5.1 in Minnesota) as the difference between men and women in areas where Progressive support is weaker (3.7 percentage points in Illinois, 4.0 in Kansas). Although women behaved as peripheral voters in their turnout – more responsive to context – they were not peripheral voters in their vote choice behavior, swinging to the party with the greatest salience and excitement in the immediate political context.

Organizing our states in terms of party context can once again provide further insight into these patterns. As Figure 6.7 indicates, in the two competitive states – that is, states without an overwhelmingly dominant party – men's and women's Republican Party support differs very little (less than one point). The same can be said of our two one-party Democratic states. In the six traditionally Republican-dominated states, however, women are more than 5 points more supportive of the GOP than are men. Over 99 percent of pooled simulations indicate higher female Republican support than male support in the one-party Republican states. In the competitive or one-party Democratic states (pooled), the comparable figure is about 60 percent, which implies no meaningful difference between men and women. Once again, we have evidence of mobilization

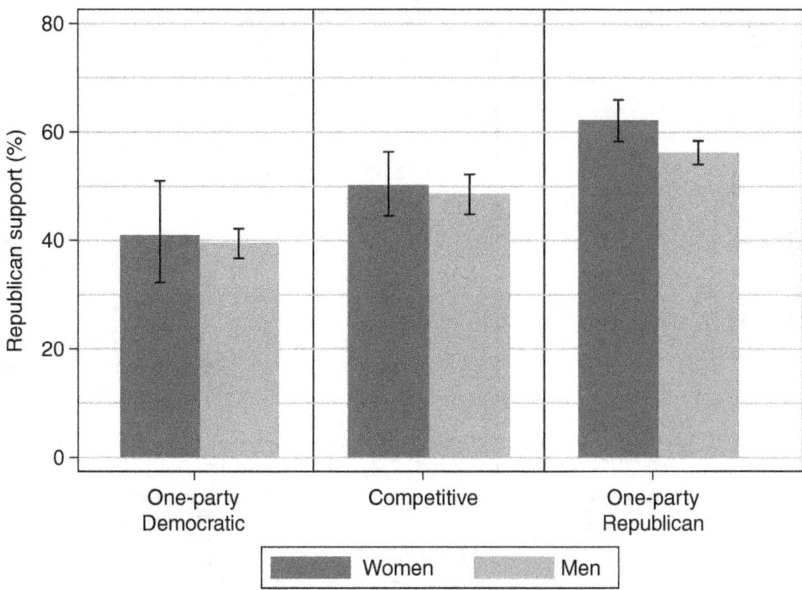

FIGURE 6.7. Partisan context and the Republican vote share of women and men, 1924.

of women into the locally dominant party in their state, consistent with the local party hypothesis, despite the Progressive Party option.

Women's consistent loyalty to or mobilization by the locally dominant party had consequences for Progressive Party mobilization of women. Progressive Party vote share is lowest, and we observe virtually no gender differences, in the competitive and one-party Democratic states (see Figure 6.8). In one-party Republican states, on the other hand, we observe dramatically higher Progressive Party support among both sexes. This may be partially a function of the states involved (e.g., lower Progressive Party interest in the one-party Democratic South), but also indicates the relative success of the Progressive Party movement in the states in our sample where Republicans had traditionally been strongest.

The surprising result is that, on average, men in the one-party Republican states were clearly more likely to support La Follette and the Progressive Party than were women. The point estimates suggest a difference of about 3 percentage points and more than 99 percent of the simulations indicate men were more likely to support La Follette in one-party Republican states. This result helps to untangle two completing explanations for the persistent Republican advantage in 1920 and 1924. In 1920, because Republicans were advantaged nationally, it is difficult to know

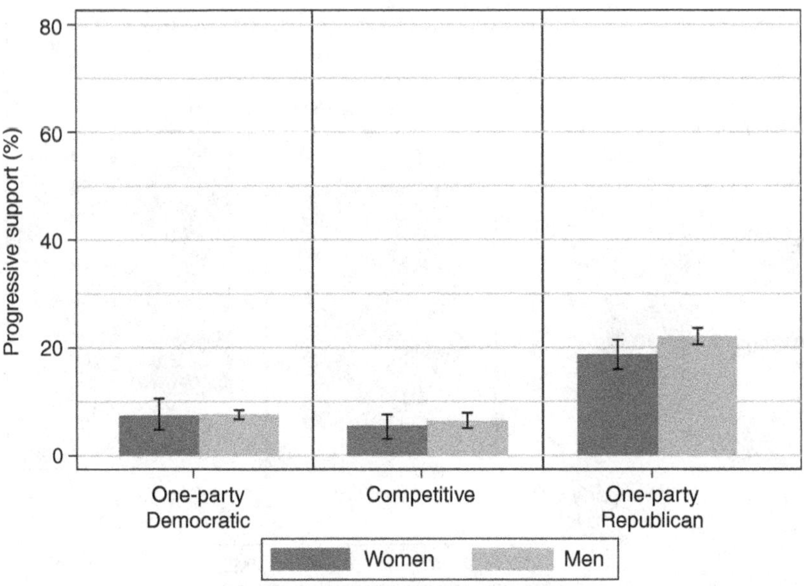

FIGURE 6.8. Partisan context and the Progressive vote share of women and men, 1924.

if the Republican advantage among women reflects loyalty to the traditionally dominant party in the state, a pro-Republican bias, or a response to election-specific forces (swing voters). But in 1924, the surge for La Follette was stronger among men in one-party Republican states, in contrast with the hypothesis that women were less loyal or dependable voters, swinging to the party most advantaged by election-specific factors. Moreover, as in 1920 – but to an even greater extent – any Republican advantage among women is limited to states where the Republican Party was dominant, suggesting that the persistent Republican advantage among women, relative to men, was not a general female preference for Republicans, but a function of loyalty to or successful mobilization by the traditionally advantaged party in the state.

The Contributions of Women to the Election of 1924

Where did Progressive voters come from? Were Progressive Party supporters largely established male and female Republican or Democratic voters? Or did the Progressive Party draw its support largely from newly mobilized voters? Did the same process generate third-party support among both women and men? To what extent did Republicans owe their reelection to men and women, and to returning and newly mobilized voters?

Uncovering the divergent contributions of mobilization (new voters), demobilization (absence of previous voters), and conversion (change among continuing voters) in accounting for electoral change, particularly major realignments, has been an ongoing challenge for social scientists and historians (for a thorough review, see Darmofal and Nardulli 2010). Like the enfranchisement of women, many of the dramatic and consequential cases of electoral realignment predate the widespread use of modern polling tools. Even when surveys exist, they rarely employ the sorts of panel designs that allow researchers to track with certainty the entrance, exit, and changing party preference of voters. Researchers have employed a number of different approaches, some of which we emulate here, to estimate the various contributions of conversion and (de)mobilization to electoral change.

Although we cannot answer the question of conversion versus mobilization decisively with our data, the next set of figures, which report the actual change (from 1920) in the number of male and female ballots cast, overall, and for each party, can reveal some features of the processes that generated Progressive vote share in 1924. In this chapter, and the two that follow, we seek to track three different sources of electoral change: mobilization, conversion, and defection. In most cases, our goal is to explain the growth in support for a particular party, be it a third-party movement (such as the Progressives in 1924) or an increase in support for an established major party (such as the Democrats in 1932).

Suppose our goal is to explain the sources of support for Party A. We conceive of mobilization as the proportion of Party A's support that can be attributed to citizens who did not cast ballots in the previous election; that is, to new voters. We define conversion as the proportion of Party A's support that can be attributed to citizens who had cast ballots for Party B in the previous election, but who cast ballots for Party A in the current election. One of our goals is to determine whether the sources of support – mobilization or conversion – for a new or newly advantaged party differ for men and women.

Defection, in our conception of the term, is related to conversion, but slightly different. Conversion is the percentage of the growth in Party's A's support that comes from previous Party B supporters. To determine this percentage we calculate the change (decline) in support for Party B from the previous election to the current election and divide that number by the change (increase) in support for Party A from the previous election to the current election. Our measure of conversion tells us how much of Party A's new support came from previous supporters of the other party. We might, however, also be interested in how likely Party B supporters were to abandon their support for Party B and switch to Party A, what we term defection. In this case, we calculate the increase in support for Party A from the previous election, subtract the number of new voters, and then divide that quantity by the number of ballots cast for Party B in the previous election. Obviously, defection is what creates conversion, but they are not the same thing. We might imagine, for example, that a very large percentage of Party B voters in the previous election switched to Party A in the current election, resulting in a high rate of defection. This would have implications for our views of the loyalty of Party B supporters. But perhaps there were few Party B supporters overall in the previous election, so that even though their rate of defection was very high, the result was a small number of converts for Party A in the current election, and Party A indeed owed more of its increased support to mobilization (previously inactive citizens) than it did to conversion. Conversely, Party A may owe a great deal of its new support to conversion (voters who changed parties), because there were so many Party B voters in the previous election, even if the actual rate of defection from Party B was quite low. These different conditions have varying implications for our conclusions about the partisan loyalty and changing political engagement of women and men.

Our estimates do not permit us to definitively determine the extent of mobilization and conversion, or the rate of defection, but can offer some insights. In this chapter, we are particularly interested in investigating the sources of Progressive Party support. The change in the number of votes cast overall and for each party, for men and women, give us some clues. For example, in a state where major party votes cast are largely unchanged but the overall number of votes cast increases substantially and to an extent similar to the number of new Progressive votes, we have reason to suspect mobilization, rather than conversion, was the key mechanism. Or consider a case where both Republicans and Democrats lose significant numbers of votes (from 1920) while Progressives gain significant numbers of votes, and the total number of ballots cast is relatively stable from 1920 to 1924. In such a case, it seems likely that conversion (voters changing their party choice from one election to the next) is responsible; that is, we assume that some or even many of those lost major party votes became Progressive Party votes. Yet, while such patterns may be *consistent* with conversion, we recognize that there could be other explanations for a Progressive surge. It is theoretically possible,

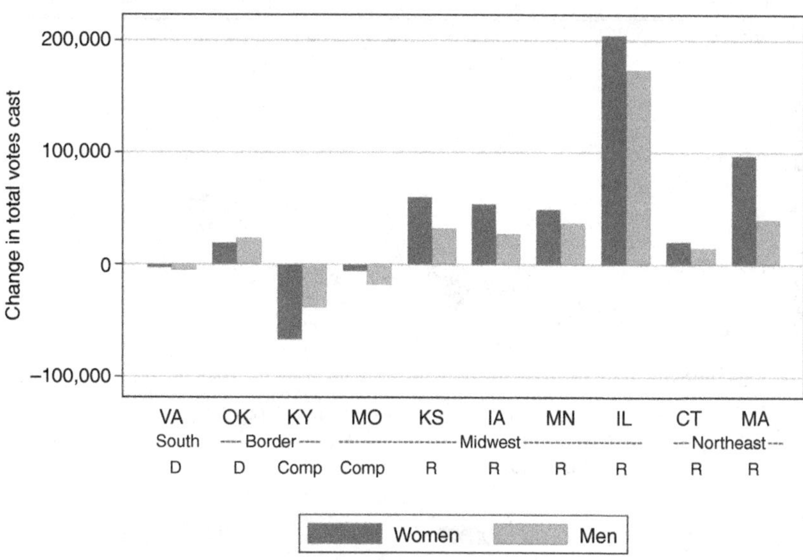

FIGURE 6.9. Change in number of votes cast by women and men, 1920 to 1924.

for example, that a major party vote decline and Progressive vote increase could be generated by significant demobilization by major party voters (that is, they withdrew from the active electorate) which was offset by a large mobilization of new voters by the Progressive Party, rather than by conversion of major party voters to the Progressive Party. For these reasons, we emphasize that our conclusions are tentative.

In terms of changes in turnout overall (see Figure 6.9), we note first that, largely as a function of population growth, there were more ballots cast by both men and women in 1924, over 1920, in every state in our sample, save three. Those three exceptions include Virginia, where turnout remains low and is virtually unchanged among both men and women, and the traditionally competitive states of Kentucky and Missouri. Even with those declines, however, Kentucky and Missouri continue to boast some of the highest rates of turnout in our sample in 1924 (see Figure 6.1).

In the other seven states where the number of ballots cast increased, the number of new ballots cast by women exceeded the number of new ballots cast by men (with the exception of Oklahoma), although differences are sometimes quite small (e.g., Minnesota, Connecticut). Thus, overall, four years of experience with the ballot did appear to generate more new female ballots (relative to new male ballots) in a number of places, with gender differences especially large in Iowa, Kansas, and Massachusetts.

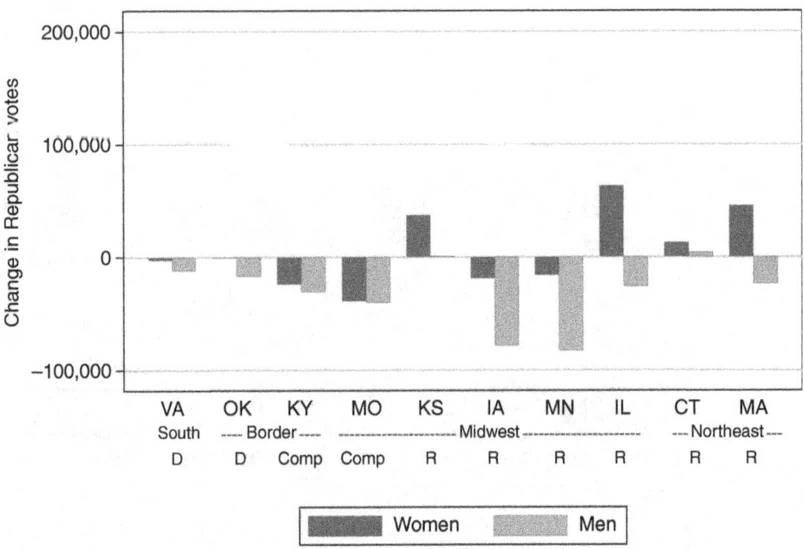

FIGURE 6.10. Change in number of Republican votes cast by women and men, 1920 to 1924.

In each of these three states, 85–90 percent of the simulations are consistent with the conclusion that women added more new votes than men. Given how many more women than men were available for mobilization in 1924, this is not surprising. Indeed, that mobilization differences were not larger and present in more states – given the dramatic undermobilization of women, relative to men, in 1920 – is the more surprising finding in Figure 6.9.

Figures 6.10 to 6.12 summarize the changes in the number of ballots cast for each party from 1920 to 1924. The Republican party lost votes among men in nearly every state (see Figure 6.10). In some states the drop in Republican ballots was large (more than 50,000 in Illinois and Iowa), but in all states the drop among men was larger than any corresponding drop among women, and sometimes much larger (e.g., Minnesota, Iowa). Of course, there were more male Republican voters in 1920 than there were female Republican voters in 1920, so more men were available to defect or demobilize. Yet, in four states – traditionally Republican-dominated Illinois, Kansas, Connecticut, and Massachusetts – Republicans actually gained female voters while the number of male Republican ballots either declined or remained relatively flat.

Patterns of Democratic and Progressive Party support (Figures 6.11 and 6.12) are more consistent across the sexes – where a party gains

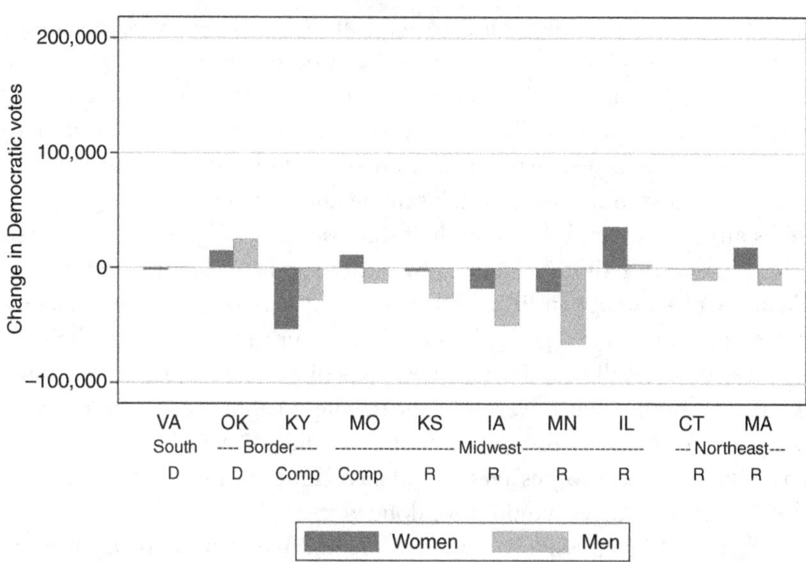

FIGURE 6.11. Change in number of Democratic votes cast by women and men, 1920 to 1924.

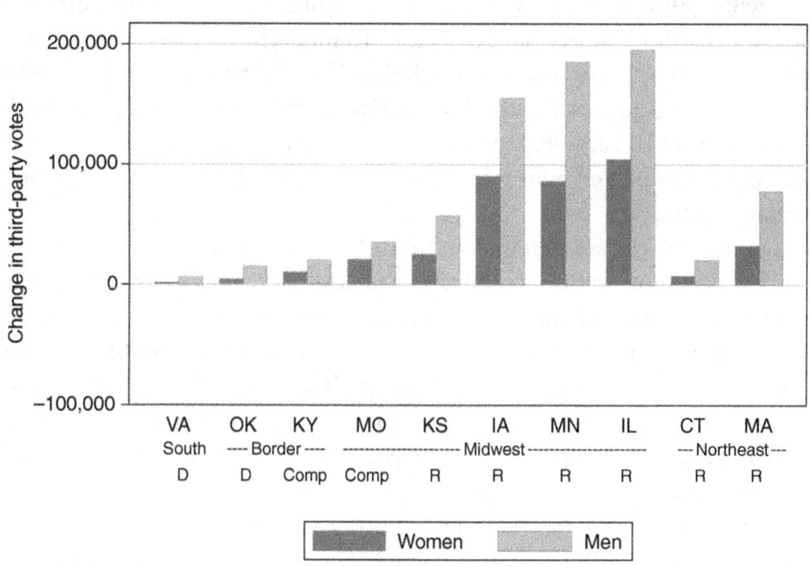

FIGURE 6.12. Change in number of Progressive votes cast by women and men, 1920 to 1924.

ballots among men, they tend to gain among women, where support from men is unchanged, it tends to be little changed among women. However, in Minnesota, Iowa, and Illinois – the states where the largest number of third-party ballots were cast – the number of third-party ballots cast by men is nearly twice the number cast by women (Figure 6.12). Indeed, in most of the states in the sample, the number of new third-party votes among women is less than half that found among men. (Because so few third-party ballots were cast by either sex in 1920, the numbers in Figure 6.12 – *change* in Progressive vote cast between 1920 and 1924 – represent nearly all Progressive votes cast in our sample states.) The twin patterns of generally similar or lower rates of Progressive support among women combined with overall lower female turnout means Progressives owed far fewer votes to women than they did to men. If the electorate had been all male, Progressives would have done even better in 1924, and the two major parties would have done worse.

Where did Progressive voters come from? We exclude from our discussion the states where Progressive vote share was less than 10 percent (Virginia, Oklahoma, Kentucky, and Missouri), as drawing inferences from the small number of Progressive votes in those states is a significant challenge. Where Progressives made a strong showing, our estimates suggest that both conversion (previous Democratic and Republican supporters switching to vote Progressive) and mobilization (previous nonvoters casting ballots for the Progressive Party) were at work for both sexes. However, there is reason to believe that conversion from major party support played a larger role among male voters than it did among female voters.

Minnesota, the state in our sample where Progressives were most successful, is an important example. Progressives gained more than 175,000 new male votes and more than 80,000 new female votes, an extraordinary level of third party support. At the same time, Republicans lost about 85,000 male votes and Democrats lost about 65,000 male votes, for a total decline among men of about 150,000 two-party votes. It is possible that all of those lost major party male voters just stayed home, and the Progressive Party support came entirely from new mobilization. It is more likely, we believe, that a good number of those major party voters in 1920 cast Progressive Party ballots in 1924. Yet, even if all of them did so, they would still fall short of the 175,000 male Progressive ballots cast, suggesting a mobilization of at least 25,000 new male voters for the Progressive Party (note that Figure 6.7 shows an increase of about 35,000 new male voters in Minnesota in 1924).

By contrast, mobilization seems to have played the larger role in generating Progressive votes among women in Minnesota, as we might expect of a generally undermobilized group. Republicans and Democrats lost about equal numbers of female votes in Minnesota in 1924 (totaling about 40,000), but Progressives gained about 80,000 female votes that same year. Again, keeping in mind that our assumptions could be wrong (e.g., voters lost by Republicans and Democrats might have stayed home or voted for the other major party), it seems likely that as many or more than 40,000 new female voters were mobilized to cast their first ballots for the Progressive Party (Figure 6.7 shows about 50,000 new female ballots overall in Minnesota in 1924). Indeed, if we simply assume that all lost two-party votes went to the Progressives, we could attribute about half of women's Progressive Party votes to mobilization and half to conversion. For men, on the other hand, more than 85 percent of Progressive support (again, under the same assumptions) can be attributed to conversion compared to just 15 percent attributed to new mobilization. Although the details vary, Iowa follows a similar pattern, suggesting a more significant role for conversion among men and a considerable role for mobilization among women in states where Progressives were most successful.

The states where the Progressive Party was less successful also suggest that conversion played a bigger role among men than women. In Massachusetts, for example, the major parties lost about 40,000 male votes (about 25,000 Republican and 15,000 Democratic) while Progressives picked up about 70,000 male votes. Again, we cannot assume that all major party vote loss became Progressive vote gain, but it does appear likely that conversion played a significant role (about 57 percent) in generating Progressive votes from men in Massachusetts. By contrast, both major parties experienced increased female mobilization in Massachusetts in 1924 (about 50,000 new Republican votes, about 20,000 new Democratic votes), while Progressives boasted about 30,000 new female votes. It is entirely possible that these increased numbers of ballots mask some conversion; for example, that a number of women who had voted Republican in 1920 defected to the Progressives in 1924. Yet, the total number of new female ballots cast in Massachusetts in 1924 was only about 100,000, very close to the total number of new major and Progressive Party votes cast by women (50,000 Republican + 20,000 Democratic + 30,000 Progressive = 90,000). While conversion was likely an important component of the male Progressive vote in Massachusetts, it appears that most of the female Progressive vote can be attributed to new mobilization, as female major party voters maintained (and expanded) their support from 1920.

While we generally find more evidence of conversion among men than women, Illinois is distinctive as a state where mobilization was likely an important mechanism for both female and male voters. In Illinois, both major parties gained female voters in 1924 (a total of about 100,000 across the two parties), while Progressives boasted about 90,000 new female votes. It is certainly possible – indeed, likely – that some previous female major party voters defected to the Progressives and were compensated for by major party mobilization exceeding the 90,000 reported in Figures 6.8 and 6.9. But given 200,000 new female voters overall in 1924, it appears likely that most of the female Progressive Party vote came from new voters, and not from women defecting from previous major party support. The surprising feature of Illinois was that there are also an additional 175,000 male voters. Given the small net gains among Democrats (3,500 more male votes in 1924) and small net losses among Republicans (25,000 fewer male votes in 1924), the Progressive surge in Illinois was almost certainly due mainly to mobilization, rather than conversion, among men, contrary to the pattern in other states.

The expectation that women would be more likely to support candidates associated with Progressivism derives not only from the association of women with that movement, but also from a general expectation that women would be less loyal partisans, both due to their inherent nature as well as their less extensive political experiences. Thus far we have little evidence to support this expectation in 1924. We have seen that female voters were not more likely than male voters to support the Progressive Party over the traditional major parties, that Progressives owed far more of their ballots to men than to women, and that conversion likely played a larger role in generating Progressive votes among men than it did women.

Another way to consider party loyalty is to examine the probability of defection from major party support. We focus on Minnesota and Iowa, the states with the highest level of Progressive vote share. Examining rates of (estimated) defection suggest that in 1924, men, rather than women, may have been more likely to defect from major party loyalty. In Minnesota, Republicans lost about 85,000 male votes, which is 23 percent of the votes we estimate men cast for the Republican presidential candidate in 1920. In contrast, Republicans lost about 20,000 female votes in 1924, just 9 percent of the votes women cast for the Republican candidate in 1920. In other words – keeping in mind the various caveats we have articulated – as many as one-quarter of men who voted Republican in 1920 defected to support La Follette in 1924 compared to less than 10 percent of women; more than 90 percent of simulations are consistent with the conclusion that defection from Republicans was higher among men than women in Minnesota. The comparable figures for defection among men and women who cast Democratic ballots in Minnesota in 1920 are even more impressive; we estimate that an astounding 63 percent of men and 55 percent of women defected from previous Democratic support in 1924. However, unlike defection among Republicans, the proportion of simulations consistent with the conclusion that male Democratic defection rates exceeded female does not meet our thresholds for confidence. Thus we can only conclude that among Democratic voters, men and women were equally likely to defect.

In Iowa, the state with the second highest rate of Progressive support, we estimate a Republican defection rate among men of about 20 percent compared to 7 percent among women; more than 80 percent of simulations are consistent with the conclusion that the male Republican defection rate exceeded the female. Among Democratic voters in 1920, those figures are 32 percent for men and 23 percent for women, but the simulations suggest we cannot be confident of a gender difference.

Although Progressive support was smaller in other states, we also find that more than 90 percent of the simulations are consistent with greater Republican defection to the Progressives among men than women in Illinois, Kansas, and Massachusetts, and more than 80 percent are consistent with greater Democratic defection among men than women in Illinois and Massachusetts. While, again, we cannot assume that every "lost" Republican and Democratic vote was cast for La Follette in 1924, even in these states where La Follette had such exceptional success, these results cast serious doubts on the claim that women were less loyal partisans than men in 1924.

Conclusion: Progressive Disappointment

In many ways the 1924 election is similar to 1920 in that much of the instability and change was due to the behavior of long-enfranchised male voters rather than that of inexperienced female voters: The relatively large male electorate was a source of disproportionate support for third-party candidate La Follette and the source of substantial defections from the Republican ticket. Contrary to popular conceptions of women as natural Progressive allies, both men and women gave historically high levels of support to La Follette. In no sample state (except possibly Virginia) were women more supportive of La Follette than men. Rather we find that men were actually more likely to support Progressives than were women in at least two Midwestern states. Women – long associated with the causes and organizations of the Progressive movement and supposedly characterized by weaker party allegiance – were either slightly more reluctant or no more likely to register their support for La Follette, contrary to the long-held expectations of many. These results are broadly consistent with *observed* female and male vote choice in Illinois in 1916 and 1920 – where combined female support for the Prohibition and Socialist parties was roughly three-quarters the level of male support for the same parties. In at least two states, then, Progressives would have done better had women not been enfranchised, an ironic outcome for a movement at the forefront of suffrage advocacy for so long.

Thus, the hopes of the Progressive reformers that the enfranchisement of women would transform the electorate and usher in Progressive victories went unfulfilled in 1924. However great women's activism and preference for Progressive causes such as temperance and social reform might have been, as voters women acted more like party regulars than ideologues, maintaining and expanding their support for the two major parties. Perhaps the specific form that the Progressive Party movement took in 1924 made Progressives less uniquely attractive to women than we might expect; the 1924 Progressive Party platform focused on economic issues, political reform, and especially the plight of farmers, not moral reform and Prohibition (Rosenstone, Behr, and Lazarus 1996). This outcome is somewhat surprising but entirely consistent with the 1920 findings – in one-party Republican states in the Midwest women reinforce and increase the Republican plurality. Thus rather than disrupting the system, the entrance of women voters tended to reinforce major party dominance at the state level.

The results of the election were shaped by the participation of women. For the most part, women's contribution was to shore up support for the major parties, especially the Republicans, and reduce the Progressive Party surge. For example, without female voters, Illinois would have witnessed massive third-party mobilization and consistent defection from both the Republican and (to a lesser extent) Democratic parties. In Illinois the Republicans lost nearly 26,000 male voters and third-party candidates picked up nearly 180,000 male voters. By contrast, the Republicans gained 63,000 female voters and third-party candidates picked up only about 92,000 female voters. Thus in Illinois, as we observed in other states previously, female voters stabilized the electorate and dampened the third-party surge.

That party loyalty is also reflected in the processes that generated Progressive support. Many expected women to be weaker partisans and less loyal to the major parties – because of their lesser knowledge and experience, because women were believed more committed to ideals than to (corrupt) parties, because of the Progressive critique of partisanship – yet we find evidence that women were more stable sources of major party support than were men. Although we cannot track conversion and mobilization definitively with our estimates, the changes between 1920 and 1924 suggest patterns in which the more numerous male Progressive votes tended to come from conversion while most of women's Progressive votes appeared to result from new voter mobilization. We also find evidence that men were substantially more likely to defect from 1920 Republican (and in some cases, Democratic) party vote choice than were women. In one sense, we should not be surprised: Male mobilization was already significant in many states, so there were far fewer men available to be newly mobilized. Indeed, given the level of male mobilization, many weakly partisan men were likely already voting in 1920, and thus available for conversion, while perhaps weakly partisan women stayed home in 1920, and were available for mobilization by the Progressives in 1924. Nonetheless, to the extent we can conclude women who cast major party votes in 1920 were more likely to do so again in 1924 than were men, these findings undermine expectations that women would be less dependable partisans.

Taken together, the 1920 and 1924 results tell a consistent story. When it came to turnout, women acted as peripheral voters. Long denied access to the institution of voting, and still hampered by norms against women's political participation, women behaved as expected of inexperienced voters: Overall turnout lagged behind men's (as we have consistently assumed), and women's turnout was more sensitive to shifts in the political context: Where competition (and thus mobilization, salience, and interest) was high, women's electoral participation increased to a greater extent than men's did. Similarly, where restrictive electoral laws hampered turnout, it did so more for women than it did for men. At the same time, we emphasize, as we did in Chapter 5, that the other conclusion we can draw from women's greater responsiveness to context is that all women were not so apolitical that they would not participate under any circumstances. Where the context was conducive to turnout, women were capable of significant mobilization – we estimate nearly (or more than) half of eligible women turned out to vote in Iowa, Kansas, and Missouri in 1924. There was evidence that experience also facilitated turnout, as women's turnout increased over 1920 in a number of states.

When women did vote, however, they did not behave as expected of disinterested and inexperienced peripheral voters. Rather than swinging to the party most advantaged by current electoral context, or defecting from the traditional parties to support the Progressive candidate, female voters were more likely to remain stalwarts of the major parties, at least compared to their long-enfranchised male counterparts. Women were either as likely to support the Progressives than were men, or – in the Midwest – they remained more loyal to the dominant Republican Party than did men. Our analysis of changes in the ballots cast for each party over time suggest that defection from major party loyalty was more prevalent among male voters than it was among women, despite the fact that in most states women had only had one (or at most two) previous presidential elections in which to reinforce their partisan loyalties at the ballot box. While women had been denied access to the act of voting, they had not been denied access to political information or the opportunity to develop political preferences. Thus, rather than as a source of instability (as we might expect of inexperienced and ill-informed new voters), women were a source of major party stability in 1924.

We have argued that conversion of previous major party voters played a significant role (although not always as significant as the mobilization of new voters) in generating Progressive Party support in 1924. We acknowledge it is a bit odd to use the term "conversion" in the case of the Progressive Party; conversion connotes a certain permanent, or at least long-term, shift in loyalties (such as we will observe for the Democratic Party in the 1930s), but history tells us that Progressive Party support was fleeting. For consistency with our analysis in other chapters, we use the terms conversion and defection in specific ways here, but we recognize that the surge in Progressive Party support in 1924 would be accurately understood by most as a temporary defection that was quickly corrected, as we will see in Chapter 7.

This does not mean that the Progressive surge was unimportant, however. The success of third-party movements often augurs a coming partisan realignment. By giving voice to causes and concerns not represented by the two major parties, third-party movements have, throughout American history, reflected increasing discontent with the options provided by the two-party system (Rosenstone, Behr, and Lazarus 1996). What would become the New Deal realignment got underway just four years after La Fallotte and the Progressives secured 17 percent of the vote. The presence of a large group of inexperienced and undermobilized voters would seem to suggest that the electorate could be particularly vulnerable to disruption and change. Our results, however, indicate that women were less, not more, willing to abandon the two major parties in 1924. The 1928 election provides an opportunity to confirm this result – as the New Deal realignment begins, would women continue to be rooted in the patterns of partisan attachment that characterized the "System of 1896" or receptive to the emerging Democratic majority?

ILLUSTRATION 7.1. League of Women Voters Get Out the Vote campaign, Anne Arundel county, Maryland, 1928. Collection of the League of Women Voters of the United States.

7

Female Voters and the "Rum and Religion" Election of 1928

The election of 1928 merits our attention as the first of a series of elections that led to the durable New Deal realignment and as an election characterized by an idiosyncratic surge in popular interest and passion fueled by the issues of "rum and religion" (Silva 1962). Resurgent controversy over Prohibition and the nation's first Catholic major party nominee stimulated a large increase in turnout in the North (among urban immigrants) and in the South (among native-born Protestants). New voters in the North were overwhelmingly Democratic, but opposition to Prohibition overlapped with religious bigotry to create a formidable Republican challenge for Democratic nominee Al Smith in the West and South (Peel and Donnelly 1931). Republican nominee Herbert Hoover ultimately captured more than 60 percent of the popular vote in the last demonstration of Republican hegemony before the emergence of the Democratic coalition that would dominate much of the twentieth century.

The impact of women in 1928 was the subject of considerable speculation, both at the time and by later scholars. Many expected that the central issues of the campaign – Prohibition and religion – were of particular interest to women and would send unprecedented numbers of women to the polls. Commentators and scholars claimed that urban and immigrant women, particularly Catholics, who had lagged behind their rural and native-born sisters in adapting to their new political right, would be motivated to come out to support Smith, their religious and ethnic compatriot. At the same time, rural and native-born Protestant women, long-standing Prohibition advocates, were believed to have been alarmed by the prospect of a Smith presidency, and thus especially motivated to support Hoover in opposition to the Democratic candidate. Indeed, some contemporary and later accounts specifically implicate Republican support among women in the Hoover landslide (see Lichtman 1979).

In this chapter, we review these expectations and then turn to our unique estimates to evaluate them. Our research suggests that both accounts are, in fact, quite accurate – to an extent. Many women entered the electorate for the first time in 1928. In almost every one of our sample states, female turnout increases by at least 5 points, and in the Northeast, turnout gains among women exceed 10 points in Connecticut and 15 points in Massachusetts – a truly extraordinary increase in mobilization. As previous scholars expected, women in different states responded in distinct ways to the presidential options in 1928. In Northeastern states with large immigrant populations, such as Connecticut and Massachusetts, sharp increases in turnout among women, and in Democratic support among women, contribute to large Democratic gains from 1924 to 1928. Outside of the Northeast, women in traditionally Republican states remained strong supporters of the Republican presidential candidate: In some states adding to Republican margins over 1924, but in others states remaining in the Republican column despite a shift in electoral support toward the Democrats. In the traditionally Democratic South and Border states, women moved sharply to the GOP, consistent with an expectation that Smith was a particularly unattractive candidate to Southern women.

Yet, for the most part, women's turnout and vote choice patterns did not distinguish them from men in 1928. Indeed, owing to turnout differences, changed electoral patterns owe more to male voters overall than they do to female. In every state in which women experienced turnout gains, men's turnout increased to the same extent. In every state that shifted Democratic, Democrats netted more – and often far more – new votes from men than from women. In all but one state that became more Republican, men were responsible for more new Republican votes than were women. The election of 1928 was characterized by considerable disruption of previous patterns, but it was not female voters who drove or accounted for most of the changes. Long-standing accounts that attribute electoral volatility during this period to less experienced and poorly socialized women (notably, Converse 1972, 1974) are not supported by our analysis. Rather, we find men to be as, or more, responsible for the dramatic partisan changes underway in 1928.

The Election of 1928

The incumbent Republican Party entered the 1928 election with a number of advantages, particularly widespread prosperity (Peel and Donnelly 1931). Several Republicans pursued the party's nomination when Coolidge declined to run for reelection. The selection of Commerce Secretary Herbert Hoover, yet another candidate more friendly to business interests than to agriculture, was indicative of the extent to which economic elites had come to dominate the GOP (Hicks 1960). In the Democratic Party, on the other hand, the urban interests that comprised an increasingly large component of the party's coalition in the 1920s were finally able to wrest control of the party. New York governor Al Smith embodied the emerging face of the Democratic Party (and in some ways, of the United States): urban, immigrant, Catholic, and wet (i.e., anti-Prohibition). Smith was extraordinarily polarizing; both within his own party and without, he was either vilified or idolized.

In general, the parties' nominees differed only slightly on many basic policy issues, such as economic regulation. The parties did offer a clear choice on the central issues of the campaign: "rum and religion" (Silva 1962). Political historians debate the extent to which religion or Prohibition was the overriding issue of the election (see Burner 1986). Al Smith's Catholicism and opposition to Prohibition were only aspects of a set of qualities – Irish, urban, immigrant, machine partisan – that aroused great distrust and opposition among many Americans, particularly Southerners (an important Democratic stronghold) and farmers (Fuchs 1971; Peel and Donnelly 1931). Iconic journalist Walter Lippmann remarked in 1927 that opposition to Smith was "inspired by the feeling that the clamorous life of the city should not be acknowledged as the American ideal" (quoted in Peel and Donnelly 1931, 99). Influential newspaper editor William Allen White described Smith's candidacy as a threat to "the whole Puritan civilization, which has built a sturdy, orderly nation" (quoted in Fuchs 1971, 2596).

In one sense, the dominant political outcome in 1928 – the clear electoral monopoly of the Republican Party – represented a continuation from the previous two elections. In other ways, however, 1928 did augur important national shifts. The combination of anti-Smith sentiment in the South and effective pro-Smith Democratic mobilization in the North resulted in large expansion of the electorate – an increase of nearly 7 million voters nationwide over 1924. As a result, turnout nationwide increased from 44 percent to 52 percent, an increase in the total ballots cast for president from 29 million to nearly 37 million. This remarkable expansion in participation in only four years had the potential to radically change the outcome of the election, but the overall Republican advantage over the Democrats was little changed from 1924 and the Republican plurality nationwide remained higher than 6 million votes for the third consecutive election.

This apparent stability in the Republican vote share masks considerable volatility, however. In retrospect, the election of 1928 contained the seeds of the realignment that would, four years later, catapult Democrats into majority party status for at least the next forty years. Smith made significant inroads into the Republican-dominated North, particularly in counties with large Catholic and immigrant populations (Hicks 1960; see also Harris 1954; MacRae and Meldrum 1960). Capitalizing on a revolt among dry southerners, Hoover realized gains in the traditionally Solid South in 1928 (indeed, Hoover carried more than half of the formerly Confederate states), but that support was fleeting. In contrast, Smith's mobilization of immigrant, urban, and Catholic voters, solidified by Franklin Roosevelt in the 1930s, would permanently reshape the Democratic Party coalition (Degler 1964; Harris 1954; Hicks 1960). One effect of this movement – away from the Democrats in the South and away from Republicans in the North – was to sharply decrease the regional variation in the 1928 presidential vote compared to that which had dominated the previous electoral era (Schantz 1992). These developments were not sufficient to elect Al Smith in 1928, but they laid the foundation for the realignment under Roosevelt in the 1930s.

Expectations for Female Voters in 1928

Many accounts of the election of 1928 identify women as an important part of the surge in electoral participation. *The New York Times* went so far as to claim that "This year the President of the United States will probably be chosen by women" (McCormick 1928, quoted in Greenlee 2014, 27). Both parties once again exerted considerable effort to appeal to female voters specifically, with Republicans making particularly strong efforts that the Democrats could only attempt to match. The Republican campaign drew notice from *The New York Times* as being "unusually segregated on gender lines" (quoted in Harvey 1998, 132). In reaching out to women, Republicans highlighted Hoover's work on behalf of housewives, his support for Prohibition, and his commitment to peace (Greenlee 2014;

Harvey 1998). Gender, ethnicity, and religion intersected in important ways. *The New York Times* recounted a prominent Republican addressing the Women's Republican Club in Springfield, saying, "I cannot say very much of Mrs. Smith, but if the contest were between Mrs. Hoover and Mrs. Smith..." The writer noted that "There, [the speaker] adroitly left his hearers to draw their own inferences," the presumption being that an Irish Catholic women did not fit his listeners' image of an appropriate First Lady (quoted in Peel and Donnelly 1931, 100). Other Republican writers described Mrs. Hoover as "American through and through." As Peel and Donnelly (1931, 84) note, "The implication was that Mrs. Smith lacked the essential Nordic background, and was somewhat deficient in those social graces and intellectual attainments which characterized the wife of the Republican nominee."

Democrats also appealed directly to women through women's offices and campaign committees, female speakers, and gender-specific appeals. As with the Republicans, the Democratic campaign emphasized women's traditional roles. Democratic nominee Al Smith hailed mothers as "one of our greatest national assets" (quoted in Harvey 1998, 134), and highlighted his stances on such issues as protective labor laws. Even his controversial stance on Prohibition was reframed to appeal to women, with Democrats imploring women to "Think clearly on the Prohibition issue" (Greenlee 2014; Peel and Donnelly 1931). Weekly radio broadcasts sponsored by the League of Women Voters were believed to increase political interest among women, particularly in remote and rural areas (Andersen 1996).

Contemporary observers expected that the central issues of that campaign – Prohibition and religion – would mobilize women on both sides at levels far exceeding previous elections. In *The New York Times*, for example, headlines such as "Forecasts Big Vote by Women of State" (October 7, 1928) and "This Year's Woman Vote to Set a High Record" (October 21, 1928) were common (although to be fair, journalists in search of news seemed to expect that every election would be a breakthrough year for female voters). Many states reported increases in female registration.[1]

[1] For example: "43,000,000 Have Qualified for Election Nov. 6. [AP story]" *Hartford (CT) Daily Courant*, October 29, 1928; "Twice as Many Women as Men Register Daily." *The Duluth (MN) News Tribune*, September 20, 1928; "Women Will Decide How Missouri Goes." *The New York Times*, October 27, 1928; "Women Play an Important Part in Presidential Campaign." *Santa Fe New Mexican*, October 20, 1928; "What'll Women Do? Is Chicago Election Enigma." *Chicago Daily Tribune*, October 4, 1928.

Analysis immediately following the election ratified these expectations. *The New York Times* reported that

The women's vote was undoubtedly an important factor. They took a keener interest in the issues than ever before, and they swelled the registration to unprecedented figures. The great majority of women were intent chiefly on saving prohibition, but they also gave their support to Hoover, the executive who enlisted their cooperation in food conservation during the war.[2]

Explaining the narrow Republican win in Texas, Peel and Donnelly (1931) emphasize the women's vote in particular (along with rain in the Smith counties, rebellion in the western sections, and a lukewarm endorsement from state leaders). A Democratic Party leader in Minnesota reported his assessment of the impact of female voters in a January 1929 letter to then-New York Governor Franklin D. Roosevelt:

Our worst opposition in this Midwestern country was the women. Republican farmers by the thousands voted for Governor Smith, but their wives and daughters and the great majority of single women voted against Governor Smith, largely because of his stand on the liquor issue – that is particularly true in Minnesota, Iowa, North and South Dakota. *I believe if it were not for the Nineteenth Amendment, giving women the right to vote – in other words, if the election had been left to men – Governor Smith would have been elected.* You understand, however, that I am not blaming the women except that they were made panic stricken, partly because of the liquor issue, and party on account of Governor Smith's religion (emphasis ours).[3]

Many later scholars accepted a significant mobilization of women as part of the conventional wisdom surrounding the presidential election of 1928 (e.g., Matthews 1992). Party realignment theorist Walter Dean Burnham (1974, 1015) writes, "it is widely agreed that female turnout did not begin to move much closer to male participation rates in the United States until the 1928–1936 realignment sequence." Fellow realignment scholar James L. Sundquist (1983, 192) agrees: "The 1928 increase [in turnout] was probably due mainly to the motivation of many women who, though enfranchised in 1920, had never voted until the spirited contest of 1928 brought them to the polls."

Consistent with contemporaries who expected most women would support Hoover, scholars describe native-born and rural women as especially mobilized against Smith and in defense of Prohibition and Protestantism

[2] "Fisher Analyzes Hoover's Victory." *The New York Times*, November 25, 1928, p. II, 1.

[3] Letter. Thomas E. Cashman to Franklin D. Roosevelt. January 7, 1929. *Minnesota Pre-Convention. Democratic National Campaign Committee Correspondence, 1928–1933.* Franklin D. Roosevelt Library.

in 1928 (Andersen 1996; Burner 1986). While perhaps mobilized earlier and in large numbers than urban and immigrant women, rural and native-born women were certainly not at their limit for mobilization in the mid-1920s. Defending against the specter of an Al Smith presidency may have brought out many previously inactive women, particularly when a well-organized Republican Party specifically sought their votes.

At the same time, many point out that the strong mobilization of native-born and rural women was likely counterbalanced by a surge in turnout among immigrant and urban women. Such women were believed to have been slow to mobilize (compared to native-born Protestant women) in 1920 and 1924, but finally stimulated by their enthusiasm for Smith in 1928 (Andersen 1979; Burner 1986). According to Jeffries (1979, 21), Democrats realized "spectacular" gains among new immigrants in Connecticut, "many of them, women especially, first-time voters." Burnham (1974, 1015) claims, "This 1928–1936 influx of new voters was heavily concentrated among working-class and women – particularly ethnic women – voters in large industrial states like Pennsylvania and Illinois." Lubell (1952, 40) asserts

> Smith made women's suffrage a reality for the urban poor. In better income families, women started voting in 1920 as soon as they were granted the privilege; but among the urban masses the tradition that a woman's place was in the home still held strong until 1928. That year in Massachusetts (which Smith carried along with Rhode Island) the outpouring of women lifted the number of voters by 40 per cent over 1924. The turnout in Boston was 44 per cent heavier.

Empirical verification of these claims has been limited. Focusing on ethnically homogenous neighborhoods in Boston, Gamm (1986; see Chapter 3) observes no particular surge among Italian women, African American women, or Yankee women in 1928, but does find that mobilization of women explains increasing Democratic support in Jewish and Irish neighborhoods. Italian women and African American women were mobilized only in later elections – 1932 and 1936. Consistent with accounts suggesting the earlier mobilization of native-born Protestants, Gamm finds Yankee women had already been integrated into electoral politics in 1920 and 1924.

Most of the claims about the mobilization of women in 1928 rely on data that are rather thin (a report in *The New York Times* about increased female registration in Catholic precincts in Chicago, for example; Burner 1986), limited to one city (e.g., Boston in the case of both Huthmacher 1959 and Gamm 1986), or in some cases, are made without reference to established fact (e.g., Lubell 1952). All of the claims we have located regarding 1928 ultimately cite to just a small number of sources, each based on a small amount of data, data of questionable interpretation, or no data at all. As later authors cite the earlier authors, and each other, small observations in earlier work becomes generalized conventional wisdom (e.g., Burnham 1974; Sundquist 1983). Given the challenges of data collection during this era (see Chapters 3 and 4), a few scholars have done the best they can to draw reasonable and cautious inferences from the available data, but – given the state of the evidence on which the conventional wisdom is based – to say that the impact of women on the election of 1928 is a settled question would be a considerable overstatement. Our estimates allow us a closer and broader look at the impact of female voters during the momentous election of 1928 than has been previously possible.

The Mobilization of Women in 1928

Previous commentators are correct that women's turnout rose considerably in 1928. In our sample, the rate of turnout among women grew to 46 percent, an 8-point gain over 1924, when women's turnout averaged 38 percent. Yet male turnout also posted an 8-point gain, increasing from 67 percent in 1924 to 75 percent in 1928, contrary to accounts that attributed turnout gains in 1928 largely to women (e.g., Sundquist 1983). As a result, the turnout gender gap in our sample remained steady at about 29 points.

Turnout was high in nearly every state. For the first time, the turnout of women (again, conservatively estimated as the proportion of the age-eligible population) exceeded 50 percent in nearly half of the sample states (see Figure 7.1). Democratic-dominated Oklahoma experienced the largest turnout gender gap in the sample (more than 37 points), as it had in 1920, while competitive Missouri again boasted the smallest gap between male and female turnout rates (24 points).

The level of male mobilization outside of the South in 1928 was truly remarkable – nearing or exceeding 80 percent in every state in our sample. Indeed, while we note the persistent and significant gender gap in turnout, it is worth emphasizing that women's level of electoral mobilization suffers only by comparison to the extraordinary mobilization of men during this era. In 1980, the first presidential election in which female turnout exceeds male turnout (US Census 1982), overall turnout was 59 percent, a level of mobilization our estimates suggest women in many of our states were approaching in 1928, and indeed, consistent with levels observed

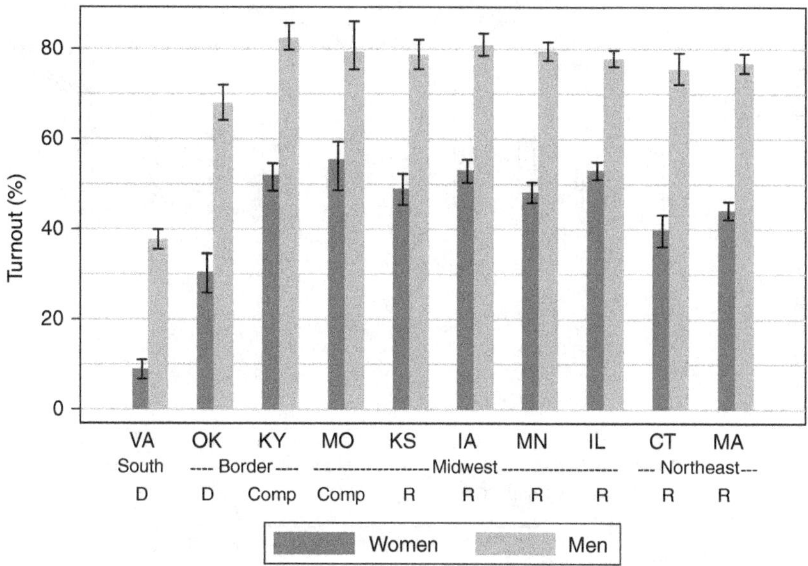

FIGURE 7.1. Turnout of women and men, 1928.

among women in competitive Missouri and Kentucky as early as 1920. Given how widespread electoral mobilization was in this period, it is appropriate to acknowledge that women were less mobilized than men. At the same time, we also note how well mobilized new women voters were by the – admittedly low – standards of the modern era.

Were women responsible for the uptick in turnout in 1928? Figure 7.2 reveals that women's turnout increased over previous years in all but one state. The increase in turnout varied considerably by region and state, ranging from 16.8 points in Massachusetts (a 60 percent increase!) to negligible changes in Iowa and Kansas. The point estimates indicate women's turnout grew more than men's in five of our ten sample states, and fell or grew less then men's elsewhere, but the credible intervals around those point estimates are so wide that we can only conclude with any confidence that men's and women's rates of turnout responded similarly to the "rum and religion" election. Contrary to expectations, women were not uniquely mobilized in 1928. Rather, in terms of percentage point increases in turnout, both men and women were mobilized by the 1928 election and largely in the same way and to the same extent.

For both men and women, the increase in turnout in our Northeastern states (Connecticut and Massachusetts) stands out as particularly stunning. As we will see (and as others have documented), Al Smith's candidacy

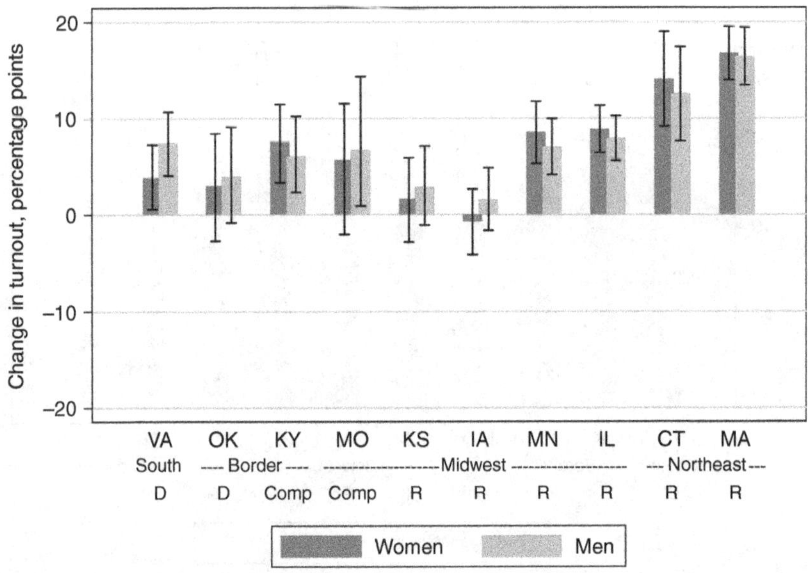

FIGURE 7.2. Change in turnout of women and men, 1924 to 1928.

transformed electoral politics in the Northeast, starting with a dramatic increase in voter mobilization (Burnham 1967). These states boasted large immigrant communities: In both Connecticut and Massachusetts, the percentage of the population that was first- or second-generation immigrant was an astounding 65 percent in 1930 (US Census 1932). Contrary to the expectations of some that women, particularly immigrant women, would be responsible for much of the increase in turnout in those states (e.g., Burnham 1974), our estimates suggest that in these heavily immigrant states, both men and women increased their rate of turnout and to the same degree.

Impact of State Context

With the massive partisan and electoral changes underway in 1928, did the political and legal context continue to weigh more heavily on the turnout decisions of women compared to men?

Partisan Context. In some ways, the impact of partisan context remains similar to what we observed in 1920 and 1924 (see Figure 7.3). Competitive states continue to boast the highest rates of turnout among both men and women compared to one-party states, with one-party Democratic states retaining distinctively low turnout levels. However, unlike 1920 and 1924, the only real turnout differences – for women and for men – are between

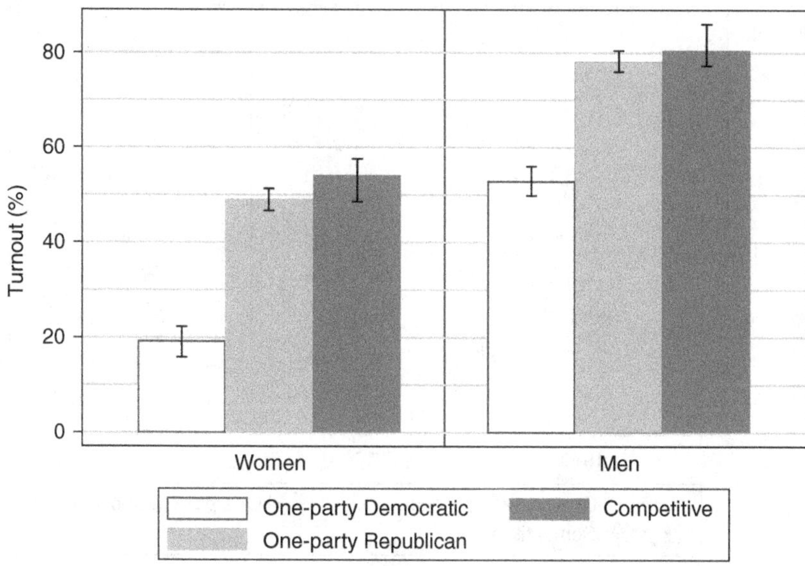

FIGURE 7.3. Partisan context and the turnout of women and men, 1928.

the one-party Democratic states and the two other partisan categories. The turnout of women in competitive states was indistinguishable from that of women in one-party Republican states, and the same can be said of men in those two categories of states. The difference between competitive and one-party Democratic states remains stark. Pooling states by partisan context, 100 percent of the simulations are consistent with women's and men's turnout in competitive states and one-party Republican states exceeding that in one-party Democratic states. Consistent with the estimates from 1920 and 1924, the effect of competition was stronger among women: A 28-point difference for men (a 52 percent increase in competitive states over one-party Democratic) versus a 35-point difference for women (a nearly 300 percent increase over turnout in one-party Democratic states). Nearly 90 percent of the simulations are consistent with the conclusion that the difference in turnout is larger for women than for men. Thus, women's turnout continues to be more affected by party context, as the peripheral voter hypothesis predicts.

The disappearing gap between turnout in competitive and one-party Republican states is one of many indicators that the 1928 election disrupted established state-level partisan context in ways that previous elections did not. As we explain in Chapter 4, we use a measure of partisan context that taps partisan state legislative lead for 1914 through 1930

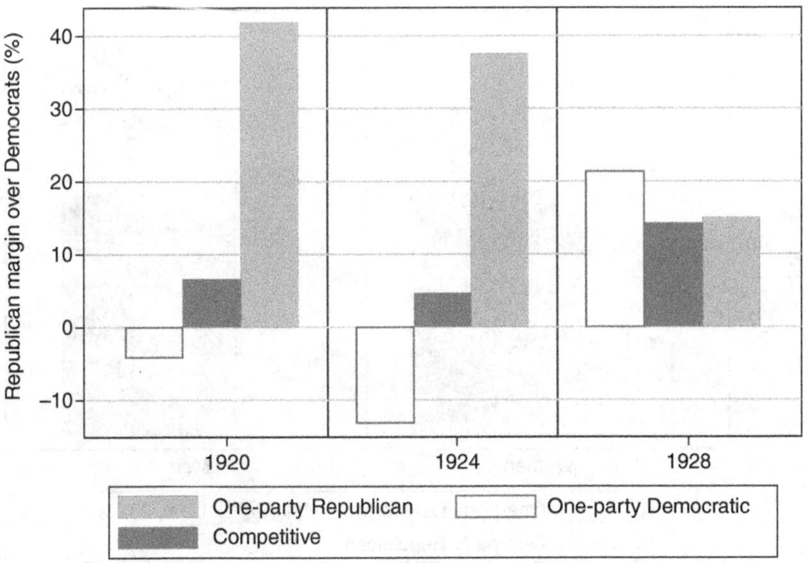

FIGURE 7.4. Partisan context and the Republican margin of victory, 1920 to 1928.

to gauge the grassroots partisan context in which women were politically socialized and first cast ballots. Those state categorizations are fairly accurate descriptions of presidential party competition in the states through the 1924 presidential election; that is, Republican presidential candidates tend to win handily in one-party Republican states, while presidential outcomes were closer in competitive states. Electoral change in 1928 is sufficient to break down those associations. Figure 7.4 reports the average margin of victory for the Republican presidential candidate in each of our categories of states in 1920, 1924, and 1928.

Clearly, 1928 is a major break from what came before. The change in Republican margin of victory in our one-party Democratic states is stunning, moving from a Republican disadvantage in 1920 and 1924 to the largest Republican advantage of states in our partisan categories in 1928. In 1920 and 1924, the Republican margin of victory in competitive states was relatively small, particularly compared to the *massive* Republican advantage in one-party Republican states. The Republican advantage in previously competitive states more than doubles in 1928 over past years. At the same time, the Republican advantage in previously one-party Republican states in 1928 falls by more than half its level in 1920 and 1924. The change in the one-party Republican states is particularly dramatic in the Northeast. In our four Midwestern one-party

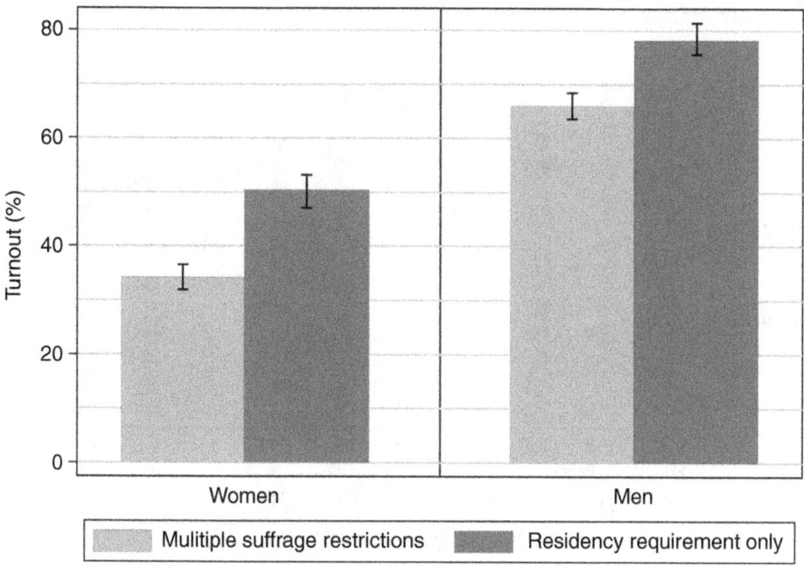

FIGURE 7.5. Legal context and the turnout of women and men, 1928.

Republican states, the Republican advantage in 1928 is 18.4 points; in our two Northeastern states, it is a mere 1.3 points.

Legal Context. Legal restrictions continue to have a large effect on women's turnout (Figure 7.5). Women's turnout was 16.3 points (32 percent) lower in states with multiple restrictions compared to those with a residency requirement only, while the similar difference among men is only 12.2 points (16 percent); more than 95 percent of simulations are consistent with the conclusion that female turnout is more affected by the legal context than is male. The relationship between legal context and turnout is smaller in 1928 than in previous elections, however. In 1920 and 1924 the difference in women's turnout between states with few and many restrictions was consistently around 25 points, compared to about 16 points in 1928. For men the difference was around 19 points, compared to about 12 points in 1928. Nonetheless, the expectation that women's turnout would be more hampered by legal restrictions than men's continues to be borne out in 1928.

The Partisan Mobilization of Women in 1928

The 1928 election represented an important break from the past as previously competitive and one-party Democratic states moved toward the

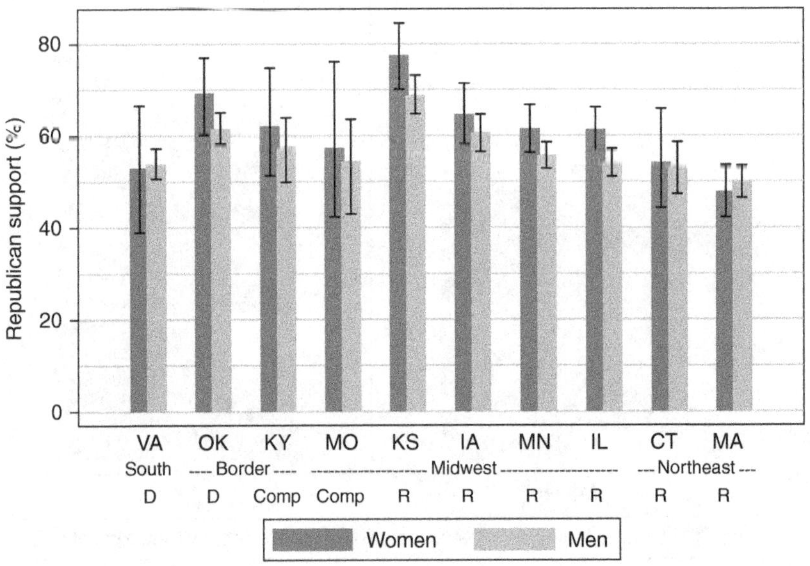

FIGURE 7.6. Republican vote share of women and men, 1928.

GOP and previous Republican strongholds became competitive or even shifted to the other side. What role did women play in this transformation? Overall, both men and women in our sample continued to favor the GOP. As in past years, women were slightly more Republican in their vote choice than were men. In our ten sample states, the Republican vote share averaged 56 percent for men, and 60 percent for women, a difference of 4 points. This was a slight increase in Republican vote share for both men and women over 1924 – a year characterized by a significant third-party vote – up from 53 percent for men (3-point increase) and 58 percent for women (2-point increase).

The state-level data (summarized in Figure 7.6) reveal that this increase in Republican support occurred over a wide range of states. Both of the traditionally competitive states – Democratic-leaning Kentucky and Republican-leaning Missouri – went Republican, and in both, men and women voted Republican to a similar degree. Amazingly, both of the traditionally one-party Democratic states in our sample (Virginia and Oklahoma) moved into the Republican column in 1928; Republican gains in Oklahoma are particularly strong. There is some indication that women in Southern/Border states may have played a distinctive role in this unusual partisan switch; while in Virginia, men and women voted Republican to a similar degree, in Oklahoma, almost 90 percent of simulations (87 percent) are consistent with greater Republican vote share among women compared to men. As many expected, we have evidence that Southern women were particularly mobilized to vote against Smith and for Hoover in 1928.

At first glance, the one-party Republican Midwest (Minnesota, Iowa, Kansas, and Illinois) shows the most stability, staying firmly on the side of the GOP. As we have seen in 1920 and 1924, women in those states continue to be more mobilized by the locally dominant Republican Party than are men, but the differences appear to be narrowing: Using the criteria outlined in previous chapters, women's Republican vote share exceeds men's in over 90 percent of our simulations in only one sample state, Illinois. About 88 percent of simulations are consistent with greater Republican support among female voters in Kansas and Iowa. In 1920, Illinois, Iowa, and Kansas met the 90 percent threshold; in 1924, all four of the one-party Republican states in the Midwest did. Not only does our confidence in a partisan gender difference in these states decline for 1928, but the size of the differences also diminishes significantly between 1924 and 1928.

Finally, traditionally one-party Republican states in the Northeast moved strongly toward the Democrats – Massachusetts actually falls into the Democratic column, and Connecticut nearly does so as well. In those two states, men and women's Republican vote share is indistinguishable, suggesting a similar response to Smith from female and male voters.

Because of the significant third party showing in 1924, tracing the process of change requires attention to shifts in both Republican and Democratic Party vote share, reported in Figure 7.7. Men and women are moving in similar ways in terms of the size of the change in both Democratic and Republican vote share, and the credible intervals are sufficiently wide that we can only conclude with any confidence that they do so to a similar extent.

As we have seen, organizing our states by grassroots party context (one-party or competitive), as we have done in previous chapters, is complicated by the changes underway in 1928. Diminishing variation in Republican support is obvious – while in previous years state-level party context strongly predicted presidential vote choice, in 1928, only roughly 3 to 8 percentage points separate male and female voters across the various partisan contexts (see Figure 7.8). The credible intervals indicate that Republican vote share – for both men and women – is indistinguishable across our competitive, one-party Democratic, and Midwestern one-party Republican states in 1928. Only male and female voters in Northeastern

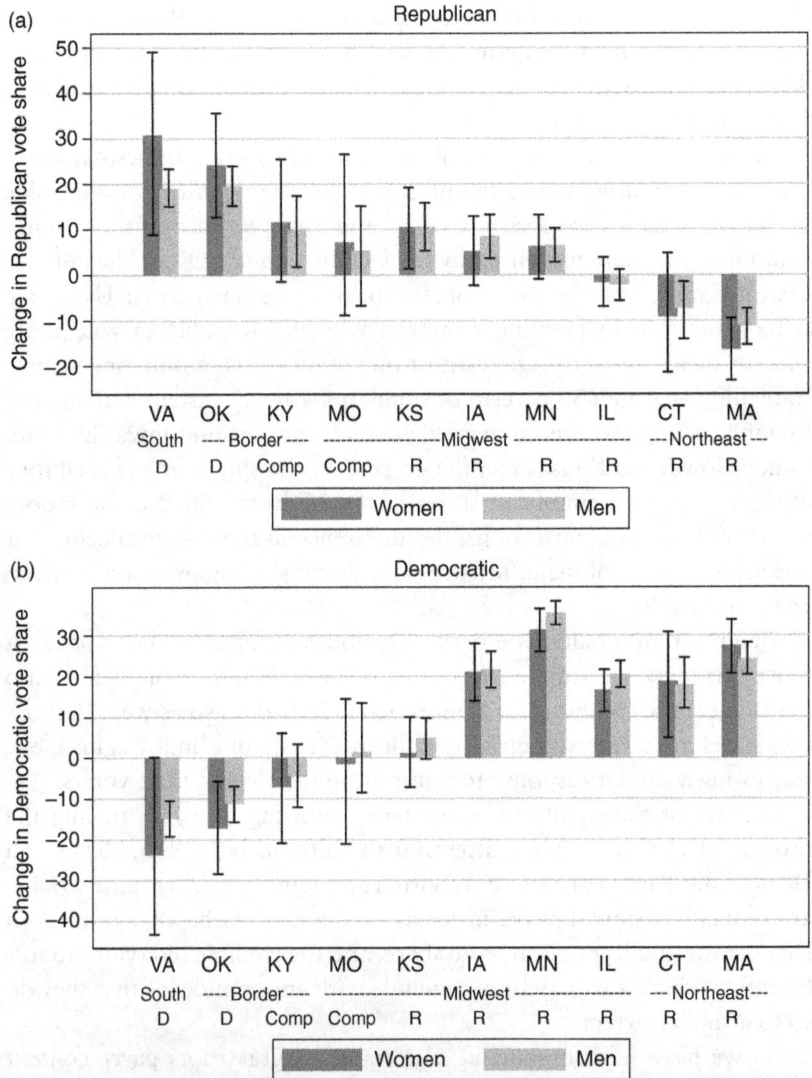

FIGURE 7.7. Change in partisan vote share of women and men, 1924 to 1928.

one-party Republican states are distinctive – voting *more* Democratic than men and women, respectively, in the other states, including states traditionally dominated by the Democratic Party!

Consistent with estimates from 1920 and 1924, the Republican vote share of women and men are similar in competitive states. And despite a dramatic swing to the Democrats, male and female vote choice in

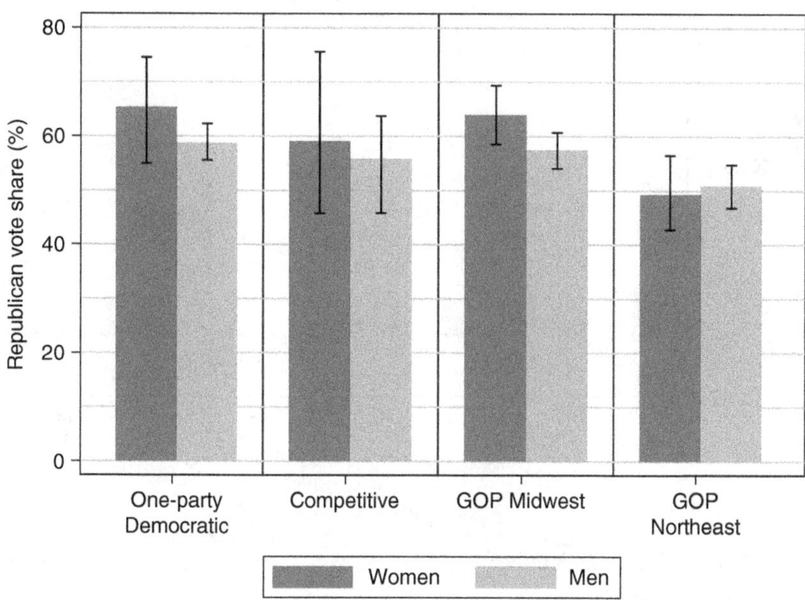

FIGURE 7.8. Partisan context and the Republican vote share of women and men, 1928.

the previously one-party Republican states in the Northeast remains indistinguishable as well. But, also consistent with 1920 and 1924, in one-party Republican states in the Midwest, women continue to be more Republican in their vote choice than men. This finding just misses our 90 percent threshold; 89 percent of the simulations are consistent with this conclusion. Persistent and high levels of Republican support among women appear to dampen the surge among men toward Democrat Al Smith in a number of Midwestern states. Previous observers attribute this outcome in 1928 to female opposition to Smith in those states. However, given the similarity to our results in 1920 and 1924, it is possible, even likely, that other longer term factors – specifically, a consistent pattern of loyalty to and/or mobilization of women by the locally dominant party in the Republican Midwest – contributed to this outcome.

There is some evidence that women also are more likely to cast Republican ballots in the one-party Democratic states (all South/Border) in our sample in 1928; 80 percent of simulations are consistent with that conclusion. Although we can be only moderately confident of the result, this greater Republican support among women in traditionally Democratic states suggests loyalty to locally dominant parties (our

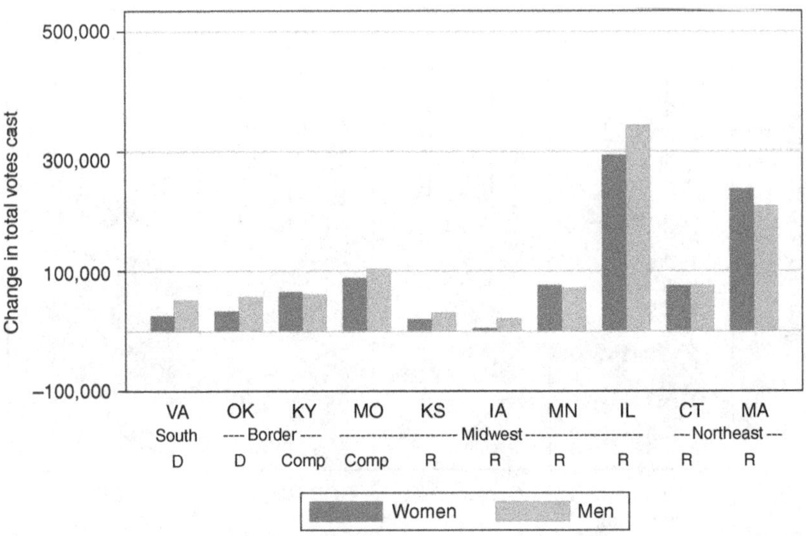

FIGURE 7.9. Change in number of votes cast by women and men, 1924 to 1928.

consistent finding among women in the Republican Midwest in 1920 and 1924) may not have characterized all elections, all contexts, or all times. Consistent with the expectations of many (see Andersen 1996; Burner 1986) that native-born white Protestant women, especially in the South, were mobilized against Al Smith, women in one-party Democratic states in the South and Border regions may have indeed been more likely to cast ballots for Republican Hoover than were men. Our findings for 1928 thus complicate attempts to generalize about the party loyalty of female voters.

The Contributions of Women to the Election of 1928

Partisan vote share can only tell us so much. We now turn to the change in the number of voters – overall and for each major party – in each sample state. We begin with changes in the number of votes cast, reported in Figure 7.9. Both men and women entered the electorate in large numbers in 1928. In most states, the number of new ballots cast by men and women is quite similar, verified by the patterns in the simulations. Given that so many more women were available for mobilization, the fact that in most states as many or more new male voters entered the active electorate in 1928 suggests a substantial and meaningful turnout surge among men.

On the whole, Figure 7.9 confirms that about the same number of new ballots came from men and women – perhaps slightly more new ballots from men in Illinois and perhaps slightly more ballots from women in Massachusetts. This outcome is unique to the 1928 election. Of the five elections we examine, the largest new mobilization of women (new votes cast) occurs, unsurprisingly, in 1920, an election in which approximately 1.3 million more new female than male voters were added to the electorate in our ten sample states; 100 percent of the pooled simulations are consistent with more new female than male voters in 1920. Similarly, 86 percent of the simulations are consistent with the same conclusion in 1924. But, in 1928, only 24 percent of the simulations indicate new female voters outnumbered new male voters, suggesting that new male mobilization may have exceeded new female mobilization. (Later elections resume the pattern of larger new female mobilization, with 80 percent and 98 percent of simulations supporting that conclusion in 1932 and 1936, respectively.) As many expected, the "rum and religion" election of 1928 mobilized many new female voters, but it brought as many or more new male voters to the polls. Although previous work (e.g., Burnham 1974; Sundquist 1983) has suggested that women were uniquely or especially responsible for the surge in turnout in 1928, we find that women accounted for a little *less* than half of the nearly two million additional (or new) ballots cast in the 1928 presidential election in our sample states.

South/Border. In the South and Border states, opposition to Smith was believed to induce many citizens to defect from Democratic loyalty, particularly women. Our estimates of the change in Republican (Figure 7.10) and Democratic (Figure 7.11) votes cast suggest little or no decline in Democratic votes cast among women in our three Southern/Border states (Virginia, Kentucky, and Oklahoma), but a notable Republican mobilization. Although we cannot say definitively, the increase in Republican votes cast by women appears to have been generated largely from new voters (Figure 7.9), given the lack of change in Democratic votes cast and the relatively small number of female Progressive votes available to be recovered from 1924 (see Figure 7.12).

Yet, Republicans gain more new male voters than female voters in all three Southern/Border states, especially in traditionally Democratic-dominated Virginia and Oklahoma. As a result, the considerable net gains Republicans experienced in Virginia and Oklahoma (see Figure 7.13) owe far more to male ballots than to female. More than

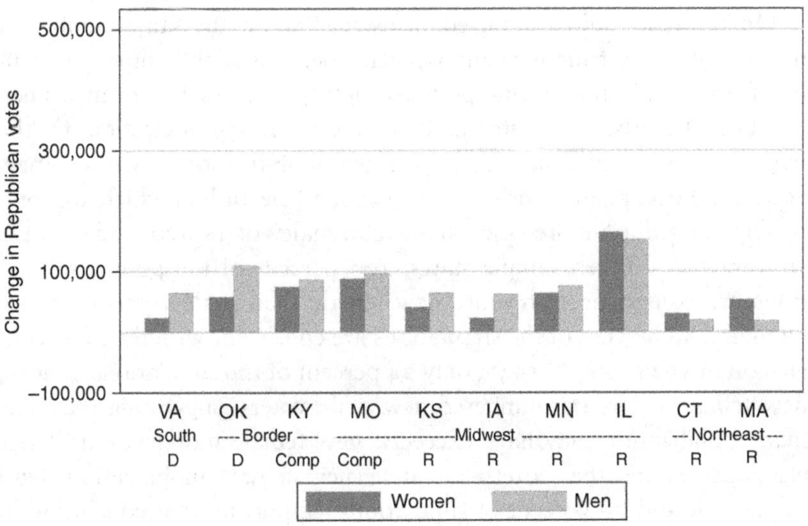

FIGURE 7.10. Change in number of Republican votes cast by women and men, 1924 to 1928.

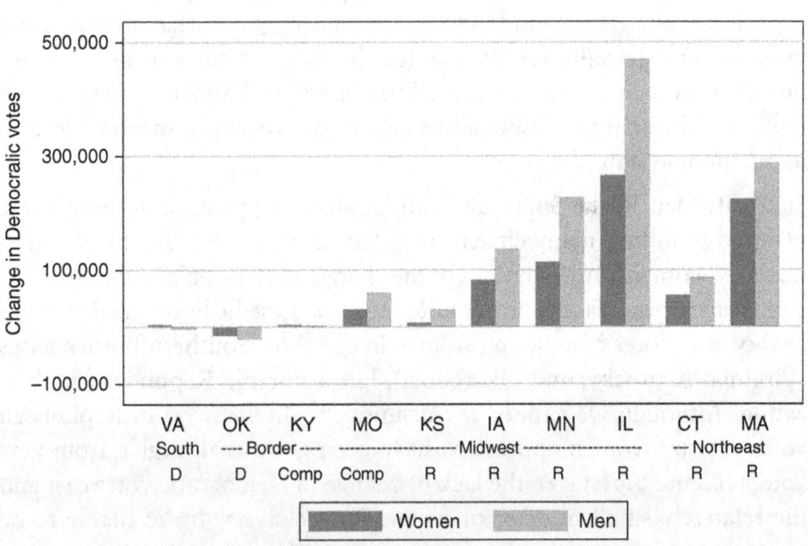

FIGURE 7.11. Change in number of Democratic votes cast by women and men, 1924 to 1928.

95 percent of the simulations support this conclusion in Virginia and about 89 percent in Oklahoma. This difference in net Republican gains in Southern states is driven largely by the greater relative Republican mobilization of new male voters compared to female voters (Figure 7.12);

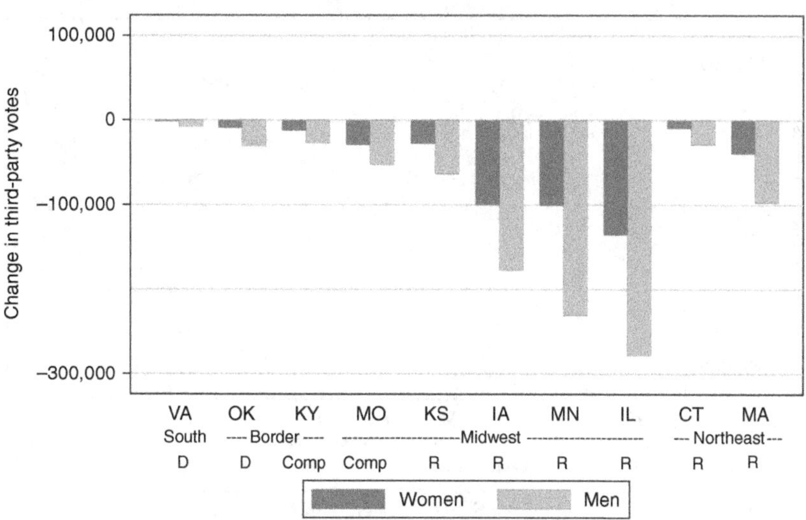

FIGURE 7.12. Change in number of Progressive votes cast by women and men, 1924 to 1928.

the change in number of new Democratic voters is both small and quite similar for men and women (Figure 7.13). Despite a higher percentage of female voters supporting the Republican candidate (recall Figure 7.9), the sheer number of male voters – far exceeding female voters over all in the region – meant that men accounted for much of the large Republican gains in Southern and Border states.

Northeast. In the Northeast, enthusiasm for Smith was expected to generate large Democratic gains, especially among undermobilized immigrant women (e.g., Jeffries 1979; Lubell 1952). Our data cannot speak directly to the behavior of immigrant (or native-born white, or any other specific subgroup of) women or men. However, as we have noted, our two Northeastern states boast enormous immigrant populations; by 1930, 65 percent of the population of both Connecticut and Massachusetts is first- or second-generation immigrant (US Census 1932).

Our estimates indicate that in the heavily immigrant Northeast, a huge number of women did indeed enter the electorate as Democrats in 1928: Nearly 240,000 new female voters cast ballots in Massachusetts alone (Figure 7.9). Another 40,000 female votes were available from women who voted Progressive in 1924 (Figure 7.12). Of the approximately 280,000 female votes available due to mobilization and defection (from Progressives) of women in 1928, Democrats captured 225,000 or about 80 percent (Figure 7.11). Republicans, by contrast, gained only

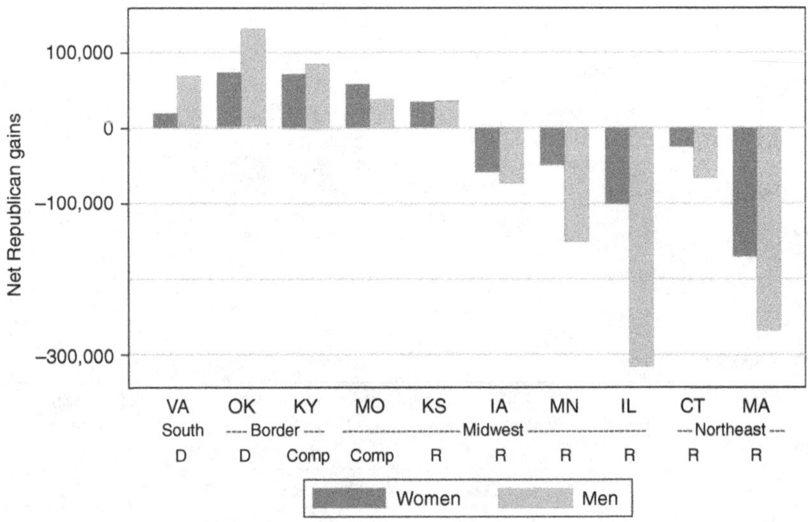

FIGURE 7.13. Change in Republican margin of victory for women and men, 1924 to 1928.

about 53,000 new female voters (Figure 7.10). Patterns are similar in Connecticut. We cannot determine definitively how many new Democratic and Republican votes can be attributed to mobilization (new voters) or conversion (previous voters for other parties, especially Progressives). But given the estimated number of new female voters (230,000) and estimated decline in female Progressive voters (40,000), mobilization appears to have played the dominant role in changing partisan patterns among women in this region. The number of presidential ballots cast by women increased dramatically in both Connecticut and Massachusetts in 1928, and the vast majority appear to have been cast for the Democratic candidate, consistent with long-held expectations.

Despite this remarkable mobilization of women in the Northeast, it was still men – participating at much higher levels – who accounted for most of the Democratic gains. Fewer men cast new Republican ballots than did women in Massachusetts and Connecticut, but men contribute more new Democratic ballots in both states, especially Massachusetts. Conversion likely played a larger role for men than it did for women in the Northeast: In both states, more male Progressive Party ballots were cast in 1924 than female, and thus many more men were available for conversion in 1928 (Figure 7.11). In Massachusetts, defecting Progressive Party voters accounted for about 97,000 male ballots and new male voters accounted for about 209,000. Of these 306,000 potential new major party votes, then, some 68 percent came from mobilization (compared to our estimate of about 86 percent for women), and 32 percent were available from previous Progressive Party voters (compared to just 14 percent among women). Democrats captured 287,000 of the votes available from new mobilization and Progressive defection, while Republicans increased only by 19,000 votes cast. As in 1924, then, we find more evidence of conversion among men than among women, but mobilization of men in the Northeast in 1928 is still considerable. The consequence is that net Democratic gains (net Republican losses) are much higher among men than women: More than 90 percent of the simulations support this conclusion in Massachusetts and more than 85 percent in Connecticut.

A closer look at Boston both confirms these general conclusions, and provides further verification of the reliability of our estimates. Consistent with Gamm's (1986) careful analysis of precinct-level voting records (see Chapter 3), our estimates reveal a remarkable level of mobilization in Boston in 1928. Combining turnout and vote choice, we find that nearly half of all age-eligible males are mobilized to support the Democratic candidate in 1928. The comparable number for women in Boston, largely a consequence of lower turnout, is only about 25 percent. Thus, Democratic shifts in the Northeast in 1928 – even where those shifts were largest – appear to be driven by male, not female, voters, contrary to expectations. Certainly there were more men available for conversion – in Massachusetts, nearly 100,000 male Progressive voters alone, compared to just 40,000 female Progressive voters. Yet far more women than men were available for mobilization: We estimate that over 60 percent of men in Massachusetts turned out to vote in 1924, but fewer than 30 percent of women. Despite that fact, men cast nearly equal numbers of new votes in Massachusetts (and Connecticut) in 1928 (Figure 7.9).

Midwest. Our five Midwestern states tell a more complicated story. The general claim has been that rural Protestant women, hostile to urban, Catholic, and anti-Prohibition Smith, shored up Republican support in the Midwest. Our estimates, however, show that while staying solidly in the Republican column, three of our five Midwestern states – Minnesota, Iowa, and Illinois – experienced a net Republican *loss* among both men and women in 1928 (Figure 7.13). Republicans gained voters in all five Midwestern states (Figure 7.10) but in those three states, Democrats gained far more (Figure 7.11). In Missouri and Kansas, on the other hand, Democratic gains were small relative to Republican gains, and Republicans experienced net gains (Figure 7.13).

What explains these two different patterns? We emphasize, once again, that our state-level summary estimates do not permit us to observe the electoral behavior of any subgroup, and we remain highly cognizant of the ecological fallacy. That being said, we note that our two groups of Midwestern states with distinctive partisan patterns in 1928 are distinguished by the size of their immigrant communities. More than one in three – and often far more – people of voting age in the three Midwestern states that swung toward the Democrats in 1928 were first- or second-generation immigrants: 40 percent in Iowa, 52 percent in Illinois, and 71 percent in Minnesota. The states that experienced a net Republican gain have comparably smaller immigrant populations – about a quarter of the voting-age population in Missouri and Kansas (US Census 1932).

As in the heavily immigrant, traditionally Republican Northeast, in the relatively heavily immigrant, traditionally Republican states in the Midwest (Minnesota, Iowa, and Illinois), women swung not to the Republicans in opposition to Smith, but to the Democrats (Figure 7.13). Like Connecticut, but unlike Massachusetts, all three states remained in the Republican column. As in the Northeast, both parties experience gains among women, but Democrats more so than Republicans. Progressives fared well in these three states in 1924, and so there is more evidence of conversion among women in these Midwestern states than in the Northeast. In Minnesota, for example, there were approximately 100,000 female Progressive voters in 1924, and about 75,000 new female votes cast in 1928. Democrats gain over 110,000 female votes in 1928, and Republicans gain about 65,000. Unfortunately, we cannot determine from our data how many Progressives votes went to Democrats or Republicans (or stayed home), or how the newly mobilized voters were distributed in 1928. We can only conclude that it is likely that both conversion and (to a slightly lesser extent) mobilization produced those new Democratic and Republican female ballots.

Yet, as in the Northeast, as much as women contributed to electoral change in the Midwest, men contributed more. In Minnesota and Illinois, more than 90 percent of the simulations indicate that net Democrat gains (net Republican losses) were larger among men than women. The Democratic Party leader quoted earlier in the chapter was correct to conclude that women were voting somewhat differently than men; but it was only the case that women remained as a relatively stable source of votes for Hoover and were lukewarm supporters of Smith, not that women shifted overwhelmingly in favor of Hoover and that Smith failed to mobilize women. As in the Northeast – but to an even greater extent – the availability of larger numbers of male Progressive voters appears to drive the difference. As we saw in Chapter 6, there were far more male than female Progressive voters in these three states. Those numerous male Progressive voters were available to be converted to major party votes in 1928: nearly 280,000 male Progressive voters in Illinois (compared to about 140,000 among women in that state) and 230,000 in Minnesota (compared to about 100,000 women).

Thus in these three states (Minnesota, Iowa, and Illinois), we observe equal numbers of new male and female voters (Figure 7.9) but many more male 1924 Progressive voters (Figure 7.12). As a result, there were more male voters available to cast ballots for the two major parties (either new voters or former Progressive voters). The number of new Republican votes cast by men and women in these three states are virtually equal. Democrats, on the other hand, gain far more new votes from men than women. In Illinois, women cast approximately 265,000 new Democratic votes in 1928 compared to approximately 470,000 new male Democratic votes. In Minnesota, women cast a little more than 114,000 new Democratic votes, compared to more than 226,000 new Democratic votes cast by men. The result is large net Democratic gains among men, far exceeding the net Democrat gains among women (Figure 7.13).

We cannot determine with certainty how the votes available from men and women – due to new mobilization or Progressive voters without a Progressive option in 1928 – were distributed among the Democratic and Republican candidates in 1928. We do know that men accounted for as many new voters as women in these Midwestern states (perhaps more in Illinois). And we know that the relatively larger Progressive support among men in these states in these states, documented in Chapter 6, had consequences beyond the 1924 election: It created a pool of men available for conversion in 1928 that far exceeded the number of women so available. Thus women's greater loyalty to the locally dominant party in 1924 – evidenced by larger Republican vote share and (surprisingly) lesser enthusiasm for the Progressive Party ticket – translated into greater relative loyalty to the traditionally dominant party in the election of 1928, in which women swing to the Democrats to a considerably lesser extent than men in these long-standing Republican strongholds.

In Missouri and Kansas, states with smaller immigrant populations and smaller Progressive vote share in 1924, the patterns are different, and the relative contributions of men and women are generally similar. Consistent with claims that rural, native-born women in the Midwest supported Hoover in opposition to Smith, we find relatively small (or nonexistent) Democratic gains, and moderate (but larger) Republican gains (see Figures 7.11 and 7.12), among women in 1928. However, women are not distinctive; the same pattern characterizes male voters, with the result that net Republican gains (Figure 7.13) are about the same for men and women in both states.

Summary. There was a great deal of electoral disruption in 1928 with clear regional patterns. In the one-party Democratic South and Border states, there was little change in Democratic votes cast among men and women, but a gain in Republican mobilization, and more so for men than for women (we are confident of this finding in Virginia, moderately confident in Oklahoma). As a result, both men and women contributed to the Republican swing in the South, but men more than women. The previously Republican-dominated Northeast experienced a huge Democratic mobilization. Conversion played a larger role among men than among women, but new male mobilization was also sizeable. Democrats netted considerably more votes from men than from women in the Northeast. Parts of the one-party Republican Midwest (Minnesota, Iowa, and Illinois) swung to the Democrats in 1928 (although not enough to change election outcomes) and Democrats netted significantly more new votes from men than from women. This gender difference was apparently a result of the greater numbers of available Progressive voters among men compared to women, as the numbers of new male and female voters (also considerable in most states) were quite similar. In other parts of the Midwest (Republican-leaning Missouri and one-party Republican Kansas) the Republicans netted more votes than Democrats, and to a fairly similar extent from men and women.

Thus, in general, despite the enthusiasm of new women voters for Republicans in states that moved Republican (Oklahoma and Virginia) and for Democrats in states that moved Democratic (Massachusetts and Connecticut, Minnesota and Illinois), men accounted for more of the surge in support for the advantaged party. Clearly, our estimates provide no support for popular scholarly narratives that give women substantial credit for electoral shifts in 1928. Given the degree to which women continued to lag men in turnout, we should not be entirely surprised to find men accounting for a greater portion of electoral volatility in 1928.

Conclusion

Both accounts outlined at the beginning of the chapter are in some ways vindicated by our estimates – the Smith candidacy seems to have mobilized women as Democrats in the Northeast and mobilized women as Republicans in the South. Patterns in the Midwest are less straightforward, with Republicans netting female votes in Missouri and Kansas, but Democrats netting more female votes than did Republicans in Minnesota, Iowa, and Illinois. While we cannot definitively attribute these different patterns to variation in nativity, we do note that the two groups of Midwestern states are distinguished on that dimension, with relatively large first- and second-generation immigrant communities in the Democratic-swinging Midwestern states, and smaller immigrant communities in Republican-swinging Missouri and Kansas.

The starkly different political behavior of women across regions and states – and the general similarity of the behavior of women and men within those same regions and states – reinforces the conclusion that women were subjected to and responded to political cues and messages not as women per se but as localized political actors. The results suggest it is folly to make general claims about women as predisposed in general to support one major party or the other – as is the case with men, in some areas women are overwhelmingly Republican, in other places overwhelmingly Democrats.

Our results for 1928 also challenge attempts to generalize about the party loyalty of women as a group. Women in the Republican-dominated Midwest were drawn in disproportionate numbers to the dominant major party in the state in the first elections after suffrage, but that pattern begins to breakdown in 1928. More importantly, we find evidence of a greater shift away from the locally dominant Democrats among women in Southern and Border states in reaction against Al Smith. Where women in the Midwest maintained their support for the dominant Republican Party, even when offered a Progressive option in 1924, women in the Democratically dominated South and Border states may have been more likely to come out for Republican Hoover in opposition to Al Smith in 1928. Women's loyalty to the major parties – like that of men – appears to be a function of the conditions and contexts of specific election contexts and not an inherent quality of their gender.

Many contemporary observers and later scholars expected that the greater number of inactive women combined with the heightened passions of the 1928 campaign would provide a large pool of new female voters in 1928 (e.g., Burnham 1974; Sundquist 1983). There is good evidence in our sample that women *were* stimulated by the election of 1928: In our ten sample states, more than twice as many women were added to the polls in 1928 (more than 924,000) than in 1924 (almost 430,000). But women were not alone in being mobilized by the election of 1928. There were only about 290,000 more male voters in our sample states in 1924, but more than 1 million in 1928! Indeed, of the five presidential elections we examine, 1928 is the only one in which there are not substantially more new female voters than new male voters. The drama of the 1928 election was not distinctly mobilizing for women, but brought both sexes to the polls in record numbers.

Many also expected that large numbers of new female voters were a major contributor to electoral change during this period. Women had had fewer opportunities than men to reinforce their partisanship through repeated voting, resulting in what Converse (1972, 277) has called "the temporary but massive dilution of the overall 'political socialization' of the electorate represented by the opening of the system to participation by women." Converse and others expected that, among other things, the impact of women's enfranchisement was considerable partisan volatility. Yet, we find that the main impact of women on the dramatic political shifts in 1928 appears to be the dampening of those partisan swings. In states that swung toward the Democratic Party, Democrats netted fewer votes from women than they did from men. In states that experienced a Republican surge, more of that surge was attributable to men's ballots than to women's. Much of that change appears attributable to the more numerous male Progressive voters from 1924. Most states witnessed an approximately equal number of new male and female ballots (remarkable, given how many more women were available for mobilization) but greater net Republican gains or losses (Figure 7.13) attributable to men. More conversion among men, particularly from those men who cast Progressive ballots in 1924, appears to explain the difference. Thus, women did not contribute to electoral change in 1928 to a greater degree than men did; if anything, women's presence stabilized the partisan electorate. In this sense, we agree (thus far) with Burnham (1974, 1015), who argued in direct opposition to Converse and others that the impact of this particular statutory change – female enfranchisement – appeared to be "*declines*, not increases" (italics original) in electoral volatility.

As many scholars have noted, the partisan shifts witnessed in 1928 – the breakdown of a highly resilient electoral pattern – might not have been maintained beyond the unique Hoover–Smith contest had the

Great Depression and related economic and political upheaval not ushered in a permanent political transformation. In Chapter 8 we turn to the momentous elections of 1932 and 1936 in which Republican ascendancy gave way to the dominant Democratic New Deal coalition. What role did female voters – now with more than a decade of experience as enfranchised citizens – play in this most consequential of electoral transformations?

8

Female Voters and the Emerging Democratic Majority, 1932–1936

The presidential elections of the 1930s are among the most consequential in American history, comprising the archetypal "critical" or "realigning" electoral era (Burnham 1970; Campbell et al. 1960). Republicans had been ascendant since the end of the Civil War, but the parties' responses to the Great Depression transformed partisan alignments in the United States and ushered in an era of Democratic dominance for much of the twentieth century. While important shifts in the parties' constituencies were underway in the preceding decades, and certainly previewed in the election of 1928 (see Key 1955), the elections of the 1930s established a new Democratic coalition that would persist for decades. Because these elections represent an unfolding process of partisan change, we examine the two elections together in this chapter.

As a set of elections with enduring and important consequences, the process of New Deal realignment has been the subject of considerable scholarly attention. Understanding this period of electoral transformation provides insight into the very nature of political order, electoral change, partisanship, and representation in the United States (c.f., Campbell et al. 1966). There is no question that the end result of the New Deal period was a dramatic reordering of partisan alignments in the United States: Previous Republican dominance was replaced by a majority Democratic coalition. More than eighty years later, students of electoral and partisan change continue to debate how that outcome was achieved.

While the New Deal realignment has received considerable attention, scholars have had less to say about the contribution of women to this process. In a sense, scholars are following the pattern of political observers of the time. As the Nineteenth Amendment's novelty faded, a powerful female voting bloc failed to materialize, and economic crisis overshadowed all else, contemporary observers became less keenly interested in the voting behavior and preferences of women. That lack of interest has been shared by many later scholars, despite their considerable attention to the contribution of other demographic groups to New Deal realignment.

Yet we have reason to expect women may have played a key role in the enormous voter mobilization during this period. From 1928 to 1936, the electorate expanded by nearly 25 percent. A large number of still politically inactive women were among those most available for mobilization. At the same time, women who *had* voted in the 1920s were – as a result of relatively fewer opportunities to have reinforced their partisanship by casting ballots – among those most available for conversion from one partisan allegiance to the other. Not only were women especially available for mobilization and conversion in the 1930s, but later scholarship on the modern gender gap also finds women are particularly hard hit by and politically responsive to economic adversity (e.g., Box-Steffensmeier, De Boef, and Lin 2004), the engine of partisan change during this period. Did women in fact contribute in unique ways to New Deal realignment?

Our estimates reveal that both mechanisms of electoral change – mobilization and conversion – were at work on male and female voters during the realignment period. Mobilization (rather than conversion) appears to have accounted for more of the ballots Democrats gained from women compared to men. However, women were both slightly more likely to defect from the dominant Republican party to the emerging Democratic party than were men between 1928 and 1932 *and* mobilized in greater numbers than men in 1936. In our sample, the number of women casting Democratic ballots increased from 1.7 million for Smith in 1928 to 3.3 million for Roosevelt in 1936 – a remarkable increase of nearly 95 percent. But, because there were many more men in the electorate at the beginning of the realignment period, men accounted for a larger *number* of converts even if defection rates were lower. Democrats managed to increase support from men by nearly 50 percent – from 3 million male ballots for Smith in 1928 to 4.5 million male votes for Roosevelt in 1936. The net result is that women and men account for roughly equal numbers – approximately 1.5 million each – of the 3 million Democratic voters added during the realigning elections in our ten sample states. These gains created a formidable – and durable – advantage in the popular vote for the Democrats.

The Presidential Elections of 1932 and 1936

The expansion of the US electorate that began in 1928 is striking. The total number of ballots cast in US presidential elections increased by 27 percent between 1924 and 1928, 8 percent between 1928 and 1932, and 15 percent between 1932 and 1936 (in our ten sample states the comparable changes are 21, 6, and 12 percent). By far the largest jump in participation occurred during the contentious and passionate contest between Smith and Hoover in 1928. That sharp increase was both maintained (an impressive enough achievement) and expanded in the next two elections, with an increase in turnout of nearly the same size across the realigning elections of the 1930s.

Herbert Hoover sought reelection in 1932 in the context of the Great Depression, ushered in by the stock market collapse of October 1929. While the Depression developed slowly, by 1931–1932 the economic crisis was grave and the extent of suffering clashed with the restrained Republican response (Freidel 1971). Hoover's popularity plummeted among all but the wealthy and business sectors of the economy (Hicks 1960). Nonetheless, at a "dull, dispirited" Chicago convention where Republicans reiterated their commitment to the present do-little course of the Republican administration, Hoover was re-nominated by the GOP (Freidel 1971, 2713).

On the Democratic side, Franklin D. Roosevelt had long been considered the front-runner, a position solidified by his innovative response to the Great Depression as governor of New York. After making huge gains in the 1930 midterm elections, Democrats were energized by the strong likelihood of victory in 1932. Roosevelt, although not without opposition, had the advantage of being uniquely acceptable to both the Northern urban and rural Southern wings of the Democratic Party (Burner 1986; Freidel 1971). It is probably fair to say that given the extent of economic crisis on his watch, there is little that Hoover could have done – and indeed, he did little – to win reelection. Roosevelt, the first Democrat to win the presidency since Woodrow Wilson left office in 1920, garnered a decisive 57 percent of the vote in 1932 (Scammon 1965).

Four years later, the emerging Democratic majority was resoundingly ratified by Roosevelt's reelection. In his 1932 nomination acceptance speech, Roosevelt had pledged "a new deal for the American people" (Freidel 1971, 2732), and in the intervening years, the first New Deal programs had transformed the role of the federal government in American life. The 1936 election was widely understood as a referendum on the

New Deal, and disagreement between party elites about the wisdom of that transformation in the size and role of the state led to a sharper ideological and policy contrast between the parties (if not the candidates) than had characterized presidential elections in the 1920s (Freidel 1971; Weed 1994).

Republicans nominated Kansas Governor Alfred (Alf) Landon, who they hoped would appeal to farmers, businesspeople, and the middle class. Landon, more Main Street than Wall Street, and more closely identified with the Progressive, rather than conservative, wing of the GOP, faced the difficult task of campaigning for the presidency despite supporting the goals and even many of the policies of his opponent. Roosevelt was largely unchallenged for his party's nomination and had become wildly popular in the intervening four years since his initial election, particularly among urban voters, organized labor, and ethnic and racial minorities. Enjoying the concrete benefits of the Democratic approach to the economic crisis, most voters were unmoved by claims that the New Deal was unconstitutional. Roosevelt's campaign strategy was simply to highlight the differences in conditions between 1932 and 1936.

Surprisingly, most contemporary observers did not expect an overwhelming victory in the months leading up to November of 1936. The widely publicized *Literary Digest* poll, which had predicted Roosevelt's 1932 margin within a percentage point, forecast a Republican victory in 1936, as did other prominent polls (Crossley 1937; Weed 1994). Ultimately, Roosevelt carried all but two states with a national margin of victory of more than 10 million votes. Roosevelt received almost 61 percent of the vote in 1936, the largest recorded landslide thus far in American history, cementing the transition to Democratic dominance and the ascendancy of the New Deal coalition (Leuchtenberg 1971).

New Deal Realignment

The electoral realignment of 1928 to 1936, the quintessential example of the critical election process that Key (1955, 1959) proposed as a model of electoral change, offers unique insights into the basic nature of partisanship and political change. As a result, this era has been the subject of a remarkable volume of scholarly work. A question of particular interest is the extent to which the shift from Republican to Democratic dominance, and to a class-based rather than regional cleavage between the parties (Kleppner 1982a), was characterized by the mobilization of previously inactive citizens or the conversion of those already active. The conversion story posits that widespread dissatisfaction with the Republican response to the economic crisis persuaded previous Republican voters to support the Democratic candidate in 1932, and then reinforce that preference by voting for FDR in subsequent elections, resulting in a long-term shift from Republican to Democratic loyalty (Brown 1988). Those particularly hard hit by the Depression – farmers and urban industrial workers – were believed the most likely candidates for conversion (Gourevitch 1984; Sundquist 1973).

Adherents to the mobilization explanation, however, highlight evidence of considerable individual-level stability of partisan attachment, a finding dating from the influential early vote studies (Berelson, Lazarsfeld, and McPhee 1954; Campbell et al. 1960, 1966; Lazarsfeld, Berelson, and Gaudet 1948) and a persistent, if contested, thesis today (e.g., Green, Palmquist, and Schickler 2002). If partisanship is an "unmoved mover" (Johnston 2006), then Democratic gains likely came less from party-switching by Republicans, and more from the mobilization of new and previously inactive citizens, such as the massive numbers of new immigrants entering the United States in the preceding decades, responding to the appeal of the Democratic Party (see Salisbury and MacKuen 1981).

Amidst debates over theory and method, scholars have found support for both mobilization (Andersen 1979; Campbell 1985; Campbell et al. 1960; Prindle 1979; Wanat 1979) and conversion (Burnham 1970; Erikson and Tedin 1981; Hawley and Sagarazu 2012; Ladd and Hadley 1975; Sundquist 1983) as the dominant mechanism for New Deal realignment. Different elections may have been characterized by different kinds of processes. Brown (1988) concludes that conversion of Republican identifiers to the Democratic Party was the dominant means to change in 1932, while mobilization characterized Democratic growth in 1936. Different groups may have participated in the New Deal realignment at different times and in different ways. In Brown's (1988) analysis, farmers, the first hit by the Depression, shifted to the Democratic Party in 1932 (both via conversion and mobilization) and then stabilized, while urban and working class voters showed relatively smaller increases in Democratic voting between 1928 and 1932, and large shifts, almost entirely via mobilization, into the Democratic column in 1936. Similarly, Gamm's (1986) careful analysis of the New Deal realignment in Boston finds differing patterns of conversion and mobilization among different racial, ethnic, class, gender, and immigrant groups, as well as over time (see Chapter 3). Conversion was predominant among Jewish voters, for example, but political change among blacks and Italians came almost entirely from mobilization. Although patterns vary, his data generally suggest conversion in the first elections followed by mobilization in later contests of the era.

It is clear from much of the work on the New Deal era that the mechanisms of conversion and mobilization operated in distinctly local ways (see Andersen 2014). While the New Deal realignment was particularly widespread geographically compared to other realignments, the shape and strength of the change varied by region (Nardulli 1995). Studies of specific states – such as Pennsylvania (McMichael and Trilling 1980), Connecticut (Jeffries 1979), Massachusetts (Gamm 1986), and Iowa (Gosnell 1942) – confirm the unique progress of New Deal realignment in specific localities. Consistent with these particular and localized accounts, we expect to observe considerable variation across states in the extent of mobilization and the pace of conversion.

Expectations for Female Voters in 1932 and 1936

The women's divisions of both parties were well-organized and active in seeking women's vote in the 1930s (Freeman 2000; Freidel 1971; Leuchtenberg 1971), but direct appeals to women tended to be less prominent than in the 1920s, particularly in 1936. The content of those appeals shifted as well. Republicans continued to emphasize women's traditional, domestic roles. Democrats, on the other hand, shifted toward greater emphasis on the economy and work, consistent with their broader message, when reaching out to female voters. Democratic women's organizations were organized around occupations and other interests. Mrs. Roosevelt was an active speaker on the campaign trail, but unlike previous (potential) First Ladies, she did not particularly emphasize her role as a mother or housewife (Greenlee 2014).

Despite the apparent reduction in gender-specific campaigns appeals in the 1930s, we have reason to expect that women were both more likely to convert from previous Republican support and more likely to be mobilized into the emerging Democratic majority during the New Deal elections. Because women had been less likely than men to turn out to vote in the elections of the 1920s, more women than men were available for mobilization – that is, there were more women who were not already members of the active electorate. Indeed, in terms of sheer numbers, there were likely more women available for mobilization than any other demographic group. At the same time, women who *had* voted during the

1920s may have been more likely to convert because their relatively short experience at the polls provided less opportunity to reinforce partisan preferences. In other words, women boasted lower levels of "political immunization" (McPhee and Ferguson 1962), the resistance to disturbance accumulated from repetition and reiteration.

Yet, women are largely absent from the dominant narratives of New Deal realignment. This is particularly surprising given the attention to the specific role of women in scholarly work on the 1928 election. As we have seen, the potential for differential mobilization of certain groups of women, particularly native-born white and immigrant white, as well as increased female turnout overall, has been proposed as a key element of changing partisan patterns in 1928 (e.g., Burner 1986; Burnham 1974; Lubell 1952; Sundquist 1973; see Chapter 7).

Fewer scholars have hypothesized about the role of female voters in the presidential elections of the 1930s. Indeed, many of the most prominent realignment and partisanship scholars have been silent on the potential conversion and/or mobilization of female voters. In his influential book, *Critical Elections and the Mainsprings of American Politics*, Burnham (1970) notes the likely differential mobilization of native and immigrant women prior to 1928 but does not implicate them in the realignment that followed. Likewise, in Sundquist's (1983) important statement on party realignment, *Dynamics of the Party System*, the chapter on New Deal realignment does not mention women. Kleppner (1982a, 89) identifies "immigrant-stock voters, the young, those toward the bottom of the economic ladder, the unemployed, reliefers, and citizens who had chosen to abstain in the 1920s" as those responsible for increased turnout during the New Deal period; while many women fell into the last category, he does not discuss women specifically with regards to the New Deal. Similarly, Gosnell (1942, 23), describing the sixfold increase in Democratic voters between 1928 and 1936 in Pennsylvania, concludes that the Democrats attracted "a huge army of new voters – the young voters and those who had formerly been non-voters through indifference." Again, we might expect many women to fall into that second camp, but they go unmentioned. Finally, and perhaps most importantly in terms of establishing the conventional wisdom, in their classic book, *The American Voter*, Campbell and his colleagues (1960, 153) implicate "the youth, the economically underprivileged, and the minority groups," but not women, as the source of the new Democratic majority. As we discuss in Chapter 1, the authors of *The American Voter* express specific doubts about the likelihood that women served as a distinctive source for partisan change during the New Deal, or any other period, due to women's lesser interest in and attention to politics, and their resultant reliance on political cues from their husbands.

A few scholars have at least allowed for the possibility of a role for female voters in the New Deal elections. Drawing explicitly on McPhee and Ferguson's (1962) concept of political immunization, Andersen (1979) identifies the enfranchisement of women as a central contributor to the large number of nonimmunized voters in the 1920s who were subsequently available for Democratic mobilization during the New Deal period. In other work, Burnham (1974, 1015) points to the heavy mobilization of women, especially "ethnic women," during the "1928–1936 realignment sequence." As we have seen, Gamm's (1986) data from the Boston wards allows him to observe male and female voters directly. He finds that women were mobilized later than men; in Gamm's Boston wards, increases in Democratic support before 1934 were a result of support from men, but after that time, women's gains surpassed those of men. The patterns vary some across racial, class, and ethnic groups, but the general conclusion (Gamm 1986, 165) is the same:

> With only the most minor exceptions, until 1934 increased male support for the Democratic party as a share of the whole period consistently outpaced female support. Conversely, after 1934 female support was more important. Democratic gains among men were more concentrated in the early years of the realignment, while those among women were more concentrated in the later years.

This differential pattern, Gamm (1986) believes, is explained by women's political inexperience and the endurance of cultural opposition to women's political participation, particularly among immigrants and racial minorities.

The general inattention to women as a factor in New Deal realignment appears to be a result of two factors. First, the conventional wisdom that female voters had failed to materialize as a unique voting bloc or to differ much from men in their political preferences had been largely accepted as conventional wisdom by the time Key (1955) had called attention to critical elections and the New Deal period in particular had become the subject of widespread scholarly interest. As a result, few scholars likely viewed women as important contributors to the process of electoral change in the 1930s.

Second, the dearth of attention to women in the previous literature on New Deal realignment highlights the methodological challenge at the core of this research. Much of the literature on New Deal realignment is characterized by meticulous data work in which scholars carefully identified counties and other geopolitical divisions with demographic populations that allowed reasonable (in most cases) inferences about the turnout and vote choice of particular groups. Key's (1955) carefully constructed graphs of electoral patterns in certain New England towns, Andersen's (1979) analysis of partisan registration in specific counties and reconstructed individual-level partisanship, Gamm's (1986) meticulous identification of ethnically homogeneous Boston wards, and Kleppner's (1982a) and Nardulli's (1995) systematic delineation of counties nationwide are all emblematic of this time- and effort-intensive historical election research (see Burnham 1986). Racial, ethnic, and immigrant residential segregation makes isolating such groups geographically far more tenable than identifying female voters separate from male (see Chapter 4). Thus data limitations likely discouraged earlier scholars from examining women's contribution to New Deal realignment. This empirical challenge does not justify the failure to so much as speculate as to the possible distinctive contribution of women to New Deal realignment, however. Rather, this lacunae in the scholarly literature (with few, important exceptions) points to a more general failure to recognize women as having a potentially unique electoral impact during this period.

The Mobilization of Women in 1932 and 1936

Mobilization of the electorate in 1932 and 1936 is truly extraordinary, particularly given the long-term trends toward declining electoral participation at the turn of the century (see Burnham 1965). Across our sample as a whole, men's turnout averages 75 percent in 1932 and 78 percent in 1936. Women's turnout averages 48 percent in 1932 (a 27-point turnout gender gap) and by 1936, more than half of the women in our sample states (54 percent) turn out to vote, a 24-point turnout gender gap. In contrast, women's turnout in 1920, the first election following ratification of the Nineteenth Amendment, averaged just 36 percent across our sample states, 32 points lower than men's in that election. With the help of both experience and the mobilizing effects of 1928 and the New Deal elections, women's turnout in our sample states grew almost 20 points between 1920 and 1936, narrowing the turnout gender gap across these five elections.

The state-level estimates highlight this remarkable mobilization. In our ten sample states, more than 70 percent of the male voting age population turns out to vote in every state save one (Virginia) in 1932 and 1936

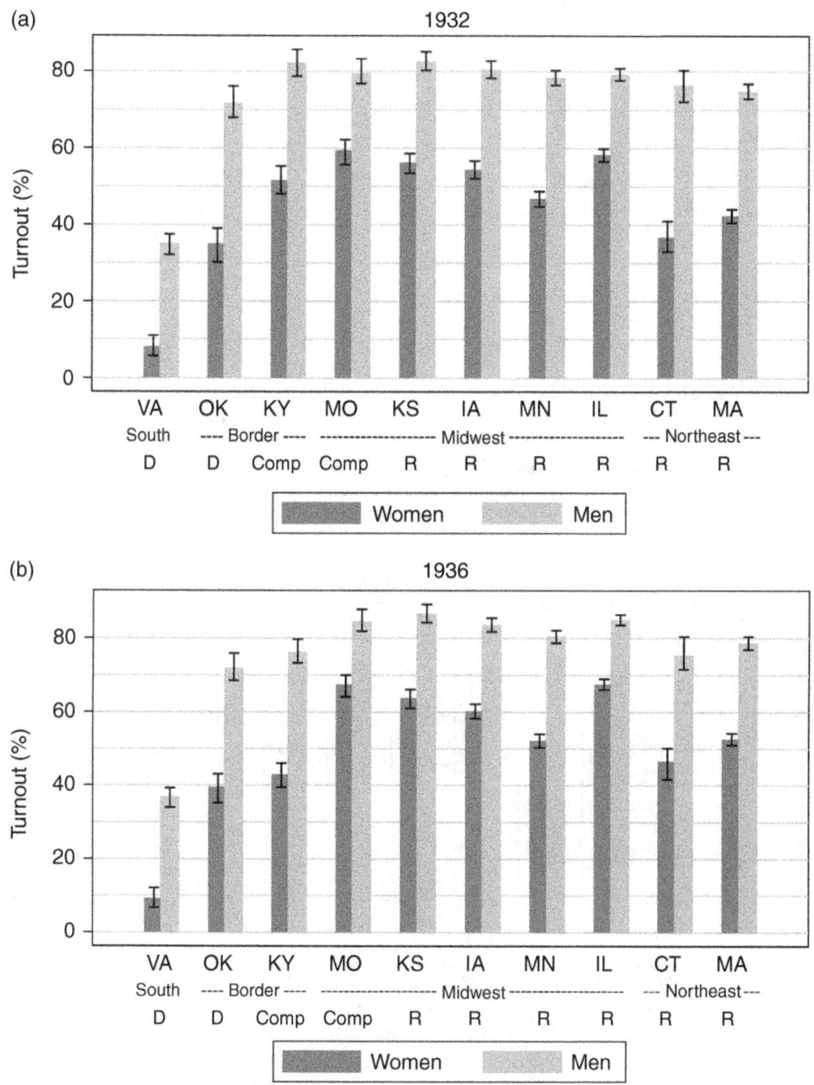

FIGURE 8.1. Turnout of women and men, 1932 and 1936.

(see Figure 8.1). Female turnout is also high: above 50 percent in half of the states in our sample in 1932 and in 6 of 10 states in 1936. Indeed, we estimate female turnout to exceed 60 percent in four Midwestern states in 1936, an extraordinary level of mobilization. As we discuss in the text that follows, turnout among women (and men) does decrease in a number of states in 1932 and 1936. But, given the dramatic increase

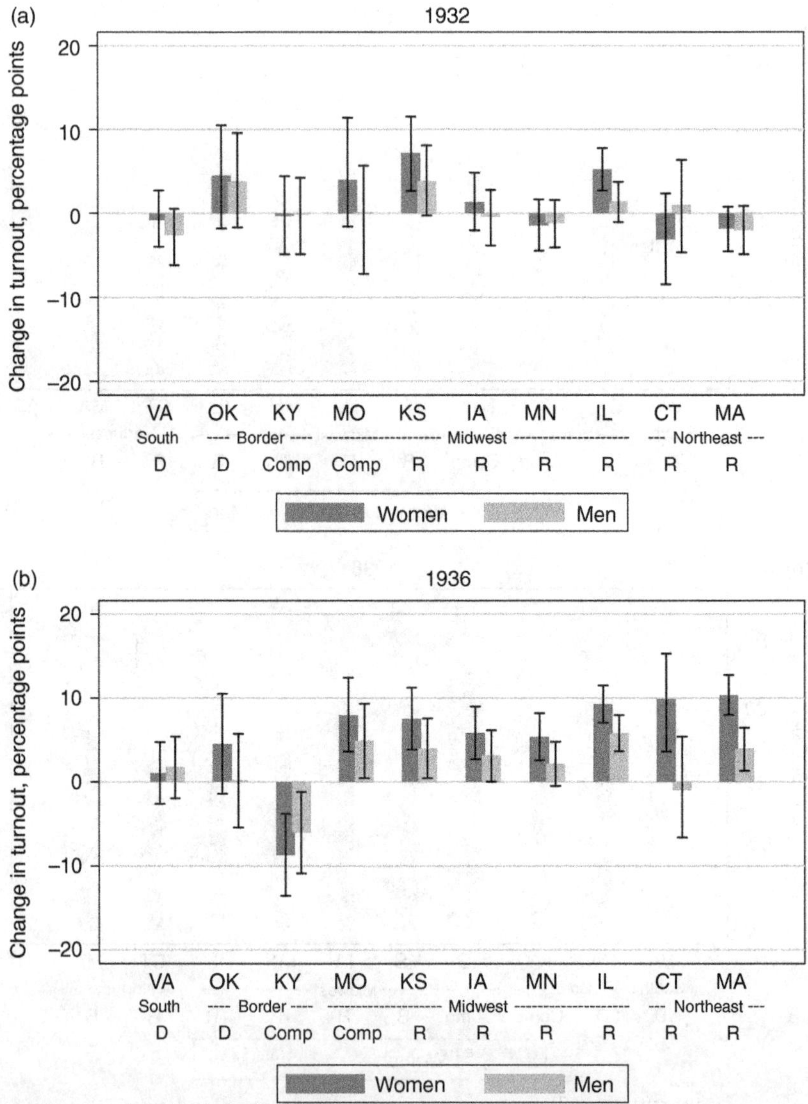

FIGURE 8.2. Change in turnout of women and men, 1928 to 1936.

in turnout in 1928, the near maintenance (and in a few cases, expansion) of the electorate in both elections is impressive.

Despite its place in history as a watershed election, in most places turnout in 1932 changed very little from 1928, drifting a few percentage points higher or lower (see Figure 8.2). In the Northeast, turnout falls among men and women and in some places the decline in women's turnout exceeds the decline in men's turnout. (Gamm [1986] observed the same outcome in his analysis of precinct-level registration by gender in Boston). The only states where we find turnout increasing by more than 5 percentage points among men or women are Illinois and Kansas, where turnout jumps sharply for women in particular. In Illinois, 90 percent of the simulations indicate that the increase in turnout among women from 1928 to 1932 exceeded the increase in turnout among men; in the case of Kansas, 73 percent of the simulations are consistent with higher turnout increases among women. In the other states, the rate of change in turnout is the same for men and women in 1932.

As previous scholars have observed (e.g., Brown 1988; Gamm 1986), new mobilization was greater in 1936 than 1932. In seven of ten states sample states – all of our states outside of the South/Border region – the increase in the proportion of age-eligible women voting was more than 5 percentage points. The point estimates suggest greater turnout growth among women than men. Taking into account the uncertainty associated with estimates in each year, we are confident of the conclusion that the increase in turnout among women exceeded the growth in turnout among men in Illinois and Connecticut (more than 90 percent of simulations), and perhaps in Kansas and Minnesota as well (80 percent or more of the simulations). In Connecticut the increase in women's turnout was, incredibly, likely more than 10 percentage points in 1936. The growth in turnout in Illinois is nearly as large.[1] Thus, the election of 1936 was characterized by more mobilization than in 1932 overall, and, more so than in 1932, there is compelling evidence of greater turnout growth among women than men in some states.

Impact of State Context

In the midst of such dramatic partisan change, did the local partisan context and voting restrictions continue to impact women's mobilization to a greater degree than they did men's?

Partisan Context. As we saw in Chapter 7, 1928 transformed the partisan politics of many of our ten sample states. Burnham (1981a) describes state partisan contexts in three distinct periods: 1896–1910, 1914–1930, and 1934–1950. We used the 1914–1930 classifications in

[1] The results in Massachusetts are similar to Illinois and Connecticut but, as discussed in the appendix to Chapter 4, the simulation for Massachusetts, 1936, failed important convergence diagnostics, so we do not report those results in the text.

our examination of the presidential elections of 1920, 1924, and 1928 in the preceding chapters. While this categorization captured the partisan context in which women first entered the electorate in the early 1920s, the partisan context in many states was considerably disrupted in the 1930s. Thus for this chapter, we use the 1934–1950 party context categories to assess the impact of partisan context on turnout. In every case of category change, the shift is away from a Republican advantage: Kentucky is reclassified from competitive Democratic to one-party Democratic, Missouri shifts from competitive Republican to competitive Democratic, Connecticut shifts from one-party Republican to competitive Democratic, and Massachusetts and Illinois shift from one-party Republican to competitive Republican.[2] Only Iowa and Kansas remain categorized as one-party Republican during the 1930s and beyond. As we have seen in previous chapters, more competitive electoral contexts are expected to be associated with increased voter turnout, particularly among low-propensity peripheral voters.

As Figure 8.3 shows, turnout continued to be lower in one-party Democratic states than in the states where both parties were competitive. However, dramatic mobilization in the remaining one-party Republican states during the 1928–1936 period resulted in rates of turnout for men and women that are indistinguishable from those in competitive states in 1932 and 1936, just as was the case in 1928. Clearly, the uniquely mobilizing elections of the realignment sequence spurred turnout even in states where the Republicans remained dominant.

Nevertheless, and consistent with the peripheral voter hypothesis, the impact of the living in a one-party Democratic state, compared to a competitive state, continues to weigh more heavily on women than it does on men: In both 1932 and 1936, the difference between women's turnout in one-party Democratic versus competitive states is almost 30 points (a 100 percent increase), compared to just 20 points for men (a 33 percent increase). More than 95 percent of the simulations are consistent with the conclusion that the difference in turnout between one-party Democratic and competitive states is larger for women than men. Given that our three one-party Democratic states are, not surprisingly,

[2] Burnham does not classify Minnesota partisan politics because the ballot for the state legislature is nonpartisan. We treat Minnesota as one-party Republican in the 1914–1930 period because the state legislature was consistently controlled by the Conservative caucus. We reclassify Minnesota as competitive in 1934–1950 because the Liberal caucus (Farmer-Labor plus Democratic) controlled the state House in two legislative sessions during that period.

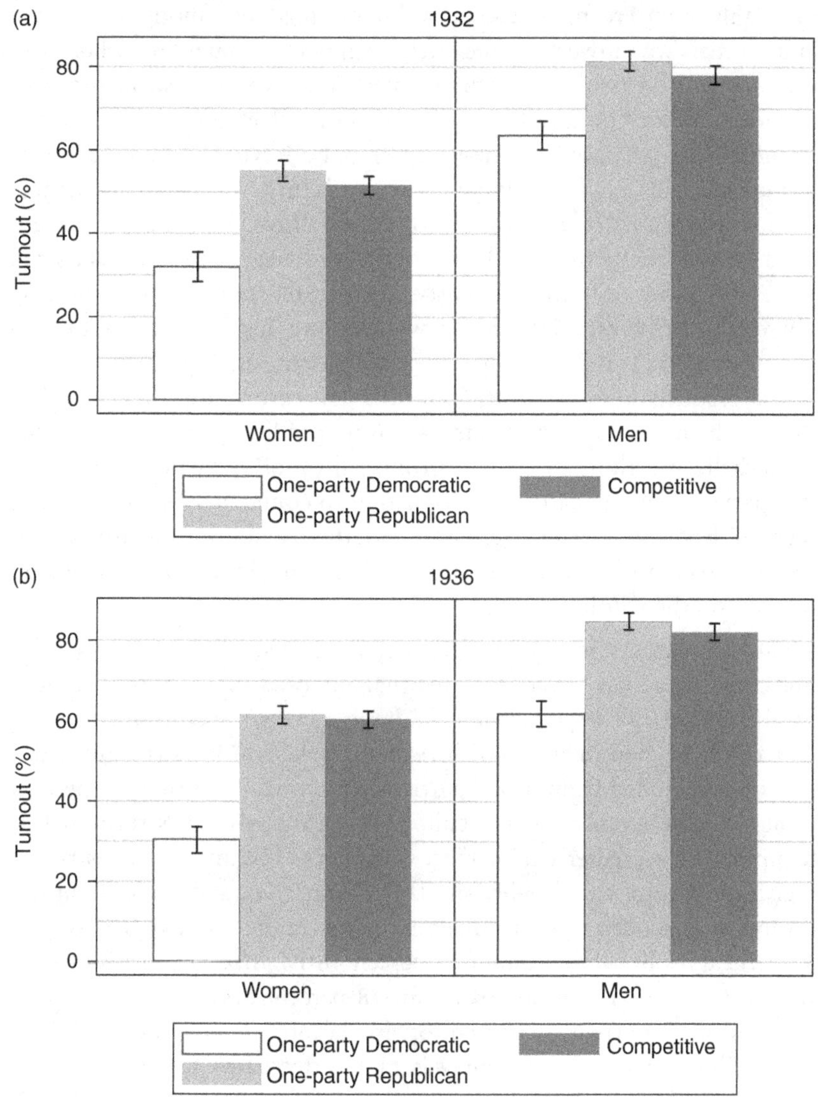

FIGURE 8.3. 1934–1950 partisan context and the turnout of women and men, 1932 and 1936.

Southern and Border states (Kentucky, Virginia, Oklahoma), we may well attribute uniquely lower turnout among women to Southern culture, rather than the demobilizing effects of one-partyism in general and on women specifically. We do not doubt that the Southern context was uniquely demobilizing for women, and women of color in particular (see Wilkerson-Freeman 2002); although turnout among both men and women was lowest in one-party Democratic states in earlier elections, it was particularly so for women. Yet, as we show, in previous chapters, before the 1928–1932–1936 series of elections dramatically upended partisan patterns, one-partyism of both types – Democratic *and* Republican – had indeed hampered women's turnout to a greater degree than it did men's. The incredible mobilization brought about by realignment in both competitive and one-party Republican states means that in 1932 and 1936, only the one-party Democratic states display uniquely low turnout, and especially so for women. As a result, we cannot determine from 1932 and 1936 if this greater effect among women is due to the uniquely antidemocratic political structure and gender norms of the South or the impact of one-partyism specifically. However, results from earlier elections showing a stronger drop-off for women than men in one-party Republican states compared to competitive states suggests that while distinctive and gendered Southern culture and institutions surely played a key role, lack of competition likely held back women's turnout on the whole as well.

Legal Context. As in earlier elections, both men's and women's turnout continue to be lower in states that imposed more restrictive electoral laws (Figure 8.4). Despite the large increases in turnout in 1928 and 1936, women in states with restrictive election laws remained distinctively excluded from broad participation, with fewer than 40 percent of age-eligible women casting ballots. As before, women's turnout was hampered to a greater extent than was men's. The impact of restrictive registration laws was roughly similar in both 1932 and 1936: women's turnout was about 20 points lower in restrictive states (an approximately 40 percent drop in 1932, about 34 percent in 1936), while men's turnout was about 14 to 15 points lower (an 18 percent drop) in more restrictive states. More than 95 percent of simulations are consistent with the conclusion that female turnout was more affected by the legal context than was male in both elections. The impact of voting restrictions, while substantially smaller than in 1920 and 1924, remained an important barrier to women's incorporation into the electorate.

The Partisan Mobilization of Women in 1932 and 1936

Across our sample as a whole, Democrats were hugely successful in 1932 and 1936 – particularly in light of Republican dominance in the 1920s.

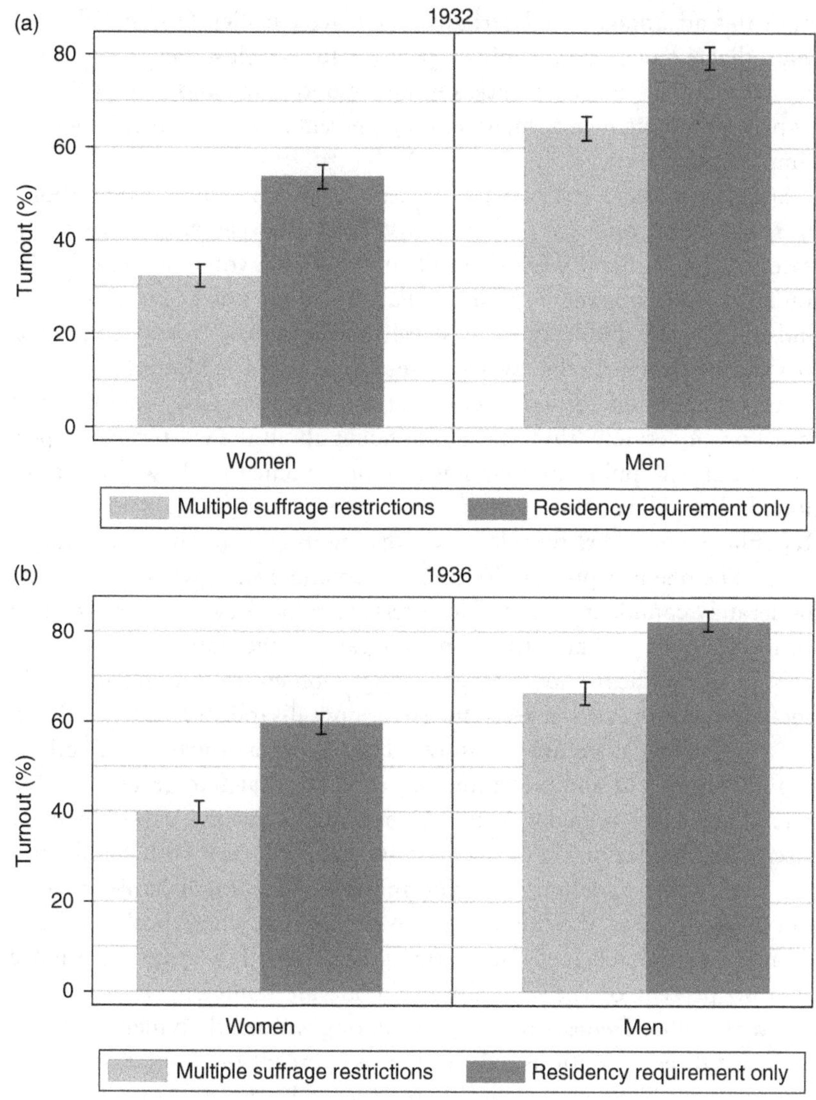

FIGURE 8.4. Legal context and the turnout of women and men, 1932 and 1936.

In the elections leading up to 1932, we observed a persistent Republican advantage among women in one-party Republican states in the Midwest. This difference is largely responsible for the small Republican advantage among women in our sample as a whole in the first three presidential elections, 1920 through 1928. The electoral disruptions of 1932 and 1936 erode this advantage – and perhaps even reverse it slightly – with the end result that women's and men's support for Roosevelt settles at about the same level by 1936. Democratic support in both 1932 and 1936 averages 57 percent among men compared to 60 percent among women in our ten sample states.

Shifts in specific states make it clear how this change came about. In 1920, 1924, and 1928, female voters in the one-party Republican states of the Midwest were more likely than male voters to support the traditionally dominant Republican Party in their state. Specifically, we find a higher Republican vote share among female voters compared to male in eleven of the twelve cases (four states – Minnesota, Iowa, Kansas, and Illinois – times three elections). We can be either highly (eight cases) or moderately (three cases) confident about the existence and persistence of a Republican advantage among women in these four traditionally Republican states across those three elections. Male and female Republican vote share were largely indistinguishable in our other sample states. The one exception is Virginia (1920 and 1924), where we can be moderately confident that female voters were more likely to cast ballots for the Democratic Party, the dominant party in the state.

That Republican advantage among women in the traditionally one-party Midwest weakens in 1928 and disappears completely in 1932 and 1936, as Figure 8.5 shows. Indeed, across those two elections and all ten of our sample states, we estimate that female *Democratic* vote share exceeds male in all but five of the twenty cases. In most cases, the simulations indicate that we can only say with confidence that male and female partisan vote share are indistinguishable in 1932 and 1936. In 1932 the one exception is Virginia, where both men and women swung back to Democratic allegiance with a vengeance; more than 80 percent of the simulations (moderate confidence) are consistent with higher Democratic support among women than men. In 1936, there are three exceptions: More than 90 percent of simulations show that women's Democratic vote share exceeded men's in Minnesota and Connecticut, and 80 percent of simulations are consistent with that conclusion in Kentucky. The Democratic advantage among female voters in Minnesota is particularly noteworthy, given that women were more likely to vote Republican than were men in that state in 1920 and 1924. This suggests a remarkable mobilization of women into the Democratic Party across the 1928–1932–1936 series of elections in Minnesota. Thus, the persistent Republican advantage among women that we observed in many Midwestern states in 1920 and 1924, and

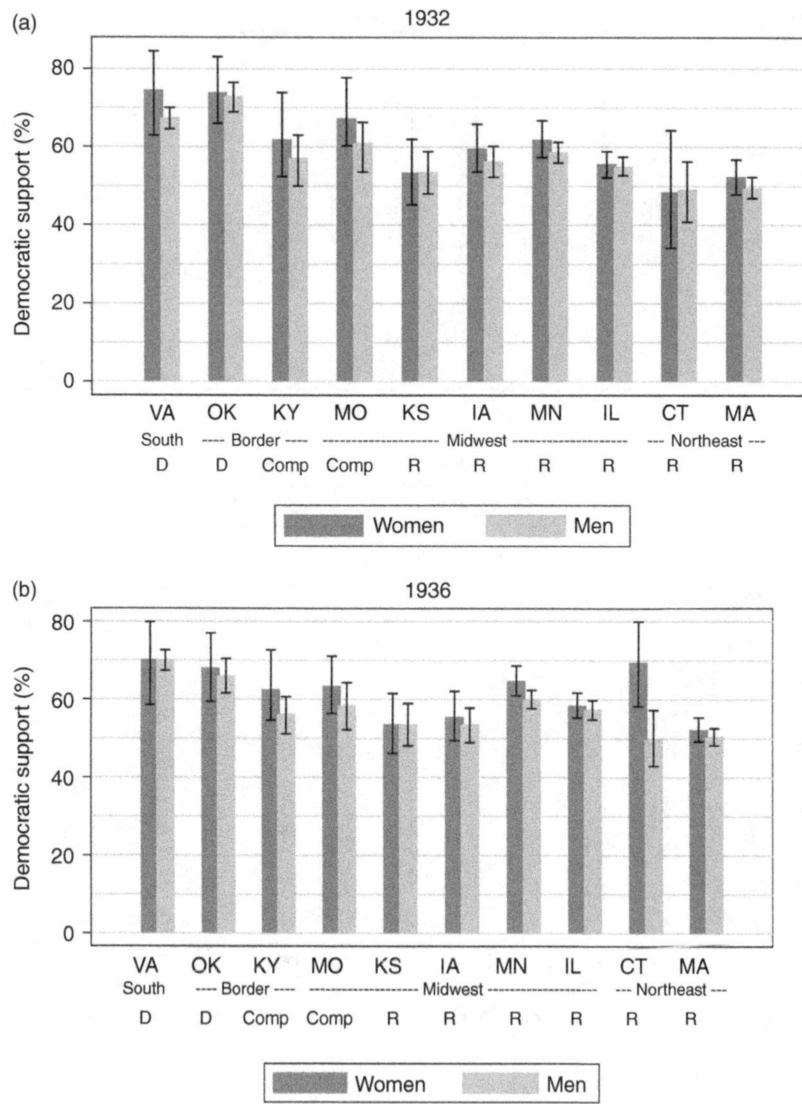

FIGURE 8.5. Democratic vote share of women and men, 1932 and 1936.

which had started to fade in 1928, was clearly eliminated, and in the cases of Minnesota, reversed, by 1936.

Figure 8.6 summarizes shifts in Democratic Party support from 1928 to 1932, and again from 1932 to 1936, by gender and state. We know that New Deal realignment occurred in unique ways in different regions

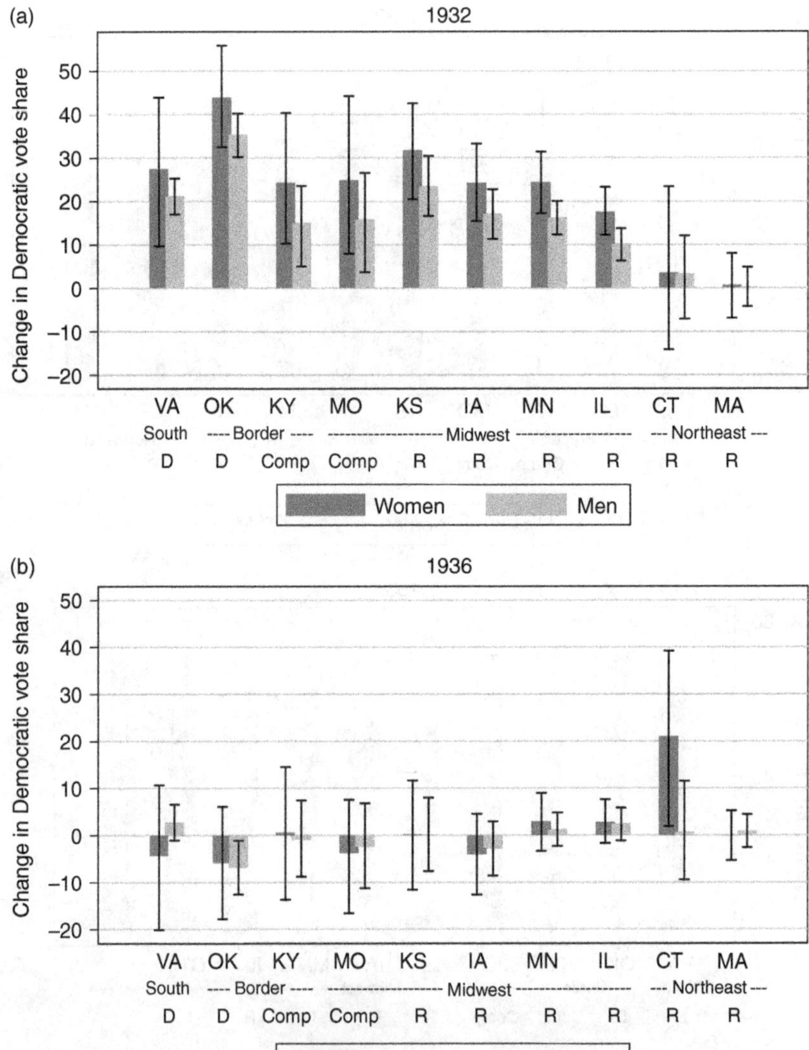

FIGURE 8.6. Change in Democratic vote share of women and men, 1928 to 1936.

and contexts (e.g., Nardulli 1995).[3] We also begin to see evidence that in some places realignment occurred a bit differently – at least in terms of the size and mechanism of the shift – for women and men. Our

[3] We omit discussion of the impact of party context on vote choice from this chapter since the party contexts used in the earlier chapters were largely disrupted in 1928. In the earlier chapters, we were interested in how long-standing partisan context and competitiveness

Northeastern states (Massachusetts and Connecticut), which moved so dramatically toward the Democrats in 1928, are basically stable between 1928 and 1932. Everywhere else, however, Democrats realized remarkable gains among female and male voters in 1932. We have evidence this shift may have been greater among women than men. In the eight non-Northeastern sample states, Democrats picked up an average of well over 20 percentage points from female voters in 1932 compared to 1928. In Oklahoma, the state-wide shift for women was stunning – from 64 percent Republican in 1928 to 73 percent Democratic in 1932 – a more than 44 point shift back to the Democrats! Our analysis suggests this shift among women in Oklahoma may have been larger than the similar shift among men: more than 80 percent of our simulations support that conclusion. In the other Southern and Border states (Virginia and Oklahoma), women also shift to the Democrats at a higher rate than men, but only about 70 percent of the simulations are consistent with this conclusion.

The turn to the Democrats in 1932 among women also appears larger than the shift among men in our formerly Republican-dominated states in the Midwest. Comparing the simulations from 1928 and 1932, the increase in women's support for the Democratic candidate exceeded the increase in men's support in more than 90 percent of the comparisons in Illinois. This was also the case for more than 80 percent of the simulations from 1928 and 1932 in Iowa, Minnesota, and Kansas. While male and female voters were equally likely to support Democrats in these states in 1932, the pro-Republican bias among women in previous years means that outcome required a larger Democratic shift among women.

By contrast, the 1936 contest, although characterized by large gains in turnout, is not nearly as disruptive as 1932 to partisan patterns in most sample states. In most states, male and female Democratic vote share changes very little (and our credible intervals are fairly wide). Only in Connecticut do we observe a larger shift toward the Democrats in 1936 than in 1932. And this shift, as the figure suggests, is driven largely by female voters. Nearly 90 percent of the simulations are consistent with the conclusion that women moved to the Democratic Party in Connecticut, while men did not. Everywhere else, there is little change in vote share, and any shifts are similar among women and men.

shaped women's socialization and mobilization into politics. Those contexts were in considerable flux in the 1930s; in 1932 and 1936, voting for president in all of the states in the sample were either competitive or overwhelmingly Democratic. In the longer-run (1934–1950), only Iowa and Kansas can be classified as one party-Republican.

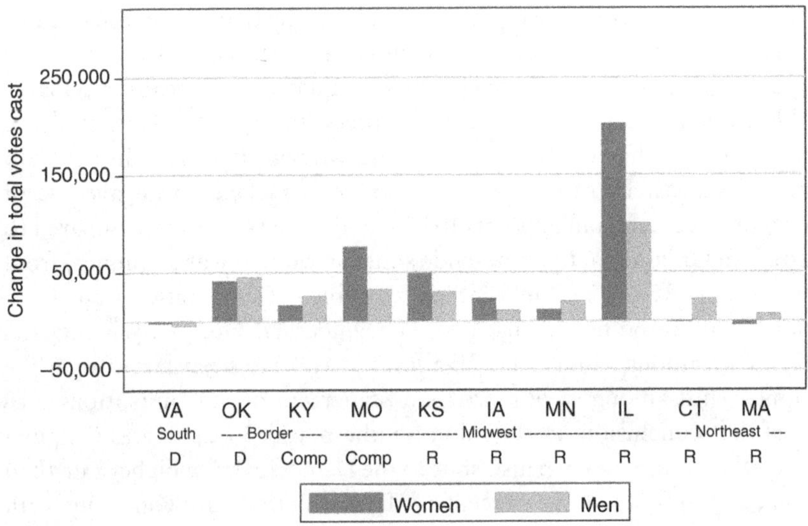

FIGURE 8.7. Change in number of votes cast by women and men, 1928 to 1932.

The Contributions of Women to New Deal Realignment

As in our earlier empirical chapters, examining the number of ballots gained and lost between elections can give us further insight into the process of electoral change for men and women. As we have discussed, the contributions of mobilization and conversion to New Deal realignment have been of keen interest to scholars. The processes appear to vary across these two elections – with little turnout change and large Democratic swings in 1932, and significant new mobilization and little change in partisan distribution in 1936 – so we discuss the overall and partisan mobilization patterns in the 1932 and 1936 elections in sequence.

The Election of 1932

Figure 8.7 summarizes the total number of female and male voters added to the electorate in 1932. With the exception of Virginia, the size of the active electorate expanded in every state, although sometimes only very slightly, over 1928. Given the extraordinary level of new voter mobilization in 1928, both maintenance and especially expansion of the size of the active electorate should be considered an impressive feat. In a handful of states in the Midwest (i.e., Missouri, Kansas, and Illinois), we estimate that nearly twice as many new female voters are added to the rolls as

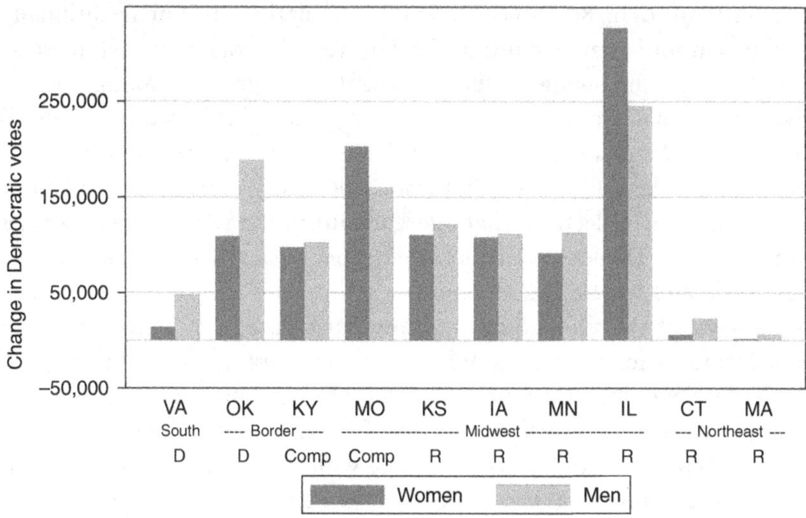

FIGURE 8.8. Change in number of Democratic votes cast by women and men, 1928 to 1932.

male voters in 1932, although only in Illinois are more than 90 percent of the simulations consistent with the conclusion that female mobilization outpaced male mobilization in 1932. (This is consistent with the finding above that over 90 percent of the simulations suggest Illinois women's rate of turnout increased more than men's). In the other states, the number of new voters is either similar or there are slightly more new female voters; we can only conclude with confidence that these states added similar numbers of new male and female voters. Massachusetts and Connecticut, both of which experienced a dramatic expansion of the electorate in 1928, stand out as states with almost no new voters introduced in 1932; here again, the simulations suggest this conclusion holds for both male and female voters. Thus, with the exception of Illinois, we estimate that roughly equal numbers of new men and women entered the electorate in 1932 consistent with our conclusions about changes in the rate of turnout in the preceding text.

Democrats overcame a considerable Republican advantage to become the majority party in 1932. Figure 8.8 summarizes the change in the number of votes cast for the Democratic presidential nominee between 1928 and 1932. Outside of the Northeast, the number of Democratic votes gained is extraordinary in every sample state. In nearly all of the states, men account for a larger number of new Democratic voters than do women but in most cases, the differences are small. Above we saw that in more than 80 to 90 percent of simulations in our traditionally Republican-dominated states in the Midwest (Illinois, Iowa, Minnesota, and Kansas), the swing to the Democrats was greater among women than men. That we do not see a similar gender difference in the number of new Democratic votes cast in these states is a function of, among other things, key differences in turnout. So many more men turned out to vote in earlier elections that a larger shift in the *percentage* of female voters casting Democratic ballots generated basically equal *numbers* of new male and female Democratic votes. Illinois is the exception: Nearly 80 percent of the simulations indicate that *women* accounted for more new Democratic voters than did men in 1932 despite the fact that, as in every state, women's turnout lagged that of men. Once again, we see evidence that New Deal realignment unfolded in uniquely local ways, and that the experience and contributions of women were as much a function of their local context as the fact of their gender.

There are two others states in which gender differences do appear, both in the Southern/Border region. In Oklahoma and Virginia more than 90 percent of the simulations are consistent with the conclusion that Democrats gained more new *male* than female voters. The findings in Oklahoma in particular highlight, once again, the interaction of turnout and vote choice when considering the contributions of men and women to electoral change. We saw above that among those who turned out to vote, the share of votes cast for Democrats (proportion) increased more among women than men in Oklahoma in 1932. However, because of gender differences in turnout (particularly large in Oklahoma), Democrats still gained more actual votes (count) from men than they did from women in Oklahoma in 1932.

Not surprisingly, the decline in Republican ballots in each state – summarized in Figure 8.9 – tells the same story. The decline in the level of support for the Republican candidate was roughly similar among men and women in most sample states. In Oklahoma and Virginia (where Democrats gained more men than women), Republican losses among men were much larger than losses among women, a conclusion supported by more than 90 percent of the simulations. More than 70 percent of the simulations support the same conclusion in Kansas and Minnesota Combined with the greater increase in mobilization of female voters in Illinois in 1932 (see Figure 8.7), confirmed by more than 90 percent of the simulations, we begin to see some evidence consistent with differing patterns of mobilization (women) and conversion (men) as explanations for partisan change among men and women in 1932.

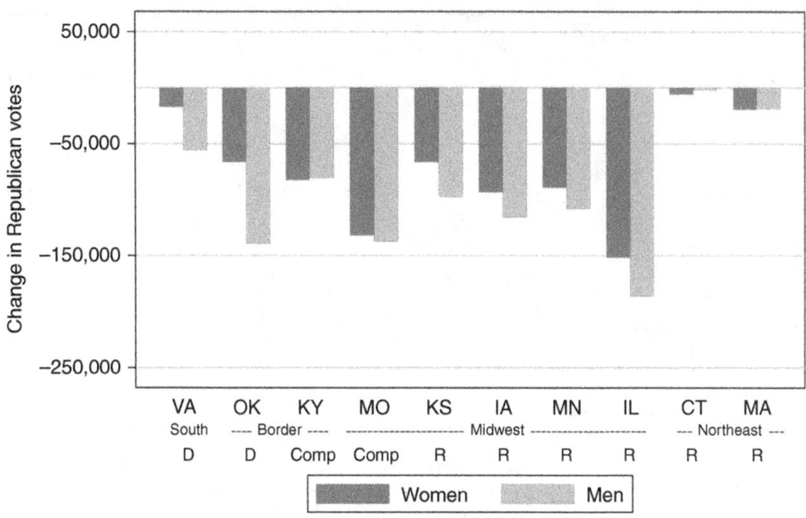

FIGURE 8.9. Change in number of Republican votes cast by women and men, 1928 to 1932.

Were women and men mobilized as or converted to Democrats in the same way in most states or by distinct paths? Keeping in mind the caveats articulated in Chapter 6, we can use the information on new votes cast overall and for each party to identify likely mechanisms behind observed partisan change. Overall, our general conclusion is clear: With the exception of the Northeastern states and Illinois, turnout gains are modest or non-existent in 1932 while the share of votes won by Democrats increases dramatically, suggesting a significant portion of those new Democratic votes likely came from voters who cast their ballots for the Republican candidate in 1928; in other words, conversion was likely the dominant mechanism overall in 1932 (Brown 1988; Hawley and Sagarzazu 2012).

The minimum number of converts required to generate the observed level of Democratic support[4] in each state in 1932 is summarized in Figure 8.10. The number represented in the figure is simply the number of new male or female Democratic votes minus the number of new male or female voters. The difference between these numbers is the minimum number of converts who must have been added to new voters to account

[4] The figure summarizes conversions from the Republican Party in 1932, which could result in increasing support for the Democratic candidate or a third party candidate. Third party support is fairly low in the sample states in 1932, about 2.5 percent, so the overwhelming number of Republican converts supported the Democratic candidate. For that reason, we refer only to conversion to Democratic support in the text.

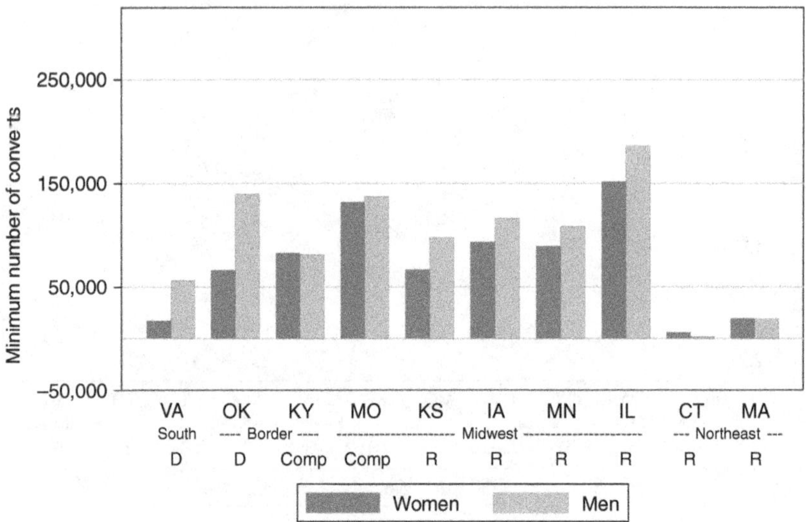

FIGURE 8.10. Minimum number of Republican converts, 1928 to 1932. ("Minimum" implies no new voters cast Republican ballots.)

for observed support for the Democratic candidate in 1932. Because the number of additional votes for Democrats is so large relative to the number of new voters in every state, it is extremely likely that there were many converts from the Republican to the Democratic Party.[5] While differences in many states are small, in most states there were more male converts (1928 Republican voters who cast Democratic or third-party ballots in 1932) than there were female.

To what extent did these likely converts (reported in Figure 8.10) contribute to the huge gains in Democratic support observed in 1932? Figure 8.11 reports the proportion of new Democratic support that we attribute to conversion (specifically, the minimum number of Republican converts divided by the change in number of Democratic voters). We exclude Virginia and Massachusetts, as well as women in Connecticut, cases where the number of available converts exceeds the gains in Democratic support, suggesting that *all* of the 1932 Democratic growth

[5] This is an estimate based on the assumption that virtually all new voters were Democrats or third party supporters. If some new voters supported the Republicans, the number of required converts would be higher. If some established voters shifted from the Democrats to or third parties to the Republican Party, the number of required converts from 1928 Republicans would be higher. On the other hand, if many Republican voters from 1928 stayed home and these voters were replaced with new Democratic voters, then the conversion numbers would be lower.

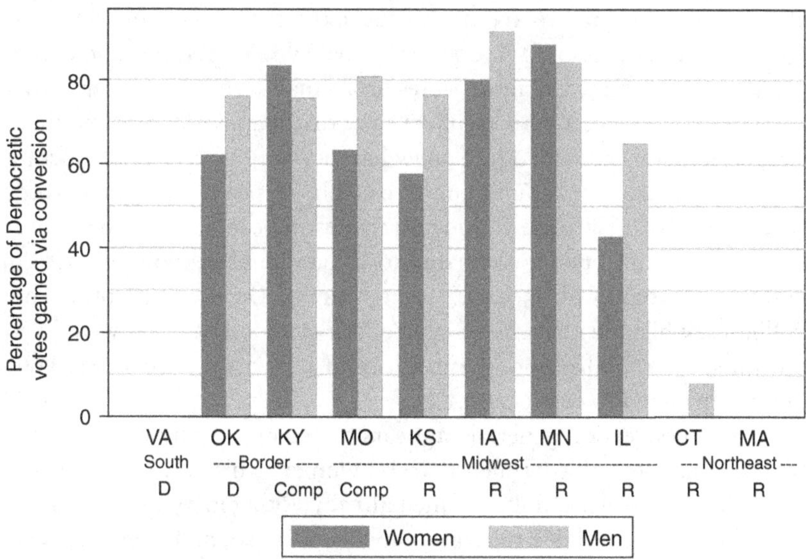

FIGURE 8.11. Percentage of new Democratic support due to conversion, 1928 to 1932.

is attributable to conversion. For this reason and others, the discussion also excludes Connecticut men.[6] In the remaining seven states, conversion accounts for more Democratic gains among men than women in five of seven cases, and often by a substantial margin. Only in Kentucky and Minnesota are more of women's Democratic gains attributable to conversion than men's, and the differences are small.

Overall, considering the total sample of ten states, we estimate there were 411,000 new female voters and 290,000 new male voters in 1932. At the same time, we estimate Democrats gained about 656,000 votes from women in 1932, and about 828,000 votes from men. If we accept the crude assumption that no new voters cast Republican ballots, conversion accounts for about 62 percent of the 1.06 million votes gained by Democrats among women in the sample states in 1932, and perhaps 75 percent of the 1.11 million votes gained by Democrats among men. Conversion was likely the dominant mechanism for both sexes in 1932, but more so for men than for women.

As noted above, Illinois stands out as an exception in important ways, and yet the general pattern holds. Clearly, Illinois had the largest number

[6] Third party ballots are not available at the Minor Civil Division (MCD) level in Connecticut in 1932, which biases our estimates of conversion. As a result, we exclude Connecticut from this analysis.

of new voters. There are about 100,000 more male voters in 1932 than 1928, and an impressive 200,000 new female voters. Yet, the Democratic Party picks up 245,000 more votes from males and, amazingly, some 330,000 from women. As a result, even with a massive level of mobilization, conversion accounted for somewhat more of men's new Democratic votes even in Illinois: A minimum of roughly 60 percent (about 145,000 of 245,000) of new male Democratic votes appear likely to have been generated by conversion, compared to a minimum of about 40 percent (estimated 130,000 of 330,000) of new female Democratic votes. Thus in Illinois, while the majority of new female Democratic votes were likely generated via mobilization, the majority of new male Democratic votes can be attributed to conversion.

In sum, conversion generally appears to account for more of the new Democratic votes cast by men than by women. This is not particularly surprising; the larger number of men already voting in 1928 implies that more men were available for conversion and, less so, mobilization. What might be surprising is that the relatively larger number of male converts occurs in spite of the fact that women are more likely to defect. The minimum number of converts (from above) as a percentage of the available 1928 electorate (reported, by state and gender, in Figure 8.12) gives a sense of the rate of defection. For example, in Minnesota, we estimate 89,000 of the 213,000 women who cast Republican ballots in 1928 did not do so in 1932, for a defection rate of 41 percent among women. In contrast, we estimate 108,000 of the 347,000 men who cast Republican ballots in 1928 did not do so in 1932, producing a male defection rate of 31 percent. Consistent with the estimates from Minnesota, women's rate of defection exceeds men's in every state. In some states, like Oklahoma and Illinois, the gender differences in defection rates are quite small. In other states, like Minnesota and Kentucky, the defection rate for women was clearly higher. Because each of the numbers in the calculation is estimated with uncertainty, the confidence intervals for these quantities are wide. Summing the numbers of minimum required converts and 1928 Republican voters available across all of the sample states, about 80 percent of the simulations are consistent with the conclusion that female defection rates exceeded male defection rates in our sample states. In one state, Minnesota, over 85 percent of the simulations are consistent with the conclusion that the percentage of Republican defectors was higher among women than men. There are no states where even more than 50 percent of the simulations are consistent with a higher minimum defection rate among men.

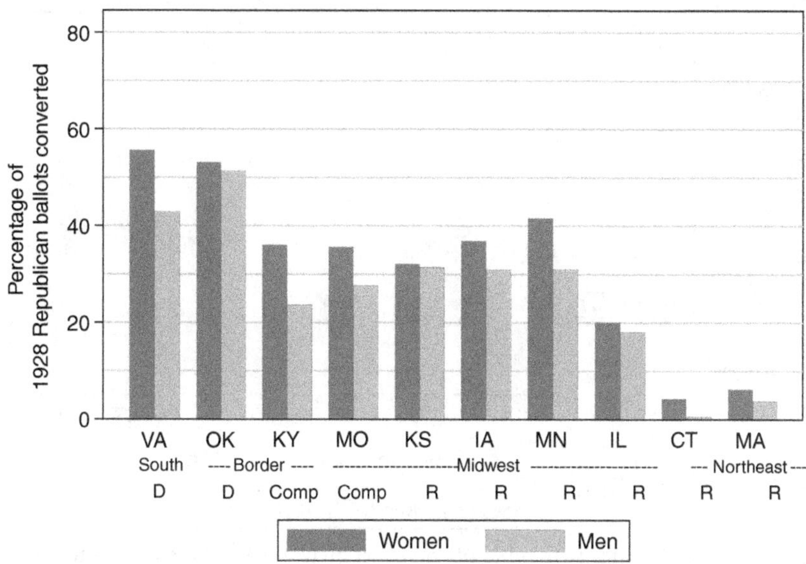

FIGURE 8.12. Minimum percentage of 1928 Republican ballots converted (defection rate), 1928 to 1932. ("Minimum" implies no new voters cast Republican ballots.)

Thus, while in 1932 mobilization was responsible for a bigger portion of new Democratic ballots cast by women, than it was for new Democratic ballots cast by men, the percentage of women who changed their vote choice from 1928 to 1932 (defection) was likely larger than the similar percentage among men. Once again, this finding highlights how our conclusions are shaped by the data and measures we examine, and particularly the interaction of turnout and vote choice. While more of the Democratic gains among men were attributable to conversion than mobilization, many fewer women voted in 1928. As a result, even with fewer converts in 1932 overall, the likelihood that a 1928 voter changed her vote from Republican to Democratic in 1932 was likely marginally higher among women than men. Substantively, the greater likelihood that women would defect in 1932 is consistent with claims that women's lesser electoral experience would mean weaker partisan ties (e.g., Converse 1969, 1976).

The Election of 1936

In 1936, the mobilization of new voters is clearly more extensive than in 1932 and in most states there are more women added to the electorate

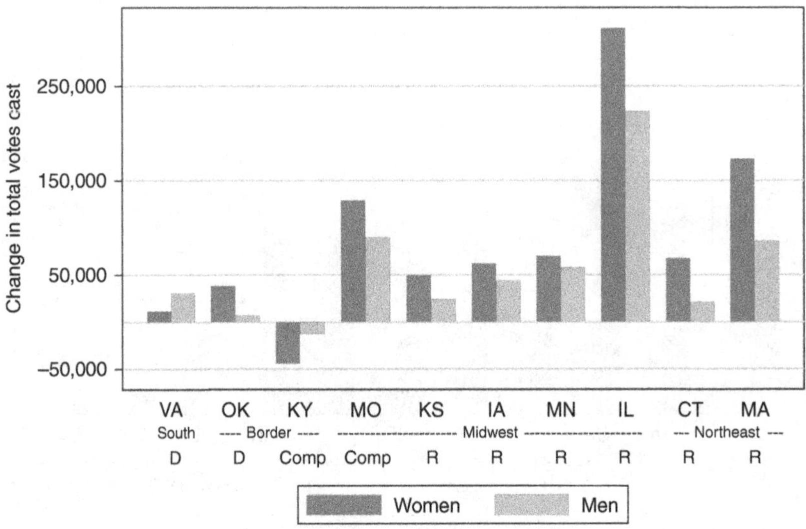

FIGURE 8.13. Change in number of votes cast by women and men, 1932 to 1936.

than men. Overall, across our ten sample states, 868,000 more women participate in 1936 than in 1932, and 570,000 more men. Figure 8.13 shows that this pattern generally holds at the state level; in nearly all of our sample states, there are more new female voters than male. We can be confident of these differences in Illinois, where more than 90 percent of the simulations support the conclusion that female mobilization was larger, and somewhat confident in Connecticut and Kansas (more than 80 percent of simulations). In another three states – Iowa, Missouri, and Oklahoma – 75 percent or more of the simulations are also consistent with this conclusion. These are, not surprisingly, the same states in which we see substantial gender differences in the size of the increase in the rate of turnout (Figure 8.2, above). Despite starting from very different turnout bases in 1932, the extent to which women's mobilization exceeded men's in these states was significant enough to show up in both the counts reported here, and in the growth rate of turnout. Thus, in most states, the expectation that the larger numbers of inactive women available for mobilization would mean women were responsible for more *new* ballots than men during the New Deal period is confirmed in a number of states in 1936, when new mobilization was considerable. (Recall that women also generated more new ballots than did men in 1932).

With the exception of Kentucky, Democrats tended to gain voters over 1932 (see Figure 8.14). In 1936 (the New Deal election characterized

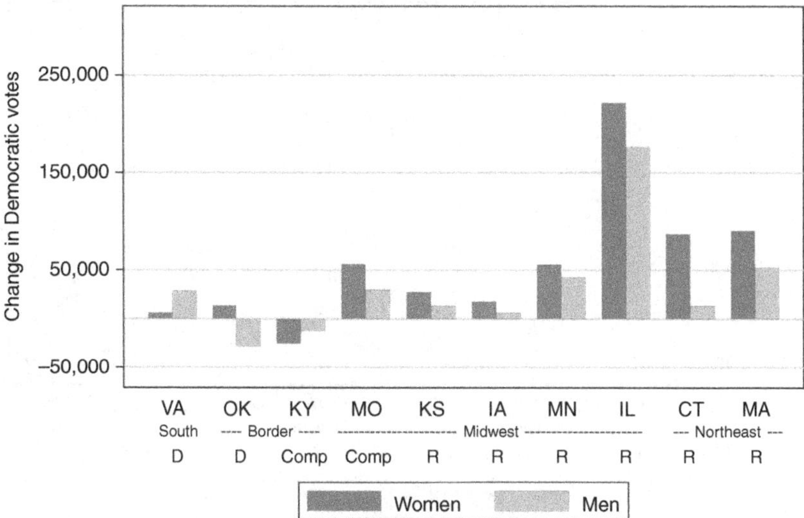

FIGURE 8.14. Change in number of Democratic votes cast by women and men, 1932 to 1936.

by greater mobilization), more of the new Democratic votes come from women than men in eight of our ten states, although again, differences are small in a number of cases. Because the uncertainty associated with these estimates are large, we can be confident about these differences only in Connecticut; over 90 percent of the simulations indicate that Democrats picked up more votes from women than from men.

The large mobilization of voters in 1936 generated gains for the Republican Party as well (see Figure 8.15). The differences between men and women are small, however, so our overall conclusion is that in 1936, in places where Republicans gained male votes, they gained a similar number of female votes.[7]

We have a harder time inferring the mechanisms for the allocation of partisan votes gained in 1936, compared to 1932, since the number of new entrants to the electorate was quite large (more than 1.4 million), but the gains for Democrats were smaller (900,000), and Republicans experienced gains as well. As a result, a variety of possible mechanisms could be at work between 1932 and 1936: Mobilization of Republicans,

[7] Massachusetts stands out as an exception, but the simulation failed to converge for Massachusetts, 1936, so we have less confidence in the estimates associated with that election.

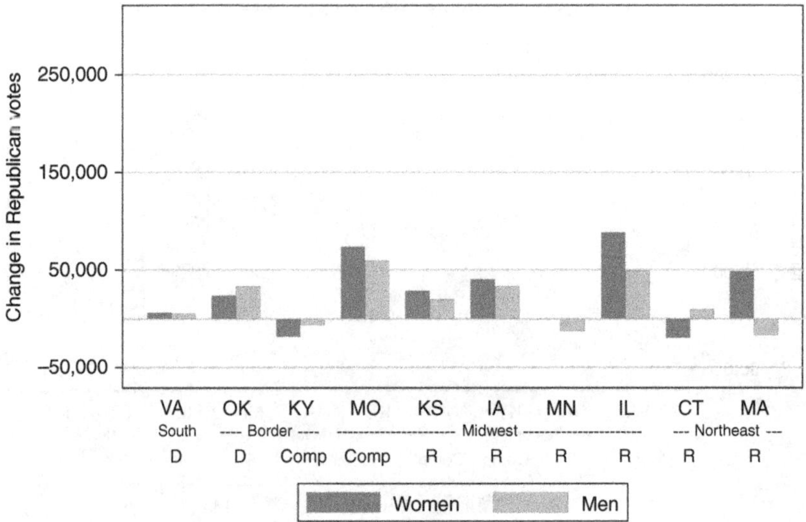

FIGURE 8.15. Change in number of Republican votes cast by women and men, 1932 to 1936.

mobilization of Democrats, conversion from Democratic to Republican, and/or conversion from Republican to Democrat. It is not possible for us to say with much confidence which mechanisms, and to what extent, explain electoral change in 1936, or if different mechanisms characterize men and women. Although they remain possible, the estimates, in the aggregate, reveal no striking gender differences in these dynamics, except for the evidence of greater turnout gains among women compared to men.

The Contributions of Women to New Deal Realignment

Overall, we find men and women contributed in roughly equal numbers, but in different ways, to New Deal realignment. In both 1932 and 1936 we find evidence that the number of new female voters entering the system exceeded the number of new male voters: In our sample, 120,000 more women than men entered the electorate in 1932 (almost exclusively attributable to Illinois) and 300,000 more women than men entered the electorate in 1936. As previous scholars have expected (e.g., Andersen 1979), women's under-mobilization relative to men translated into more new female than new male voters during the New Deal realignment period. At the same time, we find that women in the electorate prior to the 1930s were somewhat more likely to defect from their pre–New

Deal partisanship (i.e., women were more likely than men to switch from Republican ballots in 1928 to Democratic ballots in 1932), consistent with the expectation that partisanship would be less stable among female voters who had been in the active electorate for a shorter period (e.g., Andersen 1979; Converse 1969, 1976). However, because there were fewer women in the active electorate overall, mobilization accounted for more new Democratic votes among women than it did among men.

Despite the fact that more new women than new men were mobilized in these elections, the number of new *Democratic* votes overall that can be attributed to women is not substantially different than the number of new Democratic votes that can be attributed to men: In our ten sample states, we estimate that in 1932 about one million female Democratic votes (1.07 million) and a little more than one million male Democratic votes (1.11 million) were added to the electorate, and about 550,000 additional female Democratic votes and about 320,000 additional male Democratic votes in 1936. While more new female than male voters entered the active electorate in 1932 and 1936, more new male Democratic votes were generated by conversion. Thus, the combined effects of mobilization and conversion allowed the Democrats to draw nearly equal numbers of new voters from the ranks of the male and female electorate across the 1932 and 1936 elections: 1.6 million additional votes from women, and 1.4 million additional votes from men.

Conclusion: Women and the New Deal Realignment

Conventional narratives of New Deal realignment overlook the impact of new female voters on the fortunes of the Democrats. Both mechanisms of realignment – mobilization and conversion – appear to have characterized women's contribution to New Deal realignment: Due to lower turnout, many women were available for mobilization, and those who had voted previously (mostly for Republicans) lacked the reinforcement of partisanship offered by long-term political participation. And indeed, many women either converted from Republican support (particularly in 1932) or were newly mobilized by Democrats (especially in 1936).

Interestingly, although the shift in support to the Democrats – measured as the change in Democratic vote share – was smaller among men (in 1932), the male electorate was larger so the net result is that Democratic gains came in roughly equal numbers from men and women – about 1.6 million additional women and 1.4 million additional men across both elections. In our ten sample states more than 3.3 million women and

4.5 million men supported the Democratic candidate Roosevelt in 1936. Given that Democratic candidate Smith received only 1.7 million votes from women and 3 million votes from men in the same states in 1928, the joint impact of mobilization and conversion on the female electorate across the 1932–1936 period is clearly very large. By 1936, Democrats had attracted an impressive 95 percent more female voters compared to about 50 percent more male voters.

Accounts of New Deal realignment that ignore the gradual and persistent increase in women's turnout miss an important element of mobilization that accounts for a huge number of new voters in the 1930s. In some states, women were clearly well incorporated into electoral politics by the end of the realignment era – the rate of turnout for women in several sample states was nearly 65 percent by 1936. This level of mobilization would be considered remarkable in our current era.

Women shaped the size, pattern, and outcome of New Deal realignment. The massive change in the electoral fortunes of the Democratic Party in the 1930s was due, in roughly equal measure, to the ballots of men and women. Only 16 years after the extension of suffrage to women and after early accounts dismissed women's suffrage as a disappointment or failure, women were a large and increasingly important source of electoral support for the emerging Democratic majority.

ILLUSTRATION 9.1. Sophia Horne and Elizabeth Hunnicut getting out the vote in Atlanta, Georgia, 1926. Collection of the League of Women Voters of the United States.

9

Female Voters from Suffrage through the New Deal and Beyond

On November 2, 1920 – election day – the front page of the *Dallas Morning News* featured a large cartoon entitled, "Enter Mr. and Mrs. Voter." A man and a woman, both holding ballots, are shown rushing into a polling place. Scattered about the floor are scraps of paper with words like "estimate," "claims," "misrepresentation," and "figgers." Proclaims Mr. Voter: "Get out of the way; we'll settle this argument!"

The "argument," of course, was over how women would cast ballots if permitted to do so. Yet, despite Mr. Voter's claims, the presidential election of 1920 did not settle the argument. For nearly 100 years, political observers, journalists, and social scientists have sought to discern whether and with what effect women enfranchised by the Nineteenth Amendment entered polling places and cast their ballots. This effort has been hampered by the realities of the conduct of elections in the United States: With few, important exceptions, no information about the voter, including her sex, is associated with any ballot submitted for tally in American elections. In modern times, exit polls and public opinion surveys have greatly aided our understanding of who votes and how, but these tools were not available or reliable in the first elections following women's enfranchisement. Meticulous efforts have provided us with some information about how women voted in a few times and places (see Chapter 3), but these findings are limited in their coverage of time and place. In 1972 – more than fifty years after the ratification of the Nineteenth Amendment – Phillip Converse acknowledged that "definitive research on the precise effects of female suffrage remains to be done" (276).

As we now approach the one hundredth anniversary of the Nineteenth Amendment, we cannot claim to have settled this argument, or offered the "definitive" answer, with the data analysis presented in this book. We do claim to have offered a substantial advance in our understanding of the behavior and contributions of newly enfranchised women in the first elections following the ratification of the Nineteenth Amendment. Although our sample states are not fully representative of the United States as a whole, our research provides insight into whether and how women voted in more places across a longer span of time than previous scholarship has been able to do. The result is a considerably improved ability to answer a number of long-standing questions about the behavior and impact of female voters after suffrage.

Our empirical analysis thus far has been organized around specific outcomes in particular elections. In this final chapter, we summarize our findings across these five presidential elections to gauge what we can conclude about some of the central long-standing puzzles surrounding the entrance of women into the American electorate. We then place the first female voters within the context of the more than eighty years of electoral history that has followed. We examine what this set of elections, including the contributions of women, mean for American politics more broadly. Finally, we return to the question at the heart of this book: Did women's votes count?

Answering (If Not Settling) Some Arguments

The doubling of the eligible electorate raised a number of key questions about women's possible impact and behavior for contemporary observers as well as later scholars. In this section we consider what our data and estimates tell us about some of the most persistent puzzles related to how and with what consequences women cast their first ballots.

Was the Nineteenth Amendment Responsible for Declining Turnout?

Beginning in the 1880s, turnout in American elections began its long, infamous decline from the historic highs of the Reconstruction Era. Figure 9.1 shows turnout in presidential elections averaging more than 70 percent through the turn of the last century.[1] This is actually

[1] Turnout estimates combine data about the voting-age population (ICPSR 1992) and presidential vote (CQ Press 2010). As we note in Chapter 4, we rely on a conservative estimate of turnout, based on the *voting-age* population. It does not account for the exclusion of citizens from the franchise for reasons related to race, immigration status, felony convictions, and so on. The *voting-eligible* population was smaller than the voting-age population, and thus rates of turnout limited to those eligible to do so would be even higher.

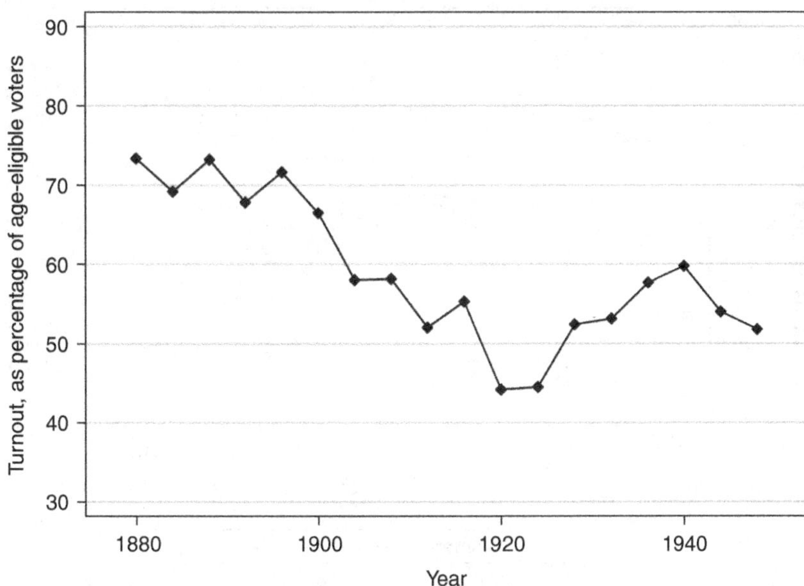

FIGURE 9.1. National turnout in presidential elections, 1880–1948.

a decrease from the 1870s when turnout exceeded 80 percent in most elections. Much of the initial deterioration can be attributed to declining turnout in the South as Reconstruction ended and systematic disenfranchisement of blacks and poor whites was enacted and enforced (Valelly 2004); outside of the South, turnout in presidential elections remained in the upper-80s until about 1900, at which point non-Southern turnout also began to decline precipitously (Burnham 1965). After diminishing dramatically with the enfranchisement of women in 1920, turnout in presidential elections stabilizes and then begins to rebound in the decades that followed. The gradual enfranchisement of women in the decades leading up to and following 1920 has been identified as a key contributor to the general decline in turnout, most notably by Phillip Converse (1972, 276) in his extended debate with Walter Dean Burnham over "The Changing Shape of the American Political Universe" (Burnham 1965):

> … the size of the national electorate was more than doubled within a decade as a result of female suffrage, and there is no question whatever but that over-all statements of turnout were drastically affected as a result … given the temporary but massive dilution of the over-all "political socialization" of the electorate represented by the opening of the political system to women.

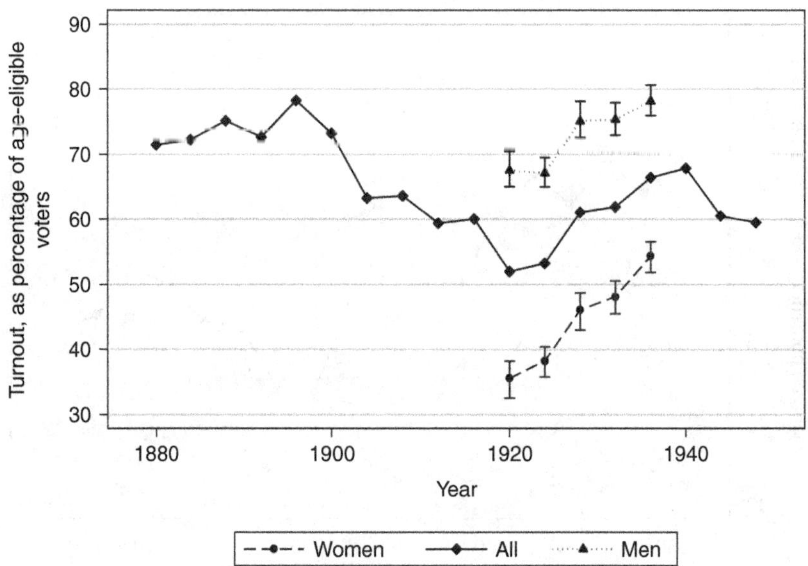

FIGURE 9.2. Total turnout and turnout of women and men, sample states, 1880–1948.

Our focus on the period after 1920 means that we cannot speak to the contribution of the piecemeal extension of female suffrage prior to the Nineteenth Amendment on the decline in turnout before 1920. We can, however, provide some insight into the contribution of women's suffrage to turnout rates in the five elections between 1920 and 1936. Figure 9.2 shows overall turnout from 1880 through 1948 in the ten states in our sample, as well as our estimates for male and female turnout in those ten states in the five presidential elections between 1920 and 1936. (Note that women were eligible to vote in the 1916 presidential election in Illinois and Kansas; overall turnout in 1916 would have been even higher had those states not been included or women not enfranchised).

We estimate that a substantial number of men entered the electorate between 1916 and 1920 (see Chapter 5). Certainly, and as expected, women's inclusion in the eligible electorate dampens overall turnout. Naively assuming male turnout in these five elections would have been the same or similar had women not been enfranchised in our ten sample states, the difference between what turnout would have been without women (i.e., male turnout) and actual turnout is about 16 points in 1920. The extent to which women dampen turnout attenuates overtime: By 1936, the difference between what turnout would have been without women and what it was with them narrows to about 12 points. Nonetheless, had women continued to be excluded from the electorate, overall turnout may well have returned to levels not seen since 1896 by 1936. With the inclusion of women, overall turnout reaches just 66 percent in these ten states by 1936, a figure which would be considered quite respectable today but that represented a significant decline from the 1880s and before.

Did Women's Turnout Increase Over Time?

That the turnout of long-enfranchised men would exceed that of newly enfranchised women is an easily defended, key assumption of our analysis (see Chapter 4). Among the many reasons why women were less likely to take advantage of the suffrage right include their lack of experience (e.g., Gerber et al. 2003; Gerould 1925; Niemi, Stanley, and Evans 1984; Plutzer 2002; Wells 1929), socialization into nonpolitical roles (Stucker 1976), and social norms discouraging political participation among women (Andersen 1990, 1996; Baker 1984; Kraditor 1981; Lane 1959; Merriam and Gosnell 1924). As women gained experience and social norms and socialization adjusted to new realities, many observers – both at the time and in later scholarship – expected that turnout would increase among women and that the gender gap in turnout would narrow over time (see Andersen 1996; Kleppner 1982b).

As we saw in Figure 9.2, there is no question that female turnout increased over the five elections in our study. Yet, the fact that male turnout is also increasing across these elections points to factors other than women's increasing experience and shifts in gender norms to explain much of this growth. Did women's turnout increase to a greater extent than men's? Figure 9.3 shows that the turnout gender gap indeed declines in every election except 1928, when the mobilization of both men and women in response to the contest between Al Smith and Herbert Hoover is exceptional (see Chapter 7). Overall, the turnout gender gap, an estimated 32 points in 1920, falls to 24 points by 1936. While the Bayesian credible intervals suggest that we can have limited confidence that the size of the gender gap varied from election to election, the difference in the size of the turnout gender gap between 1920 and 1936 is clearly real and substantial.[2] As we can see

[2] The Chicago registration data for 1932 indicate a nearly 17-point gap in the rate of registration between men and women, down from 23 points in 1920. This decrease in the gap in participation of roughly one-fourth or 6 percentage points is consistent with the broader sample estimate of a decline of roughly one-fourth or 8 percentage points.

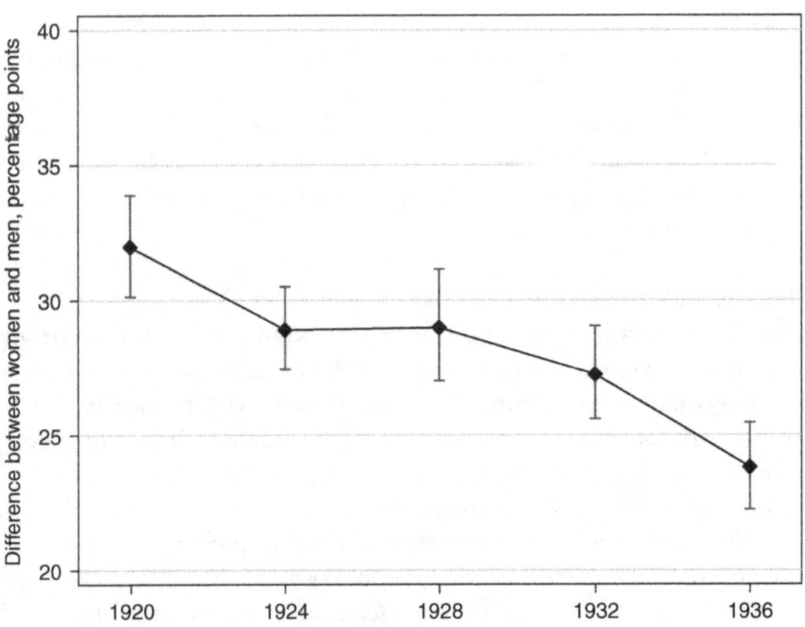

FIGURE 9.3. Difference between women's and men's turnout, sample states, 1920–1936.

in Figure 9.2, this is not due to declining male turnout but to women's turnout increasing at a slightly sharper rate.

We do find evidence, then, that women's turnout, relative to men's, increased over time. However, we want to highlight that other factors, such as variation in local context, had at least as much and in some cases a larger impact on women's turnout than did the passage of time and accumulation of experience. Across our sample states, women's turnout grew an estimated 18 points (from 36 percent in 1920 to 54 percent in 1936) over the five elections examined in this research. Yet as early as 1920, women's turnout varied more than *50 points* across the states in our sample, from a mere 5.7 percent in Virginia to an impressive 57 percent in Kentucky. Even excluding low-turnout Virginia, we still find a nearly 35-point gap between women's turnout in Kentucky and both Connecticut and Massachusetts (where women's turnout averaged around 22 percent in 1920). By 1936, female turnout remained low in Virginia (9 percent) and had fallen to 42 percent in Kentucky, as that state shifted from competitive to one-party Democratic. Yet, female turnout exceeded 67 percent in states such as Missouri and Illinois, nearly *60 points* higher than Virginia. Even if we exclude low-turnout Virginia, women's turnout in Missouri and Illinois was about 28 points higher than in Oklahoma (39 percent), at least comparable to and likely exceeding the entire growth (18 points) in average women's turnout in our ten sample states between 1920 and 1936.

Not only does the variation in female turnout across states often exceed the variation in female turnout over time, it typically exceeds the size of the gender gap in turnout in most states. That is, women often differed more from women in other states than they did from men in their own states. As we have seen, even excluding low-turnout Virginia, the difference in female turnout across states was as high as 35 points in 1920. In that same election, the turnout gender gap was as small as 24 to 28 points in Missouri and Kentucky, and topped out around 40 points in Connecticut. By 1936, the turnout gender gap varies from a low of 17 points in Missouri and Illinois to a high of 33 points in Kentucky. The size of the difference in female turnout across states (30 points, excluding Virginia) is larger than all but two state-level turnout gender gaps. Women's rates of turnout varied as much or more between women in different states than between women and men in those same states.

Thus, while continuing to lag behind what was by 1936 the incredible mobilization of men (exceeding 80 percent in at least four states, and more than 70 percent across our sample), our estimates suggest that women were capable of turning out to vote at impressive rates from the very first election following the Nineteenth Amendment through the New Deal period. Many factors contributed to variation in women's turnout across states: The social, economic, legal, and political conditions, as well as the social and economic characteristics of the women themselves. As a result, the difference in women's rates of turnout between states was often larger than the turnout gap between women and men, or the size of the growth in women's turnout over time.

What this suggests is that the first women enfranchised were not inherently incapable of mobilization into electoral politics. Disenfranchisement, socialization, and social norms did have long-lasting effects; in no cases do we have reason to expect women's turnout to meet or exceed men's during the era examined here (see Chapter 1), and available data suggests women's rates of turnout continued to lag those of men for decades (cf. Berelson, Lazarsfeld, and McPhee 1954; Campbell et al. 1960; CAWP 2014; Wolfinger and Rosenstone 1980). Yet, when given the opportunity and encouragement, women took up the right to vote as early as the very first election in which they were able at rates that would be considered impressive today.

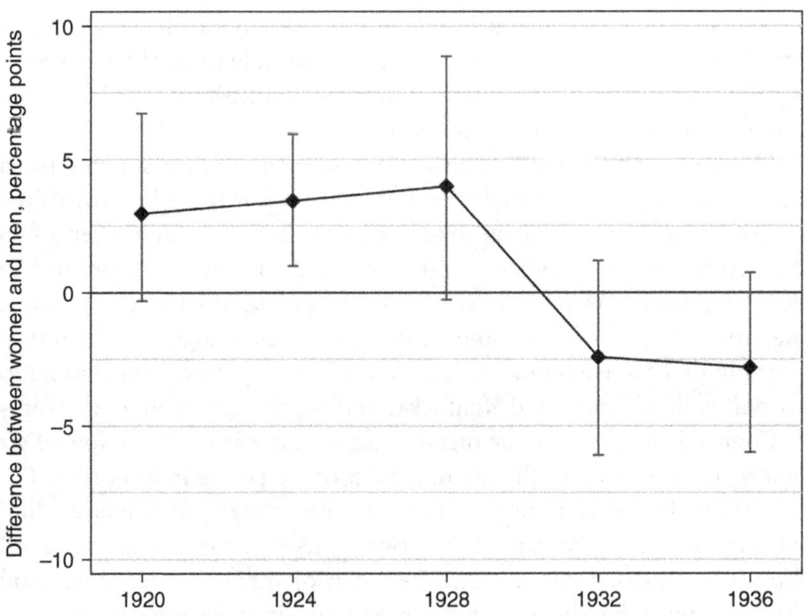

FIGURE 9.4. Difference between women's and men's support for Republican presidential candidates, sample states, 1920–1936.

Did Suffrage Advantage the Republican Party?

It is commonly believed that women's suffrage, at least initially, was a boon to the Republican Party (see, e.g., Alpern and Baum 1985; Andersen 1994; Brown 1991; Goldstein 1984; Lane 1959; Smith 1980; Willey and Rice 1924). And indeed, our analysis of the ten states in our sample provides some support for this conclusion. As Figure 9.4 shows, before 1932, female voters in our sample were slightly more likely to cast Republican ballots than men in each of the first three elections after the extension of suffrage. In the sample as a whole, the Republican advantage among women is clearest in 1924, but the 90 percent credible interval just overlaps with zero in both 1920 and 1928.

Yet, the pro-Republican bias among women in the first three elections after suffrage appears largely restricted to Midwestern states where the Republican Party boasted a significant advantage in identification and political control. This pattern is revealed in Table 9.1 which lists the states in which women voted more Republican (upper panel) or Democratic (lower panel) than did men. In 1920, we see a Republican advantage among women in three Midwestern states (and possibly a

TABLE 9.1. *States with Higher Female Support for the Republican or Democratic Presidential Candidate, 1920–1936*

Republican				
1920	1924	1928	1932	1936
Illinois	Illinois	Illinois		
Minnesota	Minnesota	Minnesota*		
Iowa	Iowa			
Kansas*	Kansas	Kansas*		
	Massachusetts*			
		Oklahoma*		
Democratic				
1920	1924	1928	1932	1936
Virginia*	Virginia*		Virginia*	
				Connecticut
				Minnesota
				Kentucky*

Note: States are listed as having higher female support if more than 90 percent of simulations support that conclusion. In states with an asterisk, more than 80 percent of simulations support the conclusion, and thus we are only moderately confident of the gender difference in those states.

fourth, Kansas, with 80 percent of simulations), and in 1924 in four (and perhaps Massachusetts with 80 percent of simulations). By 1928, the pro-Republican bias among women is found in only one state, Illinois, although we can be moderately confident about three others (Minnesota, Kansas, and Oklahoma). In the one-party South and Border states, as well as in the Republican-dominated Northeast, women were (generally) either as likely to cast Republican ballots as were men, or in the case of Virginia, perhaps even less likely than men to do so.

Moreover, whatever advantage the Nineteenth Amendment offered the GOP, it was short-lived. In 1932 and 1936, if there is any partisan advantage among women, it belongs to the Democrats. For our sample as a whole, the 90 percent confidence interval overlaps with zero (see Figure 9.4), suggesting we cannot reject the possibility that there was no gender difference in vote choice. We do, however, find evidence of a Democratic advantage among women in some states (lower panel of Table 9.1): Virginia in 1932 (over 80 percent of simulations) and Minnesota, Connecticut (both over 90 percent of simulations), and Kentucky (more than 80 percent of simulations) in 1936. The electoral shift to a Democratic majority in the 1930s characterized both female and male voters, and perhaps women more than men in a handful of cases.

Thus, the enfranchisement of women was a boon to the Republican Party, but only in the very first elections after suffrage, and our data suggests, generally only in a few, specific kinds of states. By the fourth election after the ratification of the Nineteenth Amendment, if women's votes benefited any party, it was the Democrats. Even in 1920, 1924, and 1928, our findings cast doubt on an expectation of a general Republican bias among women, but rather suggest that women may have been more mobilized by the locally dominated party in their state in the first elections after suffrage.

Were Women Peripheral Voters?

Both contemporaries and later scholars have characterized most newly enfranchised women as politically uninterested and disengaged citizens. As such, women fit the description of peripheral or low-propensity voters (e.g., Arceneaux and Nickerson 2009). Peripheral voters are mobilized to electoral participation only under the most conducive circumstances; that is, highly salient elections where mobilization efforts are extensive, election contests are exciting, and political information is easy to come by. When they do vote, peripheral voters tend to behave as "swing voters," swept up by the excitement for the party or candidate that is most advantaged by the election (see Kaufmann, Petrocik, and Shaw 2008).

In the first three elections following suffrage, we conclude that newly enfranchised women largely behaved as peripheral voters in terms of turnout, but not in terms of vote choice. In every one of the five presidential elections examined in this research, and particularly in the first three, the probability that women would turn out to vote was more strongly influenced by context, as we would expect of peripheral voters: Women were more likely to turnout in states where the partisan context was more competitive, and less likely to turnout in states with more restrictive electoral laws. Men's turnout followed these same patterns, but competitive contexts were *more* mobilizing, and electoral barriers were *more* of a hindrance, for women, consistent with expectations for a population characterized by lesser political interest, experience, and knowledge. As a result, the difference in women's rate of turnout between competitive and noncompetitive partisan contexts, and between more and less restrictive legal contexts, was greater than the difference among men in every election we analyze, as Figure 9.5 shows. The one possible exception is

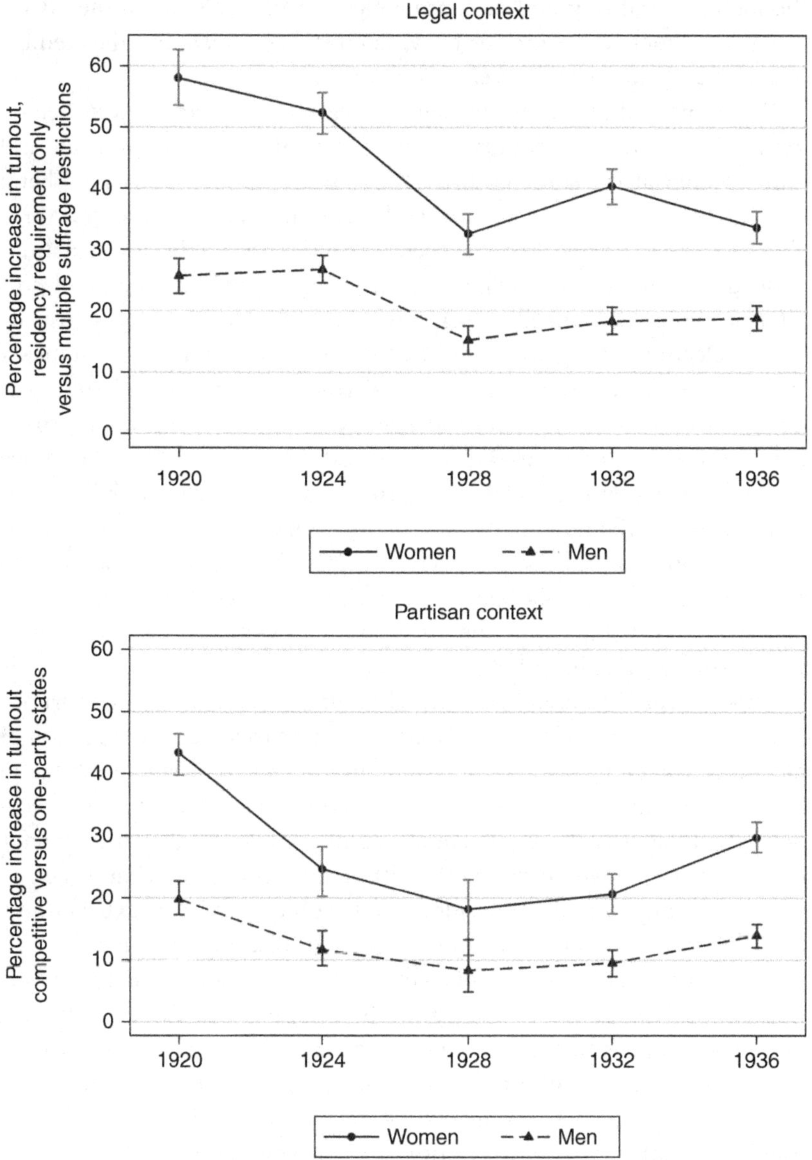

FIGURE 9.5. Effects of partisan context and voting restrictions on turnout of women and men, 1920–1936.

the highly mobilizing and disrupting election of 1928, when the effects of partisan context are greater for women than for men, but the credible intervals around those differences do overlap.

While we find persuasive evidence of peripheral voter turnout behavior in the reaction of women, compared to men, to the partisan and legal context at the state level, we find less clear evidence of peripheral turnout behavior among women at the national level. Of the first three elections after suffrage, 1928 was clearly the most highly salient nationwide, dominated by compelling issues of religion, immigration, and prohibition (Peel and Donnelly 1931; Silva 1962; Sundquist 1983) – just the sort of election setting we would expect to overcome deficits of interest and knowledge, and mobilize peripheral voters. Many believed 1928 was highly mobilizing for women (Andersen 1996; Burner 1986; Lubell 1952; Sundquist 1983), and our evidence suggests they were right. Yet, as we showed in Chapter 8, the election of 1928 was also hugely mobilizing for men. Indeed, given how many more women than men were available for mobilization (that is, how many more women than men had not voted in previous elections), the finding of nearly equal numbers of new female and male voters is striking, and not consistent with expectations that women were more likely to be peripheral voters.

This conclusion about 1928 is highlighted when we examine turnout change across all five elections. Figure 9.6 summarizes the mobilization of men and women in each election, measured as the percentage change in turnout over the previous presidential election. In every presidential election, including 1928, the percentage point change in turnout is greater for women than men (although the difference is non-significant in 1932). Given the larger pool of un-mobilized women, and the expectations regarding the effects of time and experience (discussed previously), this is unsurprising. The high salient election of 1928 is not unique, however; we find greater female turnout growth relative to men's in every election (save 1932) and the difference in male and female turnout growth in 1928 is not much different from other election years. Thus the figure reveals two important conclusions: First, women and men respond in roughly similar ways in each election, with increased turnout in each election (all values exceed zero), especially 1928. Second, women do in fact experience greater turnout growth but they do so in every election in this period. The consistency of their turnout growth, relative to men's, in all five elections suggests this greater increase is due to women's undermobilization and the effects of experience, not the response of less interested peripheral voters to particularly salient elections such as 1928.

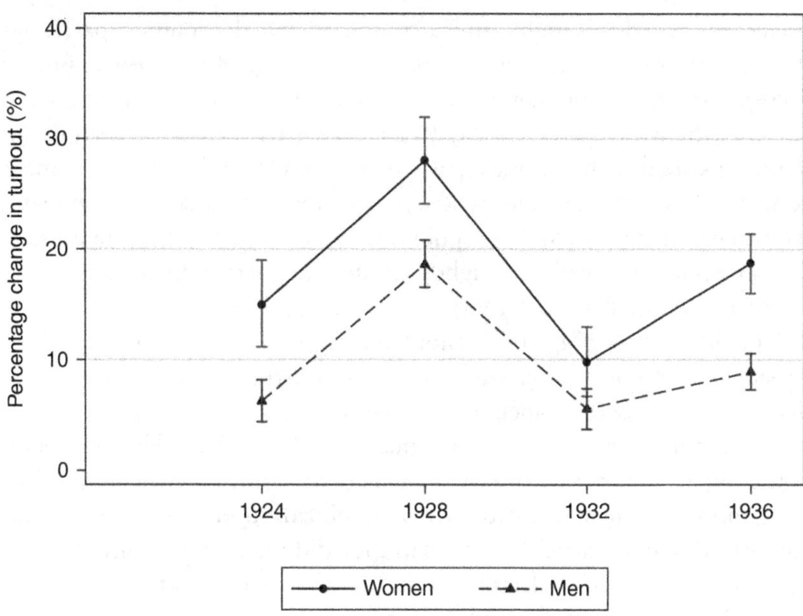

FIGURE 9.6. Percentage change in turnout of women and men, 1920–1936.

Thus, one conclusion is that the excitement and salience of the election of 1928 does not appear to have been *uniquely* mobilizing for women, despite their supposed lesser attention and interest in politics, and thus contrary to the peripheral voter hypothesis. On the other hand, the fact that women's turnout continued to lag behind men's (we estimate the overall turnout gender gap in our sample states as 29 points in 1928), even in an election as salient and compelling as 1928, also may be taken to indicate that the proportion of eligible voters who – due to lack of interest, knowledge, or engagement, as well as social norms that discouraged women's participation – could not be persuaded to exercise their voting rights was larger among women than men.

We have some, albeit mixed, evidence then that women behaved as peripheral voters in terms of turnout, especially in responding to state context. However, we find that women do not behave as peripheral voters in terms of vote choice, at least not initially. Women were slightly more likely to support the victorious Republican Party in the elections of 1920, 1924, and (to a lesser extent) 1928. Yet, this is not a general pattern among women; that is, it does not reflect a general preference among women for the party advantaged in the current election, as we would expect of peripheral voters. Similarly, it does not appear to reflect a general preference for the Republican Party among female voters ("particular partisanship hypothesis"), as others expected (e.g., Brown 1991; Burner 1986). Rather, a gender gap in favor of the Republican Party is limited to states in the Midwest where the Republican Party had long been dominant, consistent with the "local party hypothesis" (see Chapter 1). In more competitive states and states where the Democratic Party was dominant, women either supported the Republican Party to the same extent as men, or may even have exhibited slightly greater support for the locally dominant Democratic Party (e.g., Virginia in 1920 and 1924).

The different findings for turnout versus vote choice in the first three presidential elections after suffrage follow a certain logic. As a result of disenfranchisement, women lacked knowledge and experience in the act of casting of ballots. Thus, women tended to behave like peripheral voters when it came to turnout; competitive contexts, where elections were more salient and greater voter mobilization efforts were present, stimulated female turnout more than they did men's, and contexts characterized by restrictive electoral laws had a more debilitating impact on women's turnout than they did on men's. Even in a highly salient election such as 1928, significant proportions of women continued to eschew the voting booth.

But women did not necessarily lack experience or knowledge when it came to politics in general (see Chapter 2). Women were active in various political movements, clubs, and organizations prior to, and after, enfranchisement (Clemens 1997; Goss 2013). In the late nineteenth and early twentieth century, the political sphere expanded to encompass areas – consumer safety, moral purity, social reform – where women were expected to have particular expertise (Baker 1984). Political and partisan competition was highly salient and intense during the Progressive Era that preceded women's entrance into the electorate, exposing women to political debate and information (Andersen 1996). Thus the first women to enter polling places following the ratification of the Nineteenth Amendment did not behave as uninformed swing voters, but rather tended to support parties to the same extent as long-enfranchised men, or to display even greater affinity for the locally dominant political party.

Our conclusions about the extent to which women behave as peripheral voters shift somewhat when we turn to the New Deal elections of the 1930s. Women's turnout continues to be stimulated by state-level competition and hampered by state-level electoral laws to a greater extent than is men's, as we would expect of peripheral voters. Contrary to 1928, we do have some evidence of women's overall rate of turnout being more responsive than men's to the highly salient New Deal elections. We see this most strikingly in 1936, when overall turnout grew substantially (contrary to 1932, when both female and male turnout gains were minimal). In at least three states (Illinois, Massachusetts, and Connecticut), we find women's rate of turnout growing more than men's (90 percent of simulations) and perhaps in another two (Kansas and Minnesota) as well (80 percent of simulations). Thus, the general pattern of women being more likely than men to exhibit turnout behavior consistent with the peripheral voter hypothesis witnessed in the first three elections continues and is accelerated in 1932 and 1936.

Female vote choice, however, follows a different pattern in the New Deal elections, compared to the elections of the 1920s. When the country as a whole swung to the Democratic Party in 1932, we do find that women as a whole became slightly more Democratic than men. Again, however, the effect is limited to specific states. In 1932, women are more likely to vote Democratic than men in only one state, Virginia, and we can be only somewhat confident of that conclusion (over 80 percent of simulations). Virginia was a long-time one-party Democratic state, suggesting that, as with Republican bias in the earlier elections, this outcome may be more a function of the locally dominant party than a peripheral voter effect. On the other hand, we do have evidence of a greater pro-Democratic swing (change from 1928 to 1932) among women than men in Illinois (90 percent of simulations) and perhaps Oklahoma, Iowa, Minnesota, and Kansas as well (80 percent of simulations). With the exception of Oklahoma, these are all traditionally Republican Midwestern states where we had earlier observed a Republican bias among women. The greater Democratic swing is necessary to move from a Republican advantage among women in those states to an equal distribution of male and female Democratic voters in 1932. It also is evidence of greater movement (change) among women toward the party advantaged in the election, consistent with the peripheral voter hypothesis.

In 1936, the pro-Democratic bias among women is a bit more widespread: Female voters are more likely to vote for the Democrats than are male voters in Minnesota and Connecticut (90 percent of simulations) and perhaps in Kentucky (80 percent of simulations). In no states do we have strong evidence of a greater swing (change) among female voters, however. With the exception of Kentucky, these are not states in which Democrats had been traditionally dominant, so unlike the earlier elections, we cannot attribute the pro-Democratic bias among women in these states in this election to loyalty to the locally dominant party or to the relative strength of state and local Democratic organizations. In sum, contrary to the first three presidential elections, we do have some evidence of greater swing voter behavior among women in 1932 and of a bias in favor of the party advantaged in the election among women (not limited to traditionally Democratic states) in 1936.

Thus, in the 1930s, we have some indicators of peripheral voter behavior among women in terms of both turnout *and* vote choice, in contrast to the first three elections when peripheral voter behavior appears largely limited to turnout. How might we explain this difference? We argued that in 1920–1928, women were new to voting (and thus behaved as peripheral voters in their turnout behavior) but not new to politics and political knowledge (thus not peripheral voters in terms of vote choice). The elections of the 1930s, on the other hand, were a response to political knowledge that was new – in a very real sense – to *everyone*, both male and female. The economic system collapsed to an extent unprecedented in US history, and the Republican Party – the stalwart of economic management and capitalist hegemony (Bensel 2000) – both oversaw the crisis and appeared unable or unwilling to quell it. The political upheaval was extensive (Nardulli 1995). Despite this turmoil, women and men reacted largely in the same way and to the same extent as men: Both mobilized and converted in large numbers to the Democratic Party. As some (e.g., Andersen 1979) have expected, however, we do find some evidence of a greater swing to the Democrats among presumably less experienced and engaged female voters in reaction to the considerable salience of the New Deal elections.

We have evidence, then, that when politics was extraordinarily new and transformed, women may have responded more strongly to the party most advantaged in those salient elections, as the peripheral voter hypothesis would expect. More broadly, our complex conclusions regarding the peripheral voters hypothesis, and the turnout and vote choice of women more generally, highlight once again the contingent and varied nature of women's electoral behavior after suffrage. The contexts – both in terms of locale and in terms of the specific election – in which women had the opportunity to cast ballots shaped their behavior in ways that defy easy generalizations or conclusions.

Were Women Less Loyal Partisans and More Volatile Voters?

As we have seen, characterizations of women as politically disengaged and uninterested peripheral voters leads to expectations of swing voter behavior in response to election-specific factors (Kaufmann, Petrocik, and

Shaw 2008). A similar logic predicts that women's lack of suffrage experience also may point toward less partisan loyalty. Converse (1969, 1976) famously highlighted the importance of repeated electoral experience for reinforcing partisan loyalties, predicting that those enfranchised later in life would be characterized by weaker partisan attachments. Women's association with Progressivism (and its critique of party machines), as well as assumptions about the less dependable, or more independent, nature of women, also led many contemporaries to expect women to fail to behave as loyal partisan voters (see Andersen 1990; Barnard 1928c; Monoson 1990; Rogers 1930).

A corollary to less partisan loyalty is higher electoral volatility. Peripheral voters are a source of considerable instability in American elections, due to both their erratic exit and entrance into the electorate, as well as their tendency to swing to different parties based on election-specific characteristics, rather than maintaining party loyalty over time. Women's assumed lack of interest in politics, their relative inexperience with voting, and their presumed undependable, even impulsive attitudes toward politics led many to expect women would be a source of considerable electoral instability once enfranchised (Converse 1969, 1976; Lemons 1973; Rusk 1974; Russell 1924; cf. Burnham 1974; Claggett 1982).

Our finding of women's greater support for – or loyalty to – Republican candidates in states where Republicans were dominant in the first three elections examined contradicts the presumption of lesser partisan loyalty among women. Further evidence of women's partisan loyalty can be found in the election of 1924 when we conclude that women were not more likely to defect from major party loyalties and cast a vote for a relatively successful third party Progressive candidate; if anything, men are more likely to support La Follette's candidacy than are women. Moreover, estimated defection rates suggest that men were far more likely than women to defect from their 1920 partisan vote choice to support the Progressive candidate in 1924 than were women (see Chapter 6). Thus in these first three elections in particular, we conclude that what differential party support we observe between women and men is consistent with the expectation that women would be mobilized by the locally dominant party (see Harvey 1998). The possible reasons for these patterns are many; perhaps the tendency of some women to be restricted to the domestic sphere meant they had less opportunity to learn about the Progressive Party option, for example (see discussion in Chapter 1). Regardless, women's electoral behavior in 1924 is not consistent with the long-held assumption of lesser party loyalty and dependability among women.

On the other hand, we find more evidence of women's willingness to defect and be less loyal partisans during the transformative New Deal elections, and the election of 1932 in particular. As we have seen, while women's Democratic vote share is indistinguishable from men's in each of our states in 1932 (with the possible exception of Virginia), the *change* (or swing) in women's vote toward the Democrats appears bigger than men's in a number of states. More important for our evaluation of women's partisan loyalty is where these new Democratic votes came from – new voter mobilization or the conversion of voters from one party to the other – and the extent to which women were likely to defect from previous party loyalty. We find that new mobilization accounts for more of the ballots that Democrats gained among women than it did among men, as we might expect, given that more women were available for mobilization. However, women also had limited previous opportunities to reinforce their party preference through the repeated casting of ballots. And indeed, our estimates also suggest (although we cannot conclude definitively) that women who had voted Republican in 1928 were more likely than men who voted Republican in 1928 to abandon the Republican Party and move into the Democratic column. That is, women who voted Republican in 1928 do appear to exhibit less loyalty than men in 1932. Thus, while the first three presidential elections largely tell a story about the loyalty of women to the locally dominant party, the dramatic Democratic tides of the New Deal do appear to have been sufficient to generate a larger swing and perhaps more defection among less-experienced and less-"immunized" female voters in 1932, the New Deal election characterized by the most conversion overall (McPhee and Ferguson 1962; see Andersen 1979; Converse 1969, 1976).

This pattern characterizes women's contribution to electoral volatility as well. Figure 9.7 shows the average Republican vote share of female and male voters in the presidential elections from 1920 through 1936. Overall, the evidence of greater volatility in women's vote choice, compared to men's, is minimal. As we have seen, women in our sample states are slightly more Republican than men in 1920, 1924, and 1928, but the shifts from election to election are virtually identical among women and men. Similarly, the shift in Republican vote choice (now a minority position among both men and women) from 1932 to 1936 is extremely similar for women and men. Only between 1928 and 1932 do we find any evidence, in our sample, of greater volatility among women. As noted previously, female voters did swing more dramatically to the Democrats in 1932 than did men. In some states, this swing simply shifted women

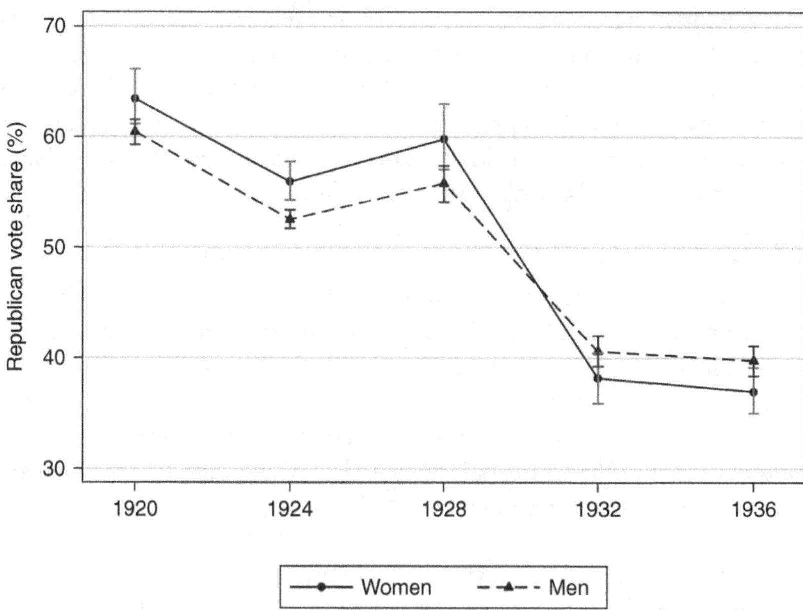

FIGURE 9.7. Average Republican vote share of women and men, sample states, 1920–1936.

from a position of greater Republican support, compared to men, to virtually identical Democratic support. In other places, women emerged as slightly more Democratic than their male counterparts, leading to the small Democratic advantage among women in 1932 and 1936 reflected in the figure.

What, then, do we conclude? Women were not more or less loyal to the major political parties than were men as a general rule. In some elections and some places, they are less likely to defect and less likely to support third party movements. In other elections, they are more likely to defect and more likely to support newly dominant parties. These differential patterns reflect responses to specific political circumstances and contexts, rather than an inherent tendency for or against loyalty among women as a whole.

Female Voters Then and Now

In 2020, Americans will celebrate the 100th anniversary of the Nineteenth Amendment to the US Constitution. After nearly a century of enfranchisement, the electoral behavior of women continues to be a source of public and scholarly interest. Just as newspapers in the 1920s and 1930s repeatedly predicted that *this* would be the election in which women were determinative, twenty-first century journalists continue to forecast and speculate as to the role of women in presidential elections today. For example, in the run-up to the 2012 presidential election, popular political analyst Nate Silver (2012) claimed that the "Although polls disagree on the exact magnitude of the gender gap ... the consensus of surveys points to a large one this year – rivaling the biggest from past elections." And indeed, as many commentators noted after the election, without the Nineteenth Amendment, Mitt Romney may well have been elected president in 2012 (e.g., Jones 2012; Omero and McGuinness 2012). Exit polls showed Romney securing 52 percent of men's votes, while 55 percent of the women cast their ballots for Barack Obama.[3] How does our expanded understanding of the behavior and impact of the first female voters relate to the experiences of female voters in the 80-some years that have followed?

Turnout

Women's rate of turnout in presidential elections continued to lag behind men's for decades after the ratification of the Nineteenth Amendment. Figure 9.8 displays reported male and female turnout from the start of the American National Election Studies (ANES) in 1948 through 2008. Note that while women's rate of turnout does not exceed men's in the ANES series until 2004, other reports, most notably the Current Population Studies (CPS) conducted by the U.S. Census Bureau, show women's turnout exceeding men's by 1980, and due to women's greater share of the population, more women than men entering polling places by 1964 (CAWP 2014).[4] The reasons for women's lower turnout through most of the twentieth century include the lingering effects of disenfranchisement, socialization and social norms that discouraged women's political activity, and women's lesser access to the resources (such as education, high-status employment, and income) associated with political activity (e.g., Andersen 1996; Burns, Schlozman, and Verba 2001; Firebaugh and Chen 1995; Lane 1959).

[3] "President Exit Polls." *The New York Times*. http://elections.nytimes.com/2012/results/president/exit-polls (Accessed May 20, 2014).

[4] Discrepancies between ANES and CPS turnout estimates are problematic, but we choose to report the ANES measures since the series extends back to 1948 while the CPS data begin in 1964. Both series lead to the same general conclusions about gender differences in turnout: Women's turnout lagged men's turnout by about 5 percentage points in 1964, and men's turnout lagged women's turnout by about 5 percentage points by 2012.

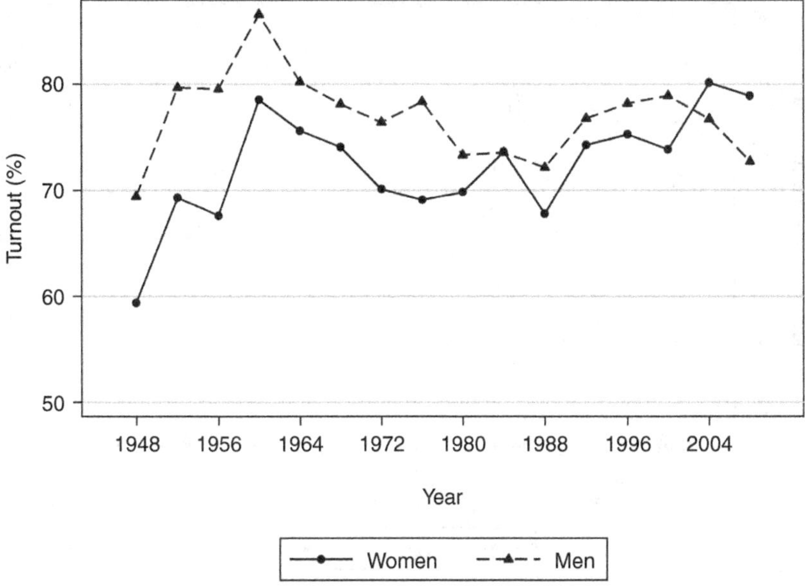

FIGURE 9.8. Turnout of women and men, American National Election Studies, 1948–2008.

The process by which women's and men's turnout rates converged and then diverged again over the twentieth century is complex, and largely outside the scope of this book. It is important to note, however, that the changing behavior of both women and men contributed to this process. Data from the nationally representative ANES indicate that the gap between men and women continued to diminish after 1936; according to the ANES, the turnout gender gap was about 10 percentage points by 1948, compared to the 24 point gap we estimate in our ten state sample in 1936 (ANES 2010). (Unlike the ANES, our sample is not nationally representative and thus the comparison of the two gaps is approximate). This narrowing of the turnout gender gap appears to be a function of both increasing rates of turnout among women, and a decline in men's turnout from realignment era highs: The 1948 ANES finds reported female turnout at just over 59 percent, while in our ten state sample, we estimate female turnout at 54 percent in 1936, plausibly indicating an approximately five point increase in female turnout over twelve years. Reported male turnout in 1948 was over 69 percent nationwide, according to the ANES, a more than ten point decline from our estimate of 78 percent male turnout in 1936 in our ten sample states. While female

FIGURE 9.9. Democratic vote share of women and men, American National Election Studies, 1948–2008.

and male turnout continues to move generally together after 1948 (similar to the pattern we observed in our sample between 1920 and 1936; see Figure 9.2), when turnout declines, women's declines less and men's more, and when turnout increases, women's increases more and men's less, leading to the eventual convergence and then reversal of the turnout gender gap we witness in Figure 9.8 and other data.

Vote Choice

What we know about the gender gap in presidential vote choice since suffrage also is consistent with our finding for the 1920s and 1930s: The gender gap varies over time in size and direction, and in response to the political, economic, and social conditions and characteristics of women's and men's lives. Figure 9.9 reports the percent of female and male voters casting ballots for the Democratic nominee in presidential elections from 1948 through 2008, again based on reported vote choice in the ANES. From 1948 through 1960, women are again slightly more likely to support the Republican candidate than are men, but these small differences are not statistically significant, except in 1956 (ANES 2010). The situation reverses after 1964, with women becoming slightly more Democratic in their presidential vote choice than men in every election (except 1976) through 2008, although differences are not statistically significant in 2004 or 2008. Thus, we have evidence that women have been – at varying times – as, more, and less Democratic in their presidential vote choices than men across the almost 100 years of their enfranchisement.

A full accounting of the causes of the postwar gender gap is beyond the scope of this research. Yet, we highlight that while the existence and direction of the partisan gender gap in presidential voting has shifted over the almost 100 years since the ratification of the Nineteenth Amendment, the consistency of popular explanations is striking. Contemporaries and later scholars relied on assumptions about the inherent nature and interests of women to predict support for Progressives (which we do not find; see Chapter 6) and explain the Republican advantage among the first female voters. Republicans were associated with the Progressive movement, and Progressive causes were a natural fit with women's supposedly inherent preferences for moral purity and social reform (see Chapters 1 and 2). Similar supposed female values – particularly women's presumed inclination toward care, compassion, and moral values – have long been offered as a rationale for women's greater support for social welfare policies, and thus for Democrats, since the 1960s. This characterization of women remains popular today; describing the 2012 Obama campaign's attempts to mobilize female voters, *New York Times* columnist Ross Douthat (2012) claims that "women are more likely to be communitarian [compared to greater individualism among men], and this creates ... a *natural* 'divergence in preferences for social welfare policies' " (emphasis ours).[5]

While in recent years women are indeed more likely to support social welfare policies, and these policy preferences do help explain the recent partisan gender gap (e.g., Kaufmann and Petrocik 1999), empirical support for the grounding of these policy and party preferences in fundamental gender differences in care and compassion has been weak or non-existent (see Huddy, Cassese, and Lizotte 2008). Similarly, in the same way that many expected women to reward the Republican Party for its support of women's suffrage (see Chapter 5), commentators often

[5] Ironically, Ross Douthat is quoting a blog post by one of the authors (Wolbrecht 2012). However, contrary to Douthat's claims, that blog post does not suggest women's greater support for social welfare policies is "natural," but rather notes that the literature finds that "Men's and women's different relationships to the social welfare state, employment patterns, and economic vulnerability are among the reasons given for these preference differences, as well as for the gender gap itself." That Douthat would read the blog post to indicate "natural" differences between men and women is indicative to the continuing strength of those stereotypes and assumptions.

have expected women to favor candidates and parties who endorse specific women's issues, such as abortion rights or the Equal Rights Amendment. Yet research consistently has discredited these expectations (Chaney, Alvarez, and Nagler 1998; Cook and Wilcox 1991; Klein 1984; Mansbridge 1985).

Contemporaries and scholars also expected newly enfranchised women to be a key cause of electoral change and instability, both overall (see discussion above) and in specific elections. Motivated by concern over "rum and religion" (Silva 1962), women were expected to have played a major role in the surge in turnout and dramatic shifts in vote choice during the highly charged 1928 election, for example (see Chapter 7). Similarly, when the modern gender gap in favor of the Democratic Party came to public and scholarly attention following the 1980 presidential election, explanations focused almost exclusively on the behavior of women themselves: What caused *women* to shift their vote choice toward the Democratic Party? Yet, scholars have since shown that much of the initial divergence in the partisan preferences of men and women in the second half of the twentieth century can be attributed to the defection of male voters from the Democratic Party, while female partisanship remained fairly stable (see Kaufmann and Petrocik 1999; Norrander 1999; Wirls 1986).[6] Similarly, we found that while the presidential contest of 1928 did indeed bring many new women to the polls and shifted the vote choice of large numbers of them, even more men were added to the electoral rolls in 1928 than were women, despite the fact that so many more women were available for mobilization. The unstated presumption that male behavior is standard, normal, and consistent, while women's is not, may lead us to attribute more change and disruption to women than is supported by the available evidence, both then and now.

More Similar than Different

We emphasize that our analysis shows that, from the very start, women have been more similar to men in their electoral behavior than they have been different. Although women's propensity to turn out to vote trailed men's substantially in the first five elections after suffrage (and for decades to come), women's patterns of turnout were not dramatically different from those of men: Where and when men were more likely to turnout to

[6] The precise contributions of women and men to the trajectory of the partisan gender gap remain contested and appears to vary over time and among different groups of women and men (Gillion, Ladd, and Meredith 2015; Kaufmann 2006).

vote, so were women, suggesting that both sexes responded to the same incentives and disincentives to vote and mostly – although not entirely – in the same way. Similarly, where and when men were Republican voters, so were women, and vice versa. We did uncover gender gaps in vote choice – in particular, favoring the GOP in a number of Midwestern states in 1920 through 1928, and favoring the Democrats in some states in 1936, but the size of these differences were not large.

The same can be said of the political engagement and preferences of men and women today. Differences exist: Women are somewhat less likely to participate in some forms of political activism, but more likely to engage in others (Burns, Schlozman, and Verba 2001), women express different policy preferences (e.g., Huddy, Cassese, and Lizotte 2008; Shapiro and Mahajan 1986), and women are more likely to identify with and vote for Democrats (e.g., Kaufmann and Petrocik 1999). Yet gender differences are not stark relative to differences in political behavior observed between other politically relevant groups. Gender differences still may be substantively significant; as we have argued, women made unique contributions from the very first elections after suffrage, and we have seen that in the current context of closely contested elections, small differences in vote choice can lead to women having decisive impacts on election outcomes. Yet on the whole, the evidence of the past 100 years supports a characterization of women as citizens and political actors more similar than different from men.

Some have viewed the general similarity of female and male electoral behavior as an indicator of the failure of the Nineteenth Amendment. Evaluating the impact of women's suffrage, writer Charles Edward Russell (1924, 725) famously declared, "Nothing has changed, except that the number of docile ballot-droppers has approximately been doubled" (also Blair 1925; Rice and Willey 1924; Russell 1924; Tarbell 1924). Others have concluded that similar electoral behavior, particularly vote choice, resulted from women simply following the guidance of their husbands and other men (Alpern and Baum 1985; Berelson, Lazarsfeld, and McPhee 1954; Campbell et al. 1960; Chafe 1972; Converse 1964 Flanagan 1995; Russell 1924). Our data cannot tell us if this was the case, and we do not doubt that some women did in fact turn to their long-enfranchised husbands for guidance on the casting of their ballots.

Another perspective, however, sees women participating in politics in similar ways as men did as a success. The electorate expanded by nearly 100 percent, and the American political system had the capacity to integrate and incorporate those voters with virtually no disruption at all; indeed, if anything, our analysis suggests women initially stabilized the electorate. Women were able to access information about how, where, and when to vote, as well as to learn about and choose among the available candidates and parties. The fact that women's turnout and vote choice generally followed patterns similar to that of men is in fact an impressive achievement. Women were denied access to the ballot for more than a century because of the widespread and long-standing belief that women were "*by nature unsuited* to politics" (italics original, Andersen 1990, 196; see Chapter 2), views that have not entirely been eliminated (Burns, Schlozman, and Verba 2001). The experience of disenfranchisement systematically denied women the opportunity to develop and reinforce political allegiances and habits (Converse 1969, 1976; Firebaugh and Chen 1995; Gerber, Green, and Shachar 2003; Plutzer 2002). From suffrage through today, women have had less access to the resources associated with political action and engagement (e.g., Burns, Schlozman, and Verba 2001). Yet, despite the legacy of disenfranchisement and the gender ideology that sustained it, despite persistent stereotypes about appropriate roles for women, and despite meaningful economic and social disparities, women have shown themselves, from the very first elections, as capable of engaging in electoral politics in much the same way as men.

American Politics Writ Large

The period examined here featured fundamental changes that would shape American politics for decades, if not centuries, to come. Women's relationship to the state was fundamentally transformed by the ratification of the Nineteenth Amendment (Andersen 1996). Partisan politics was transformed by the emergence of the New Deal coalition. And the American political system was transformed by the expanded social welfare state that the New Deal period produced. Our focus has been on understanding women's behavior and contributions as voters. Yet, it is worth highlighting how these broader, related changes interacted during this period, with long-lasting consequences.

These developments were fundamentally interwoven, both at the time and going forward. Women's shaping of the new Democratic majority with their ballots is only part of the story. The model of an expanded, activist state that emerged out of the New Deal had its roots in the Progressive Movement in which women, some of whom also campaigned for suffrage, had been so active. Women's organizations and advocacy, before and after suffrage, helped bring about the early maternalist social policies that laid the groundwork for the modern social welfare state that is the legacy of the New Deal (Goss 2013; Skocpol 1992). The nineteenth century made it clear that women did not require suffrage to be politically active, but it is also the case that, counter to some narratives, women did not disappear from political activity upon the achievement of the suffrage goal, but continued to shape politics and policy, although often via less public (Goss 2013) or even "stealth" activism (Wilkerson-Freeman 2003). Many women entered the workforce via an expanded social welfare bureaucracy, largely created by the New Deal and later the Great Society programs. These women have been identified as a factor in the emergence of the modern partisan gender gap (Erie and Rein 1988), as well as an oft-unrecognized source of feminist activism and influence during the second wave of the women's movement (Banaszak 2010).

The New Deal realignment and ascendancy of the Democratic Party transformed twentieth century politics, nationalizing party organizations and loyalties (e.g., Burnham 1967). Yet the eventual decline of the New Deal system, the well-documented challenges in replacing it, and the emergence of a new party system characterized by both economic and social cleavages also show the continuing contributions of women to political and social life. Indeed, women were central to the changing nature of political debate and political outcomes in the second half of the twentieth century. Gendered issues ranging from equal pay to abortion inspired social movements, divided the political parties, and transformed public policy (Wolbrecht 2000). And – bringing things full circle – the identification of the so-called gender gap in the presidential election of 1980 meant that female voters were finally recognized as a force in electoral politics, inspiring attention to women as targets for political mobilization to a degree not seen since the early days of suffrage ratification (Bonk 1988; Greenlee 2014).

As we approach the 100th anniversary of the ratification of the Nineteenth Amendment, the American political system, women's roles, and indeed the world have been transformed in ways none could have expected or predicted in 1920. Yet, the behavior and impact of female voters, both in elections and within politics writ large, remains in many ways as contested and salient as they were when national suffrage was first extended to women.

Did Women's Votes Count?

"What'll Women Do? Is Chicago Election Enigma" declared an October 4, 1928 *Chicago Daily Tribune* headline. How the first women granted the right to vote would use their ballots – not just in Chicago, but nationwide – has remained an enigma for almost 100 years. The title of this book, *Counting Women's Ballots*, describes both the methodological challenge and the substantive questions driving this research. Our central empirical task is to observe – or count – women's votes, separately from those of men, when official vote records failed to report such information (with one important exception) and opinion surveys were not available to compensate for the omission. By applying advances in ecological inference methodologies and computing power to a combination of census data and election returns, we have been able to produce reliable estimates of the turnout and vote choice of women for a broader set of places (ten diverse states) over a longer period of time (five presidential elections) than had been possible previously. The result is a considerable advance in our understanding of women's turnout and vote choice after suffrage, removing some of the mystery that has characterized the first women to enter polling places.

The title of the book also signals our key substantive concern: Did women's votes count? Several generations of activists dedicated themselves to the cause of obtaining the most basic democratic right of citizens – the right to participate in the selection of political representatives – for half of the population. To what end? As we discuss in Chapter 1, scholars have effectively challenged and complicated our understanding of the impact of suffrage (e.g., Andersen 1996; Cott 1990; Goss 2013; Schuyler 2006). This scholarship has emphasized, among other things, that women fulfilled many political roles – activist, organizers, policy demanders – both before and after suffrage. But women could not act as voters prior to the ratification of the Nineteenth Amendment (or state-level enfranchisement) and it is that role which is the focus of this research.

Two conflicting narratives have long characterized popular and scholarly understanding of women's use of the ballot after suffrage. In one, suffrage is a failure, as women generally failed to turn out to vote, and when they did, cast ballots that were indistinguishable from those of men. In the other, women played distinct roles overall and in specific elections: They voted more Republican than did men initially. They supported candidates associated with Progressive causes. They were highly mobilized to turn out and to cast ballots for or against ethnic, Catholic Al Smith in 1928. They were politically under-mobilized and under-immunized and thus played a significant role in the transformative New Deal elections. Overall, women lacked political knowledge, interest, and experience, and thus were likely to be less dependable and more variable voters than were men.

As we argue in Chapter 1, early and persistent claims that women's suffrage was a failure rest almost entirely on an unreasonable standard of dramatic political change – that significant numbers of women would vote and vote radically differently from men so as to transform election outcomes. As expected, we have no evidence of such an impact. As we have just argued, women's electoral behavior has not varied dramatically from that of men, nor would we expect it to. That does not mean it did not vary at all, or was not significant.

The more interesting (and plausible) claims concern variation in the behavior and contributions of women in the elections that followed suffrage. We conclude that women's entrance into the American electorate was highly contingent and variable, shaped by the political, economic, and social context across time and place. In some places, women's turnout was in fact incredibly low, and often stayed quite low for some time. In other places, however, we find that the turnout of women was impressively high – 57 percent in Kentucky as early as 1920, and more than 60 percent in four Midwestern states by 1936 – contradicting the allegation that women simply failed to take advantage of their new right. Context was clearly key. For example, places, such as Virginia, where women's turnout was exceptionally low, and stayed low, highlight the impact of race on the opportunity for African American women and men to exercise their suffrage rights, as well as the ways in which Southern social and political structures discouraged electoral participation in general during this era. In some places and at some times, the gender gap in turnout was dramatic; in others, more narrow, suggesting that the circumstances in which women made the decision to turn out to vote mattered as much or more as the fact that they were women.

In some places, women's vote choice is indistinguishable from men's, again consistent with the suffrage-as-failure indictment. As we note, however, similar male and female vote choice does not necessarily mean that women failed to cast thoughtful, independent ballots. In other places (the Republican-dominated Midwest, in particular), we find that the first female voters did *not* vote exactly like men, but were in fact more likely to cast Republican ballots as some had claimed. In some places, women also were as or less likely to support a Progressive candidate in 1924, contrary to expectations. Women were indeed highly mobilized by the "rum and religion" (Silva 1962) election of 1928, but even more men were so mobilized. In some places, women were more likely to defect from the Republican Party and experienced a bigger swing toward the Democrats than did men during the New Deal elections of the 1930s.

Overall, women appeared to be more loyal partisans in the first elections after suffrage, but more likely to defect and to be mobilized by the realigning elections of 1932 and 1936.

Women's contributions were such that elections were different because women participated in them. The mobilization of women into the dominant political party in their state – particularly in the one-party Republican Midwest – stabilized outcomes in the first elections after suffrage. In 1920, solidly Republican states became overwhelmingly Republican and the Republican surge was tempered in Democratic-dominated states. In 1924, La Follette would have done even better in a number of states had women not been enfranchised. Rather, women dampened the Progressive surge, a great irony for the movement that promoted the cause of women's suffrage long before it was broadly popular. In 1928, an election in which many have attributed partisan change to women, we find something closer to the opposite: The main impact of women appears to be the dampening of localized partisan swings. In states that moved toward the Democratic Party, Democrats netted fewer votes from women than they did from men. In states that experienced Republican gains, more of that shift was attributable to men's ballots than to women's.

Women also contributed significantly – and in a different way – to the transformative New Deal elections. After decades of Republican ascendency, the parties' responses to the crisis of the Great Depression ushered in a period of Democratic hegemony that would persist throughout most of the twentieth century. A shift of that magnitude required considerable electoral change, both mobilization and conversion. The first New Deal election, 1932, came just twelve years after the ratification of the Nineteenth Amendment, and was only the fourth presidential election in which women nationwide were eligible to vote. New Deal realignment required a particularly dramatic transformation among women. By 1936, Democrats had attracted about 50 percent more male voters than they had in 1928 (from 3 million to 4.5 million), but an amazing 95 percent more female voters (from 1.7 million to 3.3 million). In our ten sample states, we find that Democratic gains came in roughly equal numbers from men and women – about 1.6 million additional women and 1.4 million additional men across the presidential elections of the 1930s.

A central benefit of expanding the scope of research on female voters after suffrage to more states and elections is the ability to see clearly the considerable variation in women's propensity to cast ballots and for whom. Where and when and under what conditions women cast their first – and second and third and fourth and fifth – ballots mattered as much as the fact that they were women. This does not mean women do not merit careful attention as a politically relevant social group in American politics. Women were excluded from electoral participation on the basis of their sex, and the gender ideology and biases that justified that exclusion continued to shape women's own political participation – and how observers and scholars understood that participation – through the current day. Our analysis demonstrates that the electoral behavior of the first women enfranchised was indeed shaped by their status as women, but by other factors and conditions as well.

The subheading of the 1928 *Chicago Daily Tribune* headline reads: "Vote of Feminine Element is a Vital Factor." We agree. The ratification of the Nineteenth Amendment ushered in the largest expansion of the electorate in American history, and transformed, in a real and direct way, the relationship between female citizens and the state (Andersen 1996). Above all, it permitted women's voices to be heard at the ballot box. Whether few or many women turned out to vote, whether they supported the same candidates to the same extent as men or not, the choices of women would be tallied and contribute to the outcome of elections. We find that women stabilized outcomes in some states and elections, minimized third party surges in others, and contributed substantially to realignment in still others. Context – both across time and place – shaped whether and to what extent women's votes contributed to electoral stability and change. By counting women's ballots, we can finally see the many ways in which women's ballots count.

References

Abbott, Edith. 1915. "Are Women a Force for Good Government? An Analysis of the Returns in the Recent Municipal Election in Chicago." *National Municipal Review* IV(July):437–447.

Aldrich, John H. 1993. "Rational Choice and Turnout." *American Journal of Political Science* 37(February):246–278.

Allen, Florence E. 1930. "The First Ten Years." *The Woman's Journal* August:5–7, 30–32.

Allen, Frederick Lewis. 1957. *Only Yesterday: An Informal History of the Nineteen-Twenties*. New York: Harper & Row.

Alpern, Sara, and Dale Baum. 1985. "Female Ballots: The Impact of the Nineteenth Amendment." *Journal of Interdisciplinary History* 26(Summer):43–67.

Alt, James A. 1994. "The Impact of the Voting Rights Act on Black and White Voter Registration in the South." In *Quiet Revolution in the South: The Impact of the Voting Rights Act, 1965–1990*, eds. Chandler Davidson and Bernard Groffman, 351–377. Princeton, NJ: Princeton University Press.

American National Election Studies (ANES). 2010. Cumulative Data File, 1948–2008. Release Version: 20100624. June 24.

Andersen, Kristi. 1979. *The Creation of a Democratic Majority, 1928–1936*. Chicago: University of Chicago Press.

1990. "Women and Citizenship in the 1920s." In *Women, Politics, and Change*, eds. Louise Tilly and Patricia Gurin, 177–198. New York: Russell Sage Foundation.

1994. "Women and the Vote in the 1920s: What Happened in Oregon." *Women & Politics* 14(4):43–56.

1996. *After Suffrage: Women in Partisan and Electoral Politics before the New Deal*. Chicago: University of Chicago Press.

2014. "Constructing a New Majority: The Depression, the New Deal, and the Democrats." In *The CQ Guide to U.S. Political Parties*, eds. Majorie R. Hershey, Barry C. Burden, and Christina Wolbrecht, 103–115. Washington, DC: Congressional Quarterly Press.

Arceneaux, Kevin, and David W. Nickerson. 2009. "Who Is Mobilized to Vote? A Re-Analysis of 11 Field Experiments." *American Journal of Political Science* 53(January):1–16.

Arneson, Ben A. 1925. "Non-Voting in a Typical Ohio Community." *American Political Science Review* 19(November):816–825.

Arneson, Ben A., and William H. Eels. 1950. "Voting Behavior in 1948 as Compared with 1924 in a Typical Ohio Community." *American Political Science Review* 44(June):432–434.

Bagby, Wesley M. 1962. *The Road to Normalcy: The Presidential Campaign and Election of 1920*. Baltimore: The Johns Hopkins University Press.

Baker, Paula. 1984. "The Domestication of Politics: Women and American Political Society, 1780–1920." *American Historical Review* 89(June):620–647.

Banaszak, Lee Ann. 1996. *Why Movements Succeed or Fail: Opportunity, Culture, and the Struggle for Woman Suffrage*. Princeton, NJ: Princeton University Press.

2010. *The Women's Movement Inside and Outside the State*. New York: Cambridge University Press.

Barnard, Eunice Fuller. 1928a. "Women Who Yield Political Power." *The New York Times Magazine* (September 2):6–7, 23.

1928b. "Women in the Campaign." *The Woman's Journal* 13(December):7ff.

1928c. "The Woman Voter Gains Power." *The New York Times Magazine* (12 August):1–2, 20, 28.

Beard, Mary R. 1946. *Woman as Force in History: A Study in Traditions and Realities*. New York: The Macmillan Company.

Beck, Paul Allen, and M. Kent Jennings. 1991. "Family Traditions, Political Periods, and the Development of Partisan Orientations." *Journal of Politics* 53(August):742–763.

Becker, Susan D. 1981. *The Origins of the Equal Rights Amendment: American Feminism Between the Wars*. Westport, CT: Greenwood Press.

Beckwith, Karen. 1986. *American Women and Political Participation: The Impacts of Work, Generations, and Feminism*. New York: Greenwood Press.

Bensel, Richard Franklin. 2000. *The Political Economy of American Industrialization, 1877–1900*. New York: Cambridge University Press.

2004. *The American Ballot Box in the Mid-Nineteenth Century*. New York: Cambridge University Press.

Berelson, Bernard R., Paul F. Lazarsfeld, and William N. McPhee. 1954. *Voting: A Study of Opinion Formation in a Presidential Election*. Chicago: University of Chicago Press.

Berinsky, Adam J. 2006. "American Public Opinion in the 1930s and 1940s: The Analysis of Quota-Controlled Sample Survey Data." *Public Opinion Quarterly* 70(Winter):499–529.

Berinsky, Adam J., Eleanor Neff Powell, Eric Schickler, and Ian Brett Yohai. 2011. "Revisting Public Opinion in the 1930s and 1940s." *PS: Political Science and Politics* 44(July):515–520.

Berman, David R. 1993. "Gender and Issue Voting: The Policy Effects of Suffrage Expansion in Arizona." *Social Science Quarterly* 74(December):838–850.

Blair, Emily Newell. 1925. "Are Women a Failure in Politics?" *Harper's Magazine* 151(October):513–522.

1926. "Men in Politics as a Woman See Them." *Harper's Magazine* 152(May): 703–709.

1931. "Why I Am Discouraged About Women in Politics." *The Woman's Journal* January:20–22.

Blakey, Gladys C. 1928. *A Handy Digest of Election Laws*. Washington, DC: League of Women Voters.

Bonk, Kathy. 1988. "The Selling of the 'Gender Gap:' The Role of Organized Feminism." In *The Politics of the Gender Gap: The Social Construction of Political Influence*, ed. Carol M. Mueller, 82–101. Newbury Park, CA: SAGE.

Box-Steffensmeier, Jan, Suzanna De Boef, and Tse-Min Lin. 2004. "The Dynamics of the Partisan Gender Gap." *American Political Science Review* 98(August):515–528.

Breckinridge, Sophonisba P. 1933. *Women in the Twentieth Century: A Study of their Political, Social and Economic Activities*. New York: MGraw-Hill Book Company.

Brewer, Mark D., and Jeffrey M. Stonecash. 2009. *Dynamics of American Political Parties*. New York: Cambridge University Press.

Brown, Courtney. 1988. "Mass Dynamics of U.S. Presidential Competitions, 1928–1936." *American Political Science Review* 82(December):1153–1181.

1991. *Ballots of Tumult: A Portrait of Volatility in American Voting*. Ann Arbor: University of Michigan Press.

Bunche, Ralph J. 1973. *The Political Status of the Negro in the Age of FDR*. Chicago: University of Chicago Press.

Burner, David. 1971. "Election of 1924." In *History of American Presidential Elections, 1789–1968*, eds. Arthur M. Schlesinger, Jr. and Fred L. Israel, 2458–2581. New York: Chelsea House Publishers in Association with McGraw-Hill Book Co.

1986. *The Politics of Provincialism: The Democratic Party in Transition, 1918–1932*, 2nd ed. Cambridge, MA: Harvard University Press.

Burnham, Walter Dean. 1965. "The Changing Shape of the American Political Universe." *American Political Science Review* 59(March):7–28.

1967. "Party Systems and the Political Process." In *The American Party Systems: Stages of Political Development*, eds. William Nesbit Chambers and Walter Dean Burnham, 277–307. New York: Oxford University Press.

1970. *Critical Elections and the Mainsprings of American Politics*. New York: W. W. Norton.

1974. "Theory and Voting Research: Some Reflections on Converse's 'Change in the American Electorate.'" *American Political Science Review* 68(September):1002–1023.

1980. "The Appearance and Disappearance of the American Voter." In *Electoral Participation: A Comparative Analysis*, ed. Richard Rose, 35–73. Beverly Hills, CA: SAGE.

1981a. "The System of 1896: An Analysis." In *The Evolution of American Electoral Systems*, eds. Paul Kleppner, Walter Dean Burnham, Ronald P.

Formisano, Samuel P. Hays, Richard Jensen, and William G. Shade, 147–202. Westport CT: Greenwood Press.

1981b. "Printed Sources." In *Analyzing Electoral History: A Guide to the Study of American Voting Behavior*, eds. Jerome M. Chubb, William H. Flanigan, and Nancy H. Zingale, 42–70. Beverly Hills, CA: SAGE.

1986. "Those High Nineteenth-Century American Voting Turnouts: Fact or Fiction?" *Journal of Interdisciplinary History* XVI(Spring):613–644.

Burns, Nancy, Kay Lehman Schlozman, and Sidney Verba. 2001. *The Private Roots of Public Action: Gender, Equality, and Political Participation*. Cambridge, MA: Harvard University Press.

Butler, Sarah Schuyler. 1924. "Women Who Do Not Vote." *Scribner's Magazine* 76(November):529–533.

Cain, Bruce E., D. Roderick Kiewiet, and Carole J. Uhlaner. 1991. "The Acquisition of Partisanship by Latinos and Asian Americans." *American Journal of Political Science* 35(May):390–422.

Campbell, Angus. 1960. "Surge and Decline: A Study of Electoral Change." *Public Opinion Quarterly* 24(Fall):397–418.

1964. "Voters and Elections: Past and Present." *Journal of Politics* 26(November): 745–757.

1966. "A Classification of the Presidential Elections." In *Elections and the Political Order*, eds. Angus Campbell, Philip E. Converse, and Donald E. Stokes, 63–77. New York: John Wiley & Sons.

Campbell, Angus, Philip E. Converse, Warren E. Miller, and Donald E. Stokes. 1960. *The American Voter*. New York: John Wiley & Sons.

1966. *Elections and the Political Order*. New York: John Wiley & Sons.

Campbell, David. 2008. *Why We Vote: How Schools and Communities Shape Our Civic Life*. Princeton, NJ: Princeton University Press.

Campbell, James E. 1985. "Sources of the New Deal Realignment: The Contributions of Conversion and Mobilization to Partisan Change." *Western Political Quarterly* 38(September):357–376.

Carroll, Susan J. 2006. "Voting Choices: Meet You at the Gender Gap." In *Gender and Elections: Shaping the Future of American Politics*, eds. Susan J. Carroll and Richard L. Fox, 74–96. New York: Cambridge University Press.

Catt, Carrie Chapman. 1925. "What Women Have Done with the Vote." *The Independent* 115(October 17):447–448, 456.

Center for American Women and Politics (CAWP). 2014. "Fact Sheet: Gender Differences in Voter Turnout." Center for American Women and Politics, Eagleton Institute of Politics, Rutgers University.

Chafe, William H. 1972. *The American Woman: Her Changing Social, Economic, and Political Roles, 1920–1970*. New York: Oxford University Press.

Chaney, Carole Kennedy, R. Michael Alvarez, and Jonathan Nagler. 1998. "Explaining the Gender Gap in U.S. Presidential Elections, 1980–1992." *Political Research Quarterly* 51:311–339.

Cho, Wendy K. Tam, and Brian J. Gaines. 2004. "The Limits of Ecological Inference: The Case of Split-Ticket Voting." *American Journal of Political Science* 48(1):152–171.

Claggett, William. 1980. "The Life Cycle and Generational Models of the Development of Partisanship: A Test Based on the Delayed Enfranchisement of Women." *Social Science Quarterly* 4(March):643–650.

1982. "Life Cycle Model of Partisanship Development: An Analysis of Aggregate Electoral Instability Following the Enfranchisement of Women." *American Politics Quarterly* 10(April):219–230.

Clemens, Elisabeth S. 1993. "Organizational Repertoires and Institutional Change: Women's Groups and the Transformation of U.S. Politics, 1890–1920." *American Journal of Sociology* 98(January):755–798.

1997. *The People's Lobby: Organizational Innovation and the Rise of Interest Group Politics in the United States, 1890–1925*. Chicago: University of Chicago Press.

Converse, Phillip E. 1964. "The Nature of Belief Systems in Mass Publics." In *Ideology and Discontent*, ed. David Apter, 206–261. New York: The Free Press.

Converse, Philip E. 1969. "Of Time and Partisan Stability." *Comparative Political Studies* 2(July):139–171.

1972. "Change in the American Electorate." In *The Human Meaning of Social Change*, eds. Angus Campbell and Philip E. Converse, 263–337. New York: Russell Sage Foundation.

1974. "Comment on Burnham's 'Theory and Voting Research.'" *American Political Science Review* 68(September):1024–1027.

1976. *The Dynamics of Party Support: Cohort-Analyzing Party Identification*. Beverly Hills, CA: SAGE.

Cook, Elizabeth Adell, and Clyde Wilcox. 1991. "Feminism and the Gender Gap—A Second Look." *Journal of Politics* 53:1111–1122.

Corder, J. Kevin. 2005. "Ecological Inference." In *Polling America: An Encyclopedia of Public Opinion*, eds. Samuel Best and Benjamin Radcliff, 166–170. Westport, CT: Greenwood.

Corder, J. Kevin, and Christina Wolbrecht. 2006. "Political Context and the Turnout of New Women Voters After Suffrage." *Journal of Politics* 68(February):34–49.

Cott, Nancy F. 1975. *The Bonds of Womanhood: Woman's Sphere in New England, 1790–1835*. New Haven, CT: Yale University Press.

1987. *The Grounding of Modern Feminism*. New Haven, CT: Yale University Press.

1990. "Across the Great Divide: Women in Politics Before and After 1920." In *Women, Politics, and Change*, eds. Louise Tilly and Patricia Gurin, 153–176. New York: Russell Sage Foundation.

CQ Press. 2010. *Guide to U.S. Elections*, 6th ed. Washington, DC: CQ Press.

Crawford, William H. 1924. "A Big Woman Vote Seen by Mrs. Sabin." *The New York Times*, 27 October, p. 8.

Crossley, Archibald M. 1937. "Straw Polls in 1936." *Public Opinion Quarterly* 1(January):24–37.

Darmofal, David, and Peter F. Nardulli. 2010. "The Dynamics of Critical Realignments: An Analysis of Time and Space." *Political Behavior* 32:255–283.

Degler, Carl N. 1964. "American Political Parties and the Rise of the City: An Interpretation." *Journal of American History* 51(June):41–59.

Douthat, Ross. 2012. "President in Shining Armor." *The New York Times*, October 27.

DuBois, Ellen Carol. 1978. *Feminism and Suffrage: The Emergence of an Independent Women's Movement in America, 1848–1869*. Ithaca, NY: Cornell University Press.

1998. *Woman Suffrage and Women's Rights*. New York: New York University Press.

Dugan, William E., and William A. Taggart. 1995. "The Changing Shape of the American Political Universe Revisited." *Journal of Politics* 57(May):469–482.

Duncan, Otis Dudley, and Beverly Davis. 1953. "An Alternative to Ecological Correlation." *American Sociological Review* 18:665–666.

Duverger, Maurice. 1955. *The Political Role of Women*. Paris: United Nations Educational, Scientific, and Cultural Organization (UNESCO).

Edwards, Rebecca B. 1997. *Angels in the Machinery: Gender in American Party Politics from the Civil War to the Progressive Era*. New York: Oxford University Press.

Epstein, Lee, and Thomas G. Walker. 1995. *Constitutional Law for a Changing America: Institutional Powers and Constraints*, 2nd ed. Washington, DC: CQ Press.

Erie, Steven P., and Martin Rein. 1988. "Women and the Welfare State." In *The Politics of the Gender Gap: The Social Construction of Political Influence*. Newbury Park, CA: SAGE.

Erikson, Robert S., and Kent L. Tedin. 1981. "The 1928–1936 Partisan Realignment: The Case for the Conversion Hypothesis." *American Political Science Review* 75:951–962.

Erwin, Marie H. 1946. *Wyoming Historical Blue Book: A Legal and Political History of Wyoming, 1868–1943*. Denver: Bradford-Robinson Printing Co.

Evans, Sara M. 1989. *Born for Liberty: A History of Women in America*. New York: The Free Press.

Ferree, Karen. 2004. "Iterative Approaches to R x C Ecological Inference Problems: Where They Can Go Wrong and One Quick Fix." *Political Analysis* 12:143–159.

Firebaugh, Glenn, and Kevin Chen. 1995. "Vote Turnout of Nineteenth Century Women: The Enduring Effect of Disenfranchisement." *American Journal of Sociology* 100(January):972–996.

Fisher, Marguerite J. 1947. "Women in the Political Parties." *The Annals of the American Academy of Political and Social Science* 251(May):87–93.

Flanagan, Maureen A. 1995. "The Predicament of New Rights: Suffrage and Women's Political Power from a Local Perspective." *Social Politics* 2(Fall):305–330.

Flexner, Eleanor. 1959. *Century of Struggle: The Women's Rights Movement in the United States*. Cambridge, MA: Harvard University Press.

Freedman, Estelle. 1979. "Separatism as Strategy: Female Institution Building and American Feminism, 1870–1930." *Feminist Studies* 5(Fall):512–529.

Freeman, Jo. 2000. *A Room at a Time: How Women Entered Party Politics.* Lanham, MD: Rowman & Littlefield.

Freidel, Frank. 1971. "Election of 1932." In *History of American Presidential Elections, 1789–1968*, eds. Arthur M. Schlesinger, Jr. and Fred L. Israel, 2706–2806. New York: Chelsea House Publishers in Association with McGraw-Hill Book Co.

Fuchs, Lawrence H. 1955. "American Jews and the Presidential Vote." *American Political Science Review* 49(June):385–401.

1971. "Election of 1928." In *History of American Presidential Elections, 1789–1968*, eds. Arthur M. Schlesinger, Jr. and Fred L. Israel, 2584–2704. New York: Chelsea House Publishers in Association with McGraw-Hill Book Co.

Gamm, Gerald. 1986. *The Making of the New Deal Democrats: Voting Behavior and Realignment in Boston, 1920–1940.* Chicago: University of Chicago Press.

Gerber, Alan S., Donald P. Green, and Ron Shachar. 2003. "Voting May Be Habit-Forming: Evidence from a Randomized Field Experiment." *American Journal of Political Science* 47(July):540–550.

Gerould, Katharine Fullerton. 1925. "Some American Women and the Vote." *Scribner's Magazine* 127(May):449–452.

Gill, Jeff. 2002. *Bayesian Methods: A Social and Behavioral Sciences Approach.* Boca Raton, FL: Chapman and Hall.

Gillion, Daniel Q., Jonathan M. Ladd, and Marc Meredith. 2015. "Party Polarization, Ideological Sorting, and the Emergence of the Partisan Gender Gap." Georgetown University, Working Paper, July 2.

Gilmore, Glenda Elizabeth. 1996. *Gender and Jim Crow: Women and the Politics of White Supremacy in North Carolina, 1896–1920.* Chapel Hill: The University of North Carolina Press.

Ginsberg, Benjamin, Theodore J. Lowi, and Margaret Weir. 2009. *We the People: An Introduction to American Politics.* Shorter 7th ed. New York: W. W. Norton.

Glaser, William A. 1962. "Fluctuations in Turnout." In *Public Opinion and Congressional Elections*, eds. William N. McPhee and William A. Glaser, 19–51. New York: The Free Press of Glencoe.

Goldstein, Joel H. 1984. *The Effects of the Adoption of Woman Suffrage: Sex Differences in Voting Behavior Illinois, 1914–21.* New York: Praeger.

Goodman, Leo. 1953. "Ecological Regressions and Behavior of Individuals." *American Sociological Review* 18:663–664.

Gordon, Felice D. 1986. *After Winning: The Legacy of the New Jersey Suffragists, 1920–1947.* New Brunswick, NJ: Rutgers University Press.

Gosnell, Harold F. 1927. *Getting Out the Vote: An Experiment in the Stimulation of Voting.* Chicago: University of Chicago Press.

1930. *Why Europe Votes.* Chicago: University of Chicago Press.

1942. *Grassroots Politics: National Voting Behavior of Typical States.* Washington, DC: American Council on Public Affairs.

Gosnell, Harold F., and Norman N. Gill. 1935. "An Analysis of the 1932 Presidential Vote in Chicago." *American Political Science Review* 29(December):967–984.

Goss, Kirstin A. 2013. *The Paradox of Gender Equality: How American Women's Groups Gained and Lost Their Public Voice.* Ann Arbor: University of Michigan Press.

Gould, Louis L. 2003. *Grand Old Party: A History of the Republicans.* New York: Random House.

Gourevitch, Peter Alexis. 1984. "Breaking with Orthodoxy: The Politics of Economic Policy Responses to the Depression of the 1930s." *International Organization* 38(Winter):95–129.

Green, Donald P., Bradley Palmquist, and Eric Schickler. 2002. *Partisan Hearts and Minds: Political Parties and the Social Identity of Voters.* New Haven, CT: Yale University Press.

Green, Elna C. 1996. *Southern Strategies: Southern Women and the Woman Suffrage Question.* Chapel Hill: University of North Carolina Press.

Greenlee, Jill S. 2014. *The Political Consequences of Motherhood.* Ann Arbor: University of Michigan Press.

Greiner, D. James, and Kevin Quinn. 2009. "R x C Ecological Inference: Bounds, Correlations, Flexibility, and Transparency of Assumptions." *Journal of the Royal Statistical Society, Series A* 172:67–81.

Harris, Louis. 1954. *Is There a Republican Majority? Political Trends, 1952–1956.* New York: Harper & Brothers.

Harvey, Anna L. 1998. *Votes Without Leverage: Women in Electoral Politics, 1920–1970.* Cambridge: Cambridge University Press.

Hawley, George, and Inaki Sagarazu. 2012. "Where Did the Votes Go? Reassessing American Party Realignments via Vote Transfers between Major Parties from 1860 to 2008." *Electoral Studies* 31:726–739.

Heard, Alexander, and Donald S. Strong. 1950. *Southern Primaries and Elections, 1920–1949.* Tuscaloosa: University of Alabama Press.

Hicks, John D. 1960. *Republican Ascendancy, 1921–1933.* New York: Harper & Row.

Hillygus, D. Sunshine. 2005. "Campaign Effects and the Dynamics of Turnout Intention in Election 2000," *Journal of Politics* 66(1):50–68

Hofstadter, Richard. 1955. *The Age of Reform: From Bryan to F.D.R.* New York: Alfred A. Knopf.

Holbrook, Thomas M., and Emily Van Dunk. 1993. "Electoral Competition in the American States." *American Political Science Review* 87(December):955–962.

Huckfeldt, Robert, Paul Allen Beck, Russell J. Dalton, and Jeffrey Levine. 1995. "Political Environments, Cohesive Social Groups, and the Communication of Public Opinion." *American Journal of Political Science* 29(November): 1025–1054.

Huddy, Leonie, Erin Cassese, and Mary-Kate Lizotte. 2008. "Gender, Public Opinion, and Political Reasoning." In *Political Women and American Democracy*, eds Christina Wolbrecht, Karen Beckwith, and Lisa Baldez, 31–49. New York: Cambridge University Press.

Huthmacher, J. Joseph. 1959. *Massachusetts People and Politics, 1919–1933*. Cambridge, MA: The Belknap Press of Harvard University Press.

Inter-university Consortium for Political and Social Research (ICPSR). 1992. Historical, Demographic, Economic, and Social Data: The United States, 1790–1970 [Computer file]. Ann Arbor, MI: Inter-university Consortium for Political and Social Research [producer and distributor].

Inter-university Consortium for Political and Social Research (ICPSR). 1999. United States Historical Election Returns, 1824–1968 [Computer file]. 2nd ICPSR ed. Ann Arbor, MI: Inter-university Consortium for Political and Social Research [producer and distributor].

Jeffries, John W. 1979. *Testing the Roosevelt Coalition: Connecticut Society and Politics in the Era of World War II*. Knoxville: University of Tennessee Press.

Jennings, M. Kent, and Gregory B. Markus. 1984. "Partisan Orientations over the Long Haul: Results from the Three-Wave Political Socialization Panel Study." *American Political Science Review* 4(December):1000–1018.

Jensen, Joan M. 1981. "'Disenfranchisement is a Disgrace': Women and Politics in New Mexico, 1900–1940." *New Mexico Historical Review* 56(1):5–35.

Jensen, Richard. 1986. "The Changing Shape of Burnham's Political Universe." *Social Science History* 10(Fall):209–219.

Johnston, Richard. 2006. "Party Identification: Unmoved Mover or Sum of Preferences?" *Annual Review of Political Science* 9:329–351.

Jones, Jeffrey M. 2012. "Gender Gap in 2012 Vote Is Largest in Gallup's History." *Gallup on-line* www.gallup.com/poll/158588/gender-gap-2012-vote-largest-gallup-history.aspx (Accessed July 30, 2014).

Judd, Dennis R., and Todd Swanstrom. 1994. *City Politics: Private Power and Public Policy*. New York: HarperCollins.

Kaufmann, Karen M. 2006. "The Gender Gap." *PS: Political Science and Politics* 39(July):447–453.

Kaufmann, Karen M., and John R. Petrocik. 1999. "The Changing Politics of American Men: Understanding the Sources of the Gender Gap." *American Journal of Political Science* 43:864–887.

Kaufmann, Karen M., John R. Petrocik, and Daron R. Shaw. 2008. *Unconventional Wisdom: Facts and Myths about American Voters*. New York: Oxford University Press.

Kenton, Edna. 1924. "Four Years of Equal Suffrage." *Forum* 72:37–44.

Kerber, Linda K. 1976. "The Republican Mother: Women and the Enlightenment—American Perspective." *American Quarterly* 28(Summer): 187–205.

1980. *Women of the Republic: Intellect and Ideology in Revolutionary America*. Chapel Hill: University of North Carolina Press.

1985. "The Republican Ideology of the Revolutionary Generation." *American Quarterly* 37(Autumn):474–495.

1988. "Separate Spheres, Female Worlds, Woman's Place: The Rhetoric of Women's History." *Journal of American History* 75(June):9–39.

Kerber, Linda K., Nancy F. Cott, Robert Gross, Lynn Hunt, Carroll Smith-Rosenberg, and Christine M. Stansell. 1989. "Beyond Roles, Beyond Spheres:

Thinking about Gender in the Early Republic." *William and Mary Quarterly* 41(July):565–581.

Key, V. O., Jr. 1949. *Southern Politics in State and Nation*. New York: Alfred A. Knopf.

1955. "A Theory of Critical Elections." *Journal of Politics* 17(February):3–18.

1959. "Secular Realignment and the Party System." *Journal of Politics* 21(May):198–210.

Keyssar, Alexander. 2000. *The Right to Vote: The Contested History of Democracy in the United States*. New York: Basic Books.

King, Gary. 1997. *A Solution to the Ecological Inference Problem: Deconstructing Individual Behavior from Aggregate Data*. Princeton, NJ: Princeton University Press.

King, Gary, Ori Rosen, and Martin Tanner. 1999. "Binomial-Beta Hierarchical Models for Ecological Inference." *Sociological Methods and Research* 28:61–90.

King, Gary, Ori Rosen, and Martin Tanner, eds. 2004. *Ecological Inference: New Methodological Strategies*. New York: Cambridge University Press.

Klein, Ethel. 1984. *Gender Politics: From Consciousness to Mass Politics*. Cambridge, MA: Harvard University Press.

Kleppner, Paul. 1982a. *Who Voted? The Dynamics of Electoral Turnout, 1840–1940*. New York: Praeger.

1982b. "Were Women to Blame? Female Suffrage and Voter Turnout." *The Journal of Interdisciplinary History* 12(Spring):621–643.

Klinghoffer, Judith Apter, and Lois Elkis. 1992. "'The Petticoat Electors': Women's Suffrage in New Jersey, 1776–1807." *Journal of the Early Republic* 12(Summer):159–193.

Kousser, J. Morgan. 1974. *The Shaping of Southern Politics: Suffrage Restriction and the Establishment of the One-Party South, 1880–1910*. New Haven, CT: Yale University Press.

Kraditor, Aileen S. 1968. *Up from the Pedestal: Selected Writings in the History of American Feminism*. Chicago: Quadrangle Books.

1981. *The Ideas of the Woman Suffrage Movement, 1890–1920*, 2nd ed. New York: W. W. Norton.

Ladd, Everett C. 1997. "Media Framing of the Gender Gap." In *Women, Media, and Politics*, ed. Pippa Norris, 113–128. New York: Oxford University Press.

Ladd, Everett C., and Charles D. Hadley. 1975. *Transformation of the American Party System: Political Coalitions from the New Deal to the 1970's*. New York: W. W. Norton.

Lane, Robert E. 1959. *Political Life: Why People Get Involved in Politics*. Glencoe, IL: Free Press.

Lau, Olivia, Ryan T. Moore, and Michael Kellerman. 2007. "eiPack: RxC Ecological Inference and Higher Dimension Data Management." *R News*. 7:43–47.

Lawson, Steven F. 1999. *Black Ballots: Voting Rights in the South, 1944–1969*. Lanham, MD: Lexington Books.

Lazarsfeld, Paul R., Berelson, Bernard R., and Hazel Gaudet. 1948. *The People's Choice*. New York: Columbia University Press.

Lebsock, Suzanne. 1993. "Woman Suffrage and White Supremacy: A Virginia Case Study." In *Visible Women: New Essays on American Activism*, eds. Nancy A. Hewitt and Suzanne Lebsock, 61–100. Urbana: University of Illinois Press.

Lemons, J. Stanley. 1973. *The Woman Citizen: Social Feminism in the 1920s.* Charlottesville: University Press of Virginia.

Lerner, Gerda. 1969. "The Lady and the Mill Girl: Changes in the Status of Women in the Age of Jackson." *Midcontinent American Studies Journal* 10(Spring):5–15.

Leuchtenburg, William E. 1971. "Election of 1936." In *History of American Presidential Elections, 1789–1968*, eds. Arthur M. Schlesinger, Jr. and Fred L. Israel, 2808–2914. New York: Chelsea House Publishers in Association with McGraw-Hill Book Co.

Lewinson, Paul. 1932. *Race, Class, and Party: A History of Negro Suffrage and White Politics in the South.* London: Oxford University Press.

Lewis, Jan. 1995. "'Of Every Age Sex & Condition': The Representation of Women in the Constitution." *Journal of the Early Republic* 15(Fall):359–387.

Lichtman. Allan J. 1979. *Prejudice and the Old Politics: The Presidential Election of 1928.* Chapel Hill: University of North Carolina Press.

Lippman, Walter. 1928. "Lady Politicians: How the Old-Fashioned Illusion That Women Would Redeem Politics Has Been Destroyed." *Vanity Fair* 29(January):43, 104.

Lubell, Samuel. 1952. *The Future of American Politics.* New York: Harper & Brothers.

MacKay, Kenneth Campbell. 1947. *The Progressive Movement of 1924.* New York: Columbia University Press.

MacRae, Duncan Jr., and James A. Meldrum. 1960. "Critical Elections in Illinois: 1888–1958." *American Political Science Review* 54(September):669–683.

Mannheim, Karl. 1952. "The Problem of Generations." In *Essays on the Sociology of Knowledge*, ed. Paul Kecskemeti, 276–322. London: Routledge & Kegan Paul.

Mansbridge, Jane J. 1985. "Myth and Reality: The ERA and the Gender Gap in the 1980 Election." *Public Opinion Quarterly* 49:164–178.

Marilley, Suzanne M. 1996. *Woman Suffrage and the Origins of Liberal Feminism in the United States, 1820–1920.* Cambridge, MA: Harvard University Press.

Martin, Andrew D., Kevin M. Quinn, and Jong Hee Park. 2011. "MCMCpack: Markov Chain Monte Carlo in R." *Journal of Statistical Software.* 42(9):1–21.

Martin, Anne. 1925. "Feminists and Future Political Action." *The Nation* 120(February 18):185–186.

Matland, Richard E., and Gregg R. Murray. 2012. "An Experimental Test of Mobilization Effects in a Latino Community." *Political Research Quarterly* 65(1):192–205.

Matthews, Glenna. 1992. *The Rise of Public Woman: Woman's Power and Woman's Place in the United States, 1630–1970.* New York: Oxford University Press.

McConnaughy, Corrine M. 2013. *The Woman Suffrage Movement in America: A Reassessment.* New York: Cambridge University Press.

McCormick, Anne O'Hare. 1928. "Enter Woman, The New Boss of Politics." *The New York Times Magazine* October 21:3 and 22.

McCoy, Donald R. 1971. "Election of 1920." In *History of American Presidential Elections, 1789–1968*, eds. Arthur M. Schlesinger, Jr. and Fred L. Israel, 2348–2455. New York: Chelsea House Publishers in Association with McGraw-Hill Book Co.

McDonagh, Eileen L., and H. Douglas Price. 1985. "Woman Suffrage in the Progressive Era: Patterns of Opposition and Support in Referenda Voting, 1910–1918" *American Political Science Review* 79(2):415–435.

McGerr, Michael. 1990. "Political Style and Women's Power, 1830–1930." *The Journal of American History* 77(December):864–885.

McMichael, Lawrence G., and Richard J. Trilling. 1980. "The Structure and Meaning of Critical Realignment: The Case of Pennsylvania, 1928–1932." In *Realignment in American Politics: Toward a Theory*, eds. Bruce A. Campbell and Richard J. Trilling, 21–51. Austin: University of Texas Press.

McPhee, William N., and Jack Ferguson. 1962. "Political Immunization." In *Public Opinion and Congressional Elections*, eds. William N. McPhee and William A. Glaser, 123–154. New York: Free Press of Glencoe.

Merriam, Charles E. 1929. *Chicago: A More Intimate View of Urban Politics*. New York: The Macmillan Company.

Merriam, Charles E., and Harold F. Gosnell. 1924. *Non-voting: Causes and Methods of Control*. Chicago: University of Chicago Press.

Mickey, Robert. 2015. *Paths Out of Dixie: The Democratization of Authoritarian Enclaves in America's Deep South, 1944–1972*. Princeton, NJ: Princeton University Press.

Miller, Warren E., and J. Merrill Shanks. 1996. *The New American Voter*. Cambridge, MA: Harvard University Press.

Minor v. Happersett. 1874. 88 U.S. 162.

Monoson, S. Sara. 1990. "The Lady and the Tiger: Women's Electoral Activism in New York City before Suffrage." *Journal of Women's History* 2(Fall):100–135.

Nardulli, Peter F. 1995. "The Concept of Critical Realignment, Electoral Behavior, and Political Change." *American Political Science Review* 89(March):10–22.

2005. *Popular Efficacy in the Democratic Era: A Re-examination of Electoral Accountability in the U.S., 1828–2000*. Princeton, NJ: Princeton University Press.

Neal, R. M. 2003. "Slice sampling." (with discussion). *Annals of Statistics* 31: 705–767.

Nichols, Carole. 1983. "Votes and More for Women: Suffrage and After in Connecticut." *Women & History* 5:1–92.

Nickerson, David W. 2008. "Is Voting Contagious? Evidence from Two Field Experiments." *American Political Science Review* 102(February):49–57.

Niemi, Richard G., G. Bingham Powell, Jr., Harold W. Stanley, and C. Lawrence Evans. 1985. "Testing the Converse Partisanship Model with New Electorates." *Comparative Political Studies* 18(October):300–322.

Niemi, Richard G., Harold W. Stanley, and C. Lawrence Evans. 1984. "Age and Turnout among the Newly Enfranchised: Life Cycle versus Experience Effects." *European Journal of Political Research*. 12:371–386.

Niemi, Richard G., and Herbert F. Weisberg. 1984. "What Determines Turnout?" In *Controversies in Voting Behavior*, 2nd ed. eds. Richard G. Niemi and Herbert F. Weisberg, 23–33. Washington, DC: Congressional Quarterly.

Niven, David. 2001. "The Limits of Mobilization: Turnout Evidence from State House Primaries." *Political Behavior* 23(December):335–349.

2004. "The Mobilization Solution? Face-to-Face Contact and Voter Turnout in a Municipal Election." *Journal of Politics* 66(August):868–884.

Norrander, Barbara. 1999. "The Evolution of the Gender Gap." *Public Opinion Quarterly* 63(Winter):566–576.

Ogburn, William F., and Inez Goltra. 1919. "How Women Vote: A Study of An Election in Portland, Oregon." *Political Science Quarterly* 34:413–433.

Ogden, Frederic D. 1958. *The Poll Tax in the South*. Tuscaloosa: University of Alabama Press.

Ogg, Frederic A., and R. Orman Ray. 1932. *Essentials of American Government*. New York: The Century Co.

Omero, Margie, and Tara McGuinness. 2012. "How Women Changed the Outcome of the Election." *Center for American Progress* www.americanprogress.org/issues/women/report/2012/12/12/47916/how-women-changed-the-outcome-of-the-election/ (Accessed July 30, 2014).

O'Neill, William L. 1971. *Everyone Was Brave: A History of Feminism in America*. New York: Quadrangle.

Orren, Karen, and Stephen Skowronek. 2004. *The Search for American Political Development*. New York: Cambridge University Press.

Pateman, Carole. 1980. "Women, Nature, and the Suffrage." *Ethics* 90(July): 564–575.

1994. "Three Questions about Womanhood Suffrage." In *Suffrage and Beyond: International Feminist Perspectives*, eds. Caroline Daley and Melanie Nolan, 331–348. New York: New York University Press.

Patterson, Samuel C., and Gregory Caldeira. 1983. "Getting Out the Vote: Participation in Gubernatorial Elections." *American Political Science Review* 77(September):675–689.

Peel, Roy V. and Thomas C. Donnelly. 1931. *The 1928 Campaign: An Analysis*. New York: Richard R. Smith.

Plummer, Martyn, Nicky Best, Kate Cowles, and Karen Vines. 2006. "CODA: Convergence Diagnosis and Output Analysis for MCMC." *R News* 6(1):7–11.

Plutzer, Eric. 2002. "Becoming a Habitual Voter: Inertia, Resources, and Growth in Young Adulthood." *American Political Science Review* 96(March):41–56.

Pollock, James K. 1939. *Voting Behavior*. Ann Arbor: University of Michigan Press.

Powell, G. Bingham, Jr. 1986. "American Voter Turnout in Comparative Perspective." *American Political Science Review* 80(March):17–43.

Prindle, David F. 1979. "Voter Turnout, Critical Elections, and the New Deal Realignment." *Social Science History* III(Winter):144–170.

Raftery, Adrian E. 1995. "Bayesian Model Selection in Social Research." *Sociological Methodology* 24:111–163.

Rice, Stuart A., and Malcolm M. Willey. 1924. "American Women's Ineffective Use of the Vote." *Current History* 20(July):641–647.

Robert, Christian A., and George Casella. 2004. *Monte Carlo Statistical Methods*. 2nd ed. New York: Springer.

Robinson, William S. 1950. "Ecological Correlation and the Behavior of Individuals." *American Sociological Review* 15:351–357.

Rogers, Edith Nourse. 1930. "Women's New Place in Politics." *Nation's Business* 18:39–41, 124.

Roosevelt, Eleanor. 1940. "Women in Politics" (Second of three articles). *Good Housekeeping* 110 (March):45ff.

Rosen, Ori, Wenxin Jiang, Gary King, and Martin A. Tanner. 2001. "Bayesian and Frequentist Inference for Ecological Inference: The R × C Case." *Statistica Neerlandica* 55(2):134–156.

Rosenstone, Steven J., Roy L. Behr, and Edward H. Lazarus. 1996. *Third Parties in America: Citizen Response to Major Party Failure.*, 2nd ed. Princeton, NJ: Princeton University Press.

Rosenstone, Steven J., and John Mark Hansen. 1993. *Mobilization, Participation, and Democracy in America.* New York: Macmillan.

Rossi, Alice S., ed. 1973. *The Feminist Papers: From Adams to de Beauvoir.* New York: Columbia University Press.

Rubenstein, Sondra Miller. 1994. *Surveying Public Opinion.* Belmont, CA: Wadsworth.

Rusk, Jerold G. 1970. "The Effect of the Australian Ballot Reform on Split Ticket Voting." *American Political Science Review* 64(December):1220–1238.

1974. "Comment: The American Electoral Universe: Speculation and Evidence." *American Political Science Review* 68(September):1028–1049.

Russell, Charles Edward. 1924. "Is Woman-Suffrage a Failure?" *The Century Magazine* 35:724–730.

Rymph, Catherine E. 2006. *Republican Women: Feminism and Conservatism from Suffrage through the Rise of the New Right.* Chapel Hill: University of North Carolina Press.

Sainsbury, Diane. 1999. "Beyond the 'Great Divide': Women in Partisan Politics before and after the Federal Suffrage Amendment." *Women & Politics* 20(2):59–80.

Salisbury, Robert H., and Michael MacKuen. 1981. "On the Study of Party Realignment." *Journal of Politics* 43:523–530.

Sarvasy, Wendy. 1992. "Beyond the Difference versus Equality Policy Debate: Postsuffrage Feminism, Citizenship, and the Quest for a Feminist Welfare State." *Signs: Journal of Women in Culture and Society* 17(Winter):329–362.

Scammon, Richard M., ed. 1965. *America at the Polls: A Handbook of Presidential Election Statistics, 1920–1964.* Pittsburgh: University of Pittsburgh Press.

Schantz, Harvey L. 1992. "The Erosion of Sectionalism in Presidential Elections." *Polity* 24(Spring):355–377.

Schattschneider, E. E. 1960. *The Semi-sovereign People.* New York: Holt, Rinehart and Winston.

Schuyler, Lorraine Gates. 2006. *The Weight of Their Votes: Southern Women and Political Leverage in the 1920s.* Chapel Hill: University of North Carolina Press.

Scott, Anne Firor. 1964. "After Suffrage: Southern Women in the Twenties." *Journal of Southern History* 30:298–318.

1972. *The Southern Lady: From Pedestal to Politics, 1830–1930*. Chicago: University of Chicago Press.

Shapiro, Robert Y., and Harpreet Mahajan. 1986. "Gender Differences in Policy Preferences: A Summary of Trends from the 1960s to the 1980s." *Public Opinion Quarterly* 50:42–61.

Shively, W. Phillip. 1971–1972. "A Reinterpretation of the New Deal Realignment." *Public Opinion Quarterly* 35(Winter):621–624.

Siegel, Reva B. 2002. "She the People: The Nineteenth Amendment, Sex Equality, Federalism, and the Family." *Harvard Law Review* 115(February):947–1046.

Silva, Ruth C. 1962. *Rum, Religion, and Votes: 1928 Re-examined*. University Park: Pennsylvania State University Press.

Skocpol, Theda. 1992. *Protecting Soldiers and Mothers: The Political Origins of Social Policy in the United States*. Cambridge, MA: Belknap Press of Harvard University Press.

1994. "The Origins of Social Policy in the United States: A Polity-Centered Analysis." In *The Dynamics of American Politics: Approaches and Interpretations*, eds. Lawrence C. Dodd and Calvin Jillson, 182–206. Boulder, CO: Westview Press.

2003. *Civic Engagement in American Democracy: From Membership to Management in American Civic Life*. Norman: University of Oklahoma Press.

Smith, Jean M. 1980. "The Voting Women of San Diego, 1920." *The Journal of San Diego History* 26(Spring):133–154.

Smith, Rogers M. 1997. *Civic Ideals: Conflicting Visions of Citizenship in U.S. History*. New Haven, CT: Yale University Press.

Spain, Daphne. 2001. *How Women Saved the City*. Minneapolis: University of Minnesota Press.

Stoker, Laura, and M. Kent Jennings. 2008. "Of Time and Partisan Polarization." *American Journal of Political Science* 52(July):619–635.

Stucker, John J. 1976. "Women's Political Role." *Current History* 70(May): 211–214.

Sumner, Helen. 1909. *Equal Suffrage: The Results of an Investigation in Colorado made for the Collegiate Equal Suffrage League of New York State*. New York: Harper and Brothers.

Sundquist, James L. 1983. *Dynamics of the Party System: Alignment and Realignment in the United States*, rev. ed. Washington, DC: The Brookings Institution.

Swisher, Idella Gwatkin. 1933. "Election Statistics in the United States." *American Political Science Review* 27(June):422–432.

Tarbell, Ida M. 1924. "Is Woman's Suffrage a Failure?" *Good Housekeeping* October:18.

Terborg-Penn, Rosalyn. 1978. "Discrimination against Afro-American Women in the Woman's Movement, 1830–1920." In *The Afro-American Woman: Struggles and Images*, eds. Sharon Harley and Rosalyn Terborg-Penn, 17–27. Port Washington, NY: Kennikat Press.

1998. *African American Women in the Struggle for the Vote, 1850–1920.* Bloomington: Indiana University Press.

Thelen, David P. 1976. *Robert M. La Follette and the Insurgent Spirit.* Boston: Little, Brown, and Company.

Tingsten, Herbert. 1937. *Political Behavior.* Totowa, NJ: Bedminster.

Titus, Charles H. 1976. *Voting Behavior in the United States: A Statistical Study.* Berkeley, CA: University of California Press.

Toombs, Elizabeth O. 1929. "Politicians, Take Notice." *Good Housekeeping* March:14–15.

Tyler, Pamela. 1996. *Silk Stockings & Ballot Boxes: Women & Politics in New Orleans, 1920–1963.* Athens, GA: University of Georgia Press.

Unger, Nancy C. 2000. *Fighting Bob LaFollette: The Righteous Reformer.* Chapel Hill: University of North Carolina Press.

US Census. 1912. *Thirteenth Census of the United States: 1910. Population.* Volumes I, II, and III. Washington, DC: United States Printing Office.

1922. *Fourteenth Census of the United States: 1920. Population.* Volumes I, II, and III. Washington, DC: United States Printing Office.

US Census. 1932. *Fifteenth Census of the United States: 1930. Population.* Volumes I, II, and III. Washington, DC: United States Printing Office.

1982. *Current Population Reports, Population Characteristics, P-20. Voting and Registration in the Election of 1980.* Washington, DC: United States Printing Office.

US Census. 1998. *Current Population Reports, Population Characteristics, P20-504. Voting and Registration in the Election of 1996.* Washington, DC: United States Printing Office.

Valelly, Richard M. 2004. *The Two Reconstructions: The Struggle for Black Enfranchisement.* Chicago: University of Chicago Press.

Wakefield, Jon. 2004. "Ecological inference for 2 × 2 tables (with discussion)." *Journal of the Royal Statistical Society*, 167:385–445.

Wanat, John. 1979. "The Application of Non-Analytic, Most Possible Estimation Technique: The Relative Impact of Mobilization and Conversion of Votes in the New Deal." *Political Methodology* 6(3):357–374.

Weed, Clyde P. 1994. *The Nemesis of Reform: The Republican Party during the New Deal.* New York: Columbia University Press.

Wells, Marguerite M. 1929. "Some Effects of Woman Suffrage." *The Annals of the American Academy* 143:207–216.

Welter, Barbara. 1966. "The Cult of True Womanhood: 1820–1860." *American Quarterly* 18(Summer):151–174.

Wheeler, Marjorie Spruill. 1993. *New Women of the New South: The Leaders of the Woman Suffrage Movement in the Southern States.* New York: Oxford University Press.

1995. *One Woman, One Vote: Rediscovering the Woman Suffrage Movement.* Troutdale, OR: NewSage Press.

Wilkerson-Freeman, Sarah. 2002. "The Second Battle for Woman Suffrage: Alabama White Women, the Poll Tax, and V.O. Key's Master Narrative of Southern Politics." *Journal of Southern History* 68(May):333–374.

2003. "Stealth in the Political Arsenal of Southern Women: A Retrospective for the Millennium." In *Southern Women at the Millennium: A Historical Perspective*, eds. Melissa Walker, Jeanette R. Dunn, and Joe P. Dunn, 42–82. Columbia, MO: University of Missouri Press.

Willey, Malcolm, M., and Stuart A. Rice. 1924. "A Sex Cleavage in the Presidential Election of 1920." *Journal of the American Statistical Association* 19: 519–520.

Wirls, Daniel. 1986. "Reinterpreting the Gender Gap." *Public Opinion Quarterly* 50(Autumn):316–330.

Wolbrecht, Christina. 2000. *The Politics of Women's Rights: Parties, Positions, and Change*. Princeton, NJ: Princeton University Press.

Wolfinger, Raymond E., and Steven J. Rosenstone. 1980. *Who Votes?* New Haven, CT: Yale University Press.

Wong, Janelle S. 2000. "The Effects of Age and Political Exposure on the Development of Party Identification among Asian American and Latino Immigrants in the United States." *Political Behavior* 22(4):341–371.

Young, Louise M. 1975. "Women's Place in American Politics: The Historical Perspective." *Journal of Politics* (200 Years of the Republic in Retrospect: A Special Bicentennial Issue) 38(August):295–335.

1989. *In the Public Interest: The League of Women Voters, 1920–1970*. New York: Greenwood Press.

Index